KATYAYANA'S SARVANUKRAMANI

OF THE

RIGVEDA

KATYAYANA'S SARVANUKRAMANI

OF THE

RIGVEDA

WITH EXTRACTS FROM

SHADGURUSISHYA'S COMMENTARY

ENTITLED

VEDARTHADIPIKA

EDITED

WITH CRITICAL NOTES AND APPENDICES

BY

A. A. MACDONELL, M.A., PH. D.

GYAN

Published by

Gyan Publishing House
5, Ansari Road
Daryaganj, New Delhi-110002
Phone: 011-47034999, 9811692060
E-mail: books@gyanbooks.com

Distribution Network
gyanbooks.com
India, USA, Canada, UK, Australia

ISBN: 978-93-6208-658-7 (PB)
First Published, 1886

2nd Impression 2024

Printed at: Gyan Press, Delhi.

KATYAYANA'S SARVANUKRAMANI OF THE RIGVEDA
Editor: A. A. MACDONELL

Anecdota Oxoniensia

TEXTS, DOCUMENTS, AND EXTRACTS

CHIEFLY FROM

MANUSCRIPTS IN THE BODLEIAN

AND OTHER

OXFORD LIBRARIES

ARYAN SERIES. VOL. I—PART IV

KÂTYÂYANA'S SARVĀNUKRAMAṆÎ ETC.

EDITED BY

A. A. MACDONELL

Oxford

AT THE CLARENDON PRESS

1886

KÂTYÂYANA'S SARVÂNUKRAMANÎ

OF THE

*RI*GVEDA

WITH EXTRACTS FROM

SHA*D*GURU*S*ISHYA'S COMMENTARY

ENTITLED

VEDÂRTHAḌÎPIKÂ

EDITED

WITH CRITICAL NOTES AND APPENDICES

BY

A. A. MACDONELL, M.A., PH. D.

MEMBER OF THE GERMAN ORIENTAL SOCIETY
AND OF THE ROYAL ASIATIC SOCIETY OF GREAT BRITAIN AND IRELAND

Oxford

AT THE CLARENDON PRESS

1886

TO

THE MEMORY OF

THEODOR BENFEY,

MY FIRST TEACHER IN SANSKRIT,

THIS WORK IS INSCRIBED

AS A TOKEN OF GRATITUDE.

CONTENTS.

PREFACE.

INDIAN tradition at the time of Sha*d*guru*s*ishya, who completed his commentary to the Sarvânukrama*n*î, the Vedârthadîpikâ, about the year 1187[1], ascribed that index to Kâtyâyana, and named *S*aunaka as the composer of five other works specially entitled Anukrama*n*îs. These, as enumerated by Sha*d*guru*s*ishya in the introduction to his commentary[2], are:—

1. The Ârshânukrama*n*î; 2. the *Kh*ando*-*nukrama*n*î; 3. the Devatânukrama*n*î; 4. the Anuvâkânukrama*n*î; 5. the Sûktânukrama*n*î.

The first, quoted fifteen times by Sha*d*guru*s*ishya, is composed in verse, and contains about 320 *s*lokas. The only MS. of it known to exist, is described by Râjendra Lâla Mitra in his Notices of Sanskrit MSS. for 1881–1882 (p. 176, no. 2112). The owner being unwilling to part with it, Râjendra Lâla Mitra promised to have it copied for me. My hopes of receiving this MS. have, however, hitherto been disappointed.

The *Kh*ando*-*nukrama*n*î is also composed in *s*lokas. The only MS. of this index known to exist is in the possession of Râjendra Lâla Mitra. To his kindness I am indebted for a copy of it, which he sent me from Calcutta. Unfortunately this copy (and presumably the original) omits the index of metres for the first ma*nd*ala completely.

As the work in this fragmentary state comprises 238 verses, the whole work must have contained about 300, assuming the index to the first ma*nd*ala to have been of about the same length as that to the tenth (viz. 65 *s*lokas). At the end of each ma*nd*ala there is here an enumeration in figures, of the number of verses in each metre, besides the total number of verses and of hymns in each ma*nd*ala. I have found these data of considerable value in corroborating my calculations for the table given below, which shows the distribution of the various metres in each ma*nd*ala. Unfortunately in addition to the absence of the first ma*nd*ala, individual figures also are omitted here and there. Sha*d*guru*s*ishya

[1] See conclusion, p. 168, verses 13–14, and Weber in Ind. Stud., vol. viii, p. 160, note.

[2] See Max Müller, Ancient Sanskrit Literature, p. 234. This introduction is not printed in this edition for the reason stated below.

has only two quotations from this anukrama*n*î. Of these I was able to verify the second only, the first occurring in ma*nd*ala I.

Of the Devatânukrama*n*î no MS. appears to have been found, but judging by the ten quotations in Sha*d*guru*s*ishya, it was composed in the mixed verse[1] peculiar to *S*aunaka's works, and showed similar irregularities of metre to those of the Anuvâkânukrama*n*î[2]. It must have been a work not unlike the B*ri*haddevatâ, though, no doubt, much shorter.

The Sûktânukrama*n*î is neither known to exist, nor is it quoted by Sha*d*guru*s*ishya. There is, however, no reason to suppose that it did not exist in Sha*d*guru*s*ishya's time, like the remaining eight works which he attributes to *S*aunaka, and all[3] of which are still extant. (The tenth, the Smârta Sûtra of *S*aunaka, is stated by Sha*d*guru*s*ishya to have been destroyed[4] by that author in favour of his pupil Â*s*valâyana[5].) Judging from the subject-matter of the other anukrama*n*îs, this was probably chiefly an index of pratîkas, and as such would not call for quotation.

The Anuvâkânukrama*n*î is not only thrice quoted by Sha*d*guru*s*ishya, but was specially commentated on by him. Both the text and the commentary are printed in this edition. Several MSS. of this index exist, six having been collated by me.

Besides the above five among the ten books of *S*aunaka, there is another well-known work, which though not called an anukrama*n*î is practically one, the B*ri*haddevatâ, which contains about 1050 *s*lokas. Sha*d*guru*s*ishya calls it an anukrama*n*î in his comm. on *Ri*gv. X, 71, and indeed speaks of all *S*aunaka's works as anukrama*n*îs in another passage[6]. The editing of this index, though it exists in several MSS., will prove a matter of considerable difficulty owing to the widely divergent readings it contains. Professor Max Müller possesses three fairly correct MSS. of it, which have been of great service to me for collating with the numerous and often extensive quotations from this work in the Vedârthadîpikâ.

Lastly, there is another anukrama*n*î work attributed to *S*aunaka. It is quoted by Sha*d*guru*s*ishya as 'another' in his commentary to the Sarvânukrama*n*î[7], where he quotes the whole introduction (with the exception of the first two verses), which treats of the Ati*kkh*andas metres.

[1] Cp. the quotation in comm. on I, 165.

[2] See comm. on I, 112. The Ârshânukrama*n*î seems to contain similar irregularities; see p. 86, line 1.

[3] See what is said below about the Pâdânukrama*n*î.

[4] Cp. Meyer, *Ri*gvidhâna, p. ii, note 4.

[5] Max Muller, A. S. L., p. 235.

[6] Introd., § 1, 1.

[7] Introd., § 11, 6.

This passage is also quoted by Max Müller, *R*igv. Prâti*s*âkhya, pp. cccxxv and ccclviii. Of this anukrama*n*î only one MS. exists in Europe. It belongs to the India Office Library, and is written on palm leaves in the Grantha character. Though not dated, it is apparently of the seventeenth century. It is described in Burnell's small Sanskrit Catalogue, where the first seven lines of the introduction, as well as the first two lines of section 2, are printed[1]. This MS. I have copied and transliterated into the Nâgarî character. The work is here called the Pâdânukrama*n*î. Râjendra Lâla Mitra possesses another MS. of this work in Nâgarî, a copy of which he was kind enough to send me. The work is here entitled the Pâdavidhâna[2]. It is short, occupying only four pages of twenty lines each, besides an introduction of seven verses (omitted in this copy), and is composed in *s*lokas mixed with trish*t*ubhs. In the latter MS. this part is followed by a kind of commentary (six pages and a half), which gives the whole of each pâda mentioned in the former part by its pratîka, and this second part is called the Pâdavidhânânukrama*n*ikâ. This work, then, would appear to be identical with the Pâdavidhâna mentioned by Sha*d*guru*s*ishya as one of the ten works of *S*aunaka. It is not ready for publication, as I have not yet discovered on what principle this anukrama*n*î is based. I hope to be able to publish this together with the Ârshânukrama*n*î and the *Kh*ando-nukrama*n*î in a future appendix to this edition.

That anukrama*n*îs existed as a branch of literature several centuries before the beginning of our era, is shown by an unmistakeable reference to the Anuvâkânukrama*n*î in the Dharma Sûtra of Âpastamba (I, iii, 11, 6). Prof. Bühler in his introduction to his translation of this sûtra[3] has furnished a tolerably convincing proof that the composition of this sûtra cannot be placed later than the third century B.C., and even makes it probable that its date should be placed 150 or 200 years earlier. Thus the composition of the Anuvâkânukrama*n*î would reach back to the fifth century. Apart from the evidence of the tradition in Sha*d*guru*s*ishya, the probability is great that this index, owing to the similarity of style, was composed by *S*aunaka, the author of the *Ri*gveda Prâti*s*âkhya. It is at the same time extremely likely that the

[1] Part I, Vedic MSS., p. 6, no. iv.

[2] It begins with the words, अथ शौनकोक्तं पादविधानं लिख्यते । ऋक्षु संशायिकाः पादा भवंति etc.

[3] Sacred Books of the East, vol. ii.

remaining anukrama*n*îs mentioned above are closely connected in time with those two works. For on the one hand it is probable that when fixing the canon of the *Ri*gveda became a desideratum, the want was supplied almost simultaneously in the various directions of the indexes attributed to *S*aunaka, while all of them on the other hand, like the Prâti*s*âkhya, have a metrical form, several of them (the pâda- and the devatâ-, besides the Anuvâkânukrama*n*î and the B*ri*haddevatâ[1]), containing an occasional admixture of trish*t*ubh, such as appears in the Prâti*s*âkhya. That most of them at least were anterior to the Sarvânukrama*n*î, is tolerably clear, for the latter, on Sha*d*guru*s*ishya's showing from the quotations which he adduces, is based on them, and, as embodying the substance of all of them[2], is for the sake of brevity composed in sûtras. That the desire to condense the matter contained in the various indexes into a single work of a comprehensive character should soon have arisen, is in itself likely; and that this task should have been undertaken by Kâtyâyana, himself the author of a Prâti*s*âkhya and of a *S*rauta Sûtra, is highly probable. The date of the Sarvânukrama*n*î would thus be about the middle of the fourth century B. C. To lay stress on the numerous archaisms[3] in the diction of the Sarvânukrama*n*î pointed out by Sha*d*guru*s*ishya, as an argument for its early date, might justly be considered weak; for that the grammarian who completed and corrected Pâ*n*ini should have been anything but intentionally archaistic, can hardly be assumed.

As regards the contents[4] of the Sarvânukrama*n*î, the main part of the work is preceded by an introduction in twelve paragraphs[5] (pp. 1–5). § 1 shortly describes the scope of the work and the good resulting from a knowledge of its contents. §§ 2 and 12 contain the paribhâshâs necessary as a key to the sûtras of the main portion of the work. §§ 3–11 contain a treatise on the metres of the *Ri*gveda[6], which coincides almost word for word with the corresponding portion of the Vâ*g*asaneyi Anukrama*n*î[7]. The main part of the work (pp. 5–46) contains, for every hymn of the *Ri*gveda in their order, according to the recension of the

[1] See comm. on III, 5-6 and IV, 57. [2] Max Müller, A. S. L., p. 235.

[3] Upwards of thirty are discussed in the comm.; see Index, s. v. *kh*ândasa.

[4] Given at the end of Max Müller's and Aufrecht's editions of the *Ri*gveda.

[5] This part has already been printed by Prof. E. Windisch in 'Zwölf Hymnen des *Ri*gveda.'

[6] See Weber, Ind. Stud. VIII, pp. 137–144.

[7] See Weber's Vâ*g*asaneyi Sa*m*hitâ, appendix.

*S*âkala *S*âkhâ, the first word or words (pratîka), the number of verses, the name of the poet and of the deity, as well as the metres of the whole hymn or of its various parts. Occasionally, in order to make the meaning of the hymn clearer, an itihâsa is briefly sketched[1], which Sha*d*guru*s*ishya in his commentary always relates in detail, usually by a quotation from the B*ri*haddevatâ. Here and there paribhâshâs are inserted which refer to a limited number of hymns[2].

The conclusion of the various ma*nd*alas I have indicated with Sha*d*guru*s*ishya's words in small type.

In order to facilitate the use of the text, I have indicated the number of the hymn in each ma*nd*ala with small figures above the line on the left of the pratîka. At the top of each page the ma*nd*ala is given, after it on the left the number of the first hymn on the page, on the right the number of the last hymn on that page.

Every adhyâya begins with a new line, and its number is placed at the end of the paragraph.

In the choice of readings for the text I have given the chief weight to Sha*d*guru*s*ishya's authority, in order to obtain the exact text which this commentator had before him in the twelfth century. There are a few instances in which the text is slightly in conflict with the commentary. Here I have considered it right to correct the former in accordance with the latter. These slight variations are only such as might easily escape the attention. For instance, in the sûtra on X, 179 all the MSS. read aindra*h*, but the commentary, which discusses the formation of this patronymic, shows that Sha*d*guru*s*ishya read aindri*h*, and that consequently the i has dropped out since his time. All such cases are of course discussed in the notes[3].

Quotations are not frequent in the Sarvânukrama*n*î. In the introduction, § 1, a passage from the Ârsheya Brâhma*n*a is quoted, in § 2, 7 two verses from the *Ri*gveda itself, then in the main part of the work, VII, 32, the *S*â*t*yâyanaka and the Tâ*nd*aka, two passages from '*S*ruti' (III, 31 and III, 36), and twice the opinion of certain persons (IV, 13 and V, 27).

The diction of the Sarvânukrama*n*î contains numerous forms which Sha*d*guru*s*ishya characterises as actually Vedic, the references to which

[1] I, 51, 166, 170, 179; II, 1, 43; III, 1; V, 61; VI, 52; VII, 32; VIII, 1, 91; X, 9, 33, 47, 50, 57–60, 95, 102, 108.

[2] See I, 14, 15, 64, 139; III, 6; V, 1; VIII, 1; IX, 1, 67; X, 56, 110, 111–114.

[3] For other instances see I, 132 and IV, 57.

will be found in the index of words under *kh*ândasa. This chiefly applies to dvandva compounds of the names of gods which have often V*ri*ddhi in one element only, while according to Pâ*n*. VII, 3, 21 it is required in both words. In one or two instances where I had followed this rule of Pâ*n*ini for the sake of consistency, I have restored the 'Vedic' form in the list of corrigenda.

With regard to the Sandhi it is to be noticed that the MSS. follow very consistently two grammatical rules of *S*âkalya. Firstly, ă remains unchanged before *ri*, and â is shortened before it[1]; and, secondly, au becomes âv before all words except u, but becomes â before u[2]. The only exceptions to the former rule are the particles vâ, yathâ, *k*a, which are contracted, and the compound brahmarshi.

In preparing this edition of the Sarvânukrama*n*î I have used nine MSS., and at the same time always carefully collated the quotations in Sâya*n*a. It appears that the latter commentator cites the Sarvânukrama*n*î inaccurately, especially as regards the order of the words; words and whole sûtras are occasionally omitted. To notice all these variations among the critical notes, I considered unnecessary. The MSS. collated by me are:—

(1) A MS. belonging to the Wilson Collection (No. 379) in the Bodleian Library, briefly described in Aufrecht's Sanskrit Catalogue. It contains Sha*d*guru*s*ishya's commentary to both the Anuvâkânukrama*n*î and the Sarvânukrama*n*î, the text always preceding the commentary by parts of verses in the former and by sûtras in the latter. The Anuvâkânukrama*n*î occupies leaves 1 to 4 a (incl.), the Sarvânukrama*n*î 46 to 74 a. This is on the whole a first-class MS., and it is not too much to say that it would have been impossible without it to produce an approximately correct edition of Sha*d*guru*s*ishya. However, both the beginning, especially parts of Sha*d*guru*s*ishya's introduction, and the end contain many mistakes. The accuracy of this MS. in comparison with all the others becomes most apparent in the quotations, notably in the references to the sûtras of Pâ*n*ini. Its date (A.D. 1599) and the name of the writer are thus stated at the end: **संवत् १६५६ वर्षे ज्येष्ठ वदि सप्तमी रविवसरे विशालनागरज्ञातीयव्यासश्रीहरिनाथसुतव्यासपुरुषोत्तमेन लिखितं परोपकारार्थं। शुभमस्तु । श्रीः । श्रीः । श्रीः ॥**

[1] Cp. Max Muller, *Ri*gv. Pr. p. 12 and sûtras 136 and 168; Pâ*n*. VI, i, 128.

[2] Cp. Max Müller, *Ri*gv. Pr. p. 11 and sûtra 135; also Aufrecht, Ait. Br., notes, p. 427.

(2) C: a MS. of the same contents as W 1, which belongs to the Chambers Collection in the Royal Library of Berlin, and is described at great length in Weber's Sanskrit Catalogue, pp. 12–15. It is 134 years younger than W 1, and is far less correct. It repeats all the mistakes of W 1 in such a manner that there can be no doubt as to its having been copied from that MS. Any doubts on this point will be removed by referring to the critical note to the commentary on the word 'Rau*s*adas*v*a' in the sûtra on X, 179. This MS. I therefore found to be of very little value for purposes of collation, except in the few cases where letters or words had become indistinct or illegible in W 1. There is, moreover, a great lacuna in this MS., embracing ma*nd*alas VI, VII, VIII, besides part of V and of IX.

(3) A MS. of the Bodleian Library, containing only the text of the Sarvânukrama*n*î and of the Anuvâkânukrama*n*î. It is tolerably correct, and dates from 1659 A. D. It is briefly described in Aufrecht's Catalogue under Wilson 502.

(4) I 1: a MS. of the India Office (No. 132), which contains the text only; it contains 19 leaves, and is correct, for it is, as is stated at the end, likhitam svârtham parârtha*m k*a. It is dated A. D. 1745 (Samvat 1802).

(5) I 2: also from the Library of the India Office (No. 1823), into whose possession it came in 1822. It contains no statement as to the copyist, nor as to the place or time of its origin, but is without doubt a recent MS., probably not more than a century old. It concludes simply with the words, *S*rîsîtârâma*k*andrârpa*n*am astu, *s*ubham astu, *s*rîr astu. It consists of 140 leaves, and contains the text and the commentary of Sha*d*guru*s*ishya to the Sarvânukrama*n*î, but omits Sha*d*guru*s*ishya's introduction. It begins with the words, *S*rîga*n*e*s*âya nama*h*. Atha *ri*gvedâmnâye, etc. It is an incorrect MS. There can be no doubt that it is copied from P 2 (described below), even the most absurd mistakes of which it repeats with faithful accuracy. It is therefore of no independent value.

(6) I 3, a MS. of the India Office (No. 1636), contains the commentary of another writer, named *G*agannâtha, on the Sarvânukrama*n*î. This commentary is much shorter than the Vedârthadîpikâ, as it contains no stories or discussions. It is probably not more than 140 years old at the most, being dated Samvat 184, which is probably meant for either 1804 or 1840. Although this MS. does not contain the text

of the Sarvânukrama*n*î, it nevertheless proved of some service with regard to the spelling of names and to the contents generally.

(7) I 4: a MS. of the India Office Library (No. 2396) in 173 leaves, containing both the text of the Sarvânukrama*n*î and the commentary of Sha*d*guru*s*ishya, but omitting the introduction. It begins with the words, *S*rîga*n*e*s*âya nama*h*. Sarasvatyai nama*h*. *S*rîbhairavâya nama*h*. Atha *ri*gvedâmnâye, etc. There is some confusion in the date, which is given as both *S*aka 1602 (A.D. 1680) and Samvat 1812 (A.D. 1755). It has the appearance of being about two hundred years old, so that the former is probably the correct date. The conclusion in full is as follows: सख्या ग्रंथय नविंशतं । सहस्रं विंशतादूर्ध्वं त्रिंशद्वेवं ततः परं (sic) ॥ इति सर्वानुक्रमणीभाष्यं समाप्तः ॥ छ ॥ इति चतुःपष्टिरध्यायः सपूर्णः ॥ छ ॥ विश्वेरार्पणमस्तु ॥ छ ॥ इति श्रीत् शके ॥ १६०२ ॥ संवतः १८१२ ॥ शमैनामका तीका चदी दुइ जीवा रवी ह मै ॥ This specimen will suffice to show that it is an incorrect MS. An examination of the critical notes to the commentary will show that I 4 is more nearly connected with P 1 and P 2 than with W 1, though occasionally, but less frequently, it agrees with W 1, as opposed to these two. It thus stands between the two groups P 1, P 2, I 2, and W 1, C, but nearer to the former than to the latter. The various readings in the text of the Sarvânukrama*n*î of I 4 and of the following two MSS. are to be found in the critical notes to the Vedârthadîpikâ, as I did not receive these three MSS. till after the text of the Sarvânukrama*n*î had been printed.

(8) P 1: a MS. belonging to the Deccan College at Poona, and lent to me through the Indian Office. For an Indian MS. it is very old, dating from the year 1392 A.D. (Samvat 1449). The paper looks very old (being of a brownish yellow colour turning to dark brown near the edges), and is very brittle and much worn away at the margin. It consists of 178 loose leaves, and contains the text of the Sarvânukrama*n*î with the commentary of Sha*d*guru*s*ishya, omitting his introduction. It begins with the words, सर्वानु° गणेशाय नमः । अथ ऋग्वेदाम्नाये etc. The last leaf contains an abstract (18 lines) of the Anuvâkânukrama*n*î, the words इति सर्वानुक्रमवृत्तिः समाप्ताः (sic) being followed by अथानुवाकाः ॥ अग्निमीळे सुरूपकृत्नुमेंद्रसानसिं etc., i. e. the pratîkas of the anuvâkas, to which is added an abstract of the numerical statements, together with one or two of the actual verses (43 a and 45 a) of the Anuvâkânukrama*n*î. The

MS. ends with the words, स्वस्ति सं १४४९ वर्षे आ° शु° रवौ नंदपंडे द्विवे (two letters obliterated) जैगसुतमुरारे (several letters worn away at the edge) संवत् १५१४ वर्षे अषाढा दि ७४ आश्विन वदि (the concluding line being obliterated with ink). The second date probably is that of the sale of the MS., and the obliterated words the name of the then owner. The writing of this MS. is still very clear. One of its peculiarities is worth noticing. The medial diphthongs e and o are not written above the line, but with perpendicular strokes at the side of the consonant; e.g. ाक=ke, ाका=ko; similarly kai would be ाके, and kau, ाको. It is not a correct MS., being very corrupt in many difficult passages. It is especially untrustworthy in grammatical quotations. I nevertheless found it a very valuable MS. for Sha*d*guru*s*ishya, because owing to its great age, being separated from that commentator's time by only two centuries, it was bound to contain many old readings.

(9) P 2, which also belongs to the Deccan College, is about 250 years younger than P 1, being dated 1638 or 1645 A.D. (Saka 1560 or 1567)[1]. It consists of 147 leaves, but 2 leaves, 122 b to 124 a, are missing. It has the same contents as P 1. It begins with the words, सर्वानुक्रमभाष्य श्रीगणेशाय नमः। अथ ऋग्वेदाम्नाये etc.; and ends, ग्रंथसंख्या ३९३० ॥ शुभमस्तु ॥ शके १५६७ (०?) गणेशभट्टकवीश्वरेण लिखितं ॥ There can hardly be a doubt as to its being lineally descended from P 1. An examination of the critical notes will show that its mistakes coincide in a remarkable manner with those of that MS. The lacunae of P 1 are generally filled up, and often wrongly. One passage in particular will make pretty clear the connexion of P 2 with P 1[2]. P 1, however, contains two long quotations from the B*ri*haddevatâ not to be found in P 2 or in any other of the MSS.

Besides the above-mentioned MSS., I have used three of the B*ri*haddevatâ, kindly lent me by Professor Max Müller, for collating with the quotations from that work in the Vedârthadîpikâ. I have called them M 1, M 2, and M 3. They are all quite young MSS., the latter two being dated 1845 and 1866 A.D. respectively. M 2 and M 3 are almost identical (the latter probably being a copy of the former), while M 1 diverges from them to some extent; but as a rule, the readings of all three agree where they differ from those of Sha*d*guru*s*ishya.

[1] It is difficult to make out whether the last figure is a 7 or a 0.

[2] See note on comm. to Introd., § 2, 22.

For the quotations from the B*ri*haddevatâ, I have also in a few cases collated a MS. (named N), belonging to Professor Max Müller, of the Nîtima*ñg*arî, a modern work containing tales, some of them taken from the B*ri*haddevatâ, the purpose of which is to point a moral.

THE ANUVÂKÂNUKRAMA*N*Î.

This anukrama*n*î is composed in verse, partly trish*t*ubh, partly anush*t*ubh. The first verse, which is a trish*t*ubh, has a modern look, and is probably not by the author of the anukrama*n*î. It is only to be found in those MSS. which contain 'Sha*d*guru*s*ishya's commentary, but is not commented on, nor indeed is the second, which mentions *S*aunaka by name. The introduction (verses 1–14) begins with a statement of the contents of the anukrama*n*î, and then adds some remarks on the course of Vedic study. The work is stated by the author (verse 9) to belong to the *S*ai*s*irîya branch of the *S*âkala *S*âkhâ of the *Ri*gveda. He then enumerates the ten poets of the Âprî hymns and the pratîkas of these hymns. Then follow some remarks on the last Âprî hymn (X, 110), composed by *G*amadagni, which is also to be found in the Vâ*g*asaneyi Sa*m*hitâ (XXIX, 24–36) and in the Taittirîya Brâhma*n*a (III, vi, 3), in both of which passages, however, the second verse of the Âprî hymn, composed by Vasish*th*a (VII, 2), is introduced. Only three of the six MSS. I have collated contain these *s*lokas (11–14); and the readings in 13 b being corrupt, the text had to be amended. In accordance with my emendation I translate verses 13 and 14 as follows:—

'All *Ri*shi families use the Samiddha hymn (X, 110) with the exception of the *S*unakas and the Vasish*th*as. Objection to Tanûnapât (is met) by the second verse of the *g*ushasva hymn, as this verse is to be found in the Ya*g*urveda in the midst of the Samiddha hymn (X, 110). With regard to the animal sacrifice, these verses of the *G*amadagni hymn (X, 110) are employed in all cases (i. e. by all *Ri*shi families, even by the *S*unakas and the Vasish*th*as) according to the Sûtra of Â*s*valâyana "yatharshi vâ[1]."' Judging by the last remark, the author seems to have considered Â*s*v. *S*r. Sûtra III, ii, 7 and 8 to be *one* sûtra.

Of this introduction, one of the six MSS. collated by me (I 4) has nothing; one (W 2) has only one verse, the third; three (W 1, C, C 1) have the whole, while the Grantha manuscript (B) contains only verses

[1] With regard to the Âprî hymns, see Max Müller, A. S. L., pp. 463-469.

3–10 (inclusive). The tenth and eleventh verses *S*ha*d*guru*s*ishya must have considered genuine, for he comments on them. On the other hand, one might be tempted to ascribe verses 13 and 14 to Sha*d*guru*s*ishya himself, as there is not a single word of comment, though these lines are difficult. It is worth noticing that the metre from 11 b to 14 is iambic in the first pâda, whereas the preceding *s*lokas scan regularly according to the *later* form of the anush*t*ubh[1]. Meyer, *Ri*gvidhâna, p. xxvii, is of opinion that the end of the work (37–46) is not genuine. In that case verses 5 and 6 would not be genuine either, as these state the contents of the latter part of the anukrama*n*î. There does not seem to me to be any sufficient reason to assume this. The very last line, in fact, which contains the particle vâva, on the contrary, looks old.

With verse 15 begins the main part of the Anuvâkânukrama*n*î, which comprises 31 verses and a line. Of these verses 14½ are anush*t*ubh: 15–21 c and 38–44. The metre is irregular, seven lines ending with three long syllables, one with – – – –, and two with – ⏑ – –. The introduction does not show *this* irregularity, and its versification has, therefore, probably undergone revision. 42 b seems to consist of a trish*t*ubh pâda and of an anush*t*ubh pâda. The remaining 34 half-verses are trish*t*ubh. Among these only 18 have 22 syllables; of the remaining 16, two have 20 syllables, one 21, seven 23, four 24, one 25, and one 18 (or 20). The last line seems to be prose; I cannot, at least, discover any metre in it. It has 20 syllables.

As regards the contents, verses 15–21 contain the pratîkas of the anuvâkas and the number of hymns contained in these anuvâkas for ma*nd*ala I; 22 a the same for II; 22 b and 23 a for III; 23 b and 24 a for IV; 24 b and 25 a for V; 25 b and 26 a for VI; 26 b and 27 a for VII; 27 b and 28 for VIII; 29 for IX; 30 and 31 for X.

32 states the number of anuvâkas in the various ma*nd*alas: I has 24; II, 4; III, 5; IV, 5; V, 6; VI, 6; VII, 6; VIII, 10; IX, 7; X, 12. [Total 85.]

33–35 contain the number of hymns in the various ma*nd*alas: I has 191; II, 43; III, 62; IV, 58; V, 87; VI, 75; VII, 104; VIII, 92; IX, 114; X, 191. [Total 1017.]

36 states the total number of hymns to be 1017, whereas in the Bâshkala recension there are 8 additional hymns (i.e. 1025). In the

[1] Cp. Oldenberg, on the *S*loka, Zeitschrift der morgenländischen Gesellschaft, vol. xxxv.

*S*ai*s*iriya branch of the *S*âkala *S*âkhâ no anuvâkas are stated for the Khilas.

37: in the ten ma*n*d*alas there are 85 anuvâkas.

38: 64 adhyâyas, 10 ma*n*d*alas, 2006 vargas.

39: without counting the Khilas there are 1017 hymns.

40–42 state the number of the vargas according to the number of verses which they contain:—

	Vargas	Verses
Varga with 1 verse	1	1
" " 9 verses	1	9
Vargas " 2 "	2	4
" " 3 "	97	291
" " 4 "	174	696
" " 5 "	1207	6035
" " 6 "	346	2076
" " 7 "	119	833
" " 8 "	59	472
	2006	10417[1]

43 states the total number of verses in the *R*igveda to be 10580 and one pâda[2].

44: the number of half-verses is 21232 [$=10614\frac{1}{4}$][3]; of the padas, 153,826.

45: of the *k*ar*k*âpadas, 110,704. The last line gives the number of the syllables as 432,000.

The six MSS. collated by me for the Anuvâkânukrama*n*î are:—

(1) W 1, (2) C, both already described.

(3) C 1, a MS. belonging to the Royal Library of Berlin (No. 1405 in Weber's new Sanskrit Catalogue), contains the Anuvâkânukrama*n*î with Sha*d*guru*s*ishya's commentary, followed by that writer's introduction to his Vedârthadîpikâ. It consists of 7 leaves, and is dated A. D. 1525 (Samvat 1582). The commentary in this MS. is more correct than in W 1, but it is no better than that MS. in Sha*d*guru*s*ishya's introduction. It begins, **श्रीविश्वेश्वराय नमः। अथ गद्यात्मक** (sic) **अनुवाकानुक्रमणिका लिख्यते।** and the comm. to the Anuvâkânukrama*n*î ends, **इत्यनुवाकानुक्रमणी समाप्ता। संवत् १५८२ वर्षे लिखितमस्ति। श्रीविश्वेश्वरार्पणमस्तु॥**

[1] This table is given in A. S. L., p. 220.

[2] This pâda, according to Sha*d*guru*s*ishya, is *R*igv. X, 20, 1. See the comm. on this verse and on Anuvâkânukrama*n*î, ver. 43. Cp. Ind. Stud. X, 132.

[3] See A. S. L., p. 221.

(4) B: a Grantha manuscript, belonging to the India Office, which only contains the text. It omits verses 1, 2, 11–14. Its date is not stated, but it is probably about two centuries old. It is tolerably correct. It is described in Burnell's small Catalogue, pp. 5–6, where 14 verses from it are printed.

(5) W 2, containing the text only, is tolerably correct; only the old irregular ones are in this MS. almost always corrected so as to have the regular form of the classical anush*t*ubh. The introduction, with the exception of the third verse, is wanting. Two verses and a half are also omitted from the main part of the work. This MS. has already been partly described.

(6) I 4, a MS. belonging to the India Office, containing the text only, is incorrect. It has many points of similarity with W 2, leaving out the whole of the introduction, the same two verses and a half, and replacing the old irregular verses in the same way, as will appear from the various readings of verses 15 and 21.

THE *KH*ANDA*H*SAṄKHYÂ.

This short index must be considered a pari*s*ish*t*a to the *Kh*ando*nu-krama*n*î. For the latter, though stating the number of verses in each metre besides the aggregate number of verses of all metres for every ma*n*d*ala, does not supply the totals of every metre for the whole *R*igveda. This omission the *Kh*anda*h*saṅkhyâ, as I have entitled it, supplies. It is obviously wrong in two items: the number of paṅktis being stated to be 312 instead of only 248 (see Index of Metres, Appendix III), and that of the dvipadâs as 17 instead of 127. The latter error may be due to the calculations of this index being based on totals in figures, as in the *Kh*ando*nukrama*n*î (see above), and being written in words after the 2 of 127 had dropped out. The remaining totals agree very nearly with those I have arrived at by adding up the aggregates of the metres in each ma*n*d*ala. My aggregates of all verses contained in each ma*n*d*ala, tally both with those of the *Kh*ando*nu-krama*n*î (excepting three slight variations, which will be explained below) and with the statements of Dayânanda Sarasvati in his *R*igveda-bhâshya (pp. 1–8), except in ma*n*d*alas VIII and IX, but in these two cases my totals agree with those of the *Kh*ando*nukrama*n*î. In the former case the cause of the error is evident, as hymn 20 of ma*n*d*ala VIII is stated to have 36 verses, whereas it has 26. The grand total of verses in the *S*âkala recension of the *Ri*gveda resulting from the addition of the totals for each ma*nd*ala is thus 10442, which is the exact sum I obtain by adding up the aggregates of each metre, whereas the same calculation for the aggregates of the *Kh*anda*h*sankhyâ produces only 10402 [1]. Dayânanda Sarasvati, though his totals for each would give only 10521, states the grand total to be 10589. My total by counting the dvipadâs (127) twice [2] would be 10569, only eleven less than the figure of the Anuvâkânukrama*n*î. I think it is not at all improbable that the apparent inconsistencies [3] in the numerical statements of this ancient index will be removed by taking into consideration all the verses of the *Ri*gveda which are repeated. If this should prove to be the case, it will indeed be one of the most remarkable facts in the history of literature that a people should have preserved its sacred book without adding or substracting a single word for 2300 years, and that too chiefly by means of oral tradition. The subjoined table shows the distribution of the metres in detail :—

Ma*nd*.	G.	U.	A.	B.	P.	T.	*G.*	Atig.	*S.*	Atis.	A.	Aty.	D.	Atidh.	Dv.	Ek.	B.Pr.	K. Pr.	M.Pr.	Total
I.	472	21	117	5	61	742	356	..	..	5	4	80	1	1	31	..	80	..	..	1976
II.	37	..	14	1	..	230[4]	142[5]	..	..	4	1	..	..	..	..	..	..	..	..	429
III.	104	10	27	19	2	399	50	..	..	..	..	..	..	..	..	..	6	..	..	617
IV.	119[6]	2[7]	27	..	..	403[8]	33	1	1[8]	..	1	..	1	..	..	1	..	..	..	589[8]
V.	79	19[9]	155	6	54	284[10]	103	11	1[11]	..	..	..	..	..	4	3[12]	4	4	..	727[13]
VI.	137	9	45	14	5	478	39[14]	1	6[15]	1	..	..	..	..	3	1[16]	20	4	2	765[17]
VII.	61	1	44	4	1	586	39	..	1	..	..	..	..	..	40	..	64	..	..	841
VIII.	733[18]	228	112[19]	89[20]	33[21]	81	65	3	7	..	..	..	..	..	13	..	188[22]	84	..	1636[23]
IX.	600	42	55	10	20	149	166	..	..	..	..	3	..	..	27	..	22	14	..	1108[24]
X.	108	12	260	32	72	901	351	..	4	..	..	..	..	..	9	1	4	..	..	1754
Total	2450	344	856	180	248	4253	1344	16	20	10	6	83	2	1	127	6	388	106	2	10442

[1] See the table in A. S. L., p. 222; cp. Ind. Stud., vol. viii, p. 51.

[2] See comm. on Introd. to Sarv., § 12, 10.

[3] See A. S. L., p. 222.

[4] *Kh*ando-n. 229.

[5] *Kh.* 143.

[6] *Kh.* 120.

[7] *Kh.* 1.

[8] The total of the *Kh.* is 588, 402 T., 2 *S.*, and no ekapadâ. The explanation is that a trish*t*ubh and the following ekapadâ are here considered a *s*akvarî. It is the same in ma*nd*alas V and VI.

[9] Omitted in *Kh.*

[10] *Kh.* 281.

[11] *Kh.* 5.

[12] None *Kh.*

[13] *Kh.* 724. See note 8.

[14] *Kh.* 40.

[15] *Kh.* 7.

[16] None *Kh.*

[17] *Kh.* 764.

[18] *Kh.* 717.

[19] *Kh.* 104. The difference in these cases is exactly made up for by 8 anush*t*ummukhas (= 8 an. and 16 gây.), (cp. Sarv. Introd., § 11, 6), which, though not mentioned in the *Kh.* Sankhyâ, are given in the Sarv. VIII, 68 and 74.

[20] *Kh.* 93.

[21] *Kh.* 35.

[22] *Kh.* 19 (= 38).

[23] Dayân. Sarasv. 1726.

[24] Dayân. Sarasv. 1097.

The *Kh*anda*h*saṅkhyâ I have found in two MSS. only; in W 2, already described, and in I 5, a MS. belonging to the India Office, in which it comes immediately after the text of the Sarvânukrama*n*î. The latter part of this MS. I have not collated, having obtained it after the text of the Sarvânukrama*n*î was printed.

THE VEDÂRTHADÎPIKÂ.

Sha*d*guru*s*ishya, who five times[1] gives the above title to his commentary, lived in the middle of the period of the revival of Vedic studies in India, almost half-way between Kumârila and Sâya*n*a. He flourished, as he tells us himself (see p. 168, verses 13–14), in the latter half of the twelfth century. His commentary on the Sarvânukrama*n*î shows him to have been a man of some originality and of considerable learning, grammatical no less than Vedic. In the conclusion of his commentary (p. 168, verses 16–17) he enumerates the seven works in which he was specially instructed by his six teachers. In Appendix V there is given a complete list of the quotations to be found in his commentary with the sole exception of the continual references to the sûtras of Pâ*n*ini's grammar[2]. Quotations from nearly all the works of *S*aunaka occur, but the lion's share among these falls to the B*ri*haddevatâ, which is mentioned twenty-five times, and from which no fewer than 46 *s*lokas are cited. Besides occasional references to the Sa*m*hitâs and Brâhma*n*as of the other Vedas, to Manu, the Bhagavadgîtâ, the Mahâbhârata, and other works, the great majority of the quotations naturally come from the Aitareya Brâhma*n*a and Âra*n*yaka, and from the *S*rauta and G*ri*hya Sûtras of Â*s*valâyana. The Aitareya Brâhma*n*a is in the conclusion (p. 168, ver. 16) called the *K*atvâri*ms*adbrâhma*n*a, while the Bhagavadgîtâ is once referred to as the Gîtopanisha*kkh*ruti. It is worthy of notice that Sha*d*guru*s*ishya always refers to the fifth Âra*n*yaka as the fourth, apparently looking upon the fourth and fifth as one book. Piṅgala's *Kh*anda*h* Sûtras he mentions under the title of the *Kh*andovi*k*iti at the end of his work[3], where he

[1] Twice in the introduction, ver. 6: सर्वानुक्रमणीवृत्तिर्नाम्ना वेदार्थदीपिका, and vers. 65-6: वृत्तिर्नाम्ना वेदार्थदीपिका . . . सर्वानुक्रमणीवृत्तिः; and in his conclusion, p. 167, ver. 12, and p. 168, vers. 13 and 18.

[2] A few passages of little or no importance, quoted vaguely with उक्तं, स्मर्यते, श्रूयते, will be found by looking up those words in the Index.

[3] See comm. on X, 191.

quotes the last sûtra of that author in illustration of the practice of repeating the last word or words of a work to show that it is concluded.

Sha*d*guru*s*ishya's commentary does not consist merely of a bare amplification[1] explaining the obscurities arising from the brevity of the sûtra style, but introduces many tales from Vedic mythology[2]. These are frequently quoted from the B*ri*haddevatâ; but even when he relates these stories in his own words, he generally does so in *s*lokas, and in one passage[3] of considerable length he even uses the trish*t*ubh metre. In fact this commentator has a way of breaking into verse even when speaking of far drier matters; he does not even shrink from working sûtras of Pâ*n*ini into a poetical form[4]. Besides these itihâsas, there are frequent discussions on the diction and the construction of the sûtras of the Sarvânukrama*n*î.

The present edition supplies practically the whole of the Vedârthadîpikâ. Its bulk has, however, been considerably reduced by the omission of the fuller pratîka (which is invariably given by Sha*d*guru*s*ishya), of all that can easily be supplied by using the paribhâshâs, of commonplace grammatical remarks, and of the continual repetitions from the introduction explaining unusual metres. I have been careful to retain matter of any importance or interest, such as all quotations, grammatical explanations of unusual or difficult forms, itihâsas, and discussions bearing on the construction and wording of the sûtras. I have paid especial attention in this respect to the formation of proper names in connexion with the ga*n*as, thinking that this might prove to be of some value in the criticism of the ga*n*apâ*th*a, the present state of which is far from satisfactory. All references to the various ga*n*as will be found in the index of words at the end.

In his commentary on the treatise on metre (Sarv. Introd., §§ 3–11), Sha*d*guru*s*ishya quotes a number of examples (mostly identical with those in the *Ri*gveda Prâti*s*âkhya) for the various metres enumerated and explained in the text. A list of these verses is given in Appendix IV.

I have collated five MSS. in preparing this edition of the Vedârthadîpikâ, viz. W 1, I 2, I 4, P 1, P 2 (and in a few instances C also), which have already been described.

[1] Like that of *G*agannâtha.
[2] A list of these is given in Appendix VI.
[3] Comm. on II, 33.
[4] See comm. on II, 11.

Sha*d*guru*s*ishya's introduction to the Vedârthadîpikâ, which, as is well known, possesses considerable interest and value for the history of Sanskrit literature, consists of 66 verses. I was obliged to refrain from publishing it owing to the hopelessly corrupt state of several passages. This part of Sha*d*guru*s*ishya's work occurs in three MSS. only; but C, as has been shown, has no independent value, while C 1, though slightly better than W 1, has on the whole the same or similar corruptions. W 1, otherwise so good a MS., fails here completely. I had entertained hopes that P 1 and P 2 would contain this introduction, but on the arrival of these MSS. from India, my hopes were disappointed. However, almost all that is of importance in it, nearly two-thirds of the whole, has already been printed; the first seven verses in Weber's Catalogue, verses 25–56 in Max Müller's History of Ancient Sanskrit Literature, pp. 236–239, and verses 56–60 in Meyer's *Ri*gvidh., p. xx. Sha*d*guru*s*ishya's real name is not known, for he mentions only the names of his six teachers. These are enumerated in the first verse of the introduction [1], and repeated with two variations in the conclusion [2].

The Vedârthadîpikâ was apparently intended to be a work of much wider scope than a mere commentary of the Sarvânukrama*n*î, for it concludes with the statement that it is only the end of the first adhyâya [3].

The commentary to the Anuvâkânukrama*n*î, also composed by Sha*d*-guru*s*ishya, but not forming part of the Vedârthadîpikâ, being short, has been printed in full. The text itself contains no further quotations than the two references to the Ya*g*urveda and the Â*s*valâyana *S*rauta Sûtra, in verses 13 and 14, already mentioned; nor does the commentary cite anything more than a passage from the *Ri*gveda [4] itself, a sûtra of the Â*s*va-lâyana G*ri*hya [5], another of the *S*rauta [6], a passage from a lexicographical work [7], a rule of Bhâguri [8], and, lastly, a passage from the Âra*n*yaka [9].

Besides the appendices already mentioned, I have added, with a view to facilitate the use of the commentary, some explanatory notes, too long for insertion among the foot-notes, discussing difficulties or explaining the reasons for my emendations of corrupt passages.

The critical notes to the commentary do not contain all the various readings; I have kept for possible future reference upwards of thirty

[1] See Weber's Catalogue, p. 12. [2] Page 168, ver. 15.
[3] **वेदार्थदीपिकायां प्रथमोऽध्यायः समाप्तः**, p. 168. [4] Verse 7.
[5] Ver. 8. [6] Ver. 10. [7] Ver. 9. [8] Ver. 35. [9] Ver. 46.

pages of such, consisting for the most part of trivial mistakes or omissions, the larger proportion of which do not find a place among the footnotes. The space occupied by the latter is quite large enough already.

The printed text of the Sarvânukramaṇî, together with an introduction and a short autobiography in German, I offered as a dissertation for the degree of Ph. D. in the University of Leipzig, at Easter 1884. I desire to take this opportunity of thanking my examiners, Profs. Hildebrand, Leskien, and Windisch, for their courtesy to me on the occasion of my oral examination at Leipzig, and the latter also for some transcripts from Berlin MSS. of the introduction to the Sarvânukramaṇî, which he was kind enough to lend me. I am indebted to my friend Prof. E. Leumann, of Strassburg, for some useful hints he gave me, while in Oxford, with regard to the arrangement of the notes. Prof. Julius Eggeling I have to thank for a note about the Âprî hymns. To Prof. Max Müller I must express my gratitude for the help derived from the very wide knowledge of Vedic literature which the editor of the *Ri*gveda and of Sâya*n*a possesses, in finding the clue to obscure references in Sha*d*guru*s*ishya's commentary. To his guidance in my Sanskrit studies I owe so much, that although I never attended any of his lectures, with the exception of a few informal ones on the Lalita Vistara, given some six years ago for the benefit of two young Japanese priests, who had come to study Sanskrit under him at Oxford, I cannot but look upon myself as a pupil of his in the real sense of the word.

I cannot conclude without congratulating the Delegates on possessing the services of an Oriental Reader who performs his duties so excellently well as Mr. J. C. Pembrey of the University Press.

A. A. M.

OXFORD,
August 20th, 1886.

KÂTYÂYANA'S

SARVÂNUKRAMA*N*Î

ETC.

ABBREVIATIONS.

A. S. L. = Ancient Sanskrit Literature.
Ait. = Aitareya.
Âr. = Âra*n*yaka.
Â*s*v. = Â*s*valâyana.
Ath. = Atharva.
BD. or B*ri*. Dev. = B*ri*haddevatâ.
Br. = Brâhma*n*a.
Comm. = comment or commentary.
G*ri*h. = G*ri*hya.
Ind. Stud. = Indische Studien.
Kâty. = Kâtyâyana.
M. M. = Max Müller.
Pâ*n*. = Pâ*n*ini.
*Ri*gv. = *Ri*gveda.
*Ri*gvidh. = *Ri*gvidhâna.
*Ri*gv. Pr. = *Ri*gveda Prâti*s*âkhya.
Sa*m*h. = Sa*m*hitâ.
*S*âṅkh. = *S*âṅkhâyana.
Sây. = Sâya*n*a.
Sha*d*g. = Sha*d*guru*s*ishya.
*S*r. = *S*rauta.
Taitt. = Taittirîya.
Up. = Upanishad.
Vâ*g*. = Vâ*g*asaneyi.
Vârt. = Vârtika.

The symbols designating MSS. are explained in the preface. The abbreviations for the metres in the table (p. xviii) are in the order in which the metres are given in Appendix III.

॥ अथ भगवत्कात्यायनविरचिता सर्वानुक्रमणी ॥

॥ श्रीगणेशाय नमः ॥

अथ ऋग्वेदाम्नाये शाकलके सूक्तप्रतीकऋक्संख्यऋषिदैवतछंदांस्यनुक्रमिष्यामो यथोपदेशं। न ह्येतज्ज्ञानमृते श्रौतस्मार्तकर्मप्रसिद्धिः। मंत्राणां ब्राह्मणार्षेय[1]छंदोदैवतविद्याजनाध्यापनाभ्यां श्रेयो[2]ऽधिगच्छतीति[3]। एताभ्यामेवानेवंविदो यातयामानि छंदांसि भवंति[4]। स्थाणुं वर्छति[5] गर्तं वा पात्यते प्रमीयते वा पापीयान्भवतीति विज्ञायते[6] ॥१॥

अथ ऋषयः ॥१॥ शतर्चिन आद्ये मंडलेऽंत्ये क्षुद्रसूक्त[7]महासूक्ता मध्यमेषु माध्यमाः ॥२॥ क्वचित्कथंचिदविशेषितं ब्रह्मर्षिमस्त्रियमनुक्तगोत्रमांगिरसं विद्यात्॥३॥ यस्य वाक्यं स ऋषिः॥४॥ या तेनोच्यते सा देवता ॥५॥ यदक्षरपरिमाणं तच्छंदः ॥६॥ अर्थेप्सव ऋषयो देवताश्छंदोभिरुपाधावन्[8] ॥७॥ तिस्र एव देवताः क्षित्यंतरिक्षद्युस्थाना अग्निर्वायुः सूर्य इति ॥८॥ एवं व्याहृतयः प्रोक्ता व्यस्ताः ॥९॥ समस्तानां प्रजापतिः ॥१०॥ ओंकारः सर्व-

[1] W 1, C, I 1; ब्राह्मणार्षेयः W 2; ब्राह्मण आर्षेयः I 2. [2] स श्रेयो C 81. [3] W 1; °च्छति W 2, I 1, I 2, C. [4] भवंत्यधस्तु विपरीते W 2, C 55, 56. [5] W 2, I 1, C 55, 56, 81; °मृच्छति W 1, C. [6] See Max Müller, A. S. L. p. 226, note 2. [7] I 1, I 2 क्षुद्रसूक्ता. [8] C 81 °रभ्यधावन्.

देवत्यः पारमेष्ठ्यो वा ब्राह्मो दैव आध्यात्मिकः[1] ॥११॥ तत्तत्स्थाना अन्यदेवतास्[2]तद्विभूतयः ॥१२॥ कर्मपृथक्त्वाद्धि पृथगभिधानस्तुतयो भवंति ॥१३॥ एकैव वा महानात्मा देवता ॥१४॥ स सूर्य इत्याचक्षते ॥१५॥ स हि सर्वभूतात्मा ॥१६॥ तदुक्तमृषिणा सूर्य आत्मा जगतस्तस्थुषश्चेति[3] ॥१७॥ तद्विभूतयोऽन्या देवताः ॥१८॥ तदप्येतदृचोक्तं ॥१९॥ इंद्रं मित्रं वरुणमग्निमाहुरिति ॥२०॥ यथाभिधानं त्वनुक्रमिष्यामः ॥२१॥ प्रायेणैंद्रे मरुतः ॥२२॥ राज्ञां च दानस्तुतयः ॥२३॥२॥

अथ छंदांसि ॥१॥ गायत्र्युष्णिगनुष्टुब्बृहतीपंक्तित्रिष्टुब्जगत्यतिजगतीशक्वर्यतिशक्वर्यष्ट्यत्यष्टिधृत्यतिधृतयः[5] ॥२॥ चतुर्विंशत्यक्षरादीनि चतुरुत्तराणि ॥३॥ ऊनाधिकेनैकेन[6] निचृद्भुरिजौ ॥४॥ द्वाभ्यां विराट्स्वराजौ ॥५॥ पादपूरणार्थं तु क्षैप्रसंयोगैकाक्षरीभावान्व्यूहेत् ॥६॥ आद्ये तु सप्तवर्गे पादविशेषात्संज्ञाविशेषाः ॥७॥ ताननुक्रामंत एवोदाहरिष्यामः ॥८॥ विराड्रूपा विराट्स्थानाश्च बहूना अपि त्रिष्टुभ एवेत्युद्देशः ॥९॥ तत्र दशैकादशद्वादशाक्षराणां वैराजत्रैष्टुभजागता इति संज्ञाः ॥१०॥ अनादेशेऽष्टाक्षराः पादाः ॥११॥ चतुष्पदाश्चर्चः ॥१२॥३॥

[1] W 2 reads पारमेष्ठ्यो वा after आध्यात्मिकः.
[2] °ना अन्यास्तद्वि° W 2, I 1.
[3] *Rigv.* I, 115, 1.
[4] *Rigv.* I, 164, 46 (cf. Weber, Ind. Stud. V, p. iv).
[5] After this sûtra the Vs. Anukr. and MSS. W 2, C insert a sloka from the *Rigvedaprâtisâkhya* (M. M., *Rigv.*-Prât. cccxxiv, 56): कृतिः प्रकृतिराकृतिर्विकृतिः संकृतिस्तथा । षष्ठी चाभिकृतिर्नाम सप्तम्युत्कृतिरुच्यते ॥ MS. W 1 has on the margin: कृतिः प्रकृ° च्यते. See Weber, Ind. Stud. VIII, p. 137.
[6] एकेनोनाधिकेन W 2.

प्रथमं छंदस्त्रिपदा गायत्री ॥१॥ पंचकाश्चत्वारः षट्कश्चैकश्च-तुर्थश्चतुष्को वा पदपंक्तिः ॥२॥ षट्सप्तैकादशा उष्णिग्गर्भा ॥३॥ त्रयः सप्तकाः पादनिचृत् ॥४॥ मध्यमः षट्कश्चेदतिनिचृत् ॥५॥ दशकश्चेद्यवमध्या ॥६॥ यस्यास्तु षट्सप्तकाष्टकाः सा वर्धमाना ॥७॥ विपरीता प्रतिष्ठा ॥८॥ द्वौ षट्कौ सप्तकश्च[1] ह्रसीयसी ॥९॥४॥

द्वितीयमुष्णिक् त्रिपदांत्यो द्वादशकः ॥१॥ आद्यश्चेत्पुर-उष्णिक् ॥२॥ मध्यमश्चेत्ककुप् ॥३॥ त्रैष्टुभजागतचतुष्काः ककुम्न्यंकुशिरा ॥४॥ एकादशिनोः परः षट्कस्तनुशिरा ॥५॥ मध्ये चेत्पिपीलिकमध्या ॥६॥ आद्यः पंचकस्त्रयोऽष्टका अनुष्टुब्गर्भा ॥७॥ चतुःसप्तकोष्णिगेव ॥८॥५॥

तृतीयमनुष्टुप् ॥१॥ पंच पंचकाः षट्कश्चैको महापदपंक्तिः ॥२॥ जागतावष्टकश्च कृतिः ॥३॥ मध्ये चेदष्टकः पिपीलिकमध्या ॥४॥ नवकयोर्मध्ये जागतः काविराट् ॥५॥ नववैराजत्रयोदशैर्नष्टरूपा ॥६॥ दशकास्त्रयो विराट् ॥७॥ एकादशका वा ॥८॥६॥

चतुर्थं बृहती तृतीयो द्वादशकः ॥१॥ आद्यश्चेत्पुरस्ताद्बृहती ॥२॥ द्वितीयश्चे[2]न्न्यंकुसारिण्युरोबृहती वा[3] स्कंधोग्रीवी वा ॥३॥ अंत्यश्चेदुपरिष्टाद्बृहती ॥४॥ अष्टिनोर्मध्ये दशकौ विष्टारबृहती ॥५॥ त्रिजागतोर्ध्वबृहती ॥६॥ त्रयोदशिनोर्मध्येऽष्टकः पिपीलिकम-

[1] W2, I1, I2; चेति W1, C, Vs. Anukr.

[2] चेन्यंकु॰ W1, W2, I1, I2, C.

[3] Vs. Anukr. omits वा.

ध्या ॥७॥ युजावष्टकावयुजौ नवैकादशिनौ बृहती विषमपदा[1] ॥८॥ चतुर्नवका बृहत्येव ॥९॥७॥

पंचमं पंक्तिः पंचपदा ॥१॥ अथ चतुष्पदा[2] ॥२॥ विराड् दशकैः[3] ॥३॥ अयुजौ जागतौ सतोबृहती ॥४॥ युजौ चेद्विपरीता ॥५॥ आद्यौ चेत्प्रस्तारपंक्तिः ॥६॥ अंत्यौ चेदास्तारपंक्तिः ॥७॥ आद्यांत्यौ चेत्संस्तारपंक्तिः ॥८॥ मध्यमौ चेद्विष्टारपंक्तिः ॥९॥८॥

षष्ठं त्रिष्टुप् त्रैष्टुभपदा ॥१॥ द्वौ तु जागतौ यस्याः सा जागते जगती ॥२॥ त्रैष्टुभे त्रिष्टुप् ॥३॥ वैराजौ जागतौ चाभिसारिणी ॥४॥ नवकौ वैराजस्त्रैष्टुभश्च द्वौ वा वैराजौ नवकस्त्रैष्टुभश्च विराट्स्थाना ॥५॥ एकादशिनस्त्रयोऽष्टकश्च विराड्रूपा ॥६॥ द्वादशिनस्त्रयोऽष्टकश्च ज्योतिष्मती ॥७॥ यतोऽष्टकस्ततो ज्योतिः ॥८॥ चत्वारोऽष्टका जागतश्च महाबृहती ॥९॥ मध्ये चेद्यवमध्या ॥१०॥ आद्यौ दशकावष्टकास्त्रयः पंक्त्युत्तरा विराट्पूर्वा वा ॥११॥९॥

सप्तमं जगती जागतपदा ॥१॥ अष्टिनस्त्रयः स्वौ च द्वौ महासतोबृहती ॥२॥ अष्टकौ सप्तकः षट्कौ दशको नवकश्च षळष्टका वा महापंक्तिः ॥३॥१०॥

अथ प्रगाथाः ॥१॥ बृहतीसतोबृहत्यौ बार्हतः ॥२॥ ककुप् चेत्पूर्वा काकुभः ॥३॥ महाबृहतीमहासतोबृहत्यौ महाबार्हतः ॥४॥

[1] W 1, W 2, C; नवकाष्टकैकादशाष्टिनो विषमपदा Vs. Anukr.; नवकाष्टकैकादश्यष्टिनो विषमपदा I 1, I 2, and Sây. *Rigv.* VIII, 46 introd. See Ind. Stud. VIII, p. 143. [2] °पादा Vs. Anukr. [3] W 1, I 2, C; दशकाः Vs. Anukr.; वैराजैर्विराट् W 2, C 55, 56. See Ind. Stud. VIII, p. 143.

बृहतीविपरीते विपरीतोत्तरः ॥५॥ अनुष्टुब्गायत्र्यौ चानुष्टुभोऽनुष्टुम्मुखास्तृचा इत्युक्ते ॥६॥११॥

सूक्तसंख्यानुवर्तेत आन्यस्याः सूक्तसंख्यायाः ॥१॥ ऋषिश्चान्यस्मादृषेरवाविशिष्टः ॥२॥ तुहिहवैतच्छब्दविशिष्टान्यृषिदैवतच्छंदांसि द्वित्रिचतुःपंचषट्सूक्तभांजि यथासंख्यं ॥३॥ अनिरुक्ता संख्या विंशतिः ॥४॥ अनादेशे त्विंद्रो देवता ॥५॥ त्रिष्टुप् छंदः ॥६॥ प्रगाथा बार्हताः ॥७॥ विंशतिका द्विपदा विराजः ॥८॥ तदर्धमेकपदाः ॥९॥ द्विर्द्विपदास्त्वृचः[1] समामनंति ॥१०॥ अयुक्ष्वंत्या द्विपदैव[2] ॥११॥ मंडलादिष्वाग्नेयमैंद्रात् ॥१२॥ त्रिष्टुबंतस्य सूक्तस्य शिष्टा[3] जगत्यः ॥१३॥ आदौ गायत्रं प्राग्घैरण्यस्तूपीयात्[4] ॥१४॥१२॥

॥ इति द्वादशकांडी तु परिभाषा प्रवर्णिता ॥

[१]अग्निं नव मधुच्छंदा वैश्वामित्रः। [२]वायो वायव्यैंद्रवायवमैत्रावरुणास्तृचाः। [३]अश्विना द्वादशाश्विनैंद्रवैश्वदेवसारस्वतास्तृचाः। सप्तैताः प्रउगदेवताः। [४]सुरूपकृत्नुं दशैंद्रं। [५]आ तु। [६]युंजंत्यादहेत्येताः षण्मारुत्यो वीळु चिदिंद्रेणेत्यैंद्र्यौ च। [७]इंद्रमित्। [८]एंद्र सानसिं। [९]इंद्रेहि। [१०]गायंति द्वादशानुष्टुभं तु। [११]इंद्रमष्टौ जेता माधुच्छंदसः। [१२]अग्निं द्वादश मेधातिथिः काण्व आग्नेयमग्निनेति पादो द्व्यग्निदैवतो निर्मथ्या[5]हवनीयौ[6]। [१३]सुसमिद्ध इतीध्मः समिद्धो

[1] C, W 1; तृचः I 1, I 2; °दा स्तृचः W 2, C 55, 56, 81. [2] See Ind. Stud. VIII, p. 144. [3] शेषा I 1. [4] W 1, W 2, C; °ग्घिरण्यस्तूपात् I 1, I 2, C 55, 56, Sây. Introd. to *Rigv.* I, 1. [5] W 1, W 2, C; निर्मैथ्य I 1; निर्मैथ्य I 2 and Sây. [6] °श्च आहवनीयश्च Sây.

वाग्निस्तनूनपान्नराशंस इळो बर्हिर्देवीर्द्वार उषासानक्ता दैव्यौ
होतारौ प्रचेतसौ तिस्रो देव्यः सरस्वतीळाभारत्यस्त्वष्टा वनस्पतिः
स्वाहाकृतय इति प्रत्यृचं देवताः[1]। एतदाप्रीसूक्तं। एतेनान्यान्युक्त-
दैवतानि। एकादशकानि तु नाराशंसान्याग्रशब्दोक्तान्यतनूनपांति।
[१४]ऐभिर्वैश्वदेवं। [१५]इंद्र सोममृतव्यं। तत्रैंद्री मारुती त्वाष्ट्र्याग्नेय्यैंद्री
मैत्रावरुणी चतस्रो द्रविणोदस आश्विन्याग्नेयीत्यृतुदेवताः सर्वत्र।
[१६]आ त्वा नव। [१७]इंद्रावरुणयोरैंद्रावरुणं युवाकु पादनिचृतौ।
[१८]सोमानमिति पंच ब्राह्मणस्पत्याश्चतुर्थ्यामिंद्रश्च सोमश्च पंचम्यां
दक्षिणा चान्याः सादसस्पत्या नाराशंसी वांत्या[2]। [१९]प्रति त्यमाग्नि-
मारुतं ॥१॥

[२०]अयमष्टावाभेवं। [२१]इह षळैंद्राग्नं। [२२]प्रातर्युजा सैका चतस्र
आश्विन्यस्तथा सावित्र्य आग्नेय्यौ द्वे देवीनामेकैकेंद्राणी[3]वरुणा-
न्यग्नायीनां द्यावापृथिव्ये पार्थिवी षड्वैष्णव्योऽतो देवा दैवी वा।
[२३]तीव्राश्चतुर्विंशतिर्वायव्यैकेंद्रवायव्यौ मैत्रावरुणमरुत्वतीयवैश्व-
देवपौष्णास्तृचाः शिष्टा[4] आप्योऽंत्याध्यर्धाग्नेय्यप्स्वंतः पुरउष्णिक्
परानुष्टुभिस्तिस्रश्चांत्या एकविंशी प्रतिष्ठा। [२४]कस्य पंचोनाजीगर्तिः
शुनःशेपः स कृत्रिमो वैश्वामित्रो देवरातो वारुणं तु त्रैष्टुभमादौ
काय्याग्नेय्यौ सावित्रस्तृचो गायत्रोऽस्यांत्या[5] भागी वा। [२५]यच्चित्सै-
का। [२६]वसिष्व[6] दशाग्नेयं तु। [२७]अश्वं सप्तोना गायत्रेऽंत्या दैवी

[1] W 1, I 2, C; °ता Sây. [2] I 1, I 2, Sây.; W 1 corrected to वा; चांत्या C, W 2.
[3] I 1, Sây.; °मेकेंद्रा° W 1, W 2, I 2, C. [4] शेषा I 1, I 2, Sây. [5] °ता I 1, Sây.
[6] Sây. °ष्वा (Sa*m*hita).

त्रिष्टुप्। [२८]यत्र ग्रावा नव षळनुष्टुबादि यच्चिद्धौलूखल्यौ परे
मौसल्यौ च प्रजापतेर्हरिश्चंद्रस्यांत्या चर्मप्रशंसा वा। [२९]यच्चित्सप्त[1]
पांक्तं। [३०]आ वो द्व्यधिकास्माकं पादनिचृच्छम्वन्त्रिष्टुप्परौ तृचा-
वाश्विनोषस्यौ[2]। [३१]त्वमग्ने द्व्यूना हिरण्यस्तूप आग्नेयं त्रिष्टुबंत्याष्ट-
मीषोळश्यौ च। [३२]इंद्रस्य पंचोना ॥२॥

[३३]एत। [३४]त्रिश्चिद्द्वादशाश्विनं नवम्यंत्ये[3] त्रिष्टुभौ। [३५]ह्वयाम्ये-
कादश सावित्रं नवमी जगत्याद्या च लिंगोक्तदैवतपादा[4]। [३६]प्र
वो विंशतिः कण्वो घौर[5] आग्नेयं प्रागाथमूर्ध्व ऊ षु यौप्यौ।
[३७]क्रीळं पंचोना मारुतं हि गायत्रं तु। [३८]कद्ध। [३९]प्र यद्दश प्रागाथं
तु। [४०]उत्तिष्ठाष्टौ ब्राह्मणस्पत्यं। [४१]यं रक्षंति नव वरुणमित्रार्यम्णां
मध्ये तृच आदित्येभ्यो गायत्रं हि। [४२]सं पूषन्दश पौष्णं। [४३]कद्रुद्राय
नव रौद्रं तृतीया मैत्रावरुणी चांत्यस्तृचः सौम्योऽंत्यानुष्टुप्। [४४]अग्ने
षळूना प्रस्कण्वः काण्व आग्नेयं तु प्रागाथमाद्यो द्वृचोऽश्व्युषसां
च। [४५]त्वमग्ने दशानुष्टुभमर्धर्चोऽंत्यो दैवः। [४६]एषो पंचोनाश्विनं तु
गायत्रं ॥३॥

[४७]अयं दश प्रागाथं तु। [४८]सह षोळशोषस्यं तु। [४९]उषश्चतुष्क-
मानुष्टुभं तु। [५०]उदु त्यं सप्तोना सौर्यं नवाद्या गायत्र्योऽंत्यस्तृचो
रोगघ्न उपनिषत्[6]। [५१]अभि त्यं पंचोना सव्यो द्वित्रिष्टुबंतं। आंगिरा

[1] यच्चिद्धि Sây. [2] °नोषस्यं W 2. [3] °म्यंते Sây. [4] W 1, C; °ताः पादास्त्रयः Sây. and W 2. I 2 has देवतापवादः (!), but com. दैवतपादाः। I 1 °दैवतपाद्य. [5] घोर W 2, I 2. [6] The words अंत्योऽर्धर्चः शत्रुघ्नश्च are added by MSS. C, W 2, I 3; supplied on the margin in W 1; omitted in Sây., I 1, I 2. Sha*d*guru*s*ishya makes no comment on them; cf. *Rig*vidh. I, 19, 2.

इंद्रतुल्यं पुत्रमिच्छन्नभ्यध्यायत्सव्य इतींद्र एवास्य पुत्रोऽजायत ।
[५२]त्यं सु त्रयोदश्यंत्ये त्रिष्टुभौ । [५३]न्यू ष्वेकादशांत्ये त्रिष्टुभौ । [५४]मा
नोऽंत्या त्रिष्टुप् षष्ठ्यष्टमी नवमी च । [५५]दिवश्चिदष्टौ जागतं हि ।
[५६]एष प्र षट् । [५७]प्र मंहिष्ठाय । [५८]नू चिन्नव नोधा गौतम आग्नेयं हि
चतुस्त्रिष्टुबंतं । [५९]वया इत्सप्त वैश्वानरीयं । [६०]वह्निं पंच । [६१]अस्मा
इदु षोळश ॥४॥

[६२]प्र सप्तोना । [६३]त्वं नव । [६४]वृष्णे पंचोना मारुतं त्रिष्टुबंतं ।
परमाग्नेयमैंद्रात् । [६५]पश्वा दश पराशरः शाक्त्यो द्वैपदं तत् । [६६]रयिः ।
[६७]वनेषु । [६८]श्रीणन् । [६९]शुक्रः । [७०]वनेमैकादश । [७१]उप प्र दश । [७२]नि
काव्या । [७३]रयिर्न । [७४]उपप्रयंतो नव गोतमो राहूगणो गायत्रं तु ।
[७५]जुषस्व पंच । [७६]का ते । [७७]कथा । [७८]अभि त्वा गायत्रं तु । [७९]हि-
रण्यकेशो द्वादशाद्यौ तृचौ त्रैष्टुभौष्णिहौ पूर्वोऽग्नये वा मध्यमाय ।
[८०]इत्था षोळशैंद्रं पांक्तं हि ॥५॥

[८१]इंद्रो नव । [८२]उपो षु षड् जगत्यंतं । [८३]अश्वावति जागतं ।
[८४]असावि विंशतिः षळनुष्टुभ औष्णिहपांक्तगायत्रत्रैष्टुभास्तृचाः
प्रगाथः । [८५]प्र ये द्वादश मारुतं ह पंचम्यंत्ये[1] त्रिष्टुभौ । [८६]मरुतो दश
गायत्रं । [८७]प्रत्वक्षसः षड् जागतं । [८८]आ विद्युन्मद्भिराद्यांत्ये प्रस्तार-
पंक्ती पंचमी विराड्रूपा । [८९]आ नो दश वैश्वदेवं तु पंचाद्याः सप्तमी
च जगत्यः षष्ठी विराट्स्थाना । [९०]ऋजुनीती नव गायत्रमंत्या-
नुष्टुप् । [९१]त्वं सोम त्र्यधिका सौम्यं पंचम्यादि गायत्र्यो द्वादशोष्णिक्
च । [९२]एता उ त्या द्व्यूनोषस्यं चतुर्जगत्यादि षळुष्णिगंतं तृचोऽंत्य

[1] W2, I1, I2; °ते Sây., W1, C.

अश्विनः । ९३ अग्नीषोमौ द्वादशाग्नीषोमीयमाद्यास्तिस्रोऽनुष्टुभ
उपांत्यास्तिस्रो गायत्र्योऽष्टमी जगती वा । ९४ इमं षोळश कुत्स
आग्नेयं तद्द्वित्रिष्टुबंतं पूर्वो देवास्त्रयः पादा दैवास्ततो मित्रोऽर्धर्चो
लिंगोक्तदेवतो[1] यद्देवत्यं[2] वा सूक्तं ॥६॥

९५ द्वे एकादशौषसाय[3] वाग्नये । ९६ स प्रत्नथा नव द्रविणोदसे ।
९७ अप नोऽष्टौ शुचये गायत्रं । ९८ वैश्वानरस्य तृचं वैश्वानरीयं ।
९९ जातवेदस एका जातवेदस्यमेतदादीन्येकभूयांसि सूक्तसहस्रमेत-
[4]त्कश्यपार्षं । १०० स यो वृषैकोना वार्षागिरा ऋज्राश्वांबरीषसहदेवभ-
यमानसुराधसः । १०१ प्र मंदिन एकादश कुत्स आद्या गर्भस्राविण्यु-
पनिषच्चतुस्त्रिष्टुबंतं[5] । १०२ इमां तेऽंत्या त्रिष्टुप् । १०३ तत्तेऽष्टौ । १०४ यो-
निर्नव । १०५ चंद्रमा एकोनाप्त्यस्त्रितो वा वैश्वदेवं हि पांक्तमंत्या
त्रिष्टुबष्टमी[6] महाबृहती यवमध्या । १०६ इंद्रं मित्रं सप्त त्रिष्टुबंतं ।
१०७ यज्ञस्तृचं । १०८ य इंद्राग्नी सप्तोनैंद्राग्नं तु । १०९ वि ह्यष्टौ । ११० ततं
नवार्भवं तु पंचम्यंत्ये[7] त्रिष्टुभौ । १११ तक्षन्पंचांत्या त्रिष्टुप् । ११२ ईळे
पंचाधिकाश्विनमाद्यौ पादौ लिंगोक्तदेवतावंत्ये त्रिष्टुभौ ॥७॥

११३ इदं विंशतिरुषस्यं द्वितीयोऽर्धर्चो रात्र्याश्च । ११४ इमा एकादश
रौद्रं द्वित्रिष्टुबंतं । ११५ चित्रं षट् सौर्यं । ११६ नासत्याभ्यां पंचाधिका
कक्षीवान्दैर्घतमस उशिक्प्रसूत आश्विनं वै । ११७ मध्वः । ११८ आ
वामेकादश । ११९ आ वां रथं दश जागतं । १२० का राधद्द्वादशांत्या

1 W 1, Sây.; °देवत्यो C; °दैवतो W 2, I 2. 2 W 1, W 2, C; यद्दैवत्यं I 1, I 2, Sây.
3 °शोपसाय W 2, I 2. 4 W 1, W 2, C; °तमु I 1, I 2, Sây. 5 W 1, C; कुत्सश्चतुस्त्रिष्टु-
बंतमाद्या गर्भस्राविण्युपनिषत् W 2, I 1, I 2, Sây. 6 त्रिष्टुबंतं W 2. 7 °ते Sây., C.

दुःस्वप्ननाशिन्याद्या गायत्री द्वितीया ककुप्तृतीयाचतुर्थ्यौ काविरा-
ण्नष्टरूप्यौ पंचमी[1] तनुशिरा षष्ठ्यक्षरैरुष्णिग्विष्टारबृहती कृति-
र्विराट् तिस्रो गायत्र्यः[2]। १२१ कदित्था पंचोना वैश्वदेवं वा ॥८॥
१२२ प्र वो वैश्वदेवमा वो विराड्रूपे[3]। १२३ पृथुः सप्तोनोषस्यं तु।
१२४ उषा उच्छंती। १२५ प्राता रत्नं सप्त स्वनयस्य दानस्तुतिरुप[4]
जगत्यौ। १२६ अमंदानिति कक्षीवान्दानतुष्टः पंचभिर्भावयव्यं तुष्टा-
वांत्ये अनुष्टुभौ भावयव्यरोमशयोर्दंपत्योः संवादः। १२७ अग्निमेका-
दश परुच्छेपो दैवोदासिराग्नेयं तु पारुच्छेपं सर्वमात्यष्टं तत्राति-
धृतिः षष्ठी। १२८ अयं जायताष्टौ। १२९ यं त्वमेकादश षष्ठ्यैंदवी प्रप्रा
वोऽतिशक्वर्यावष्टिरंत्या[5]। १३० एंद्र याहि दशांत्या त्रिष्टुप्। १३१ इंद्राय
सप्त। १३२ त्वया[6] षळ्युवंतमैंद्रापार्वतोऽर्धर्चः। १३३ उभे सप्तादौ त्रिष्टुप्ति-
स्रोऽनुष्टुभो गायत्री धृतिः। १३४ आ त्वा षड्वायव्यं त्वंत्याष्टिः। १३५ स्तीर्णं
नव चतुर्थ्याद्याः पंचैंद्र्यश्चोपांत्ये अष्टी। १३६ प्र सु सप्त मैत्रावरुणं
त्वंत्ये लिंगोक्तदेवत्ये[7] अंत्या त्रिष्टुप् ॥९॥
१३७ सुषुम तृचमतिशाक्वरं। १३८ प्रप्र चतुष्कं पौष्णं। १३९ अस्तु श्रौ-
षळेकादश वैश्वदेवी मैत्रावरुण्याश्विन्यस्तिस्र ऐंद्राग्नेयी मारुत्यैं-
द्राग्नी बार्हस्पत्या वैश्वदेव्यंत्या त्रिष्टुप्पंचमी बृहती वैश्वदेवमेतदेव-
मन्यासामपि सूक्तप्रयोगे वैश्वदेवत्वं सूक्तभेदप्रयोगे यल्लिंगं सा

1 °म्यौ W 2. 2 W 2, I 1, I 2, I 3, Sây.; का राधद्वादशांत्या दुःस्वप्ननाशिनी गायत्र्यनुष्टुभौष्णिहा द्वृचा विष्टारबृहती कृतिर्विराट् तिस्रो गायत्र्यो द्वितीयोष्णिग्वा तृतीयाचतुर्थ्यौ काविराण्नष्टरूप्यौ पंचमी तनुशिरा वा W 1, C. 3 MSS.; Sây. omits आ वो विराड्रूपे. 4 उप चरंति W 1. 5 I 1, I 2, Sây.; °ष्ट्यंत्या W 1, W 2, C. 6 त्वया वयं Sây. 7 W 1, C; °ते I 1, I 2, W 2, Sây.

देवता। १४०वेदिषदे सप्तोना दीर्घतमा औचथ्य आग्नेयं तु द्विचिष्टुबंतं
तु चिष्टुब्दशमी वा। १४१बळित्था। १४२समिद्ध आप्रिय आनुष्टुभ-
मंत्यैंद्री। १४३प्र तव्यसीमष्टावाग्नेयं तु तत्त्रिष्टुबंतं। १४४एति प्र सप्त
जागतं। १४५तं पृच्छत पंचांत्या चिष्टुप्। १४६चिमूर्धानं। १४७कथा।
१४८मथीद्यत्। १४९महः स वैराजं। १५०पुरु तृचमौष्णिहं। १५१मित्रं
नव मैत्रावरुणं हि जागतं मैत्र्याद्या। १५२युवं सप्त। १५३यजामहे
चतुष्कं। १५४विष्णोः षड्वैष्णवं हि। १५५प्र वो जागतं त्वैंद्रश्चाद्यस्तृचः।
१५६भव पंच। १५७अबोधि षळाश्विनं त्वंत्ये चिष्टुभौ ॥१०॥

१५८वसू अंत्यानुष्टुप्। १५९प्र द्यावा पंच द्यावापृथिवीयं[1] तु जागतं
तु। १६०ते हि। १६१किमु श्रेष्ठः षळार्भवं चिष्टुबंतं। १६२मा नो
द्व्यधिकाश्वस्तुतिस्तु तृतीयाषष्ठ्यौ जगत्यौ। १६३यदक्रंदः सप्तोना।
१६४अस्य द्विपंचाशदल्पस्तवं त्वेतत्संशयोत्थापनप्रश्नप्रतिवाक्यान्यत्र
प्रायेण ज्ञानमोक्षाक्षरप्रशंसा च पंचपादं साकंजानां यज्ञायचेऽयं
स शिंक्ते सप्तार्धगर्भा गौरीरिति जगत्यः। एतदंतं[2] वैश्वदेवं तस्याः
समुद्रा इति वाचः समुद्रा आपोऽक्षरं सा प्रस्तारपंक्तिः शकमय-
मिति शकधूम उक्षाणं पृश्निमिति सोमस्त्रयः केशिन इत्यग्निः सूर्यो
वायुश्च केशिनश्चत्वारि वाग्वाच इंद्रं मित्रं सौर्यौ द्वादशेति संवत्स-
रसंस्थं कालचक्रवर्णनं यस्ते सरस्वत्यै यज्ञेन साध्येभ्यः परानुष्टु-
प्सौरी पर्जन्याग्निदेवता वांत्या सरस्वते सूर्याय वा। १६५कया
पंचोना संवादोऽगस्त्यैंद्रमरुतां[3] तृतीयाद्ययुजो मरुतां वाक्य-

[1] MSS.; °थिव्यं Sây. [2] °तं तु I 1, Sây. [3] W 2; ऽगस्त्यैंद्रमरुतां supplied on the margin in W 1; omitted in C, I 1, I 2, and Sây.

मंत्यस्तृचोऽगस्त्यस्य शिष्टा इंद्रस्यैकादशी च मरुत्वांस्त्विंद्रो[1] देव-
ता ॥११॥

१६६ तन्वगस्त्यो मारुतं हि द्विचिष्टुबंतं मित्रावरुणयोर्दीक्षित-
योरुर्वशीमप्सरसं दृष्ट्वा वासतीवरे कुंभे रेतोऽपतत्ततोऽगस्त्य-
वसिष्ठावजायेतां। १६७ सहस्रमेकादशाद्यैंद्री। १६८ यज्ञायज्ञा दश त्रि-
ष्टुबंतं। १६९ महोऽष्टौ द्वितीया विराट्[2]। १७० न नूनं पंचागस्त्येनैंद्रे
हविषि मरुतामुद्यत इंद्रागस्त्ययोः संवाद ऐंद्रस्तत्राद्या तृतीया चेंद्र-
वाक्यं चतुर्थी वांदौ[3] बृहती तिस्रोऽनुष्टुभः। १७१ प्रति वः षण्मारुतं
तु चतस्रोऽंत्या मरुत्वतीयाः। १७२ चित्रस्तृचं गायत्रं। १७३ गायत्स-
म्नोना। १७४ त्वं राजा दश। १७५ मत्सि षळानुष्टुभं तु त्रिष्टुबंतं त्वाद्या
स्कंधोग्रीवी। १७६ मत्सि नः। १७७ आ चर्षणिप्राः पंच। १७८ यद्ध स्या।
१७९ पूर्वीः षड् जायापत्योर्लोपामुद्राया अगस्त्यस्य च द्वृचाभ्यां रत्यर्थे
संवादं श्रुत्वांतेवासी ब्रह्मचार्यंत्ये बृहत्यादी अपश्यत्। १८० युवोर्द-
शाश्विनं वै। १८१ कदु नव। १८२ अभूदिदमष्टौ षष्ठ्यंत्ये त्रिष्टुभौ।
१८३ तं युंजाथां षट् ॥१२॥

१८४ ता वां। १८५ कतरैकादश द्यावापृथिवीयं। १८६ आ नो वैश्वदेवं।
१८७ पितुं न्वन्नस्तुतिर्गायत्रं त्वाद्यानुष्टुब्गर्भा तृतीया[5] पंचम्याद्याश्च
तिस्रोऽनुष्टुभोऽंत्या च बृहती वा[6]। १८८ समिद्ध आप्रियः। १८९ अग्ने
नयाष्टावाग्नेयं। १९० अनर्वाणं बार्हस्पत्यं। १९१ कंकतः षोळशोपनिष-

[1] तु omitted in W 2. [2] W 1, C add पंक्तिः। [3] C, W 1, I 3; च W 2, I 1, I 2, and Sây. [4] Cf. *Rigvidh*. I, 26, 6. [5] तृतीयांत्ये Sây. [6] Sây. omits बृहती वा; all the MSS. have it (even I 3: चांत्या बृहतीयानुष्टुभा (sic)).

दानुष्टुभमम्नृणसौर्ये विषशंकावानगस्त्यः प्राब्रवीद्दशम्याद्यास्तिस्रो[1] महापंक्तयो महाबृहती च ॥

॥ शतर्चिनां मंडलं तु समाप्तं प्रथमं त्विति ॥

य आंगिरसः शौनहोत्रो भूत्वा भार्गवः शौनकोऽभवत्स गृत्स-
मदो द्वितीयं मंडलमपश्यत् । [१]त्वमग्ने जागतं तु । [२]यज्ञेन सप्तोना ।
[३]समिद्ध एकादशाग्रं सप्तमी जगती[2] । [४]हुवे नव सोमाहुतिर्भार्गवो
ह । [५]होताष्टावानुष्टुभं । [६]इमां मे गायत्रं हि । [७]श्रेष्ठं षट् । [८]वा-
जयन्निवांत्यानुष्टुप् ॥१३॥

[९]नि होता । [१०]जोहूत्रः । [११]श्रुधि सैकेंद्रं विराट्स्थानमृतेऽंत्यां ।
[१२]यो जातः पंचोना[3] । [१३]आतुः सप्तोनांत्या त्रिष्टुप् । [१४]अध्वर्यवो
द्वादश । [१५]प्र घ दश । [१६]प्र वो नवांत्या त्रिष्टुप् । [१७]तदस्मै द्वि-
त्रिष्टुबंतं । [१८]प्रातः । [१९]अपायि । [२०]वयं ते स नो विराड्रूपा[3] ।
[२१]विश्वजिते षट् त्रिष्टुबंतं । [२२]त्रिकद्रुकेषु चतुष्कमष्ट्याद्यतिशाक्कर-
मंत्याष्टिर्वा । [२३]गणानामेकोना ब्राह्मणस्पत्यं ह[4] बार्हस्पत्यास्तु
दृष्टलिंगाः पंचदश्यंत्ये त्रिष्टुभौ ॥१४॥

[२४]सेमां षोळशांत्या त्रिष्टुब्द्वादशी च सैंद्री च । [२५]इंधानः पंच
जागतं तु । [२६]ऋजुश्चतुष्कं । [२७]इमा[5]स्त्र्यूना कूर्मो गार्त्समदो हि

[1] C, W 1, W 2, I 2; °द्याश्च तिस्रो Sây., I 1. [2] I 1, I 2, and Sây.; पञ्चादि जगत्यः W 2, C; W 1 the same, but जगत्यः corrected on the margin to जगत्यौ. [3] W 1, W 2, C, I 1; स नो विराड्रूपा omitted by I 2, Sây. [4] MSS.; Sây. has तु. [5] I 1, I 2, and Sây. give the fuller pratîka इमा गिरः ।

वादित्येभ्यः[1]। २८इदमेकादश वारुणं[2]। २९धृतव्रताः सप्त वैश्वदेवं।
३०ऋतमेकादश जगत्यंतं षष्ठ्यैंद्रासौमी[3] सरस्वति त्वमिति सार-
स्वतोऽर्धर्चो यो नो बार्हस्पत्या तं वो[4] मारुती। ३१अस्माकं सप्त
वैश्वदेवं त्रिष्टुबंतं। ३२अस्य मेऽष्टौ जागतं त्र्यनुष्टुबंतं द्यावापृथिव्यैका
द्वे ऐंद्र्यौ त्वाष्ट्र्यौ वा द्वे द्वे राकासिनीवाल्योरंत्या लिंगोक्तदेवता।
३३आ ते पंचोना रौद्रं। ३४धारावरा मारुतं त्रिष्टुबंतं। ३५उपेमपो-
नप्त्रीयं[5]। ३६तुभ्यं षडृतव्यं तु जागतं तु ॥१५॥

३७मंदस्व। ३८उदु ष्य एकादश सावित्रं। ३९ग्रावाणेवाष्टावाश्विनं।
४०सोमापूषणा षट् सोमापौष्णमंत्योऽर्धर्चोऽप्यदितेः। ४१वायो सैका
गायत्रमुक्ता देवताः प्रउगेणाद्ये तु तृचेऽंत्यैंद्रवायवी द्यावापृथिव्यो
ऽंत्यस्तृचो हाविर्धानो वा तृतीयः पादो वाग्नेयोऽंबितमेऽनुष्टुभौ
बृहती च। ४२कनिक्रदत्तृचं। ४३प्रदक्षिणिज्जागतं मध्येऽतिशक्कर्य-
ष्टिर्वा। एताभ्यामृषिरध्वनि वाश्यमानं शकुंतं तुष्टाव[6] ॥

॥ इति गार्त्समदं द्वितीयं मंडलं समाप्तं ॥

कुशिकस्त्वैषीरथिरिंद्रतुल्यं पुत्रमिच्छन्ब्रह्मचर्यं चचार तस्येंद्र
एव गाथी पुत्रो जज्ञे[7] गाथिनो विश्वामित्रः स तृतीयं मंडलम-

[1] W 1, W 2, C, I 2; °त्यं Sây., I 1. [2] C, W 1, W 2, Sây.; उपांत्या दुःस्वप्ननाशिनी added in I 1, I 2, I 3; Shadg. makes no comment on these words. See *Rig*vidh. I, 30, 1. [3] W 1, C; °सोमी W 2, I 1, I 2, I 3, Sây. [4] I 1, I 2, (I 3), Sây.; बृहस्पतिस्तवोऽंत्या W 1, W 2, C. [5] I 1, I 2, and Sây.; °त्रियं W 1, C; °त्र्यं W 2. [6] See M. M., *Rig*v. vol. ii, p. xl; cf. *Rig*vidh. I, 31, 3, 4. [7] Sây. on *Rig*v. I, x, 11 quotes so far, omitting the rest.

पश्यन्। ¹सोमस्य ष्यधिका। ²वैश्वानराय पंचोना वैश्वानरीयं तु जागतं तु। ³वैश्वानरायैकादश। ⁴समित्समिदाप्रियः। ⁵प्रत्यग्निः। ⁶प्र कारवः। इत्याग्नेययोरन्यासामपि निपातो दृश्यते ॥१६॥

⁷प्र ये। ⁸अंजंति यूपस्तुतिः षष्ठ्याद्याभिर्बहवोऽंत्या व्रश्चिन्यष्टमी वैश्वदेवी वा तृतीयासप्तम्यावनुष्टुभौ। ⁹सखायो नव बार्हतं त्रिष्टुबंतं। ¹⁰त्वामग्न औष्णिहं। ¹¹अग्निर्होता गायत्रं तु[1]। ¹²इंद्राग्नी ऐंद्राग्नं। ¹³प्र वः सप्त ऋषभस्त्वानुष्टुभं। ¹⁴आ होता। ¹⁵वि पाजसा कात्य उत्कीलस्तु[2]। ¹⁶अयमग्निः षट् प्रागाथं। ¹⁷समिध्यमानः पंच कतो वैश्वामित्रस्तु। ¹⁸भवा नः। ¹⁹अग्निं होतारं गाथी ह। ²⁰अग्निमुषसमाद्यांत्ये[3] वैश्वदेव्यौ। ²¹इमं न उपाद्ये अनुष्टुभौ विराड्रूपा सतोबृहती चांत्या। ²²अयं स उपांत्यानुष्टुप्पुरीष्येभ्यो ऽग्निभ्यः। ²³निर्मथितो देवश्रवा देववातश्च भारतौ तृतीया सतोबृहती। ²⁴अग्ने सहस्व गायत्रमाद्यानुष्टुप्। ²⁵अग्ने दिवो वैराजमुपांत्याग्नेंद्री। ²⁶वैश्वानरं नव तृचौ वैश्वानरीयमारुतौ जागतौ तृच आत्मस्तुतिर्वा पूर्वात्मगीतांत्योपाध्यायस्तुतिः। ²⁷प्र वः पंचोना गायत्रं त्वृतव्या वाद्या। ²⁸अग्ने जुषस्व षट् तृतीयाद्युष्णिक्त्रिष्टुब्जगत्यः। ²⁹अस्तीदं षोळशाद्याचतुर्थीदशमीद्वादश्योऽनुष्टुभः षष्ठ्येकादश्युपांत्ये च जगत्यः पंचम्यृत्विग्भ्यो वा ॥१७॥

³⁰इच्छंति द्व्यधिकैंद्रं। ³¹शासत्कुशिको विश्वामित्र एव वा श्रुतेः। ³²इंद्र सोमं त्र्यूना। ³³प्र पर्वतानां सप्तोना संवादो नदीभिर्वि-

[1] MSS.; Sây. omits तु. [2] C, W 1 corrected; कात्यो उत्कीलस्तु I 1; कात्योत्कीलस्तु Sây., W 2, I 2. [3] W 2, I 1, I 2; °त्ते W 1, C, Sây.

श्वामित्रस्योत्तितीर्षोस्तत्र नदीवाक्यं चतुर्थीषष्ठ्यष्टमीदशम्यः षष्ठी-
सप्तम्योस्त्विंद्रस्तुतिरंत्यानुष्टुप्। [३४]इंद्रः पूर्भिदेकादश। [३५]तिष्ठा हरी।
[३६]इमामू षूपांत्यां घोरोऽपश्यत्सा निर्देहेच्छस्यमानेति श्रूयते।
[३७]वार्त्रहत्याय गायत्रमंत्यानुष्टुप्। [३८]अभि तष्टेव दश प्रजापतिः
स वैश्वामित्रो वाच्यो वा द्वौ वा तौ न वैकोऽपि। [३९]इंद्रं
मतिर्नव ॥१८॥

[४०]इंद्र त्वा गायत्रं हि। [४१]आ तू नः। [४२]उप नः। [४३]आ याह्यष्टौ।
[४४]अयं ते पंच बार्हतं तु। [४५]आ मंद्रैः। [४६]युध्मस्य। [४७]मरुत्वान्।
[४८]सद्यो ह। [४९]शंसा महां। [५०]इंद्रः स्वाहा। [५१]चर्षणीधृतं द्वादशाद्यांत्यौ
तृचौ जागतगायत्रौ। [५२]धानावंतमष्टौ पूर्वार्धं गायत्रं षष्ठी जगती।
[५३]इंद्रापर्वता चतुर्विंशतिराद्यैंद्रापार्वती पंचदश्यादिद्वे वाचे सस-
पर्यै चतस्रो रथांगस्तुतयोऽंत्या अभिशापास्ता[1] वसिष्ठद्वेषिण्यो
न वसिष्ठाः शृण्वंति। दशमीषोळश्यौ जगत्यौ त्रयोदशी गायत्री
द्वादशीविंशीद्वाविंश्योऽनुष्टुभोऽष्टादशी बृहती। [५४]इमं महे द्याधि-
कोक्तगोत्रः प्रजापतिर्हि वैश्वदेवं ह। [५५]उषसः ॥१९॥

[५६]न ताष्टौ। [५७]प्र मे षट्। [५८]धेनुर्नवाश्विनं। [५९]मित्रो मैत्रं
चतुर्गायत्र्यंतं। [६०]इहेह वः[2] सप्तार्भवं जागतं तृचोऽंत्य ऐंद्रश्च। [६१]उष
उषस्यं[3]। [६२]इमा उ द्यूनैंद्रावरुणबार्हस्पत्यपौष्णसावित्रसौम्यमैत्रा-
वरुणास्तृचा अंत्यो जमदग्न्यार्षो वा चतुर्थ्याद्या गायत्र्यः ॥

॥ तृतीयं मंडलं समाप्तं ॥

[1] C, W 1, W 2, I 2; °पार्यास्ता I 1, Sây. [2] C, W 1, W 2, I 2; वः omitted by I 1, Sây. [3] MSS.; औषस्यं Sây.

वामदेवो गौतमश्चतुर्थं मंडलमपश्यत्। [१]त्वां ह्यग्ने विंशति-
रष्ट्यतिजगतीधृतय आद्या उपाद्याश्चतस्रो वारुण्यश्च वा। [२]यो
मर्त्येषु। [३]आ वः षोळशाद्या रौद्री[1]। [४]कृणुष्व पंचोना रा-
क्षोघ्नं ॥२०॥

[५]वैश्वानराय वैश्वानरीयं। [६]ऊर्ध्व ऊ ष्वेकादश। [७]अयमिहादौ
जगती पंचानुष्टुभः। [८]दूतं वोऽष्टौ गायत्रं तु। [९]अग्ने मृळ। [१०]अग्ने
तमद्य पदपांक्तं पंचमी महापदपंक्तिरंत्योष्णिक् चतुर्थी षष्ठ्युपांत्या
वा सप्तम्याः पंचकौ मुख्यौ तृतीयः सप्तको नवकश्चाष्टम्याः पंचकः
पादश्चतुष्कः सप्तकस्त्रैष्टुभश्च। [११]भद्रं षट्। [१२]यस्त्वां। [१३]प्रत्यग्निः पंच
लिंगोक्तदैवतं त्वेके। [१४]प्रत्यग्निः। [१५]अग्निर्होता दश गायत्रमृषिर्बो-
धदित्याभ्यां[2] सोमकं साहदेव्यमभ्यवदत्पराभ्यामस्याश्विनावायुर-
याचत। [१६]आ सत्यः सैकेंद्रं। [१७]त्वं महाँ असिन्नन्यामेकपदा। [१८]अयं
पंथाः सप्तोना संवाद इंद्रादितिवामदेवानां ॥२१॥

[१९]एवैकादश। [२०]आ नः। [२१]आ यातु। [२२]यन्नः। [२३]कथोपांत्या-
स्तिस्र ऋतदेव्यो वा। [२४]का सुष्टुतिरुपांत्यानुष्टुप्। [२५]को अद्याष्टौ।
[२६]अहं मनुः सप्ताद्याभिस्तिसृभिरिंद्रमिवात्मानमृषिस्तुष्टावेंद्रो वा-
त्मानं परा नवाष्टौ वा श्येनस्तुतिः। [२७]गर्भे नु पंचांत्या शक्वरी।
[२८]त्वा युजेंद्रासौमं[3] वा। [२९]आ नः स्तुतः। [३०]नकिश्चतुर्विंशतिर्दिव-
श्चित्तृच उषस्यश्च गायत्रं ह्यष्टम्यंत्ये[4] अनुष्टुभौ। [३१]कया पंचो-

[1] C, W1, W2, I1, I2, I3; आद्या रौद्री omitted in Sây. See M.M., *Rigv.* vol. vi, p. xxii.
[2] इति द्वाभ्यां I1, I2, Sây.
[3] ०द्रासोमं MSS. See Pâṇini VII, iii, 21.
[4] ०न्ते C.

नाभी षु पादनिचृत् । [३२] आ तू नश्चतुर्विंशतिरंत्याभ्यामिंद्राग्नी स्तुतौ ॥२२॥

[३३] प्र ऋभुभ्य एकादशार्भवं वै । [३४] ऋभुर्विभ्वा । [३५] इहोप नव । [३६] अनश्वोऽंत्या त्रिष्टुप् । [३७] उप नोऽष्टौ चतुरनुष्टुबंतं । [३८] उतो हि दश दाधिक्रं हि द्यावापृथिव्याद्या । [३९] आशुं षळंत्यानुष्टुप् । [४०] दधिक्राव्णः पंच चतस्रोऽंत्या जगत्योऽंत्या सौरी । [४१] इंद्रा को वामेकादशैंद्रावरुणं तु । [४२] मम द्विता दश त्रसदस्युः पौरुकुत्स्यः षळाद्या आत्मस्तवः[1] । [४३] क उ श्रवत्सप्त पुरुमीळ्हाजमीळ्हौ सौहोत्रौ त्वाश्विनं हि । [४४] तं वां । [४५] एष स्य त्रिष्टुबंतं । [४६] अग्रं वायव्याद्यैंद्रवायवं तु गायत्रं । [४७] वायो चतुष्कमाद्या वायव्यानुष्टुभं तु । [४८] विहि पंच वायव्यं । [४९] इदं वां षळैंद्राबार्हस्पत्यं गायत्रं । [५०] यस्तस्तंभैकादश बार्हस्पत्यमंत्ये ऐंद्र्यौ चोपांत्या जगती ॥२३॥

[५१] इदमुषस्यं तु । [५२] प्रति ष्या सप्त गायत्रं । [५३] तद्देवस्य सावित्रं तु जागतं । [५४] अभूद्देवः षट् त्रिष्टुबंतं । [५५] को वो दश वैश्वदेवं त्रिगायत्र्यंतं तु । [५६] मही सप्त द्यावापृथिवीयं । [५७] क्षेत्रस्याष्टौ तिस्रः क्षैत्रपत्याः शुनायैका परा पुरउष्णिक् सांत्या च शुनासीराभ्यामुपांत्ये सीतायै ते चानुष्टुभावाद्याचतुर्थ्यौ च[2] । [५८] समुद्रादेकादशाग्नेयं जगत्यंतं सौर्यं वापं वा गव्यं वा घृतस्तुतिर्वा ॥

॥ इति चतुर्थं मंडलं समाप्तं ॥

1 °संस्तवः W 2. 2 W 1, C; आद्या चतुर्थी च I 2; ते अनुष्टुभावाद्या च चतुर्थी च Sây.; च omitted in W 2, I 1.

नमोऽत्रिभ्यो भौमोऽत्रिः पंचमे मंडलेऽनुक्तगोत्रमात्रेयं विद्यात्पंक्त्यंतस्य च सूक्तस्य शेषमानुष्टुभं । १अबोधि द्वादश बुधगविष्ठिरौ । २कुमारं कुमारो वृशो वा जान[1] उभौ वा शक्त्यंतं कं वीत्यृचोस्तु वृश एव । ३त्वमग्ने वसुश्रुतः । ४त्वामग्न एकादश । ५सुसमिद्धायाग्नं गायत्रं । ६अग्निं तं दश पांक्तं । ७सखाय इषः पंक्त्यंतं । ८त्वामग्ने सप्त जागतं ॥२४॥

९त्वामग्ने गयोऽंत्यापंचम्यौ पंक्ती । १०अग्न ओजिष्ठमंत्याचतुर्थौ[2] च । ११जनस्य षट् सुतंभरो जागतं । १२प्राग्नये । १३अचेतो गायत्रं तु । १४अग्निं स्तोमेन । १५प्र वेधसे पंचांगिरसो धरुणः । १६बृहत्पूरुः पंक्त्यंतं हि । १७आ यज्ञैः । १८प्रातर्मृक्तवाहा द्वितः । १९अभ्यवस्था वव्रिर्गायत्र्यावनुष्टुभौ विराड्रूपा । २०यमग्ने चतुष्कं प्रयस्वंतः पंक्त्यंतं ह । २१मनुष्वत्ससः[3] । २२प्र विश्वसामन्विश्वसामा[4] । २३अग्ने द्युम्नो विश्वचर्षणिः । २४अग्ने त्वं गौपायना लौपायना वा बंधुः सुबंधुः श्रुतबंधुर्विप्रबंधुश्चैकर्चा द्वैपदं । २५अच्छा वो नव वसूयव आनुष्टुभं । २६अग्ने गायत्रमंत्या लिंगोक्तदेवता[5] । २७अनस्वंता षट् त्रैवृष्ण[6]पौरुकुत्स्यौ द्वौ त्र्यरुणत्रसदस्यू राजानौ भारतश्चाश्वमेधोऽंत्यास्तिस्रोऽनुष्टुभो नात्मात्मने दद्यादिति सर्वास्वत्रिं केचिदंत्यैंद्राग्नी । २८समिद्धो विश्ववारात्रेयी त्रिष्टुब्जगती त्रिष्टुबनुष्टुब्गायत्र्यौ । २९त्र्यर्यमा पंचोना गौरिवीतिः

1 MSS. (I 3 जनपुत्रो वृशः); जारः Sây. 2 W 1, C, I 1, Sây.; अंत्या चतुर्थी च W 2, I 2. 3 मनुष्वच्छसः W 2. 4 W 2, I 1, I 2, Sây.; प्र विश्वसामा W 1, C. 5 C, W 2; अंत्या लिंगोक्तदेवता added on the margin in W 1, omitted in I 2, Sây.; अंत्या वैश्वदेवी I 1; I 3 explains अंत्या वैश्वदेवी वा; Shad*g*. has no comment. 6 वृष्णि° W 2.

शाक्त्य ऐंद्रमुशना यदौशनसो वा पादः। [३०]क्व स्य बभ्रुर्ऋणंचयोऽप्यत्र
राजा स्तुतः। [३१]इंद्रो रथाय सप्तोनावस्युरूपमिति कौत्स्यौशनसौ
वा पादौ पैरंद्राकौत्सी। [३२]अदर्दर्द्वादश गातुः ॥२५॥

[३३]महि दश प्राजापत्यः संवरणः। [३४]अजातशत्रुं नव त्रिष्टुबंतं।
[३५]यस्तेऽष्टौ प्रभूवसुरांगिरसः पंक्त्यंतं। [३६]स आ गमत् षट् तृतीया
जगती। [३७]सं भानुना पंचात्रिः। [३८]उरोरानुष्टुभं। [३९]यदिंद्र पंक्त्यंतं।
[४०]आ याहि नव त्र्युष्णिगाद्यंत्यानुष्टुम्मध्ये च सा सौरी तदादीति-
हासः[1] स्तुतिकर्मत्वादत्रिर्देवतैव[2]। [४१]को नु विंशतिर्वैश्वदेवं वै तत्
षोळश्याद्यतिजगत्यावंत्यैकपदा। [४२]प्र शंतमा द्व्यूनैकादशी रौद्री।
[४३]आ धेनवस्त्र्यूना। एतयोरुपांत्यैकपदा। [४४]तं प्रत्नथा पंचोना
काश्यपोऽवत्सारोऽन्ये च ऋषयोऽच दृष्टलिंगा द्वित्रिष्टुबंतं। [४५]वि-
दा एकादश सदापृणः। [४६]हयोऽष्टौ प्रतिक्षत्रोऽंत्यो द्वृचो देव-
पत्नीस्तवोऽंत्या त्रिष्टुब्द्वितीया च ॥२६॥

[४७]प्रयुंजती सप्त प्रतिरथः। [४८]कदु पंच प्रतिभानुर्जागतं। [४९]देवं
वः प्रतिप्रभोऽंत्या तृणपाणिः। [५०]विश्वः स्वस्त्यात्रेयः पंक्त्यंतं। [५१]अग्ने
पंचोना चतस्रो गायत्र्यः षडुष्णिहस्तिस्रो जगत्यस्त्रिष्टुभो वांत्ये
अनुष्टुभौ। [५२]प्र श्यावाश्व त्र्यूना श्यावाश्वो मारुतं ह तत्पंक्तिः
षष्ठ्यंत्ये च[3]। [५३]को वेद षोळश ककुब्बृहत्यनुष्टुप्पुरउष्णिक् ककुप्स-
तोबृहत्यौ गायत्री सतोबृहती ककुभौ गायत्री सतोबृहत्यौ ककु-
प्सतोबृहती। [५४]प्र शर्धाय पंचोना जागतमुपांत्या त्रिष्टुप्। [५५]प्र-

[1] Sây.; °स MSS. [2] अत्रिरेव देवः I 1, Sây. [3] W 1, W 2, C, I 1; °ते च I 2; अंत्या च Sây.

यज्यवो दशांत्या त्रिष्टुप्। ५६ अग्ने नव बार्हतं तृतीयासप्तम्यौ सतो-
बृहत्यौ। ५७ आ रुद्रासोऽष्टौ द्वित्रिष्टुबंतं। ५८ तमु। ५९ प्र वस्त्रिष्टुबंतं।
६० ईळे द्विजगत्यंतमाग्नेयं च वा। ६१ के ष्ठैकोना गायत्रं श्यावाश्वोऽत्र
वैददश्वी तरंतपुरुमीळ्हौ दाल्भ्यं रथवीतिं मरुतश्च दानतुष्टः प्रश-
शंस बुद्धा च तरंतमहिषीं शशीयसीं पंचम्यनुष्टुम्नवमी सतोबृहती।
६२ ऋतेन नव श्रुतविन्मैत्रावरुणं वै तत् ॥२७॥

६३ ऋतस्य सप्तार्चनाना जागतं। ६४ वरुणं पंक्त्यंतं तु। ६५ यश्चि-
केत षड्रातहव्यः। ६६ आ चिकितानानुष्टुभं तु। ६७ बळित्था पंच
यजतः। ६८ प्र वो गायत्रं। ६९ त्री रोचना चतुष्कमुरुचक्रिः। ७० पुरू-
रुणा गायत्रं तु। ७१ आ नस्तृचं बाहुवृक्तः। ७२ आ मित्र औष्णिहं।
७३ यदद्य दश पौर आश्विनं तदानुष्टुभं तु। ७४ कूष्ठः। ७५ प्रति नवा-
वस्युः पांक्तं। ७६ आ भाति पंचात्रिः। ७७ प्रातर्यावाणा। ७८ अश्विनौ
नव सप्तवध्रिस्त्र्युष्णिगादि चतुर्थी त्रिष्टुप्पंचानुष्टुभोऽंत्याः पंच
गर्भस्राविण्युपनिषत्[1]। ७९ महे दश सत्यश्रवा उषस्यं तु पांक्तं।
८० द्युतद्यामानं षट्। ८१ युंजते पंच श्यावाश्वः सावित्रं तु जागतं।
८२ तत्सवितुर्नव गायत्रमाद्यानुष्टुप्। ८३ अच्छ दशात्रिः पार्जन्यमुपा-
द्यास्तिस्रो जगत्य उपांत्यानुष्टुप्। ८४ बळित्था तृचं पार्थिवमानुष्टुभं।
८५ प्र सम्राजेऽष्टौ वारुणं। ८६ इंद्राग्नी षळैंद्राग्नमानुष्टुभं विराट्पूर्वांतं।
८७ प्र वो नवैवयामरुन्मारुतमतिजागतं ॥

॥ इति पंचमं मंडलं ॥

[1] W 1, W 2, C, I 1, I 2 (I 3 पंचांत्या अनुष्टुभो गर्भस्राविण्यः); अंत्याः पंच गर्भस्राविण्युपनिषत् omitted by Sây.

बार्हस्पत्यो भरद्वाजः षष्ठं मंडलमपश्यत्। [१]त्वं ह्यग्ने सप्तोना ॥२८॥

[२]त्वं ह्येकादशानुष्टुभं शक्कर्यंतं। [३]अग्ने ऽष्टौ। [४]यथा होतः। [५]हुवे सप्त। [६]प्र नव्यसा। [७]मूर्धानं वैश्वानरीयं[1] हि द्विजगत्यंतं। [८]पृक्षस्यांत्या त्रिष्टुप्। [९]अहश्च। [१०]पुरो वो द्विपदांतं। [११]यजस्व षट्। [१२]मध्ये। [१३]त्वद्विश्वा। [१४]अग्ना य आनुष्टुभं शक्कर्यंतं। [१५]इममू ष्वेकोना वीतहव्य ऋषिर्वा जागतं प्राग्दशम्यास्तृतीयापंचदश्यौ शक्कर्यौ षष्ठ्यतिशक्कर्यनुष्टुबृहत्या उपांत्ये। [१६]त्वमग्ने ऽष्टाचत्वारिंशद्गायत्रं वर्धमानाद्या षष्ठी च सप्तविंश्यनुष्टुप्त्रिष्टुप्पूर्वे चांत्ये ॥२९॥

[१७]पिब पंचोनैंद्रं त्रैष्टुभं द्विपदांतं। [१८]तमु ष्टुहि। [१९]महान्सप्तोना। [२०]द्यौर्न वि पिप्रोर्विराट्। [२१]इमा उ द्वादश नवम्येकादश्यौ वैश्वदेव्यौ। [२२]य एक एकादश। [२३]सुत इद्दश। [२४]वृषा। [२५]या ते नव। [२६]श्रुधी नोऽष्टौ। [२७]किमस्यांत्या चायमानस्याभ्यावर्तिनो दानस्तुतिः। [२८]आ गावो गव्यं द्वितीयैंद्री वांत्यश्च[2] पादोऽंत्यानुष्टुब्जागतस्तृचो द्वितीयादिः ॥३०॥

[२९]इंद्रं षट्। [३०]भूयः पंच। [३१]अभूरेकः सुहोत्रस्तु चतुर्थी शक्करी। [३२]अपूर्व्या। [३३]य ओजिष्ठः शुनहोत्रस्तु। [३४]सं च त्वे। [३५]कदा नरस्तु। [३६]सत्रा। [३७]अर्वाक्। [३८]अपात्। [३९]मंद्रस्य। [४०]इंद्र पिब। [४१]अहेळमानः। [४२]प्रत्यस्मै चतुष्कमानुष्टुभं बृहत्यंतं। [४३]यस्यौष्णिहं। [४४]यो रयिवश्चतुर्विंशतिः शंयुर्बार्हस्पत्यो द्व्यादौ षळनुष्टुभस्तिस्रश्च विराजो मध्यमैव वासां। [४५]य आनयत्त्रयस्त्रिंशद्गायत्रं पुरूतममतिनि-

[1] ॰नरं W 1. [2] W 1, I 2, I 3, Sây.; च W 2, I 1.

चृदंत्यानुष्टुभृचेऽंत्ये बृबुस्तक्षा दैवतं। [४६]त्वामिद्धि षळूना प्रागाथं। [४७]स्वादुरेकत्रिंशद्वर्गः पंचादौ सौम्योऽगव्यूत्यर्धर्चो लिंगोक्तदेवतः[1] प्रस्तोक इति त्रिष्टुबनुष्टुब्गायत्री द्विपदा सार्जयस्य प्रस्तोकस्य दानस्तुतिः परौ तृचौ रथदुंदुभिदेवत्यावैंद्रोऽंत्योऽर्धर्चो युजानो बृहती त्रिष्टुम्महि द्विपदा[2] दिवस्पृथिव्या जगती ॥३१॥

[४८]यज्ञायज्ञा द्व्यधिका शंयुस्तृणपाणिकं[3] पृश्निसूक्तं प्रगाथौ बृहती महासतोबृहती महाबार्हतबार्हतौ प्रगाथावित्याग्नेय्यः काकुभः प्रगाथः पुरउष्णिग्बृहत्यतिजगतीति मारुत्योऽंत्यास्तिस्रो वासां लिंगोक्तदेवताः काकुभः प्रगाथः पुरउष्णिग्बृहतीति पौष्णयौ बृहती महाबृहती यवमध्यांत्यानुष्टुम्मारुत्योऽंत्या[4] द्यावाभूम्योर्वा पृश्नेर्वा। [४९]स्तुषे पंचोन ऋृजिश्वा ह वैश्वदेवं ह शक्वर्यंतं। [५०]हुवे वः। [५१]उदु त्यत्षोळश त्र्युष्णिगनुष्टुबंतं। [५२]न तदूना सप्तम्याद्याः षड्गायत्र्यश्चतुर्दशी जगती। सुहोत्रादयोऽनुक्तगोत्रा भारद्वाजाः पौत्रा बृहस्पतेर्दौःषंतेर्वा भरतस्य। [५३]वयं दश पौष्णं तन्नायत्रं वै यां पूषन्ननुष्टुप्। [५४]सं पूषन्। [५५]एहि वां षट्। [५६]य एनमंत्यानुष्टुप्। [५७]इंद्रा न्वैंद्रं च। [५८]शुक्रं चतुष्कं द्वितीया जगती। [५९]प्र नु दशैंद्राग्नं तु बार्हतं चतुरनुष्टुबंतं। [६०]श्नथत्पंचोना गायत्रं तु त्रित्रिष्टुबादि

[1] °दैवतः W 1. [2] W 1, W 2; त्रिष्टुब्द्विपदा I 1, I 2. Sây. omits these three words. (I 3 explains: पंचविंशी द्विपदा त्रिष्टुप्.) [3] Cf. com. on V, 49. [4] W 1, W 2, I 2; मारुत्योऽंत्या omitted in I 1; W 1 has two marginal notes: (1) °नुष्टुबंत्या द्यावाभूम्योर्वा पृश्नेर्वेत्येव पाठः। (2) °नुष्टुप् द्यावाभूम्योरिति संहिताभाष्ये पाठः। विंश्येकविंश्योः पृश्निसूक्तमित्युक्तत्वान्मरुतां माता पृश्निर्देवतेति तस्य तत्रार्थश्च. See M. M., *Rigv*. vol. vi, p. xxiii. MS. I 3 explains: ततो मारुत्यौ। अंत्या मारुती वा। द्यावाभूमिपृश्निस्तुतिर्वा. In none of the MSS. of Sha*dg*.'s comm. is there a word about the last three verses being sacred to the Maruts.

त्रिष्टुब्बृहत्यनुष्टुबंतं । [६१]इयं षळूना सारस्वतं त्रिजगत्यादि जगती-
त्रिष्टुबंतं ॥ ३२ ॥

[६२]स्तुष एकादशाश्विनं तु । [६३]क्व त्यैकपदांतं त्रैष्टुभं[1] । [६४]उदु श्रिये
षळुषस्यं तु । [६५]एषा स्या । [६६]वपुर्न्वेकादश मारुतं । [६७]विश्वेषां
मैत्रावरुणं । [६८]श्रुष्टी वामैंद्रावरुणमुपांत्ये जगत्यौ । [६९]सं वामष्टा-
वैंद्रावैष्णवं । [७०]घृतवती षट् द्यावापृथिवीयं जागतं । [७१]उदु ष्य सा-
वित्रं त्रित्रिष्टुबंतं । [७२]इंद्रासोमा पंचैंद्रासौमं । [७३]यो अद्रिभित्तृचं
बार्हस्पत्यं । [७४]सोमारुद्रा चतुष्कं सौमारौद्रं[2] । [७५]जीमूतस्येवैको-
ना पायुर्भारद्वाजः संग्रामांगान्यृक्शोऽभितुष्टाव वर्म धनुर्ज्या-
मार्त्नी इषुधिं जगत्यर्धे सारथिमर्धे रश्मीनश्वान् रथं रथगोपाञ्ज-
गत्यां[3] लिंगोक्तदेवता द्वाभ्यामिषूः प्रतोदं हस्तघ्नं द्वाभ्यामिषूः
पराः पंक्त्यादयो लिंगोक्तदेवताः संग्रामाशिषोऽंत्यानुष्टुबृजीत
आलाक्तेति च द्वे द्वे ॥

॥ इति षष्ठं मंडलं ॥

सप्तमं मंडलं वसिष्ठोऽपश्यत् । [१]अग्निं पंचाधिका विराजो
ऽष्टादशाद्याः ॥ ३३ ॥

[२]जुषस्वैकादशाग्नं । [३]अग्निं वो दश । [४]प्र वः । [५]प्राग्नये नव
वैश्वानरीयं तु । [६]प्र सम्राजः सप्त । [७]प्र वो देवं । [८]इंधे । [९]अबोधि
षट् । [१०]उषो न पंच । [११]महान् । [१२]अगन्म तृचं । [१३]प्राग्नये वैश्वा-
नरीयं । [१४]समिधा बृहत्यादि । [१५]उपसद्याय पंचोना गायत्रं । [१६]एना

[1] W 1, W 2, Sây.; आद्या विराट् added by I 1, I 2. [2] सोमा° MSS.; see Pâṇ. VII, iii, 21. [3] MSS.; जगत्यादि Sây. [4] ताभ्यां W 2.

वो द्वादश प्रागाथं। १७ अग्ने भव सप्त द्वैपदं त्रैष्टुभं। १८ त्वे ह पंचा-
धिकेंद्रं सुदासः पैजवनस्यांत्याश्चतस्रो दानस्तुतिः। १९ यस्तिग्मशृंग
एकादश ॥ ३४ ॥

२० उग्रो दश। २१ असावि। २२ पिब नव वैराजमृतेऽंत्यां। २३ उदु
षट्। २४ योनिः। २५ आ ते। २६ न सोमः पंच। २७ इंद्रं नरः। २८ ब्रह्मा
णः। २९ अयं सोमः। ३० आ नः। ३१ प्र वो द्वादश गायत्रं त्रिवि-
राळंतं। ३२ मो षु सप्ताधिका प्रागाथं तृतीया द्विपदा सौदासैरग्नौ
प्रक्षिप्यमाणः शक्तिरंत्यं प्रगाथमालेभे[1] सोऽर्धर्चे उक्तेऽदह्यत। तं
पुत्रोक्तं वसिष्ठः समापयतेति शाट्यायनकं वसिष्ठस्यैव हतपुत्र-
स्यार्षमिति तांडकं। ३३ श्वित्यंचः षळूना संस्तवो वसिष्ठस्य सपुत्र-
स्येंद्रेण वा संवादः। ३४ प्र शुक्रा पंचाधिका वैश्वदेवं हाद्या एक-
विंशतिर्द्विपदा अब्जामहेरर्धर्चे उत्तरोऽहिर्बुध्न्याय। ३५ शं नः पंचोना
शांतिः ॥ ३५ ॥

३६ प्र ब्रह्म नव। ३७ आ वोऽष्टौ। ३८ उदु ष्य सावित्रमंत्ये वाजिन्यौ
भगमिति भागो वार्धर्चः। ३९ ऊर्ध्वः सप्त वैश्वदेवं तु। ४० ओ श्रुष्टिः।
४१ प्रातर्भागं जगत्याद्या लिंगोक्तदेवतांत्योषस्या। ४२ प्र ब्रह्माणः
षड्वैश्वदेवं तु। ४३ प्र वः पंच। ४४ दधिक्रां दाधिक्रं जगत्याद्या लिं-
गोक्तदेवता। ४५ आ देवश्चतुष्कं सावित्रं। ४६ इमा रौद्रं त्रिष्टुबंतं।
४७ आपो यमापं। ४८ ऋभुक्षण आर्भवमंत्या वैश्वदेवी वा। ४९ समु-
द्रज्येष्ठा आपं। ५० आ मां मैत्रावरुण्याग्नेयी वैश्वदेवी नदीस्तुतिर्जा-
गतमंत्यातिजगती शक्करी वा। ५१ आदित्यानां तृचमादित्यं तु।

[1] MSS. and Sây.; आरेभे marginal correction in W 1.

५२ आदित्यासः। ५३ प्र द्यावा द्यावापृथिवीयं। ५४ वास्तोष्पते वास्तो-
ष्पत्यं। ५५ अमीवहाष्टौ वास्तोष्पत्याद्या गायत्री शेषास्तूपरिष्टाद्बृ-
हत्यादयोऽनुष्टुभः प्रस्वापिन्य उपनिषत्। ५६ क ईं पंचाधिका मा-
रुतं हाद्या एकादश द्विपदाः। ५७ मध्वः सप्त। ५८ प्र साकमुक्षे षट्।
५९ यं त्रायध्वे द्वादश त्रिप्र[1]गाथादि नवम्याद्या गायत्र्योऽंत्यानुष्टु-
ब्रौद्री मृत्युविमोचनी ॥३६॥

६० यदद्य मैत्रावरुणं तु वै सौर्याद्या। ६१ उद्वां सप्त। ६२ उत्सूर्यः
षळाद्यास्तिस्रः सौर्यः। ६३ उद्वेतीति चार्धपंचमाः। ६४ दिवि पंच।
६५ प्रति वां। ६६ प्र मित्रयोरेकोना गायत्रं दशम्यादयस्त्रयः प्रगाथाः
पुरउष्णिक् चतुर्थ्याद्या दशादित्यास्तिस्रः सौर्यः। ६७ प्रति वां दशा-
श्विनं तु तत्। ६८ आ शुभ्रा नव सप्ताद्या विराजः। ६९ आ वां रथो
ऽष्टौ। ७० आ विश्ववारा सप्त। ७१ अप स्वसुः षट्। ७२ आ गोमता
पंच। ७३ अतारिष्म। ७४ इमा उ वां षट् प्रागाथं। ७५ व्युषा अष्टा
उषस्यं तु वै। ७६ उदु सप्त। ७७ उपो रुरुचे षट्। ७८ प्रति पंच।
७९ व्युषाः। ८० प्रति तृचं ॥३७॥

८१ प्रत्यु षट् प्रागाथं। ८२ इंद्रावरुणा दशैंद्रावरुणं ह जागतं तु।
८३ युवां नरा। ८४ आ वां पंच। ८५ पुनीषे। ८६ धीराष्टौ वारुणं ह।
८७ रदत्सप्त। ८८ प्र शुंध्युवमंत्या पाशविमोचनी[2]। ८९ मो षु पंच गायत्रं
जगत्यंतं। ९० प्र वीरया सप्त वायव्यं त्वैंद्र्यश्च या द्विवदुक्ताः। ९१ कुवि-
दंग। ९२ आ वायो पंच। ९३ शुचिं न्वष्टावैंद्राग्नं तु। ९४ इयं वां द्वादश
गायत्रमंत्यानुष्टुप्। ९५ प्र क्षोदसा षट् सारस्वतं तु तृतीया सरस्वते।

1 त्रि:प्र° W1. 2 MSS.; अंत्या पाशविमोचनी omitted by Sây.

९६ बृहदु प्रगाथः प्रस्तारपंक्तिः परास्तिस्रो गायत्र्यः सरस्वते। ९७ यज्ञे
दशैंद्र्यादि बार्हस्पत्यमंत्यैंद्री च तृतीयानवम्यावैंद्राब्राह्मणस्पत्ये।
९८ अध्वर्यवः सप्तोक्तदेवतांत्या। ९९ परो वैष्णवं नूरुमित्यैंद्र्यश्च तिस्रः।
१०० नू मर्तः ॥ ३८ ॥

१०१ तिस्रः षट् पार्जन्यं तु। १०२ पर्जन्याय तृचं गायत्रं। एते कुमार
आग्नेयोऽपश्यद्वसिष्ठ एव वा वृष्टिकामः[1]। १०३ संवत्सरं दश पर्ज-
न्यस्तुतिसंहृष्टान्[2]मंडूकांस्तुष्टावाद्यानुष्टुप्। १०४ इंद्रासोमा पंचाधिकेंद्रा-
सौमं[3] राक्षोघ्नं शापाभिशापप्रायं षट् सप्त वाद्या जगत्य एकविं-
शीत्रयोविंश्यौ चाष्टादशी मारुती च दशमीचतुर्दश्यावाग्नेय्यौ दैव्ये-
कादश्यंत्यानुष्टुम्नवमी द्वादशी त्रयोदशी सौम्यः सप्तदशी ग्राव्णायष्ट-
मीषोळश्यावैंद्र्यौ प्र वर्तयेति पंचैंद्र्यो मा नो रक्ष इत्यृषेरात्मन
आशीरुत्तरोऽर्धर्चः पृथिव्यंतरिक्षदैवतः ॥

॥ इति वासिष्ठं मंडलं समाप्तं ॥

परं गायत्रं प्राग्वत्सप्रेः। ऋषिश्चानुक्तगोत्रः प्राङ्मत्स्यात्काण्वः।
१ मा चिच्चतुस्त्रिंशन्मेधातिथिमेध्यातिथी ऐंद्रं बार्हतं द्विप्रगाथादि
द्वित्रिष्टुबंतमाद्यं द्वृचं प्रगाथोऽपश्यत्स घौरः सन्भ्रातुः कण्वस्य
पुत्रतामगात् प्लायोगि[4]श्चासंगो यः स्त्रीभूत्वा पुमानभूत्स मेध्यातिथये
दानं दत्वा स्तुहि स्तुहीति चतसृभिरात्मानं तुष्टाव पत्नी चास्यां-
गिरसी शश्वती पुंस्त्वमुपलभ्यैनं प्रीतांत्यया तुष्टाव। २ इदं वसो
द्विचत्वारिंशन्मेधातिथिरांगिरसश्च प्रियमेधः स्वादवोऽनुष्टुबंत्या-

[1] MSS.; वृष्टिकामः omitted by Sây.
[2] W 1, W 2, I 2; °स्तुतिः I 1 and Sây.
[3] °द्रासोमं MSS.
[4] प्रायोगि° W 2.

भ्यां मेधातिथिर्विभिंदोर्दानं तुष्टाव। ३ पिब चतुर्विंशतिर्मेध्यातिथिः प्रागाथं त्वनुष्टुप् गायत्र्यौ बृहती चांत्याः कौरयाणस्य पाकस्थाम्नो दानस्तुतिः। ४ यदिंद्र सैका देवातिथिस्तृचोऽंत्यः पुरउष्णिगंतः कुरुंगस्य दानस्तुतिस्तत्पूर्वोश्चतस्रः पौष्ण्यो वा ॥ ३९ ॥

५ दूरादेकान्नचत्वारिंशद्ब्रह्मातिथिराश्विने द्विबृहत्यनुष्टुबंते[1]ऽंत्याः पंचार्धर्चोश्चैद्यस्य कशोर्दानस्तुतिः। ६ महाँ इंद्रोऽष्टाचत्वारिंशद्वत्सस्तृचोऽंत्यस्तिरिंदिरस्य पार्शव्यस्य[2] दानस्तुतिः। ७ प्र यद्वः षट्त्रिंशत्पुनर्वत्सो मारुतं। ८ आ नस्त्र्यधिका सध्वंस आश्विनं ह्यानुष्टुभं तु। ९ आ नूनं सैका शशकर्णोऽंत्ये गायत्र्या उपाद्ये चाद्या चतुर्थी षष्ठी चतुर्दश्याद्ये च बृहत्यः पंचमी ककुब्दशम्याद्यास्त्रिष्टुब्विराड्जगत्यः। १० यत्स्थः षट् प्रगाथोऽपश्यद्बृहती मध्येज्योतिरनुष्टुबास्तारपंक्तिः प्रगाथः। ११ त्वमग्ने दश वत्स आग्नेये गायत्रेऽंत्या त्रिष्टुबाद्या प्रतिष्ठोपाद्या वर्धमाना ॥ ४० ॥

१२ य इंद्र त्रयस्त्रिंशत्पर्वत औष्णिहं तु। १३ इंद्रः सुतेषु नारदः। १४ यदिंद्र पंचोना गोषूक्त्यश्वसूक्तिनौ काण्वायनौ। १५ तम्वभि सप्तोनौष्णिहं। १६ प्र सम्राजं द्वादशेरिंबिठिः। १७ आ याहि पंचोना प्रगाथांतं। १८ इदं ह द्व्यधिकादित्यमौष्णिहमंत्[3]ष्टम्यश्विभ्यां परामि-

[1] W 1, W 2, C; °नं द्विबृहत्यनुष्टुबंतं I 1, I 2, Sây. [2] W 1, I 1, I 2; पारशव्यस्य W 2, Sây.; cp. *S*âṅkhây. *S*r. Sûtra XVI, 11, 20; Weber, Ind. Stud. IV, p. 379; Zimmer, Altindisches Leben, pp. 136, 137; Ludwig, *Rigv*. vol. iii, p. 196. [3] I 1, I 2, Sây.; चतुर्थ्याद्याश्चतस्रोऽदिते: here added in W 2 and W 1. Sha*dg*.'s com. (q. v.) does not support this reading. The com. of Jagannâtha in I 3, however, says: चतुर्थीपंचमीषष्ठीसप्तमीष्वदितिः।

सूर्यानिलानां। [१९]तं गूर्धय सप्तत्रिंशत्सोभरि[1]राग्नेयं काकुभं[2] प्रागाथं ह पितुर्न त्रिपदांत्ये ककुप्पंक्ती त्रसदस्योर्दानस्तुतिस्तत्पूर्वे उष्णिक्सतोबृहत्यावादित्येभ्यः । [२०]आ गंता षड्विंशतिर्मारुतं ॥४१॥

[२१]वयमु द्व्यूनांत्ये तृचे चित्रस्य दानस्तुतिः। [२२]ओ त्यमाश्विनं[3] त्रिप्रगाथादि बृहत्यनुष्टुबेकादश्याद्ये ककुम्मध्येज्योतिषी। [२३]ईळिष्व त्रिंशद्विश्वमना वैयश्व आग्नेयमौष्णिहं ह । [२४]सखायस्तृचोऽंत्यः सौषाम्णस्य वरोर्दानस्तुतिरंत्यानुष्टुप्। [२५]ता वां चतुर्विंशतिर्मैत्रावरुणं दशम्याद्यास्तिस्रो वैश्वदेव्य[4] उपांत्योष्णिग्गर्भा । [२६]युवोः पंचाधिका व्यश्वो वांगिरस आश्विनं विंश्याद्या वायव्यास्तत्पूर्वाश्चतस्रो गायत्र्योऽंत्यैकविंश्यौ च विंश्यनुष्टुप्। [२७]अग्निरुक्थे द्व्यधिका मनुर्वैवस्वतो वैश्वदेवं ह प्रागाथं। [२८]ये त्रिंशति पंचोपांत्या पुरउष्णिक्। [२९]बभ्रुर्दश कश्यपो वा मारीचो द्वैपदं। [३०]नहि वश्चतुष्कं पुरउष्णिग्बृहत्यनुष्टुबंतं । [३१]यो यजाति द्व्यूनाचेज्यास्तवो यजमानप्रशंसा च येत्यादिपंच दंपत्योः शिष्टास्तदाशिषोऽनुष्टुप् चतुष्पंक्त्यंतं नवम्यनुष्टुब्दशमी पादनिचृत् ॥४२॥

[३२]प्र कृतानि त्रिंशन्मेधातिथिः। [३३]वयं घैकोना मेध्यातिथिर्बार्हतं त्रिगायत्र्यनुष्टुबंतं । [३४]एंद्र याहि द्व्यूना नीपातिथिरानुष्टुभं तृचोऽंत्यो गायत्रस्तं सहस्रं वसुरोचिषोऽंगिरसोऽपश्यन्। [३५]अग्निना चतुर्विंशतिः श्यावाश्व आश्विनमौपरिष्टाज्ज्योतिषं[5] पंक्तिमहा-

[1] W 1, W 2, I 1; सौभरिः I 2; सौभरं Sây. [2] I 1, I 2; °भप्रागाथं W 1; °भः प्रागाथः W 2. [3] °मश्विनौ Sây. [4] W 1, I 1; °व्यो वोपा° I 2; °देव W 2. [5] W 1, I 1; उपरिष्टाज्ज्योतिषं W 2, I 2, I 3, Sây.

बृहतीपंक्त्यंतं । ३६ अविता सप्त शाक्करं महापंक्त्यंतं । ३७ प्रेदं महा-
पांक्तमा[1]द्यातिजगती । ३८ यज्ञस्य दशैंद्राग्नं । ३९ अग्निमस्तोषि नाभाक
आग्नेयं महापांक्तं[1] हि । ४० इंद्राग्नी द्वादशैंद्राग्नं त्रिष्टुबंतं द्वितीया
शक्करी । ४१ अस्मा ऊ षु दश वारुणं तु । ४२ अस्तभ्नात्षळर्चनाना
वा त्रैष्टुभमंत्यं वा तृचमाश्विनमानुष्टुभमपश्यत् । ४३ इमे त्रयस्त्रिं-
शद्विरूप आंगिरस आग्नेयं तु । ४४ समिधाग्निं त्रिंशत् । ४५ आ घ
द्विचत्वारिंशन्त्रिशोक आद्याग्नैंद्री ॥ ४३ ॥

४६ त्वावतस्त्रयस्त्रिंशद्वशोऽश्व्य आ स आदि कानीतस्य पृथुश्रवसो
दानस्तुतिराद्या पादनिचृत् पंचम्यादि ककुब्गायत्री बृहत्यनुष्टुप्
सतोबृहती गायत्री विपरीतोत्तरः प्रगाथो द्विपदा चतुर्विंशिका
बृहती पिपीलिकमध्या ककुम्न्यंकुशिरा विराड्गत्युपरिष्टाद्बृह-
तीबृहत्यौ विषमपदोत्तरे[2] पंक्ती[3] गायत्री पंक्तिः प्रगाथौ च[4]
वायव्यौ[5] गायत्री द्विपदोष्णिक् पंक्तिर्वायव्या गायत्री । ४७ महि
वो द्यूना त्रित आप्त्य आदित्येभ्योऽंत्याः पंचोषसेऽपि महापांक्तं ।
४८ स्वादोः पंचोना प्रगाथः सौम्यं त्रैष्टुभं पंचमी जगती । ४९ अभि[6]
प्र दश प्रस्कण्वः प्रागाथं तत् । ५० प्र सुश्रुतं पुष्टिगुः । ५१ यथा मनौ
श्रुष्टिगुः । ५२ यथा मनावायुः । ५३ उपमं त्वाष्टौ मेध्यः । ५४ एतत्ते
मातरिश्वा नो विश्व इति वैश्वदेवः प्रगाथः । ५५ भूरीत्पंच कृशः

[1] Corrected to माहापांक्तं in W 1. [2] W 1; °रा W 2; cp. M. M., *Rigv.* vol. iv, p. 32 (var. lect.) [3] W 1, W 2; उत्तरा पंक्तिः संस्तारपंक्तिः I 1, I 2; a marginal note in W 1 mentions this as an alternative reading, °तरा पंक्तिः संस्तारपंक्तिरिति पाठांतरं; I 3 explains एकविंशी पंक्तिः । द्वाविंशी संस्तारपंक्तिः । [4] W 1, I 1; च omitted in W 2, I 2. [5] बृहत्यौ च here inserted in I 2. [6] The Anukrama*n*î for the Khilas is continued in MSS. W 2 and I 1 only.

प्रस्कण्वस्य दानस्तुतिर्गायत्रं तृतीयापंचम्यावनुष्टुभौ । ५६ प्रति ते
पृषध्रोऽंत्याग्निसौरी[1] पंक्तिः । ५७ युवं देवा चतुष्कं मेध्य आश्विनं
त्रैष्टुभं[2] । ५८ इमानि वां सप्त सुपर्ण ऐद्रावरुणं जागतं । ६० अग्न आ
विंशतिर्भर्गः प्रागाथ आग्नेयं प्रागाथं तु । ६१ उभयं द्व्यूना । ६२ प्रो
अस्मै द्वादश प्रगाथः पांक्तं सप्तम्याद्यास्तिस्रो बृहत्यः । ६३ स पूर्व्यो
गायत्रमाद्या चतुर्थ्यादिद्वे सप्तमी चानुष्टुभोऽंत्या दैवी त्रिष्टुप्[3] ।
६४ उत्त्वा । ६५ यदिंद्र । ६६ तरोभिः पंचोना कलिः प्रागाथः प्रागाथ-
मंत्यानुष्टुप् । ६७ त्यान्नु सैका मत्स्यः सांमदो मैत्रावरुणिर्मान्यो वा
बहवो वा मत्स्या जालनद्धा आदित्यानस्तुवन्[4] ॥४४॥

६८ आ त्वैकोना प्रियमेध आदावनुष्टुम्मुखास्तृचाश्चत्वारोऽंत्याः
षळृक्षाश्वमेधयोर्दानस्तुतिः । ६९ प्रप्र द्व्यूनानुष्टुभं द्विबृहत्यंतं द्विती-
योष्णिक् चतुर्थ्याद्यास्तिस्रो गायत्र्यः षोळश्येकादश्यौ पंक्ती अपा-
द्वैश्वदेवोऽर्धर्चस्त्रयो वारुणाः । ७० यो राजा पंचोना पुरुहन्मा बार्हतं
त्रिप्रगाथाद्युष्णिगनुष्टुप्पुरउष्णिगंतं । ७१ त्वं नः सुदीतिपुरुमीळ्हौ
तयोर्वान्यतर आग्नेयं तु त्रिप्रगाथांतं[5] । ७२ हविर्द्व्यूना हर्यतः प्रागाथो
हविषां स्तुतिर्वा । ७३ उदीराथां गोपवन आत्रेयः सप्तवध्रिर्वाश्विनं ।
७४ विशो विशो वः पंचोनाग्नेयं त्वनुष्टुम्मुखास्तृचाश्चत्वारोऽंत्यास्ति-
स्रोऽनुष्टुभ आर्क्षस्य[6] श्रुतर्वणो दानस्तुतिः । ७५ युक्ष्वा हि षोळश

[1] W 2; अंत्या सौरी I 1. [2] ५८ is omitted in both MSS. [3] W 2, I 1, Sây.; स पूर्व्यं आद्या चतुर्थ्यादिद्वे सप्तमी चानुष्टुभो गायत्रेऽंत्या दैवी त्रिष्टुप् I 2; स पूर्व्यो गायत्रमाद्या चतुर्थ्यादिद्वे सप्तमी चानुष्टुभो गायत्रेऽंत्या दैवी त्रिष्टुप् W 1. [4] W 1, I 1, I 2, Sây.; दशम्याद्यास्तिस्रोऽप्यदितेः added by W 2. [5] त्वं नः सुदीतिः पुरुमीळ्हयो राज्ञोर्गृहपतियविष्ठयोर्वान्यतर आग्नेयं तु त्रिप्रगाथांतं I 2. [6] W 1, W 2, I 1; आर्ष्यस्य I 2, Sây.

विरूपः। ७६इमं नु द्वादश कुरुसुतिः काण्वः। ७७जज्ञान एकादश
प्रगाथांतं। ७८पुरोळाशं दश बृहत्यंतं। ७९अयं कृत्नुर्नव कृत्नुर्भार्गवः
सौम्यमंत्यानुष्टुप्। ८०न ह्यन्यं दशैकद्यूर्नौधसो गायत्रेऽंत्या दैवी
त्रिष्टुप्। ८१आ तू नो नव कुसीदी काण्वः ॥४५॥

८२आ प्र द्रव। ८३देवानां वैश्वदेवं। ८४प्रेष्ठमुशना काव्य आग्नेयं।
८५आ मे कृष्ण आश्विनं हि। ८६उभा हि पंच विश्वको वा कार्ष्णिर्जा-
गतं। ८७द्युम्नी षड्वासिष्ठो वा द्युम्नीकः प्रियमेधो वा प्रागाथं ह। ८८तं
वो दस्मं नोधाः। ८९बृहदिंद्राय सप्त नृमेधपुरुमेधौ द्व्यनुष्टुब्बृहत्यंतं।
९०आ नो विश्वासु षट्। ९१कन्या वाः सप्तात्रेय्यपालेतिहास ऐंद्र आनु-
ष्टुभं द्विपंक्त्यादि। ९२पांतं त्रयस्त्रिंशच्छ्रुतकक्षः सुकक्षो वाद्यानुष्टुप्।
९३उद्घ चतुस्त्रिंशत्सुकक्षोऽंत्यैंद्राभर्वी। ९४गौर्धयति द्वादश बिंदुः[1] पूत-
दक्षो वा मारुतं। ९५आ त्वा नव तिरश्चीरांगिरस[2] आनुष्टुभं। ९६अस्मै
सैका द्युतानो वा मारुतिस्त्रैष्टुभं[3] चतुर्थी विराळिष्यामीति मारुतः
पादः पैंद्राबार्हस्पत्या। ९७या इंद्र पंचोना रेभः काश्यपो बार्हतम-
तिजगत्युपरिष्टाद्बृहत्यावतिजगती त्रिष्टुब्जगतीत्यंततः ॥४६॥

९८इंद्राय द्वादश नृमेध औष्णिहं सप्तम्युपांत्ये च ककुभोऽंत्या-
नवम्यौ पुरउष्णिहौ। ९९त्वामिदाष्टौ प्रागाथं। १००अयं ते द्वादश
नेमो भार्गवस्त्रैष्टुभं षष्ठी जगती परास्तिस्रोऽनुष्टुभोऽयमिति तृचे-
नेंद्र आत्मानमस्तौदुपांत्ये[4] वाच्यौ। १०१ऋधक् षोळश जमदग्निर्भार्ग-

[1] MSS.; विंदुः Sây. [2] MSS.; आंगिरस omitted by Sây. [3] मारुतस्त्रै° Sây.

[4] W 1, I 1, Sây.; °मस्तौदष्टमी सौपर्णी (सौवर्णी I 2) नवमी वज्रसंस्तुतिरुपांत्ये वाच्यौ W 2, I 2.
No mention is made of verses 8 and 9 in I 3.

वो मैत्रावरुणं प्रागाथं त्रित्रिष्टुबंतं तृतीयादि गायत्री सतोबृहती
स्तोत्रं राजस्त्वृक्सपादादित्याश्विन्यौ वायव्ये सौर्यौ बृहत्युषस्या सूर्य-
प्रभास्तुतिर्वा पावमानी गव्ये। [१०२] त्वमग्ने द्व्यधिका भार्गवः प्रयोगो
बार्हस्पत्यो वाग्निः पावकः सहसः सुतयोर्वाग्न्योर्गृहपतियविष्ठ-
यो[1]र्वान्यतर आग्नेयं तु। [१०३] अदर्शि षळूना सोभरिर्बार्हतं पंचमी
विराड्रूपा सप्तम्या[2]द्ययुजः सतोबृहत्योऽष्टम्यादि युजः ककुब्भ्रसी-
यसी[3] ककुबनुष्टुबंत्याग्निमारुती ॥

॥ इत्यष्टमं मंडलं समाप्तं ॥

नवमं मंडलं पावमानं सौम्यं। [१] स्वादिष्ठया दश मधुच्छाः।
[२] पवस्व मेधातिथिः। [३] एषः शुनःशेपः। [४] सन हिरण्यस्तूपः।
[५] समिद्ध एकादश काश्यपोऽसितो देवलो वा विंशतिः सूक्तान्या-
द्यमाप्रियश्चतुरनुष्टुबंतं। [६] मंद्रया नव। [७] असृग्रं। [८] एते सोमाः।
[९] परि प्रिया। [१०] प्र स्वानासः। [११] उपास्मै। [१२] सोमा असृग्रं ॥४७॥
[१३] सोमः। [१४] परि प्रासिष्यदत्। [१५] एष धिया। [१६] प्र ते। [१७] प्र निम्नेनेव।
[१८] परि सुवानः सप्त। [१९] यत्सोम। [२०] प्र कविः। [२१] एते धावंति।
[२२] एते सोमासः। [२३] सोमा असृग्रं। [२४] प्र सोमासः। [२५] पवस्व षड्
दृळ्हच्युत आगस्त्यः। [२६] तममृक्षंतेध्मवाहो दार्ढच्युतः। [२७] एष
कविर्नृमेधः। [२८] एष वाजी प्रियमेधः। [२९] प्रास्य नृमेधः। [३०] प्र धारा

[1] I 1, I 2, I 3, Sây.; °यविष्ठ्ययोः W 1, W 2. [2] विराड्रूपा सप्तमी omitted in W 2, I 2 (text and com.) [3] I 1, I 3; गायत्री W 2; W 1 also, but corrected, by the same hand, to ह्रसीयसी in both text and com. I 2 has ह्रसीयसी in the text, but गायत्री in the com. Cp. M. M., *Rig*v. vol. iv, p. 51 (var. lect.)

बिंदुः । [३१]प्र सोमासो गोतमः । [३२]प्र सोमासः श्यावाश्वः । [३३]प्र
सोमासस्त्रितः । [३४]प्र सुवानः । [३५]आ नः पवस्व प्रभूवसुः । [३६]असर्जि ।
[३७]स सुतो रहूगणः । [३८]एष उ स्यः । [३९]आशुरर्ष बृहन्मतिः । [४०]पुनानः ।
[४१]प्र ये गावो मेध्यातिथिः । [४२]जनयन् । [४३]यो अत्य इव ॥४८॥

[४४]प्र णोऽयास्यः । [४५]स पवस्व । [४६]असृग्रन् । [४७]अया सोमः पंच
कविर्भार्गवः । [४८]तं त्वा । [४९]पवस्व । [५०]उत्ते शुष्मास उचथ्यः ।
[५१]अध्वर्यो । [५२]परि द्युक्षः । [५३]उत्ते चतुष्कमवत्सारः । [५४]अस्य प्रत्नां ।
[५५]यवंयवं । [५६]परि सोमः । [५७]प्र ते धाराः । [५८]तरत्सः[1] । [५९]पवस्व ।
[६०]प्र गायत्रेणोपांत्या पुरउष्णिक् । [६१]अया वीती त्रिंशदमहीयुः ।
[६२]एते असृग्रं जमदग्निः । [६३]आ पवस्व निध्रुविः काश्यपः । [६४]वृषा
सोम कश्यपः ॥४९॥

[६५]हिन्वंति भृगुर्वारुणिर्जमदग्निर्वा । [६६]पवस्व शतं वैखानसा
अष्टादश्यनुष्टुप्परास्तिस्र आग्नेय्यः । [६७]त्वं सोमासि द्वात्रिंशद्भरद्वाजः
कश्यपो गोतमोऽत्रिर्विश्वामित्रो जमदग्निर्वसिष्ठ इति ह तृचाः
सप्त ऋषयः शेषे पवित्रो वसिष्ठो वोभौ वा पवस्व सोम तिस्रो
नित्यद्विपदा गायत्र्योऽविता नस्तिस्रः पौष्ण्यो वा यत्ते पवित्रं
पंचाग्नेय्यः सावित्र्यग्निसावित्री वैश्वदेवी वासामंत्यास्त्रिंशी पुर-
उष्णिक् सप्तविंश्यनुष्टुबंत्ये च ते पावमान्यध्येतृस्तुती । जागतमूर्ध्वं
प्रागुशनसः । [६८]प्र देवं दश वत्सप्री[2]र्भालंदनस्त्रिष्टुबंतं ह । [६९]इषुर्न
हिरण्यस्तूपोऽंत्ये[3] त्रिष्टुभौ । [७०]त्रिरस्मै रेणुः । [७१]आ दक्षिणा नव

[1] सः omitted in W 1.
[2] C, W 1, W 2; °प्रि° I 1, I 2, I 3, Sây. See Aufrecht, *Rigv.* vol ii, p. 494, note.
[3] MSS.; °न्ते Sây.

ऋषभः । तौ वैश्वामित्रौ । [७२]हरिं हरिमंतः । [७३]स्रक्के पवित्रः ।
[७४]शिशुर्न कक्षीवांस्त्रिष्टुबष्टमी । [७५]अभि प्रियाणि पंच कविः ॥५०॥

[७६]धर्ता । [७७]एषः । [७८]प्र राजा । [७९]अचोदसः । [८०]सोमस्य वसुर्भा-
रद्वाजः । [८१]प्र सोमस्य । [८२]असावीति त्रिष्टुबंते । [८३]पवित्रं ते पवित्रः ।
[८४]पवस्व वाच्यः प्रजापतिः । [८५]इंद्राय द्वादश वेनो भार्गवो द्वि-
त्रिष्टुबंतं । [८६]प्र तेऽष्टाचत्वारिंशदृषिगणा दशर्चा अकृष्टा माषाः
प्रथमे सिकता निवावरी द्वितीये पृश्नयोऽजास्तृतीये[1]ऽत्रयश्चतुर्थे
ऽत्रिः पंचांत्या[2] गृत्समदः । [८७]प्र तु नवोशना । [८८]अयं सोमोऽष्टौ ।
[८९]प्रो स्य सप्त । [९०]प्र हिन्वानः षड्वसिष्ठः ॥५१॥

[९१]असर्जि कश्यपः । [९२]परि सुवानः । [९३]साकमुक्षः पंच नोधाः ।
[९४]अधि यत्कण्वः । [९५]कनिक्रंति प्रस्कण्वः । [९६]प्र सेनानीश्चतुर्विंश-
तिर्दैवोदासिः प्रतर्दनः । [९७]अस्य प्रेषाष्टापंचाशदाद्यं तृचं वसिष्ठो
ऽपश्यदुत्तरान्नव पृथग्वसिष्ठा इंद्रप्रमतिर्वृषगणो मन्युरुपमन्युर्व्या-
घ्रपाच्छक्तिः कर्णश्रुन्मृळीको वसुक्र इति चतुर्दश पराशरोऽंत्याः
कुत्सः । [९८]अभि नो द्वादशांबरीष ऋजिश्वा चानुष्टुभं ह बृहत्यु-
पांत्या । [९९]आ हर्यतायाष्टौ रेभसूनू काश्यपौ बृहत्याद्या । [१००]अभी
नवंते नव ॥५२॥

[१०१]पुरोजिती षोळशांधीगुः श्यावाश्वि[3]र्ययातिर्नाहुषो नहुषो
मानवो मनुः सांवरण इति तृचाः शेषे प्रजापतिरुपाद्ये गायत्र्यौ ।
[१०२]क्राणाष्टौ त्रित औष्णिहं वै । [१०३]प्र पुनानाय षड् द्वित आप्त्यः ।

[1] **तृतीये त्रयः** Sây. See Aufrecht, *Rigv.* vol. ii, p. 495, note; M. M., *Rigv.* vol. v, p. xl.
[2] Sây. inserts **तिस्रः ।** [3] C, W 1, W 2, I 1, I 2; **श्यावाश्विरंधीगुः** Sây.

१०४ सखायः पर्वतनारदौ काश्यपौ द्वे शिखंडिन्यौ वाप्सरसौ। १०५ तं
वः। १०६ इंद्रमच्छ षळूनाग्निश्चाक्षुषश्चक्षुर्मानवो मनुराप्सव इति
तृचाः पंचाग्निः। १०७ परीतः षड्विंशतिः सप्त ऋषयः प्रागाथं तृतीया-
षोळश्यौ द्विपदे अष्टम्याद्ये बृहत्यौ। १०८ पवस्व षोळश गौरिवी-
तिर्द्वृचं शक्तिरेकामूरुर्ऋजिश्वोर्ध्वसद्मा कृतयशा ऋणंचय इत्यृषयो
द्वृचास्तिस्रः शक्तिः काकुभाः प्रगाथाः स सुन्वे गायत्री यवमध्या।
१०९ परि प्र द्यधिकाग्नयो धिष्ण्या ऐश्वरयो[1] द्विपदं। ११० पर्यू षु द्वादश
त्र्यरुणत्रसदस्यू राजानौ तिस्रोऽनुष्टुभः पिपीलिकमध्याः षळूर्ध्व-
बृहत्यस्तिस्रश्च विराजः। १११ अया रुचा तृचमनानतः पारुच्छेपि-
रात्यष्टं। ११२ नानानं चतुष्कं शिशुः पांक्तं हि। ११३ शर्यणावत्येकादश
कश्यपः। ११४ य इंदोश्चतुष्कं ॥

॥ नवमं मंडलं समाप्तं ॥

१ अग्ने सप्त त्रितः। २ पिप्रीहि। ३ इनः। ४ प्र ते। ५ एकः ॥५३॥
६ अयं। ७ स्वस्ति। ८ प्र केतुना नव त्रिशिरास्त्वाष्ट्रस्तृचोऽंत्य
ऐंद्रः। ९ आपो हि सिंधुद्वीपो वांबरीष आपं गायत्रं द्यनुष्टुबंतं
पंचमी वर्धमाना सप्तमी प्रतिष्ठा। १० ओ चित्षळूना वैवस्वत-
योर्यमयम्योः संवादः षष्ठ्ययुग्भिर्यमी मिथुनार्थं यमं प्रोवाच स
तां नवमीयुग्भिरनिच्छन् प्रत्याचष्टे। ११ वृषा नवांगिर्हविर्धान
आग्नेयं तु त्रित्रिष्टुबंतं[2]। १२ द्यावा। १३ युजे पंच विवस्वान्वादित्यो[3]
हाविर्धानं[4] जगत्यंतं। १४ परेयिवांसं षोळश यमो यामं षष्ठी

1 C, W 1, W 2; ऐश्वरा I 1, Sây.; cp. M. M., *Rigv.* vol. v, p. xliii. 2 C, W 1, W 2, I 2; त्रिष्टुबंतं I 1, Sây. 3 C, W 1, I 1, I 2; वा omitted in W 2 and Sây. 4 W 1, W 2; हविर्धानं I 1, I 2, Sây.; हावर्धानं C.

लिंगोक्तदेवता पराश्च तिस्रः पित्र्या वा तृचः श्वभ्यां परा अनुष्टुभो
बृहत्युपांत्या। यामायनाः परे पंच। [१५]उदीरतां षळूना शंखः पित्र्यं
जगत्येकादशी। [१६]मैनं दमन आग्नेयं चतुरनुष्टुबंतं। [१७]त्वष्टा देवश्रवा
द्वे सरण्यूदेवते पौष्ण्यश्चतस्रः सारस्वत्यस्तिस्रः पंचाप्यो द्रप्सस्तिस्रः
सौम्यो वांत्ये[1] अनुष्टुभा उपांत्या पुरस्ताद्बृहती वा। [१८]परं मृत्यो
संकुसुकश्चतस्रो[2] मृत्युदेवताः परा धात्री परा त्वाष्ट्री पराः पितृमेधा
एकादशी प्रस्तारपंक्तिर्जगत्युपांत्यांत्यानुष्टुप् प्राजापत्या वा सा-
निरुक्ता ॥५४॥

[१९]नि वर्तध्वमष्टौ मथितो भृगुर्वा वारुणिर्भार्गवश्च्यवनो वापं
गव्यं वानुष्टुभमग्नीषोमीयो[3] द्वितीयोऽर्धर्चः[4] षष्ठी गायत्री[5]। सप्तो-
त्तराण्यैंद्रो विमदः प्राजापत्यो वा वासुक्रो वसुकृद्वा[6]। [२०]भद्रं
दशाग्नेयं तु गायत्रमाद्यैकपदा पाद एव वा शांत्यर्थः परानुष्टुबंत्ये
विराट्त्रिष्टुभौ। [२१]आग्निं नाष्टावास्तारपांक्तं। [२२]कुह पचोना पुर-
स्ताद्बार्हतं त्रिष्टुबंतं त्वं त्या चिदा नस्त्वं नोऽनुष्टुभः। [२३]यजामहे
सप्ताद्यांत्ये त्रिष्टुभौ पंचम्यभिसारिणी। [२४]इंद्र सोमं षळास्तारपांक्तं
त्वाश्विन्योऽंत्यास्तिस्रोऽनुष्टुभः। [२५]भद्रमेकादश सौम्यं। [२६]प्र हि नव
पौष्णमानुष्टुभमाद्याचतुर्थ्यौ[7] उष्णिहौ। [२७]असत्सु चतुर्विंशतिरैंद्रो
वसुक्रः। [२८]विश्वो हि द्वादशेंद्रवसुक्रयोः संवाद ऐंद्रः सूक्तस्य प्रथ-
मयेंद्रस्य स्नुषा परोक्षवदिंद्रमाहेंद्रस्य युजः शिष्टा[8] ऋषेश्चतुर्थी च।

[1] ॰ते C, W 1, I 1.
[2] Cp. M. M., *Rigv.* vol. v, p. l.
[3] ॰ग्निषोमीयो वा I 2.
[4] W 2 inserts चानुष्टुभं here.
[5] गायत्र्यैंद्री च W 2.
[6] प्राजापत्यो वासुक्रपुत्रो वा C.
[7] आद्या चतुर्थी च W 2.
[8] C, W 1, W 2; शेषाः I 1, I 2, Sây.

२९ वने नाष्टौ। ३० प्र देवत्रा पंचोना कवष ऐलूष आपमपोनप्त्रीयं वा।
३१ आ न एकादश वैश्वदेवं। ३२ प्र सु ग्मंता नव पंचाद्या जगत्यः॥५५॥

३३ प्र माद्या वैश्वदेव्येंद्रः प्रगाथः परा गायत्र्यो द्वे कुरुश्रवणस्य
त्रासदस्यवस्य दानस्तुतिः पराभिर्मृते मित्रातिथौ राज्ञि तत्स्नेहा-
दृषिरुपमश्रवसं पुत्रमस्य व्यशोकयत्। ३४ प्रावेपाः षळूना मौज-
वान्वाक्षो[1]ऽक्षकृषिप्रशंसा चाक्षकितवनिंदा[2] च सप्तमी जगती।
३५ अबुध्रं लुशो धानाको वैश्वदेवं तु द्वित्रिष्टुबंतं तु। ३६ उषासानक्ता।
३७ नमो द्वादश सौर्योऽभितपाः सौर्यं जागतं वै त्रिष्टुब्दशमी।
३८ अस्मिन्नः पंच मुष्कवानिंद्रः। ३९ यो वां षळूना काक्षीवती घो-
षाश्विनं हि त्रिष्टुबंतं। ४० रथं यांतं। ४१ समानं तृचं सुहस्त्यो[3] घो-
षेयः। ४२ अस्तेवैकादश कृष्णः। ४३ अच्छा मे द्वित्रिष्टुबंतं तु। ४४ आ
यातु त्रित्रिष्टुबादि। ४५ दिवस्परि द्वादश वत्सप्री[4]राग्नेयं तु॥५६॥

४६ प्र होता दश। ४७ जगृभ्माष्टौ सप्तगुर्वैकुंठमिंद्रं तुष्टाव। विकुंठा
नामासुरींद्रतुल्यं पुत्रमिच्छंती महत्[5]तपस्तेपे तस्याः स्वयमेवेंद्रः पुत्रो
जज्ञे। स सप्तगुस्तुतिसंहृष्ट आत्मानमुत्तरैस्त्रिभिस्तुष्टाव। ४८ अहं
भुवमेकादशांत्ये त्रिष्टुभौ सप्तमी च। ४९ अहं दामंत्योपाद्ये त्रिष्टुभौ[6]।
५० प्र वो महे सप्त द्विजगत्याद्यंतं के तेऽभिसारिण्यौ। वषट्कारेण
वृकणेषु भ्रातृषु सौचीकोऽग्निरपः प्रविश्य देवैः समवददुत्तरैस्त्रिभिः।
५१ महत्तन्नवात्र[7] युजोऽग्निवाक्यं। ५२ विश्व इत्युत्तरं च षट्कमयुजो

[1] See M. M., *Rigv.* vol. v, p. liv. [2] See ibid. p. lv. [3] °स्तो C. [4] वात्सप्रिः MSS.; but see IX, 68; cp. M. M., *Rigv.* vol. v, p. lvii. [5] महत् omitted in W 2. [6] C, W 1, W 2; °त्योपाद्ये च I 2, Sây.; °द्ये च त्रिष्टुभौ I 1. [7] W 1, I 1, C; तत्र W 2, I 2, Sây.

देवानां। ५३ यमैच्छामेत्युत्तरं चैकादशकं तदद्येति तु त्र्यृचोऽग्नेस्तंतु-
माद्या जगत्योऽष्टमीवर्जं। ५४ तां सु षड् बृहदुक्थो वामदेव्यः[1]। ५५ दूरे
ऽष्टौ। ५६ इदं ते सप्त वैश्वदेवं तु चतुर्थ्याद्यास्तिस्रो जगत्यः। पराणि
चत्वारि सूक्तान्युक्त्वा ऋषयो द्वैपदे त्वत्रिमंडले[2]। अथ हैक्ष्वाको
राजासमातिर्गौपायनान्बंध्वादीन्पुरोहितांस्त्यक्त्वान्यौ मायाविनौ
श्रेष्ठतमौ मत्वा पुरोदधे। तमितरे क्रुद्धा अभिचेरुः। अथ तौ मा-
याविनौ सुबंधोः प्राणानाचिक्षिपतुरथ हा[3]स्य भ्रातरस्त्रयः। ५७ मा
प्र गामेति षट्कं गायत्रं स्वस्त्ययनं जप्त्वा। ५८ यत्ते यममिति द्वा-
दशर्चमानुष्टुभं मनआवर्तनं जेपुः। ५९ प्र तारीति दशर्चे चतस्रो
निर्ऋत्यपनोदार्थं जेपुश्चतुर्थ्या सोमं चास्तुवन्मृत्योरपगमायोत्त-
राभ्यां दैवीमसुनीतिं सप्तम्यां लिंगोक्तदेवताः शिष्टाभिः पंक्ति-
महापंक्तिपंक्त्युत्तराभिर्द्यावापृथिव्यौ समिंद्रेतींद्रं वा[4]र्धर्चेन। ६० आ
जनमिति द्वादशर्चं आनुष्टुभे[5] चतसृभिरसमातिमस्तुवन् पंचम्येंद्रं
षष्ठ्यागस्त्यस्य स्वसा मातैषां राजानमस्तौत्पराभिः सुबंधोर्जीव-
माह्वयंस्तमंत्यया लब्धसंज्ञमस्पृशन् पंचाद्या गायत्र्योऽष्टम्याद्ये
पंक्ती। ६१ इदमित्था सप्ताधिका नाभानेदिष्ठो मानवो वैश्वदेवं
तत् ॥ ५७॥

६२ ये यज्ञेनैकादशाद्याः षळंगिरसां स्तुतिर्वांत्या त्रिष्टुप्पंचम्य-
नुष्टुप्प्रगाथोऽनुष्टुभौ गायत्री चतस्रोऽंत्याः सावर्णेर्दानस्तुतिः।

[1] MSS.; वा added by Sây. [2] See M. M., *Rigv.* vol. vi, p. 5 (var. lect.) [3] I 1, W 2; ह omitted in the text of C, W 1, I 2, but explained in the commentary. [4] वा C, W 1, I 1; च W 2, Sây.; च in the text, but वा in the commentary of I 2. [5] C, W 1, I 1; द्वादशर्चमानुष्टुभं W 2, I 2, Sây.

६३ परावतस्त्यूना गयः प्लातो द्विचिष्टुबंतं तु स्वस्ति नस्त्रिष्टुब्वा सह
सोत्तरया[1] पथ्यास्वस्तिदेवत्या। ६४ कथा यां मे चिष्टुप्। ६५ अग्निरिंद्रः
पंचोना वसुकर्णो वासुक्रस्त्रिष्टुबंतं तु। ६६ देवान्हुवे। ६७ इमां धियं
द्वादशायास्यो बार्हस्पत्यं तु। ६८ उदप्रुतः। ६९ भद्राः सुमित्रो वाध्र्यश्व
आग्नेयं द्विजगत्यादि। ७० इमां म एकादशाप्रं। ७१ बृहस्पते बृहस्प-
तिर्ज्ञानं तुष्टाव[2] नवमी जगती ॥५८॥

७२ देवानां नव लौक्यो वा बृहस्पतिर्दाक्षायण्यदितिर्वा दैव-
मानुष्टुभं। ७३ जनिष्ठा एकादश गौरिवीतिः। ७४ वसूनां षट्। ७५ प्र
सु नव सिंधुक्षित्प्रैयमेधो नदीस्तुतिर्जागतं तु। ७६ आ वोऽष्टौ सर्प
ऐरावतो जरत्कर्णो ग्राव्णोऽस्तौत्। ७७ अभ्रप्रुषः स्यूमरश्मिर्भार्गवो
मारुतं तु पंचमी जगती। ७८ विप्रासो द्वितीया पंचम्याद्याश्च तिस्रो
जगत्यः। ७९ अपश्यं सप्त सौचीकोऽग्निर्वैश्वानरो वा सप्तिर्वा वा-
जंभर आग्नेयं तु। ८० अग्निः सप्तिं। ८१ य इमा विश्वकर्मा भौवनो
वैश्वकर्मणं तु। ८२ चक्षुषः। ८३ यस्ते मन्यो मन्युस्तापसो मान्यवं तु
जगत्यादि। ८४ त्वया मन्यो चतुर्जगत्यंतं। ८५ सत्येन सप्तचत्वारिंशत्सा-
वित्री सूर्यात्मदैवतमानुष्टुभं पंचभिः सोममस्तौत्पराभिः स्वविवाहं
सप्तदश्या देवान्परया सोमार्कौ परया चंद्रमसं परा नृणां वि-
वाहमंत्राशीःप्रायाः[3] परा देहि द्वे वधूवासःसंस्पर्शमोचन्यौ[4] परा

[1] C, W 1; सा सहोत्तरया I 1; चोत्तरया W 2, Sây.; सहोत्तरया I 2. [2] तु शिष्टा W 2.
[3] W 1, W 2; °त्राशीप्रायाः C; °त्रा आशीः प्रायाः I 1, I 2. [4] W 2; संस्पर्शनिंदार्थे I 1, I 2, which is the original reading of W 1 and C, but is corrected by the same hand in both MSS. to °मोचिन्यौ (W 1) and °मोचन्यौ (C), which is the reading explained in Shadg.'s com. (q. v.) Jagannâtha, however, (I 3) says: परा देहीत्यृग्द्वये वधूवासःस्पर्शनिंदा.

यक्ष्मनाशिनी[1] दंपत्योर्नवोनवस्तिस्रोऽनुष्टुभा गृभ्णामीति द्वे द्वे यदश्विना पूषाघोरचक्षुरिति त्रिष्टुभस्त्रिष्टमुरोबृहती पूर्वापरमिह प्रियमा नः प्रजां जगत्यः[2] ॥५९॥

८६वि हि त्र्यधिकेंद्रो वृषाकपिरिंद्राणींद्रश्च समूदिरे पांक्तं। ८७रक्षोहणं पंचाधिका पायुराग्नेयं राक्षोघ्नं चतुरनुष्टुबंतं। ८८हविरेकोनांगिरसो मूर्धन्वान्वामदेव्यो वा सौर्यवैश्वानरीयं। ८९इंद्रं स्तव द्यूना रेणुः पंचम्यैंद्रासौमी[3]। ९०सहस्रशीर्षा षोळश नारायणः पौरुषमानुष्टुभं त्रिष्टुबंतं तु। ९१सं जागृवद्भिः पंचोनारुणो वैतहव्य[4] आग्नेयं। ९२यज्ञस्य शार्यातो मानवो वैश्वदेवं तु जागतं। ९३महि तान्वः पार्थः[5] प्रस्तारपांक्तं पुरस्ताद्बृहत्यंतं त्रयोदश्युपाद्ये चानुष्टुभौ[6] नवम्यक्षरैः पंक्तिरेकादशी न्यंकुसारिणी। ९४प्रैते षळूना सर्पोऽर्बुदः काद्रवेयो ग्राव्णोऽस्तौत्पंचम्यंत्ये त्रिष्टुभौ सप्तमी च ॥६०॥

९५हये द्यूनोर्वशीमैळः पुरूरवाः पूर्वोषितां[7] कामात्पुनरासाद्यावरोद्धुमैच्छत्सा तमनिच्छंती प्रत्याचष्टे हय इषुर्या कदा सुदेवोऽंतरिक्षप्रां सचेति तिस्रश्चैळवाक्यं शिष्टा उर्वश्याः। ९६प्र ते सप्तोना बरुः सर्वहरिर्वैंद्रो हरिस्तुतिर्द्वित्रिष्टुबंतं। ९७या ओषधीस्त्र्यधिकाथर्वणो भिषगोषधिस्तुतिरानुष्टुभं। ९८बृहस्पते द्वादशार्ष्टिषेणो देवापिर्वृष्टिकामो देवांस्तुष्टाव। ९९कं नो वम्रो वैखा-

[1] परा comes after यक्ष्मनाशिनी in W 2. [2] Sây. quotes only the first two words of this sûtra. [3] °सोमी C, W 2, I 1, I 3; पंचम्यैंद्रासोमी added by another hand on the margin in W 1, omitted in I 2 and Sây. [4] वीतहव्य C. [5] W 1, W 2, C, Sây.; पार्थ्यः I 2; पार्थः corrected to पार्थ्यः I 1; cp. M. M., *Rigv.* vol. vi, p. 18 (var. lect.) [6] °भौ W 2, Sây. [7] W 1, W 2, C; °तात् I 2, Sây.; °तात् corrected to °तां I 1.

नसः। १०० इंद्र दुवस्युर्वांदनो वैश्वदेवं तु त्रिष्टुबंतं[1]। १०१ उद्बुध्यध्वं बुधः
सौम्य ऋत्विक्स्तुतिर्वा नवम्यंत्ये जगत्यौ गायत्र्योर्मध्ये पंचमी बृह-
ती। १०२ प्र ते मुद्गलो भार्म्यश्वो द्रुघणेन ऋषभेण[2] चाजिं जिगायेति
द्रौघणं वाद्या तृतीयांत्या च[3] बृहत्यः। १०३ आशुः सप्तोनैंद्रोऽप्रति-
रथश्चतुर्थी बार्हस्पत्योपांत्याप्वादेव्यंत्यानुष्टुम्मारुती वा। १०४ असा-
व्येकादशाष्टको वैश्वामित्रः। १०५ कदा कौत्सो दुर्मित्रो नाम्ना सुमित्रो
गुणतः सुमित्रो वा नाम्ना दुर्मित्रो गुणत औष्णिहं हरी वज्रं
पिपीलिकमध्ये त्रिष्टुबंत्याद्या गायत्री वा ॥६१॥

१०६ उभौ भूतांशः काश्यप आश्विनं। १०७ आविर्दिव्यो दक्षिणा
वा प्राजापत्या दक्षिणां[4] तद्दातृन्वास्तौच्चतुर्थी जगती। १०८ किमि-
च्छंती पणिभिरसुरैर्निरूळ्हा[5] गा अन्वेष्टुं सरमां देवशुनीमिंद्रेण
प्रहिता[6]मयुग्भिः पणयो मित्रीयंतः प्रोचुः सा[7] तान्युग्मांत्या[8]भिर-
निच्छंती प्रत्याचष्टे। १०९ तेऽवदंत्सप्त जुहूर्ब्रह्मजाया ब्राह्मो वोर्ध्व-
नाभा वैश्वदेवं द्व्यनुष्टुबंतं। ११० समिद्ध एकादश जमदग्निस्तत्सुतो
वा राम आप्रियः। परे चत्वारो वैरूपाः। १११ मनीषिणो दशा-
ष्टादंष्ट्रः[9]। ११२ इंद्र पिब नभःप्रभेदनः। ११३ तमस्य शतप्रभेदनोऽंत्या
त्रिष्टुप्[10]। ११४ घर्मा सध्रिस्तापसो वा घर्मो वैश्वदेवं चतुर्थी जगती।
११५ चित्र इन्नव वार्ष्टिहव्य उपस्तुत आग्नेयं जागतं त्रिष्टुप्शक्वर्यंतं।

[1] W 1, C, I 1; त्र्यंत्या त्रिष्टुप् W 2, I 2, Sây. [2] वृषभेन Sây. [3] च is omitted in C and I 1. [4] Sây.; °णा C, W 1, W 2, I 2; °णाः I 1. [5] C, W 1, W 2; निगूळ्हाः I 1, I 2, Sây. [6] W 2, I 1, I 2, Sây.; प्रेषितां W 1, C. [7] स C, Sây. [8] युग्मांताभिः W 2. [9] W 1, W 2, C, I 3; °ष्टादंष्ट्रः I 1, I 2, Sây. [10] त्रिष्टुबंतं W 2, Sây.

११६ पिब स्थौरो[1]ऽग्नियुतो[2]ऽग्नियूपो वा । ११७ न वा उ भिक्षुर्ध-
नान्नदानप्रशंसाद्ये[3] जगत्यौ । ११८ अग्ने हंस्युरुक्षय आमहीयव
आग्नेयं राक्षोघ्नं गायत्रं तु । ११९ इति वै सप्तोनैंद्रो लब[4] आत्मानं
तुष्टाव ॥ ६२ ॥

१२० तदिन्नवाथर्वणो बृहद्दिवः । १२१ हिरण्यगर्भो दश हिरण्यगर्भः
प्राजापत्यः कायं । १२२ वसुं नाष्टौ चित्रमहा वासिष्ठ आग्नेयं जा-
गतमाद्यां पंचमीं चर्ते । १२३ अयं वेनो वैन्यं । १२४ इमं नो नवेंद्युत्तमा
निहवोऽग्निवरुणसोमानामाग्नेय्याद्या तिस्रश्चाग्नेरात्मस्तवः शिष्टा
यथानिपातं सप्तमी जगती । १२५ अहमष्टौ वागांभृणी तुष्टावात्मानं
द्वितीया जगती । १२६ न तं शैलूषिः[5] कुल्मुल[6]बर्हिषो वामदेव्यो
वांहोमुग्वैश्वदेवमुपरिष्टाद्बार्हतमंत्या त्रिष्टुप् । १२७ रात्री कुशिकः
सौभरो रात्रिर्वा[7] भारद्वाजी रात्रिस्तवं गायत्रं । १२८ ममाग्ने नव
विहव्यो वैश्वदेवं जगत्यंतं । १२९ नासत्सप्त प्रजापतिः परमेष्ठी भा-
ववृत्तं तु । १३० यो यज्ञो यज्ञः प्राजापत्यो जगत्याद्या । १३१ अप प्राचः
सुकीर्तिः काक्षीवतो मध्येऽनुष्टुप्सोत्तरा चाश्विन्यौ । १३२ ईजानं शक-
पूतो नार्मेधो मैत्रावरुणमाद्या लिंगोक्तदेवता न्यंकुसारिण्यंत्या
महासतोबृहत्युपाद्योपांत्ये प्रस्तारपंक्ती शेषा विराड्रूपाः । १३३ प्रो षु
सुदाः पैजवनः शाक्वरमहापांक्तावाद्यौ तृचौ त्रिष्टुबंत्या । १३४ उभे
यन्मांधाता यौवनाश्वो महापांक्तं पंक्तिरंत्या तामध्यर्धा गोधाप-

1 W 1, C, I 2, I 3; स्थौल: W 2; स्थौव: I 1; cp. M. M., *Rigv.* vol. vi, p. 23. 2 W 2, I 1, I 2, I 3; °यूतो C, W 1. 3 °सा चाद्ये W 2, I 2. 4 W 1, W 2, I 2; लव C, I 1, Sây. 5 C, W 1, I 1, I 2; °षः W 2, Sây. 6 C, W 1, W 2, I 3; कुल्मल° I 1, I 2, Sây. 7 वा omitted in C.

श्यत्। १३५ यस्मिन्कुमारो यामायनो याममानुष्टुभं हि[1]। १३६ केशी
मुनयो वातरशना जूतिर्वातजूतिर्विप्रजूतिर्वृषाणकः करिक्रत एतश
ऋष्यशृंगश्चैकर्चाः केशिनं। १३७ उत देवाः सप्त ऋषय एकर्चा वैश्वदेवं।
१३८ तव त्ये षळंग औरवो जागतं। १३९ सूर्यरश्मिर्देवगंधर्वो विश्वाव-
सुरात्मानमस्तौत्पूर्वार्धं[2] सवितारं। १४० अग्ने तवाग्निः पावक आग्नेयं
विष्टारपंक्ति[3]स्तिस्रः सतोबृहत्य उपरिष्टाज्ज्योतिः। १४१ अग्ने अच्छा-
ग्निस्तापसो वैश्वदेवमानुष्टुभं हि। १४२ अयमष्टौ द्वृचाः शार्ङ्गा जरिता
द्रोणः सारिसृक्तः[4] स्तंबमित्रश्चाग्नेयमाद्ये जगत्यौ चतस्रश्च त्रि-
ष्टुभः ॥ ६३ ॥

१४३ त्यं षट् सांख्योऽत्रिराश्विनं। १४४ अयं हि तार्क्ष्यपुत्रः सुपर्णो
यामायनो वोर्ध्वकृशनो[5] गायत्री बृहती गायत्र्यौ सतोबृहती विष्टा-
रपंक्तिः। १४५ इमामिंद्राण्युपनिषत्सपत्नीबाधनमानुष्टुभं तु पंक्त्यंतं।
१४६ अरण्यान्यैरंमदो देवमुनिररण्यानीं तुष्टाव। १४७ श्रत्ते पंच सुवेदाः
शैरीषिस्त्रिष्टुबंतं। १४८ सुष्वाणासः पृथुर्वैन्यः। १४९ सविता[6]र्चन्हैरण्यस्तूपः
सावित्रं। १५० समिद्धो वासिष्ठो मृळीक[7] आग्नेयं बार्हतमंत्ये उपरि-
ष्टाज्ज्योतिषी जगत्युपांत्या वा। १५१ श्रद्धया श्रद्धा कामायनी श्राद्ध-
मानुष्टुभं तु। १५२ शासः शासो भारद्वाजः। १५३ ईंखयंतीर्देवजामय
इंद्रमातरो गायत्रं। १५४ सोमो यमी भाववृत्तमानुष्टुभं तु। १५५ अरायि

[1] MSS.; तु Sây. [2] W 1, C, I 1, I 2; °र्धे W 2, Sây. [3] C, W 1, I 1, Sây.; विष्टारपंक्ति° corrected by another hand to आद्ये विष्टारपंक्ती on the margin in W 1; आद्ये विष्टारपंक्तो W 2; आद्या विष्टारपंक्तिः I 2. [4] W 1, W 2, C, I 2; °क्व I 1, I 3, Sây. All the MSS omit the visarga. [5] °कृशानो I 1; cp. M. M., *Rigv.* vol. vi, p. 28 (var. lect.) [6] °तार्चिनो है° I 2; °तार्चन्है° W 2. [7] C, W 1, I 1; मृळीको वासिष्ठ W 2, I 2, Sây.

शिरिंबिठो भारद्वाजोऽलक्ष्मीघ्नं द्वितीयातृतीये[1] ब्राह्मणस्पत्ये
अंत्या वैश्वदेवी । १५६ अग्निं केतुराग्नेय आग्नेयं गायत्रं । १५७ इमा नु
कं भुवन आप्त्यः साधनो वा भौवनो वैश्वदेवं द्वैपदं त्रैष्टुभं । १५८ सूर्यो
नश्चक्षुः सौर्यः सौर्यं गायत्रं । १५९ उदसौ षट् पौलोमी शच्यात्मानं
तुष्टावानुष्टुभं । १६० तीव्रस्य पंच पूरणो वैश्वामित्रः । १६१ मुंचामि
प्राजापत्यो यक्ष्मनाशनो राजयक्ष्मघ्नमंत्यानुष्टुप् । १६२ ब्रह्मणा षड्
ब्राह्मो रक्षोहा गर्भसंस्रावे प्रायश्चित्तमानुष्टुभं हि । १६३ अक्षीभ्यां
विवृहा काश्यपो यक्ष्मघ्नं । १६४ अपेहि पंच प्रचेता दुःस्वप्नघ्नं पंक्त्यंतं
त्रिष्टुम्मध्यं । १६५ देवा नैर्ऋतः कपोतः कपोतोपहतौ प्रायश्चित्तमिदं[2]
वैश्वदेवं । १६६ ऋषभमृषभो वैराजः शाक्करो वा सपत्नघ्नमानुष्टुभं
महापंक्त्यंतं । १६७ तुभ्येदं चतुष्कं विश्वामित्रजमदग्नी जागतं तृतीया
लिंगोक्तदेवता[3] । १६८ वातस्यानिलो वातायनो वायव्यं । १६९ मयोभूः
शबरः काक्षीवतो गव्यं । १७० विभ्राड्विभ्राट् सौर्यः सौर्यं जागतमा-
स्तारपंक्त्यंतं । १७१ त्वं त्यमिटो भार्गवो गायत्रं । १७२ आ याहि संवर्त
उषस्यं द्वैपदं । १७३ आ त्वा षड् ध्रुवो राज्ञः स्तुतिस्त्वानुष्टुभं तु ।
१७४ अभीवर्तेन पंचाभीवर्तः । १७५ प्र वश्चतुष्कमूर्ध्वग्रावार्बुदिर्ग्राव्णो
ऽस्तौद्गायत्रं । १७६ प्र सूनवः सूनुरार्भव आग्नेयमानुष्टुभं द्वितीया
गायत्र्याद्यार्भवी[4] । १७७ पतंगं तृचं पतंगः प्राजापत्यो मायाभेदं जग-
त्यादि । १७८ त्यमू ष्वरिष्टनेमिस्तार्क्ष्यस्तार्क्ष्यं । १७९ उत्तिष्ठतैकर्चाः शिबि[5]-

[1] W 2, I 2, Sây.; द्वितीया तृतीया W 1, C, I 1. [2] W 2, I 2, Sây.; इदं omitted in W 1, C, I 1. [3] C, W 1, I 1; वा is added by W 2, I 2, Sây. See Aufrecht, *Rigv.* vol. ii, p. 502, note 2. [4] द्वितीयं गायत्र्यार्भवी C, Sây. [5] W 1, W 2, I 2; शिवि° C, I 1, Sây.

रौशीनरः काशिराजः प्रतर्दनो रौहिदश्वो[1] वसुमना आद्यानुष्टुप्।
१८० प्र ससाहिषे जय ऐंद्रः। १८१ प्रथश्चैकर्चाः प्रथो वासिष्ठः सप्रथो
भारद्वाजो घर्मः सौर्यो वैश्वदेवं। १८२ बृहस्पतिस्तपुर्मूर्धा बार्हस्पत्यो
बार्हस्पत्यं। १८३ अपश्यं प्रजावान्प्राजापत्योऽन्वृचं यजमानपत्नी-
होत्राशिषः। १८४ विष्णुस्त्वष्टा गर्भकर्ता विष्णुर्वा प्राजापत्यो गर्भार्था-
शीर्लिंगोक्तदैवतमानुष्टुभं। १८५ महि सत्यधृतिर्वारुणिरादित्यं स्वस्त्य-
यनं गायत्रं वै। १८६ वातो वातायन उलो वायव्यं। १८७ प्राग्नये
पंचाग्नेयो वत्स आग्नेयं तु। १८८ प्र नूनं तृचमाग्नेयः श्येनो जातवेदस्यं।
१८९ आयं गौः सार्पराज्ञ्यात्मदैवतं सौर्यं वा। १९० ऋतं माधुच्छंदसो
ऽघमर्षणो भाववृत्तमानुष्टुभं तु। १९१ संसं चतुष्कं संवननः संज्ञा-
नमाद्याग्नेयी तृतीया त्रिष्टुप् तृतीया त्रिष्टुप् ॥६४॥

॥ इति कात्यायनमुनिकृता सर्वानुक्रमणी समाप्ता ॥

1 रौहिषदश्वो C. 2 °दैवत° C.

॥ अथ शौनकाचार्यकृतानुवाकानुक्रमणी ॥

॥ श्रीगणेशाय नमः ॥

सर्वं कर्म सफलं[1] यत्र तुष्टेऽतुष्टे न किंचित्तमहं नमामि ।
विनायकं गिरिराजेंद्रपुत्रीमहेश्वरप्रियसूनुं घृणाब्धिं ॥१॥
बह्वृचानां जनानां तु शौनकस्य प्रसादतः ।
अनुवाकानुक्रमणीरूपं किंचित्प्रवर्ण्यते ॥२॥
पितृदेवर्षि[2]श्राद्धेभ्यो[3] ब्राह्मणेभ्यश्च सर्वशः ।
आचार्येभ्यो गुरुभ्यश्च प्रणम्य प्रयतः शुचिः ॥३॥
मधुच्छंदःप्रभृति[4]भिर्ऋषिभिर्हि तपोबलात् ।
दृष्टानामनुवाकानामृजु[5] वक्ष्याम्यतंद्रितः ॥४॥
सूक्तादि परिमाणं तु संख्यां[6] च क्रममेव च ।
मंडले मंडले चैव यावंतो हि समीरिताः ॥५॥
सूक्तसंख्यानुवाकानां सूक्तानामृक्समाहिता[7] ।
पदाक्षरसमाम्नायं छंदस्येव प्रतिष्ठितं ॥६॥
एकैकमनुवाकं तु खिलानि ब्राह्मणानि च ।
संवत्सरे संवत्सरे पठेदहरहः शुचिः ॥७॥
श्रावणस्य तु मासस्य पौर्णमास्यामुपक्रमः ।
समाप्य तर्पयेद्देवानृषीन्पितॄननुक्रमात् ॥८॥

[1] C 1; कर्मफलं W 1, C. [2] B, C 1; °देवऋषि° C, W 1. [3] °साध्येभ्यो B; °सिद्धेभ्यो C 209 b, 3 (Weber's Catal. No. 48). [4] B, C 1; मधुछंदप्र° W 1, C. [5] °ऋषु B, C 209. [6] दृष्टानामनुवाकानां संख्यां C 209; आदिं सूक्तपरिमाणं संख्यां क्रममेव च B. [7] B omits this line.

ऋग्वेदे शैशिरीयायां संहितायां यथाक्रमं ।
प्रमाणमनुवाकानां सूक्तैः शृणुत शाकलाः ॥९॥
कण्वांगिरोऽगस्त्यशुनका विश्वामित्रोऽत्रिरेव च ।
वसिष्ठकश्यपवाध्र्यश्वा जमदग्निरथोत्तरं[1] ॥१०॥
श्लोकस्यास्य यथासंख्यं[2] सूक्तानि दश वै विदुः ।
न आ वहाग्न आ वहाद्य राजसीत्यग्निर्नि च[3] ॥११॥
समित्[4]समित्सु शोचिषे जुषस्व विश्वतस्तथा ।
इमां मे अद्य मन्विमा यथर्षिपक्ष आप्रियः[5] ॥१२॥
वसिष्ठशुनकौ विना समिद्धसर्वपक्षता[6] ।
जुषस्वादिद्वितीयया तनूनपाद्विरोधिता[7] ।
यजुःश्रुतौ[8] तथाश्रुतेः समिद्धसूक्तमध्यतः ॥१३॥
प्रजापतेः पशोः[9] सदा[10] भवेयुरद्य मन्विमाः[11] ।
इतीरितं हि बह्वृचैर्यथर्षि वेत्ति सूत्रतः[12] ॥१४॥

[1] Cp. Nârâyana on Âsv. Sr. Sûtra III, ii, 7. [2] C 1; °ख्य W 1, C. [3] C, C 1; °ग्निर्निहितः W 1. [4] C omits one समित्. [5] See Ait. Br. II, 4; Sat. Br. III, viii, 1, 2; VI, ii, 1, 28; XI, viii, 3, 5; XIII, ii, 2, 14; Kâty. Sr. Sûtra XIX, vi, 12, vii, 19; Nirukta VIII, 4 sqq.; Roth, Nir., introd. p. xxxvi, Erl. p. 122; M. M., A. S. L. pp. 463–466. [6] Cp. Âsv. Sr. Sûtra III, ii, 6. [7] जुषस्व द्वितीयया यजू याद्विरोधिनां W 1, C; जुषस्व द्वितीयया यजू यद्विरोधिनीं C 1; cp. Âsv. Sr. Sûtra V, i, 21, 22; Haug, note on Ait. Br. II, 4; Roth, note on Nir. VIII, 7. [8] C 1; श्रुतो W 1, C. See Vâg. Sanh. XXIX, 27; Taitt. Br. III, 6, 3. [9] यषो W 1; यशो C; यशः C 1. [10] यदा C 1.
[11] Âsv. Sr. Sûtra III, ii, 8; Roth, note on Nir. VIII, 5; Sây. on Rigv. X, 110, introd.
[12] Âsv. Sr. Sûtra III, ii, 7.

अग्निमीळे त्रिसूक्तस्तु सुरूपेंद्र चतुःसूक्तौ[1]।
अग्निं सोमानमित्येतौ षट्कौ कस्येति सप्तकः ॥१५॥
त्वमग्ने पंचकं विद्यात् प्र वो यह्वमथाष्टकं।
अग्ने विवस्वदभि त्यं नू चित्ते सप्तकास्त्रयः ॥१६॥
पश्वा न नवकं विद्यादुपप्रयंतो दशैकं च[2]।
खैलिकानाम[3]नादेशोऽस्मिन्ग्रंथेऽनुवाकानां[4] ॥१७॥
यस्तु चर्चायते वेदे तस्य संख्येति नः[5] श्रुतिः।
प्र ये शुंभंते नवकमिमं[6] द्वादशकं विद्यात्[7] ॥१८॥
इंद्रं मित्रं दशैवाथ नासत्याभ्यां तु पंचकं।
कदित्था षट् परः सप्ताग्निमा त्वा जुवः षट्कं[8] ॥१९॥
वेदिषदे सप्तदशाबोधीत्यष्टौ सूक्तानि[9]।
कया त्रिपंचसूक्तस्तु युवोर्द्वादशकं विद्यात्[10] ॥२०॥
इत्याद्ये मंडले दृष्टाश्चत्वारो विंशतिश्चैव[11]।
गौतमादौशिजः कुत्सः परुच्छेपादृषेः परः।
कुत्साद्दीर्घतमा इत्येष तु बाष्कलकः क्रमः[12] ॥२१॥

[1] B, C; चतुष्ककौ corrected by the same hand to चतुःसूक्तौ W 1; चतुष्ककौ W 2, C 1, I 4. [2] B, W 1, C 1; उपप्रयंतो दशैवं च C; विद्यादुपैकादशकं तथा W 2, I 4. [3] See Ind. Stud. III, p. 251; Max Müller, A. S. L., pp. 218, 222, 230; *Rig*-veda, vol. ii, p. xxxiii; Meyer, *Rig*vidhânam, p. xx. [4] B, W 1, C, C 1; ऽनुवाकानामिह स्मृतः W 2, I 4. [5] The visarga is added above the line in W 1; न W 2, C, C 1, I 4, B. [6] °मिदं I 4. [7] W 1, C, C 1; विदुः W 2, I 4; °के विदुः B. [8] W 1, C, C 1; जुवष्षट्कं B; जुवश्च षट् W 2, I 4. [9] W 1, C, C 1, B; °त्येषोऽष्टसूक्तकः W 2, I 4. [10] B, C, C 1, W 1; विदुः W 2, I 4. [11] B, W 1, C, C 1; °तिस्तथैव I 4; °तिस्तथा W 2. [12] क्रमात् C 1.

त्वं यो गणानामा ते दश तृतीय एकादशास्त्रयः परे ।
सोमस्य मा तवसं द्वादशोक्तं प्र वो देवायेति सप्तदशकं तु विद्यात् ॥ २२ ॥
इच्छंति त्वा नवेंद्रं मतिस्त्रिपंचको नवक इमं महे ।
त्वां ह्यग्ने दश भद्रं यन्नस्त्वेकादशकावुभाविमौ ॥ २३ ॥
त्रयोदशायं प्र ऋभुभ्य ईरितोऽयं पिबेत्येष चापि त्रयोदश ।
अबोध्यग्निः समिधा चतुर्दशातः परोऽष्टादशकः प्र वेधसे ॥ २४ ॥
महि महे द्वादशको विदास्तथा रुद्रासः षोळश[1] यत्त्रिपंचकः[2] ।
त्वं ह्यग्ने पंचदश त्वमष्टौ वृषा मदो विंशतिर्यो रयिवस्तु षट्कः[3] ॥ २५ ॥
द्विषड्ढुवे[4] स्तुषेऽथ[5] द्विसप्तकः षष्ठः षष्ठे मंडले योऽनुवाकः ।
अग्निं नरः सप्तदशाथ षोळश[6] त्वे ह[7] प्र शुक्रा ह्यधिका तु विंशतिः ॥ २६ ॥
क ईं व्यक्ताः पंचदशोना विंशतिरप[8] स्वसुः पंचदश प्र वीरया ।
मा चिन्महाँ इंद्र इंद्रः सुतेषु पंचाथ सप्ताष्ट वयं द्विपंचकः ॥ २७ ॥
यो यजाति द्वादशेमे ह षट्कोऽग्ने दशैकादशको य इत्युत[9] ।
त्रयोदशा तू न इंद्र द्युमंतममतः[10] परो दशको गौर्धयत्ययं[11] ॥ २८ ॥
स्वादिष्ठया त्र्यष्टसूक्तः पवस्व त्रिंशत्सषट्कः परः सप्तकोऽया[12] ।
प्राष्टादशैकादशकः[13] प्र तेऽस्य प्रेषा सप्तैकादशकः सखायः ॥ २९ ॥

[1] C 1, W 2, I 4; षोडश W 1, C, B. [2] C 1; यत्त्रि° W 1, C, B; यस्त्रि° W 2; यत् I 4. [3] रयिवः षट् B. [4] षड्दुवे B, C 1, W 2; षट् हुवे W 1, C. [5] द्विः षडस्तु य (sic) I 4. [6] B, C 1, W 2, I 4; षोडश W 1, C. [7] W 1, C, C 1; त्वे ह यत् W 2, I 4, B. [8] B; °दश ... ऊना विंश° W 1, C, C 1; °दशैकोनविंश° W 2; पंचदशेको नु विंशतिपः (sic) I 4. [9] B, W 1, C, C 1; इत्यप W 2; इत्या I 4. [10] B, W 2, I 4; इंद्र ... मतः W 1, C, C 1, omitting द्युमंतं. [11] Cp. Meyer, *Rigv.* p. xxvii, note 1. [12] ऽयाः W 2, I 4. [13] B, W 2, I 4: °कादश W 1. C. C 1.

अग्ने बृहन् षोळशकस्त्रयोदश[1] त्वष्टा प्र देवत्रेति चाष्टादशाच्छ[2] ।
अष्टाविदं षोळशकस्तु[1] भद्राः सत्येन षट् सं नवेंद्र त्रयोदश ॥३०॥
तमस्य द्यावापृथिवी अष्टकः परस्त्रयोविंशतिर्नासदासीत् ।
ऋग्वेदांत्यो द्वादशकोऽनुवाकश्चत्वारिंशच्छास इत्थेति चास्मिन्[3] ॥३१॥
आद्ये[4] चतुर्विंशतिर्हानुवाका अतः[5] परं मंडलं यच्चतुष्कं[6] ।
द्वे पंचके त्रीणि षट्कानि चैव दशाष्टमं सप्त नवमं द्वादशांत्यं[7] ॥३२॥
एकाधिका स्यान्नवतिः शतं च वदंति वै मंडलमादितो यत् ।
चत्वारिंशत्त्रीणि चाहुर्द्वितीयं सूक्ते च षष्टिं च तृतीयमाहुः ॥३३॥
अष्टापंचाशदपि यच्चतुर्थं सप्ताधिकाशीतिरतः परं स्यात् ।
पंचाधिका सप्ततिरुत्तरं तु चत्वारि वासिष्ठमथो शतं च ॥३४॥
द्वे चैव सूक्ते नवतिं च विद्यादथाष्टमं नवमं वै शतं स्यात्[8] ।
चतुर्दश त्वाहुरथाधिकान्यप्याद्ये[9] यदुक्तं दशमे तथैव ॥३५॥
एतत्सहस्रं दश सप्त चैवाष्टावतो बाष्कलकेऽधिकानि[10] ।
तान्पारणे शाकले शैशिरीये[11] वदंति शिष्टा न खिलेषु विप्राः[12] ॥३६॥
पंचाशीतिर्दाशतये[13]ऽनुवाका दृष्टाः पुराणैर्ऋषिभिर्महात्मभिः ।

[1] C 1, W 2, I 4; षोडश° W 1, C, B. [2] °दशाच्छ दशाप W 2; °दश I 4. [3] B, W 2; च्छास इत्या चास्मिन् W 1, C, C 1; चत्वारिंशच्छास इत्येति चास्मिन्नृग्वेदाते द्वादशकोऽनुवाकाः (sic) I 4. [4] आद्यं B. [5] °तिरिहानुवाका अंतः I 4. [6] B, W 2, C 1, I 4; यत् . . . अतः परं मंडल चतुष्कं W 1, C. [7] च added in W 1, C, C 1. [8] W 2 and I 4 omit 33, 34, 35 a. [9] °कानि त्वाद्ये B. [10] B, W 1, C, C 1; बाष्कलको ऽधिकारे W 2; बाष्कलाधिकारो I 4. [11] पारण्ये शाकले शैशीरीय W 2; तान्पारणे शाकले शैशिरे तु I 4. [12] B, W 1, C, C 1; शैशिरीया वदंति शिष्टानखिलेषु विप्रा इति पठंत्यन्ये Shadg.; see Max Müller, *Rig*-veda, vol. ii, p. xxxiii; Weber, Ind. Stud. III, 253; Meyer, *Rig*vidh. p. xxvii. [13] B, W 2; दाशतय्ये W 1, C, C 1, I 4.

यस्तानृग्विद्वेद चैवाप्यधीते स नाकपृष्ठं भजते ह[1] शश्वत् ॥ ३७ ॥
अध्यायानां चतुः षष्टिर्मंडलानि दशैव तु ।
वर्गाणां तु सहस्रे द्वे संख्याते च षळुत्तरे[2] ॥ ३८ ॥
सहस्रमेतत्सूक्तानां निश्चितं खैलिकैर्विना ।
दश सप्त च पठ्यंते संख्यातं वै पदक्रमं ॥ ३९ ॥
एकर्च एकवर्गः[3] स्यादेकश्च नवकस्तथा ।
द्वौ वर्गौ तु[4] द्वृचौ ज्ञेयौ त्र्यूनं तृचशतं स्मृतं[2] ॥ ४० ॥
चतुष्कं शतमेकं च चत्वारः सप्ततिस्तथा ।
पंचकानां सहस्रं तु द्वे च सप्तोत्तरे शते[5] ॥ ४१ ॥
त्रीणि शतानि षट्कानां चत्वारिंशत् षट् च[6] वर्गाः ।
शतमूनविंशतिः[7] सप्तकानां न्यूना[8] षष्टिरष्टकानां ॥ ४२ ॥
ऋचां दश सहस्राणि ऋचां पंचशतानि च ।
ऋचामशीतिः पादश्च पारणं संप्रकीर्तितं[9] ॥ ४३ ॥
अर्धर्चानां सहस्राणामेकविंशतिकं तथा ।
शतद्वयं तु द्वात्रिंशत्सपादं मुनिभिः पुरा ॥ ४४ ॥
शाकल्यदृष्टे पदलक्षमेकं सार्धं च[10] वेदे त्रिसहस्रयुक्तं ।
शतानि चाष्टौ दशकद्वयं च पदानि षट् चेति[11] हि[12] चर्चितानि ॥ ४५ ॥

[1] B, C 1, W 2, I 4; भजेतेह W 1, C. [2] Ind. Stud. III, 254. [3] °र्गै स्यात् MSS. [4] B, C 1, W 2, I 4; तु omitted in W 1, C. [5] शते omitted in I 4. [6] B; षट्कवर्गाः W 1, C, I 4; षट्कवर्गः C 1; चत्वारिंशत्षट्कवर्गाः W 2; cp. Ind. Stud. X, 133, note 1. [7] C 1; शतमूनं विंशतिः W 1, W 2, C, I 4; शतमूनविंशकं B. [8] न्यूनं त्रिषष्टिर° B. [9] पादश्चैतत्पारायणमुच्यते I 4; see Ind. Stud. III, 256. [10] च omitted in C 1. [11] चर्चे दश W 2, I 4. [12] C 1; च B; no particle in the other MSS.

एकं च शतसहस्रं दश च सहस्राणि सप्त[1] शतानि चर्चापदानि ज्ञेयानि पदानि चान्यानि चत्वारि। चत्वारि वाव[2] शतसहस्राणि द्वात्रिंशच्चाक्षरसहस्राणि द्वात्रिंशच्चाक्षरसहस्राणि ॥

॥ इत्यनुवाकानुक्रमणी समाप्ता ॥

[1] च added in B.

[2] B; या च W 1, C; च W 2; चत्वारिंशत्सहस्राणि I 4; no particle in C 1.

॥ अथ छंदःसंख्या ॥

एकपंचाशदृग्वेदे गायत्र्यः शाकलेयके।
सहस्रत्रितयं चैव[1] चत्वार्येव शतानि तु ॥१॥
त्रीणि शतानि सैकानि चत्वारिंशत्तथोष्णिहः।
अनुष्टुभां शतान्यष्टौ पंचाशत्पंचसंयुता ॥२॥
बृहतीनां शतं ज्ञेयमेकाशीत्यधिकं बुधैः।
शतानि त्रीणि पंक्तीनां द्वादशाभ्यधिकानि तु ॥३॥
पंचाशत्त्रिष्टुभः प्रोक्तास्तिस्रश्चैव ततोऽधिकाः।
सहस्राण्येव चत्वारि विज्ञेयं तु शतद्वयं ॥४॥
चत्वारिंशत्तथाष्टौ च तथा चापि शतत्रयं।
जगतीनामियं संख्या सहस्रं तु प्रकीर्तितं ॥५॥
दशैवातिजगत्योऽपि तथा सप्त न संशयः।
शक्वर्यो[2]ऽपि तथैवोक्तास्तथा नव विचक्षणैः[3] ॥६॥
नव चैवातिशक्वर्यः षळष्टयः प्रकीर्तिताः[4]।
अशीतिश्च चतस्रश्च[5] तथात्यष्टिश्चृचः[6] स्मृताः ॥७॥
धृतिद्वयं[7] विनिर्दिष्टमेकातिधृतिरेव च।
एकपदास्तु षट् प्रोक्ता द्विपदा दश सप्त च ॥८॥

[1] वैव W 2. [2] Weber, Ind. Stud. VIII, p. 51 note. [3] I 5; नवति च चक्षणैः W 2.
[4] W 2; षळष्ट्यः परिकीर्तिताः I 5. [5] अशीतिश्चतस्रश्च W 2; अशीतिश्च चतस्रश्च I 5.
[6] ०ष्टिर्ऋचः W 2, I 5. [7] धृतिर्द्वयं W 2, I 5.

प्रगाथा बार्हता येऽच तेषां शतमुदाहृतं ।
चतुर्नवतिरेवोक्तास्तद्वद्द्वृचांस्त्वसंशयः[1] ॥९॥
काकुभानां तु पंचाशद्विज्ञेया पंचसंयुता ।
महाबार्हत एवैक एवं सार्धं शतद्वयं ॥१०॥
एवं दश सहस्राणि शतानां तु चतुष्टयं ।
ऋचां ह्यधिकमाख्यातमृषिभिस्तत्वदर्शिभिः ॥११॥

॥ इति च्छंदःसंख्या समाप्ता ॥

1 °द्वर्या° W 2, I 5.

॥ अथ षड्गुरुशिष्यकृता वेदार्थदीपिका सर्वानुक्रमणीवृत्तिः ॥

१, १. अथेति मंगले प्रस्तावे वा । ऋगंशबाहुल्यादृग्वेदः । तत्राम्नाये सम्यगभ्यासयुक्ते खिलरहिते शाकलके । शाकल्योच्चारणं शाकलकं । तत्रादिः प्रतीकं । ऋक्संख्या ऋचामेकत्वादिः । ऋषिर्द्रष्टा । ऋषयोऽनागतातीतवर्तमानार्थवेदिनः । अर्तेः सनोतेश्च ऋषिशब्दो निरुच्यते[1] । दानादिसर्वकल्याणगुणयोगी पचाद्यच् देवः । देवान्नलंतात् स्वार्थे अण् दैवतं । छंदः पापेभ्यश्छादनात्[2] । छादयंतीह वा एनं छंदांसि पापात्कर्मणः[3] इति श्रुतेः । षष्ठीसमासगर्भो द्वंद्वसमासः । सूक्तानां हि प्रतीकादि । अत्र ऋत्यकः[4] । आनुपूर्व्या प्रतिपाद्यानुक्रमिष्यामः । ननु च । एको हि शौनकाचार्यशिष्यो भगवान् कात्यायनः । कथं बहुवचनं ॥

उच्यते । व्याख्येयार्थबहुत्वेन बहुमानेन चात्मनः ।
व्याख्यातॄ[5]त्मन्यथारोप्य बहुत्वं तु प्रयुज्यते[6] ॥
यथा हि निधिमासाद्य प्रयुंजानस्तु दृश्यते ।
एते वयं समृद्धार्था देवोऽस्मासु प्रसीदति ॥

इत्येतेन सर्वबहुवचननिर्देशः प्रतिपादितः । यथोपदेशं । शौनकोपदेशानुक्रमणीदशकाश्वलायनोपदेशसूत्रगृह्यचतुर्थारण्यकानतिक्रमेण[7] । अथ सर्वानुक्रमण्यारंभसंबंधेऽज्ञानदोषसंकीर्तनेन तदारंभं समर्थयते ॥

२. अग्निहोत्रादि विश्वसृजामयनांतं श्रुतिविहितं कल्पसूत्रे व्याख्यातं कर्म श्रौतं । निषेकादि श्माशानांतं स्मृतिगृह्यविहितं स्मार्तं सदाचारादि कर्म । प्रशब्द आदिकर्मणि । प्रसिद्धिः फलप्रदानं । एतज्ज्ञानमिति छांदसं व्यत्ययाच्छंदोवद्भावाच्छंद एव वा । एतस्माज्ज्ञानादृत इति यावत् । प्रकृतत्वात् सर्वानुक्रमणीगतं ज्ञानं । अस्माज्ज्ञानादृते श्रौतस्मार्तकर्मणोः फलप्रदानसंभवाय[8] वादोऽपि नास्ति । ऋष्याद्यज्ञानेन मंत्रकंटकत्वाद्यागकंटकत्वाच्चानधिकृतत्वात् सर्वत्रैव । तथा हि स्मर्यते ॥

अविदित्व ऋषिं छंदो दैवतं योगमेव च ।
योऽध्यापयेज्जपेद्वापि[9] पापीयाञ्जायते तु सः ॥

[1] Cp. Nirukta, II, 11, where it is derived from दृश्. [2] Cp. Nirukta, VII, 12; Ind. Stud. VIII, pp. 3–8. [3] Cp. Sâyana, M. M., *Rig*v. vol. i, p. 44, line 5; *S*at. Br. VIII, 5, 1, 1; *Kh*ândogya Up. I, 4, 2. [4] Pâ*n*. VI, i, 128; W 1; तत्र त्रिरित्युक्तेः the other MSS.; .n all the MSS. the words come between अनुक्रमिष्यामः and ननु च । [5] व्याख्याम् W 1; व्याख्याता the others. [6] W 1; प्रयुंजते the others. [7] W 1; शौनकोपदेशानतिक्रमेण only in the other MSS.; cp. M. M., A. S. L., p. 234. [8] °प्रदानांतत्व° W 1. [9] MSS.; also Sâya*n*a, who quotes this and the next two *s*lokas, pp. 43, 44; cp. also Burnell, Ârsheya Br., p. 4; ध्यापयेद्याजयेद्वा W 1 only.

योज्यवेदभागानां संबंधिनां ब्राह्मणादीनां ज्ञाता । याजनाध्यापनाभ्यां । करणाभ्यासाभ्यां । श्रेयः प्रशस्यतरमन्नपुत्रादिमोक्षांतं फलं । अधिगच्छतीति पाठादाधिक्येन गच्छति लभते । अथाज्ञं निंदति ॥

४. एताभ्यां याजनाध्यापनाभ्यामनेवंविदः सर्वानुक्रमण्यज्ञस्यैव पुनर्यातयामानि । यातः प्राप्तो यामः फल[1]रक्षाविषयमौदासीन्यं यैस्तानि यातयामानि । नास्य तारका वेदा इत्यर्थः । अथवा यातयामो जीर्णो भुक्तोच्छिष्टेऽपि चेति निघंटौ[2] । जीर्णे भुक्तोच्छिष्टे वान्नादौ वर्तते । यातयामशब्दो नीरसत्वादिसाम्याच्छंदःसु वर्तते । छंदांसि वेदाः । भवंति संपद्यंते ॥

५. अत एवानेवंवित् स्थाणुं वृक्षादिजातिमृच्छति प्राप्नोति । वा खलु । गर्ते नरके कूपे पंकवारिमध्ये मत्स्यमंडूककच्छपादिजातिषु पात्यते । अधश्चाल्यते । कैः । देवैः[3] । यद्देवा देवहेलनम्[4] अपभर्ता रपसो दैव्यस्येति[5] श्रुतेः । प्रमीयते वा । कदाचिदपि न वेदोक्तमायुर्भजते ॥

उक्तं हि । अनभ्यासेन वेदानामाचारस्य च वर्जनात् ।
आलस्यादन्नदोषाच्च मृत्युर्विप्राञ्जिघांसति ॥

इति भगवता मनुना[6] । पापीयान् भवतीति । दस्युम्लेच्छादिजातिषु जायते । इति विज्ञायते । इत्येवं सामवेदार्षेयब्राह्मण आम्नातं[7] । विज्ञायते विशेषेण ज्ञायतेऽवगम्यते सर्वमहर्षिभिः ॥

अतो महर्षयः सर्वे वेदविदो इति स्थिताः ।
अधीयते कर्शयंति देहं मृत्युं न भुंजते ॥

इति सर्वानुक्रमण्यारंभः समर्थितः ॥

२, १. अथेति प्रस्तावे । सामान्येनर्षयः प्रस्तूयंते । अथ ऋषय इति । ऋत्यकः[8] ॥

२. आद्यमंडलस्था ऋषयः शतर्चिन इति संज्ञिताः । ऋचां शतं शतर्च । आद्यस्यर्षेर्ऋक्शतयोगेन छत्रिन्यायेन शतर्चिनः सर्वे । ह्यधिकेऽपि शतोक्तिर्बाहुल्यात् ॥

उक्तं हि । शतर्चिसंज्ञा विज्ञेया ह्याद्यमंडलदर्शिनः ।
ददर्शादौ मधुच्छंदा ह्यधिकं यदृचां शतं ॥
तत्साहचर्यादन्येऽपि विज्ञेयास्तु शतर्चिनः ।
अच्छत्राश्छत्रिणैकेन यथा वै छत्रिणोऽभवन् ॥

नासदासीयात्[9] पूर्वं महासूक्तं परं क्षुद्रसूक्तं । सूक्तदर्शित्वादंत्ये दशमे मंडले स्थिता ऋषयः क्षुद्रसूक्तमहासूक्तनामानः । द्वितीयादिनवमांतेषु मध्यमेषु मंडलेषु स्थिता माध्यमनामान ऋषयः ॥

३. अथ परिभाषते । एवंभूतस्यर्षेर्गोत्रानुक्तौ तमांगिरसं विद्यात् सर्वानुक्रमणीजिज्ञासुरवगच्छेत् । ब्रह्मर्षिमिति । अश्वमेधनृमेधत्रसदस्युपुरुमीळ्हादिराजर्षिनामसु मा भूत् । अस्त्रियमिति ।

[1] W 1; अरसो रक्षा° I 2, P 2; उपरामो रक्षा° P 1; उपरमः फलरक्षा° I 4. [2] Not in Yâska's Nighan*t*u. [3] वेदैः W 1, I 4; दोषैः I 2, P 1, P 2. [4] Ath.-veda VI, 114. [5] *Rig*v. II, 33, 7. [6] Manu V, 4. [7] Ârsheya Br. I, 1; see M. M., A. S. L., p. 226, note 2. [8] Pâ*n*. VI, i, 128. [9] *Rig*v. X, 129.

उर्वश्यादिस्त्रीनामसु मा भूत् । क्वचिदविशेषितं । पूर्वत्र परत्र वाविशिष्टश्चेत् स एव ऋः । ऋषभस्तौ वैश्वामित्राविति[1] परत्र दर्शनाद्वैश्वामित्रत्वं । कथंचिदविशेषितं । कथादिना । गाथिन ऋषेः कौशिकत्वं कथया । अविशेषितम् अनुपपादितं । अनुक्तगोत्रत्वेऽपि नारायणस्य गोत्रं नास्ति यथोपदेशमिति संबंधादुपदेशेषु चानुपलभ्यगोत्रस्य । अथ कोऽयमृषिरित्याह ॥

४. उक्तं च । ऋषिर्दर्शनादिति[2] ॥

५. तेन वाक्येन यत्प्रतिपाद्यं वस्तु सा देवता ॥

७. अथर्षिच्छंदोदेवतानां संबंधमाह । अर्थ्यत इत्यर्थः । अर्थः फलमन्नपुत्रादिमोक्षांतं । अर्थमात्माधीनं कर्तुमिच्छंतो मधुच्छंदःप्रभृतयः संवननांता ऋषयो देवताः सूक्तहविर्भागिनीश्छंदोभिर्गायत्र्यादिभिरुपायभूतैस्तद्युक्तमंत्रैर्वाभ्यधावन् । अभ्ययागच्छन् । अर्थस्य प्राप्तावयमेवोपाय इति दृढसंकल्पाः । यादृगिव वै देवेभ्यः करोति तादृगिवास्मै देवाः कुर्वंति । भद्रा इंद्रस्य रातयः[3] स्तोतॄणामुत भद्रकृत्[4] य इंद्राय सुनवामेत्याह[5] येषामिंद्रस्ते जयंति[6] अव स्तोमेभी रुद्रं दिषीय[7] न मृषा श्रांतं यदवंति देवाः[8] यत्कामास्ते जुहुमस्तन्नो अस्तु[9] ध्रुवासो अस्य कीरयो जनासः[10] पूषन्तव व्रते वयं न रिष्येम कदा चन[11] न स जीयते मरुतो न हन्यते[12] न हन्यते न जीयते त्वोतो नैनमंह[13] इत्यादिश्रुतिशतेभ्यः समाश्रितरक्षणं देवाः कुर्वंतीति दृढबुद्धयः प्राभवंत इत्यर्थः ॥ देवता अभ्यधावन्निति प्रसंगाद्देवता आह ॥

८. क्षियंति निवसंत्यत्रेति पृथिवी क्षितिः । भूमिस्वर्गयोरंतरा मध्येऽमूर्ततयानुपलंभादंतरा क्षांत-[14]मित्येवमंतरिक्षं । क्रीडादानादिसंयुक्ता नित्यतृप्ता अत्रासत इति द्यौः स्वर्गः । सूर्यो नो दिवस्पातु वातो अंतरिक्षादग्निर्नः पार्थिवेभ्यः[15] तमू अकृण्वन् त्रेधा भुवे कं[16] बहुधा वदंत्यग्निं यमं मातरिश्वानमाहुर्[17] इति लिंगात्रिस्र एव देवताः । अग्निर्गृहपतिरिति हैक आहुरित्यादितश्च ॥

९. उक्तक्रमदेवतायोगितया व्याहृतीः प्रस्तौति । देवता इत्येवमुक्तक्रमादुक्तदेवतासंबंधिन्यः प्रोक्ताः ॥

१०. भूरादीनां समस्तानामिति दर्शनाद्देवतेति शेषः ॥

११. ओमिति शब्दः सर्वदेवताभिधायित्वेन सर्वदेवत्यः । ओंकारः परमेष्ठिनं वाभिधत्ते । परम उत्कृष्टतमे स्थाने तिष्ठतीति परमेष्ठी । ब्राह्मो वेत्येव । ब्रह्मदेवत्यो वौंकारः । दैवो वा । देवदेवत्यो वौंकारः । शरीरवर्तिप्रत्यगात्मनोऽभिधायको वौंकारः । प्रासंगिकं समाप्य प्रकृतमनुसरति ॥

१२. बृहद्देवतायां[18] निरुक्तशास्त्रव्याख्येयदेवताकांडे च पृथिव्यादिस्थानभेदेन पठ्यमाना अन्या देवतास्तद्विभूतयः । अग्न्यादीनां विभूतयो विकृतय इत्यर्थः ॥

तथा हि । आद्यं नैघंटुकं कांडं द्वितीयं नैगमं तथा ।
तृतीयं दैवतं चेति समाम्नायस्त्रिधा स्थितः ॥

[1] Cp. sûtra on III, 13, 14 and IX, 71. [2] Nirukta, II, 11. [3] *Rigv.* VIII, 62, 1. [4] VIII, 14, 11. [5] IV, 25, 4. [6] VIII, 16, 5. [7] II, 33, 5. [8] I, 179, 3. [9] X, 121, 10. [10] VII, 100, 4. [11] VI, 54, 9. [12] V, 54, 7. [13] III, 59, 2. [14] Cp. Nirukta, II, 10. [15] *Rigv.* X, 158, 1. [16] X, 88, 10. [17] I, 164, 46. [18] *Bri.* Dev. I, 69–85.

गौराद्यपारंपर्यंतमाद्यं नैघंटुकं मतं ।
जहाद्युल्बमृबीसांतं नैगमं संप्रचक्षते ॥
अग्न्यादिदेवपर्यंत्यंतं देवताकांडमुच्यते ।
तत्राग्न्यादिदेव्यूर्जाहुत्यंतः क्षितिगतो गणः ॥
वाय्वादयो भगांताः[5] स्युरंतरिक्षस्थदेवताः ।
सूर्यादिदेवपत्न्यंता द्युस्थानदेवता इति ।
गौरादिदेवपत्न्यंतं समाम्नायमधीयते[7] ॥

बृहद्देवतायामपि निघंटुवत् । ननु च । अन्याश्च देवताः संति बह्व्यः । नेत्याह ॥

१३. हीति प्रसिद्धौ । वृत्रवधसमाश्रितरक्षणवर्षणदहनपवनपचनद्योतनादिव्यापारभेदात् पृथग्नामानः पृथक्स्तवा बहुरूपाश्च ता एव तिस्रो देवता भवंति । तथा हि । नामानि ते शतक्रतो विश्वाभिर्गीर्भिरीमहे[8] इंद्रो मायाभिः पुरुरूप ईयते[9] नहि नु ते महिमनः समस्य[10] न ते महित्वमन्वश्नुवंति[11] भुवनस्य पितरं गीर्भिराभिः[12] आस्य जानंतो नाम चिद्विवक्तन[13] यस्येमे हिमवंतो महित्वा[14] सहस्राणि सहस्रशो ये रुद्रा अधि भूम्याम्[15] इत्यादिश्रुतिशतेभ्यः । अभिधानं नाम गुणावच्छिन्नं । गुणसंकीर्तनं स्तुतिः ॥

उक्तं हि । स्तुतिः स्तुत्यप्रभावोक्तिः स्तोतृभिस्तु सभक्तिका ॥

१४. एका वा देवता न तिस्रः । तस्या नाम महानात्मेति च । श्रूयते हि । तस्य नाम महद्यश इति । आत्मा वा इदमेक एवाग्र आसीदिति[16] । कः स एक इत्याह ॥

१५. उक्तत्रिकात्मिकः सूर्यो यः स एक इति वेदविदो वदंति । एतमेव बह्वृचा महत्युक्थे मीमांसंत इत्यारण्यकश्रुतेः[17] । अथोक्तमर्थमुपपादयति ॥

१६. स सूर्ये सर्वं इति नैय्यायकाः[18] पठंति प्रमाणत्वेन ॥

१७. ऋषिणा कृत्स्नेन मंत्रेण वा तदर्थरूपमुक्तं प्रतिपादितं । पुराणे च ।

दिव्यं ज्योतिः सलिलपवनैः पूरयित्वा त्रिलोकीं ।
एकीभूतं पुनरपि च तत्सारमादाय गोभिः ॥
अंतर्लीनो विशसि वसुधां तन्नतः सूयसेऽन्नं ।
तन्न[19] प्राणास्त्वमिति जगतां प्राणभृत्सूर्य आत्मा ॥

इति । जगतो जंगमस्य । तस्थुषः स्थावरस्य ॥

[1] Adhyâyas 1–3. [2] Adhy. 4. [3] Adhy. 5. [4] §§ 1–3. [5] §§ 4–6. [6] § 6. [7] See M. M., *Rigv.* vol. i, p. 38; A. S. L., p. 155 and p. 157, note. [8] *Rigv.* III, 37, 3. [9] VI, 47, 18. [10] VI, 27, 3. [11] VII, 99, 1. [12] VI, 49, 10. [13] I, 156, 3. [14] X, 121, 4. [15] Vâ*g*. Sam*h*. XVI, 53, 54. [16] Ait. Âr. II, 4, 1; cp. M. M., Upanishads, Sacred Books of the East, vol. xv, p. xvii. [17] Ait. Âr. III, ii, 3, 12. [18] [ऐतरेयकाः?]; I 2, P 1, P 2; स सूर्यः स्वग्रंथतयारण्यकं पठति प्रमाणत्वेन W 1, I 4. [19] I 1, P 1, P 2; वसुधांतर्गतः सूर्ये से नं तन्नत W 1; वसुधां तन्नतं सूर्ये से नं तन्नत I 4.

१८. देवताकांडत्रयवर्तिन्यः सूर्यव्यतिरिक्ता या अग्निवाय्वाद्यास्तद्विभूतयः । तस्य सूर्यस्य विभूतय इत्यर्थः ॥

१९. तदिति वाक्योपन्यासे । एतदर्थरूपमृचैव स्पष्टमुक्तं । कथमित्याह ॥

२०. उभयं[1] मा भूदित्याहुरित्युक्तं ॥

इह च । रससिद्धं[2] यथा ताम्रमाप्नोति हि सुवर्णतां ।
एवमर्थोऽप्यृचा स्पष्ट इति वेदे च बुध्यते ॥
सत्यं वै वागृचा स्पष्टेत्यत्र ज्ञातं महर्षिभिः ।
ऋगुदाहरणं तस्माद्ब्राह्मणे[3] बहुशः कृतं ॥

सूत्राणि च ब्राह्मणवच्छ्रुतेः[4] सूत्रयंतेऽन्वयं ॥

२१. नैकेन सूर्यशब्देन न त्रिभिरग्निवायुसूर्यैर्न पर्यायैः किंत्वभिधानमुपदेशं मंत्रद्रष्टृणामनतिक्रमेणानुक्रमिष्यामः[5] ॥

२२. ऐंद्रसूक्ते मरुतः प्रायेण बाहुल्येन निपातभाजो भवंति । ऐंद्रे तु प्रायेणानैंद्रे त्वल्पश इति प्रायशब्दार्थः । निपातो स्वागतपूजनमित्यनुक्रमणीविदः । अपि च यथैंद्रमेवात ऊर्ध्वं छंदः शस्यते तद्धि सर्वं मरुत्वतीयं भवति मंत्रलिंगात् । तेनादह सधामन्विति[6] मारुतषड्वान्वयेऽपि युंजंति ब्रध्नमरुषमित्यस्यैंद्रस्य ब्राह्मणाच्छंसिविनियोगः सिद्धो भवति ॥

[7] [8] [9]

२३. दानस्तुतिं[10] प्रति संबंधिनो राजानः । चकारोऽवधारणे । विभिंदोर्दानं तुष्टावेत्यादौ[11] विभिंद्वादीनां राजत्वं विधीयते ॥

3, १. अथेति प्रस्तावे । अनंतरं छंदांसि प्रस्तूयंत इत्यर्थः । अथैतेषां छंदसामेव चतुर्दश नामान्याह ॥

२. एषां गायत्र्यादीनां शब्दानामितरेतरयोगे द्वंद्वः । संज्ञाप्रदेशाः प्रथमं छंदस्त्रिपदा गायत्र्येवमादयः[12] । अथ तेषामेवाक्षरसंख्यामाह ॥

३. चतुर्विंशत्यादि चतुरुत्तरवृद्ध्या षट्सप्तत्यंतानि छंदांसि भवंति । चतुर्विंशतिर्गायत्री । अष्टाविंशतिरुष्णिक् । द्वात्रिंशदनुष्टुप् । षट्त्रिंशदक्षरा बृहती । चत्वारिंशदक्षरा पंक्तिः । चतुश्चत्वारिंशदक्षरा त्रिष्टुप् । अष्टाचत्वारिंशदक्षरा जगती । द्वापंचाशदक्षरातिजगती । षट्पंचाशच्छक्करी ।

[1] सौभत्यं I 2, P 1, P 2. [2] तारविद्धं I 2, P 2; चारविद्धं P 1 [स्पारविद्धं]. [3] A marginal note in MS. W 1, आश्वलायनारण्यके, apparently refers to ब्राह्मणे बहुशः कृतं । [4] °वच्छ्रुति सूत्रायते त्वयं W 1; °वत् श्रुति सूत्रायते न्वयं I 4; सूत्राणि ब्राह्मणवत्सूत्रायंते न्वयं I 2, P 1, P 2. [5] W 1; I 4 also, but ending °देशं तद्दृष्टृणामनुक्रमेणानुक्रमिष्यामः । P 2, I 2 एकेन सूर्यशब्देन त्रिभिरग्निवायुसूर्यैः किंतु उपदेशो मंत्रदृष्टनामभिः क्रमेणानुक्रमिष्यामः । P 1 the same, but ending उपदेशमंत्रदृष्टृणामतिक्रमेणानुक्रमिष्यामः । [6] *Rigv*. I, 6, 4. [7] मारुतः P 1; मारुत्यः the rest; cp. Sâyana, vol. i, p. 95. [8] *Rigv*. I, 6. [9] °च्छंसी MSS. [10] °ति I 4; °प्रत I 2, P 1, P 2. [11] See sûtra on VIII, 2. [12] § 4, 1.

षष्टिरतिशक्करी । चतुःषष्टिरष्टिः । अष्टाषष्टिरत्यष्टिः । द्वासप्ततिर्धृतिः । षट्सप्ततिरतिधृतिरित्यर्थः । अत्र विशेषमाह ॥

४. एकेनाक्षरेणोनेनैषामेव निचृद्गायत्री निचृदुष्णिग् निचृत्पदपंक्तिर्निचृत्ककुप्न्यंकुशिरा निचृज्जगतीत्यादि सर्वसंज्ञाः स्युः । तथाधिकेनैकेन भुरिग्गायत्रीत्यर्थः । त्रयोविंशतिर्निचृद्गायत्री पंचविंशतिर्भुरिग्गायत्रीत्यादि । यथा । अग्निः पूर्वेभिर्ऋषिभिरिति[1] निचृद्गायत्री । विद्वांसाविद्दुरः पृच्छेदिति[2] भुरिग्गायत्री ॥

५. ऊनाधिकेत्येव । द्वाभ्यामक्षराभ्यामूनाभ्यां विराड्गायत्रीत्यादि सर्वसंज्ञाः स्युः । तथा द्वाभ्यामधिकाभ्यां स्वराड्गायत्रीत्यादीत्यर्थः । द्वाविंशतिर्विराड्गायत्री । षड्विंशतिः स्वराड्गायत्री विराडुष्णिग्वा । यथा राजंतमध्वराणाम्[3] इति विराड्गायत्री । इंद्र जुषस्व प्र वहा याहीति[4] स्वराडनुष्टुप् सूत्रपठिता[5] । अत्र शास्त्रे निचृदादिविशेषणचतुष्टयस्य क्वचिदप्यनुक्तिर्लाघवार्था । इतरथेदमिदमिति प्रतिव्यक्त्युक्तौ बहुवक्तव्यतया शास्त्रं गुरुतरं स्यात् । न खल्वेतद्विशेषणचतुष्टयास्पृष्टं किंचिदपि सूक्तं प्रायेण विद्यते । तथाप्यस्माकमेतच्चतुष्टयं सामान्योक्तावपि सति न्यूनाधिकाभावेऽवश्यं ज्ञातव्यमेवातो योगद्वयादुपदेशेषु क्वचित्कथंचिदुपलंभाच्च । तथा हि छंदोऽनुक्रमण्यां । हिरण्यपाणिः सविता विचर्षणिर्[6] इतीयमुत्तमस्य सूक्तस्य नवमी जगती निचृदित्युच्यते । तथा हि प्रातिशाख्ये ॥

ददी रेक्ण[7] इति त्वेषा ककुप्न्यंकुशिरा निचृत्[8] ॥
त्रयो द्वादशका यस्याः सा होर्ध्वबृहती विराट् ।
महो यो अधीत्त तं मत्सीजानमिदजीजनः[9] ॥

इति च । अथोनाक्षरेषु गायत्र्यादिव्यवहारसिद्धये पादनिर्वाह[10]प्रकारमाह[11] ॥

६. क्षैप्रसंयोगो यकारवकारसंयोगः । यणसंयोग इत्यन्ये । कुत एतत् । यण् हि क्षिप्रे भवति । क्षैप्रो दध्यत्रेत्यादावेकमात्रामर्धमात्रां करोतीति[12] । एकः पूर्वपरयोरि[13]त्यधिकारे संपन्नः संधिरेकाक्षरीभावः[14] । तत्र पूर्वं द्वे अक्षरे एकमक्षरं क्रियत इति । एतान्पादपूरणार्थं व्यूहेत् पृथक्कुर्यात् । यकारं व्यूहेत् । दिवस्पृथिव्याः पर्योज उद्भृतं[15] प्रत्नो होता वरेण्यः[16] तत्सवितुर्वरेण्यं[17] इत्यादौ । वकारं व्यूहेत् । द्रुन्नः सर्पिरासुतिर्[18] दिवं गच्छ स्वःपत इत्यादौ । रेफं व्यूहेत् । एवा त्वामिंद्र वज्रिन्नत्र[19] । आनुपं[20] व्यूहेत् उपेदमुपपर्चनं[21] इंद्रो व्रधेंद्र ऋषिः[22] । एवं वृद्धं व्यूहेत् । प्र ब्रह्मैत्विति[23] । एकः

[1] *Rigv*. I, 1, 2. [2] I, 120, 2. [3] I, 1, 8. [4] Sâma-v. II, 3, 1, 22, 1. [5] W 1; सूत्रे पठिता I 4; अनुष्टुप्सु पतितत्वात् I 2, P 1, P 2. [6] *Rigv*. I, 35, 9. [7] VIII, 46, 15. [8] See M. M., *Rigv*. Pr. 892. [9] Ibid. 907 and comm. [10] निर्व्यूह I 4, P 1, P 2. [11] प्रतिज्ञाम् I 2, I 4, P 1, P 2. [12] Cp. Vâ*g*. Prât. IV, 146. [13] Pâ*n*. VI, i, 84. [14] Cp. *Rigv*. Pr. 973 and Uva*t*a in comm. [15] *Rigv*. VI, 47, 27. [16] II, 7, 6. [17] III, 62, 10. [18] II, 7, 6. [19] IV, 19, 1. [20] Pâ*n*. VI, i, 87. [21] VI, 28, 8; cp. *Rigv*. Pr. 910. [22] *Rigv*. VIII, 16, 7. [23] VII, 36, 1.

पदांतादतीति[1] पूर्वरूपं व्यूहेत् । अयासा मनसा कृतोऽयासं हव्यमूहिषेऽया नो धेहि भेषजं[2] । इंद्र वाजेषु नोऽव[3] इंद्रं सखायोऽनु सं रभध्वमिति[4] च । सवर्णदीर्घं[5] व्यूहेत् । वदन् ब्रह्मावदतो वनीयान्[6] अध्याध्या भ्वः भ्व इति[7] च । आनुपूर्व्यं व्यूहेदित्याद्येकाक्षरीभावस्योदाहरणं ॥

७. तुशब्दोऽवधारणे । चतुर्दशसु छंदःस्वाद्ये तु सप्तवर्गे गायत्र्यादिजगत्यंत एव पादविशेषात्संज्ञाविशेषा भवंति नोत्तरसप्तकेऽतिजगत्याद्यतिधृत्यंते । आद्ये सप्तके पादविशेषात्संज्ञायुक्ता ऋच इति पुनर्वेदनीयमित्याह[8] ॥

८. तान्पादकृतसंज्ञाविशेषानेवानुक्रामंतोऽग्निं नव मधुच्छंदा वैश्वामित्रो[9] वायो वायव्यमित्यादि प्रतिसूक्तमृष्यादि परिपाटीं वदंत[10] उदाहरिष्यामः । न पुनः सामान्यगायत्र्यादिशब्दान् ॥

९. त्रिष्टुभश्चतुश्चत्वारिंशदक्षरत्वे प्राप्ते सति बहुभिरक्षरैरूना हीना अपि विराड्रूपा विराट्स्थानाश्च त्रिष्टुबधिकारोक्तास्त्रिष्टुभ एव स्युः । नवकौ वैराजस्त्रैष्टुभश्च द्वौ वा वैराजौ नवकस्त्रैष्टुभश्च विराट्स्थानैकादशिनस्त्रयोऽष्टकश्च विराड्रूपेति[11] चैकोनचत्वारिंशच्चत्वारिंशदेकचत्वारिंशदिति पंचभिश्चतुर्भिस्त्रिभिरक्षरैरूना अप्यधिकारात्त्रिष्टुभ एवेत्यर्थः । किमर्थमिदमुच्यते । असत्यस्मिन्योगे ह्येकोनचत्वारिंशतो निचृत्पंक्तित्वं चत्वारिंशतः पंक्तित्वम् एकचत्वारिंशतो भुरिक्पंक्तित्वं च स्यात् । इत्युद्देशः । इतिशब्दः प्रकारे । उद्देशः संक्षेपः । पूर्वोक्तप्रकारो बहूनेषु तत्तदधिकारात्तदात्मकः सप्त छंदःसु गायत्र्यादिष्वभिमत इत्यर्थः । तेन त्रयः सप्तकाः पादनिचृदित्येकविंशत्यक्षरापि गायत्र्येव[12] मध्यमः षट्कश्चेदतिनिचृदिति[13] च विंशत्यक्षरापि गायत्र्येवेत्यादि सिद्धं भवति[14] । न वा एकेनाक्षरेण छंदांसि वियंति न द्वाभ्यामिति[15] । न ह्येकस्मादक्षराद्बाधयंतीति च । तत्र वियंतीत्यन्यत्वं गच्छंतीत्यर्थः । बाधयंतीति नश्यंतीत्यर्थः । द्व्येकयोरुपलक्षणत्वाद्बहूनेष्वपि भवति । तत्राद्यसप्तके गायत्र्यादिजगत्यंते वक्ष्यमाणे वेदितव्यं । अस्य चानंतरसूत्रे प्रयोजनाभावादनादेशेऽष्टाक्षरा[16] इत्यादि पूर्वसप्तक एव नोत्तरसप्तक इति वक्तुं तत्रोपयोगः । तेनातिजगत्याद्यतिधृत्यंते यथाध्ययनं पादाक्षरसंख्याव्यवस्थेति सिद्धं । व्यवहारलाघवाय संज्ञां करोति ॥

१०. पादानामिति शेषः । अक्षरशब्दस्य प्रत्येकं संबंधः । दशाक्षरस्य पादस्य संज्ञा वैराज इति । एकादशाक्षरस्य पादस्य त्रैष्टुभ इति । द्वादशाक्षरस्य पादस्य जागत इति वैराजादिप्रदेशाः । नवकौ वैराजस्त्रैष्टुभश्च[17] त्रिजागतोर्ध्वबृहतीत्येवमादयः[18] । सूत्र्यते पिंगलेनापि ह्ययमर्थो महात्मना । विराजो दिशः । त्रिष्टुभो रुद्राः । जगत्या आदित्या इति[19] । दशाक्षरा विराट् । एकादशाक्षरा त्रिष्टुप् । द्वादशाक्षरा जगतीति[20] श्रुतिरपि पादाभिप्रायेणैव ॥

[1] Pân. VI, i, 109. [2] Cp. Âsv. Sr.-sûtra, I, xi, 13. [3] *Rig*v. I, 7, 4. [4] X, 103, 6. [5] Pân. VI, i, 102. [6] X, 117, 7. [7] VIII, 61, 17. [8] W 1, I 4; न पुनश्चोदनीयमित्याह I 2, P 1, P 2. [9] Sûtras on I, 1 and 2. [10] W 1, I 4; परिपाट्यां वदंत I 2, P 1, P 2. [11] § 9, 5–6; cp. *Rig*v. Pr. 926 and 928. [12] Ibid. 880. [13] § 4, 5. [14] *Rig*v. Pr. 881. [15] Ait. Brâhm. I, 6. [16] See sûtra 11. [17] § 9, 5. [18] § 7, 6. [19] Piṅgala, *Kh*anda*h*-sûtra, III, 4–6. [20] Ait. Br. I, 5.

११. अक्षरसंख्यानुक्तौ पादोऽष्टाक्षरो भवतीति पूर्वसप्तके । तेन त्रिपदा गायत्रीत्यादौ त्र्यष्टकेत्यादि सिद्धं ॥

१२. तत्रानादेश इत्येव । आद्यसप्तकेऽनुक्तपादसंख्या ऋचश्चतुर्भिः पादैर्युक्ता भवंति । तेन तृतीयमनुष्टुबित्यत्र चतुष्पदा ऋचो भवंति । अथादितः सप्त छंदांसि पादविशेषात्संज्ञाविशेषान्विविच्य दर्शयितुमुपक्रमते ॥

४, १. चतुर्दश छंदसामादिभूतं गीतासु च स्वयं साक्षाद्भगवता गायत्री छंदसामहमित्युक्तत्वात्प्रधानभूतं च । गायतां त्राणाद्गायत्रीति निरुक्तं नाम छंदसः । त्रिपदा पादत्रययुक्ता । त्रित्वं चतुष्कनिवृत्त्यर्थं । पादाश्च त्रयोऽष्टाक्षराः । उदाहरणम् अग्निमीळे पुरोहितम्[2] इत्यादि । गायत्रीति प्रागुष्णिहोऽधिकारः । प्रथमं छंद इति श्रुत्यनुकरणं । एवमुत्तरत्र द्वितीयमित्यादि सप्तममित्यंतं । सकलश्रुतिदर्शी ह्ययमाचार्यः ॥

२. गायत्रीत्येव । अत्र संज्ञिनौ द्वौ पदपंक्तिरिति संज्ञा । आदितश्चत्वारः पादाः पंचकाः पंचमः षडक्षरः । एषा पदपंक्तिर्गायत्री । अधा ह्यग्ने[3] । इयं वा पदपंक्तिः । आदितस्त्रयः पंचकाश्चतुर्थश्चतुरक्षरः पंचमः षडक्षर इति । अग्ने तमद्य[4] ॥

३. प्रत्येकान्वयिनः कनो लुक् छांदसः । षट्कः सप्तक एकादशक इति त्रयः पादा यस्याः उष्णिग्गर्भा सा । ता मे अश्व्यानां[5] ॥

४. सा हि पादनिचृद्यस्यास्त्रयः पादास्तु सप्तकाः ॥

युवाकु हि शचीनाम्[6] अभी षु णः सखीनां[7] ॥

५. आद्यपादस्तृतीयश्च सप्तकौ मध्यमो यदि ।
षडक्षरः सा विज्ञेया गायत्र्यतिनिचृत्त्विति ॥

पुरूतमं पुरूणां स्तोतॄणां विवाचि[8] । ननु च ।

षट्सप्तकमध्येऽष्टावतिपादनिचृत्त्विति ।
पैंगलसूचिते शास्त्रे[9] तत् किं नैवेह सूच्यते ॥
यथा निचृत्पादनिचृद्वर्धमानादि सूच्यते ।
उदाहृतिश्च प्रेष्ठं वः[10] प्रेष्ठमु प्रियाणामिति[11] ॥

[1] Bhagavadgîtâ, X, 35. [2] *Rigv.* I, 1, 1. [3] IV, 10, 2. [4] IV, 10, 1. See *Rigv.* Pr., sûtra 877, where the order of the pâdas is not determined in the latter form of the padapaṅkti, while the former is called padapaṅkti bhuri*g*. Kâtyâyana apparently does not recognise a third form of this metre, consisting of five pâdas of five syllables, as Saunaka does in the above-mentioned sûtra. [5] *Rigv.* VIII, 25, 23. See *Rigv.* Pr. 887 and comm. [6] *Rigv.* I, 17, 4. [7] IV. 31, 3; cp. *Rigv.* Pr. 880. [8] *Rigv.* VI, 45, 29; cp. *Rigv.* Pr. 881. [9] Piṅgala's *Kh*anda*h*-sûtra, III, 11; cp. Ind. Stud. VIII, pp. 239–241. [10] *Rigv.* VIII, 84, 1. [11] VIII, 103, 10; cp. *Rigv.* Pr. 882.

उच्यते। व्यूहेनैते हि गायत्र्याविवत्र तत्र सूच्यते[1]।
सावित्रीति तदित्याद्या गायत्री व्यूहनाश्रया ॥

६. मध्यम इत्येव।
आद्यः पादस्तृतीयश्च सप्तको मध्यमो यदि।
दशाक्षरः सा गायत्री यवमध्या प्रकीर्तिता ॥

स सुन्वे यो वसूनां[3] ॥

७. यस्याः पादाः क्रमेण स्युः षट्सप्तकाष्टकास्त्रयः।
सा गायत्री वर्धमाना पादैकाक्षरवर्धनात् ॥

त्वमसि प्रशस्यः[4] त्वमग्ने यज्ञानामिति[5] ॥

८. अष्टकः सप्तकः षट् इति यस्यास्तु पादकाः।
क्रमेण सा प्रतिष्ठोक्ता त्वमग्ने व्रतपा असि[6] ॥

९. द्वौ षट्कौ सप्तकश्चांत्यः प्रेष्ठं[7] सा तु ह्रसीयसी।
इति पादविभागेन नव गायत्र्य ईरिताः[8] ॥

५, १. उष्णिगिति प्रागनुष्टुभोऽधिकारः। अत्र चतुरुत्तरवृद्ध्यारंभादूर्ध्वं विज्ञातीयुष्णिगिति निरुच्यते। उक्ताद्यपेक्षया गायत्र्याश्च चतुरुत्तरवृद्ध्यान्वयेनोष्णिक्त्वं पंकजादिवद्योगरूढित्वात्। अंत्यो द्वादशक इत्यष्टाक्षरत्वापवादः। त्रिपदेति चतुष्पदापवादः परिभाषयैव सिद्धत्वात्।
आद्यावष्टाक्षरौ पादौ तृतीयो द्वादशाक्षरः[9]।
सोष्णिगुदाहृतिः प्रोक्ता य इंद्र सोमपातमः[10] ॥

२. द्वादशक इत्येव।
आद्यो द्वादशकः पादस्त्वष्टकावपरौ यदि।
पुरउष्णिगिति प्रोक्ता सा ह्यप्स्वंतर्[11] उदाहृतिः ॥

[1] इति अत्र न सूच्यते I 2, I 4, P 1, P 2; इति तत्र तत्सूच्यते W 1. [2] *Rigv.* III, 62, 10. [3] IX, 108, 13; *Rigv.* Pr. 886. [4] *Rigv.* VIII, 11, 2. [5] VI, 16, 1; *Rigv.* Pr. 883. [6] *Rigv.* VIII, 11, 1. [7] VIII, 103, 10. This verse is twice quoted in the *Rigv.* Pr., 882 and 1000. In the former sûtra it is represented as consisting optionally of pâdas of 6 + 8 + 7 (Sha*d*g., § 4, 5: 7 + 6 + 7) syllables, with vyûha of the second pâda, instead of 6 + 6 + 7, as in 1000. In the latter sûtra it is said to be shorter (ह्रसीयसी) than another verse. This expression may probably, as M. M. suggests, have originated the name given to it by Kâtyâyana. [8] It is to be noticed that of these nine gâyatrî metres, two (pratish*th*â and hrasîyasî) are not mentioned in the Prâtisâkhya, whereas the latter has six which are omitted in the Sarvânukrama*n*î (cp. the list of metres, p. cccelvi in M. M.'s *Rig*v. Pr.). [9] Cp. *Rigv.* Pr. 888. [10] *Rigv.* VIII, 12, 1. [11] I, 23, 19.

३. द्वादशक इत्येव ।

द्वादशाक्षरको मध्ये त्वष्टकावभितो यदि ।
सोष्णिक्ककुबिति प्रोक्ता वयमु त्वामपूर्व्य[1] ॥

४. एकादशाक्षरस्त्वाद्यो द्वितीयो द्वादशाक्षरः ।
चतुष्कोऽपीति यस्यां सा ककुभ्न्यंकुशिरा मता ॥

दद्री रेक्णस्तन्वे ददिर्वसु[2]। ननु चतुर्थारक्षके दद्री रेक्ण इति द्विपदा नूनमर्चेत्येकपदे[3]त्येतद्विरुध्यते। न। एतस्या एव ऋच्यर्धे द्विपदैकपदात्वविधेः ॥

५. एकादशाक्षरावाद्यौ तृतीयस्तु षडक्षरः ।
यस्याः सैषा तनुशिरा प्र या घोष[4] उदाहृतिः ॥

६. मद्ध्य इत्येव ।

एकादशाक्षरः षट्कः पुनरेकादशाक्षरः ।
सा पिपीलिकमध्योक्ता हरी यस्येत्युदाहृतिः[5] ॥

७. आद्यः पंचाक्षरः पादस्त्रयस्त्वष्टाक्षराः परे ।
अनुष्टुब्गर्भा सा प्रोक्ता पितुं नु स्तोषमित्यसौ ॥

८. चतुर्भिः सप्तकैः पादैर्युक्ताप्युष्णिगिहोच्यते ।
नदं व ओदतीनां[7] मंसीमहीत्युदाहृतिः[8] ॥

द्वितीयमुष्णिक् त्रिपदांत्यो द्वादशक इत्यत्र चतुःसप्तका चेति लाघवाय वाच्येऽत्र गुरुसूत्रकरणं चतुःसप्तकोष्णिहोऽल्पप्रयोगत्वसूचनार्थमित्याहुः। कथं पुनः प्र प्र वस्त्रिष्टुभमिषम्[9] अर्चत प्रार्चत[10] यो व्यतींरफाणयद्[11] इति तृचानन्वनुक्रम्य प्रशास्ता अनुष्टुभः शंसतीति ब्राह्मणं[12] तृचा आनुष्टुभा इति च सूत्रं[13] नदं व[14] इत्यस्या उष्णिक्त्वं नोपपद्यते। तेषु हीयमपि पठ्यते। उच्यते।

अनुष्टुप्पादसाम्येन गुणवादोऽयमुष्णिहः ।
रहस्यब्राह्मणेऽप्येवं संयगाम्नायते खलु ॥

नदं व ओदतीनामित्युष्णिगक्षरैर्भवत्यनुष्टुप्पादैरिति[15]।

इत्युष्णिहोऽष्टावुद्दिष्टाः सम्यक् पादविभेदतः[16] ॥

[1] *Rigv.* VIII, 21, 1. [2] VIII, 46, 15; *Rigv.* Pr., 982, calls this verse निचृत् because the number of syllables is 27 instead of 28. [3] Ait. Âr. V, ii, 5. [4] *Rigv.* I, 120, 5; *Rigv.* Pr. 894. [5] *Rigv.* X, 105, 2; *Rigv.* Pr. 893. [6] *Rigv.* I, 187, 1; *Rigv.* Pr. 895. [7] *Rigv.* VIII, 69, . [8] X, 26, 4; *Rigv.* Pr. 891, where this metre is said to be anush*t*ubh by pâdas or ush*n*ih by syllables. [9] *Rigv.* VIII, 69, 1. [10] VIII, 69, 8. [11] VIII, 69, 13. [12] Ait. Br. IV, iv, 4; cp. Haug, Ait. Br., vol. ii, p. 261. The words तृचानन्वनुक्रम्य do not occur in the text of either Haug or Aufrecht (cp. comm.). [13] Âsv. *S*r.-sûtra, VI, ii, 9. [14] *Rigv.* VIII, 69, 2. [15] The *Rigv.* Pr. 891 sayc the same of this verse as well as of X, 26, 4. [16] The *Rigv.* Pr. has exactly the same eight varieties of ush*n*ih.

६, १. आ बृहत्या अनुष्टुबधिकारः ।

चतुर्भिरष्टकैः पादैर्युक्तानुष्टुबिहोच्यते ॥
गायंति त्वा गायत्रिणो[1] इंद्रं विश्वा अवीवृधन्[2] ।
अनादेशाच्चतुष्पात्त्वं पादाश्चाष्टाक्षरास्तथा ॥

२. पंच पंचाक्षरा यस्याः षष्ठश्चैकः षडक्षरः ।
सोक्ता महापदपंक्तिस्तव स्वादिष्ठ[3]येत्युदाहृतिः ॥

३. द्वादशाक्षरकावाद्यौ तृतीयोऽष्टाक्षरः कृतेः ।
मा कस्मै धातमित्येषा कृत्यनुष्टुबुदाहृतिः[4] ॥

४. यस्या द्वादशकस्त्वाद्यस्त[5]थाष्टद्वादशाक्षरौ ।
सा पिपीलिकमध्योक्ता पर्यू षु प्रे[6]त्युदाहृतिः ॥

५. चेदित्येव ।

नवाक्षरो द्वादशको नवाक्षरक एव चेत् ।
इति पादास्त्रयो यस्याः सा प्रोक्ता काविराडिति ॥

ता विद्वांसा हवामहे वां[7] ॥

६. पादैर्युक्तेति शेषः ।

नवाक्षरो दशाक्षरस्त्रयोदशाक्षरस्तथा ।
इति त्रयो हि यत्रैव नष्टरूपा तथेह सा ॥

वि पृच्छामि पाक्या३न देवान्[8] ॥

७. दशाक्षरास्त्रयः पादा यस्याः सा हि विराड् भवेत् ।
त्रयोग्रहस्त्वनादेशाच्चतुष्पात्त्वं तु मास्म भूत् ॥

पिबा सोममिंद्र मंदतु त्वा[9] ॥

८. त्रय इत्येव विराडिति च ।

एकादशाक्षरा यस्यास्त्रयः सापि विराड्भवेत् ।

दुहीयन्मित्रधितये युवाकु[10] ॥

इत्यनुष्टुभ उद्दिष्टा अष्टौ पादप्रभेदतः[11] ॥

७, १. आ पंक्तेर्बृहत्यधिक्रियते ।

आदितोऽष्टाक्षरौ पादौ तृतीयो द्वादशाक्षरः ।
चतुर्थोऽष्टाक्षरश्चेति बृहती खलु वै भवेत् ॥

[1] *Rigv.* I, 10, 1. [2] I, 11, 1. [3] IV, 10, 5. [4] I, 120, 8. [5] °श्चो-स्त्य° MSS. [6] *Rigv.* IX, 110, 1. [7] I, 120, 3. [8] I, 120, 4. [9] VII, 22, 1. [10] I, 120, 9. [11] The eight forms of anush*t*ubh are identical with those of the *Rigv.* Pr. 896–903.

अभि त्वा शूर नोनुम[1] उत्तिष्ठ ब्रह्मणस्पते[2]।
अष्टाक्षरचतुष्पात्त्वमनादेशेन लभ्यते ॥

२. द्वादशक इत्येव ।

द्वादशाक्षर आदौ चेदष्टकाश्च परे त्रयः ।
पादा यस्या हि सा प्रोक्ता पुरस्ताद्बृहतीति वै ॥

महो यस्पतिः शवसो असाम्या[3] कुह श्रुत इंद्रः[4] ॥

३. द्वादशक इत्येव ।

आदितोऽष्टाक्षरः पादो द्वितीयो द्वादशाक्षरः ।
पादावथाष्टकौ सोक्ता त्रिभिरेव तु नामभिः ॥
ऋषीणां मतभेदो हि नामभेदेऽस्ति कारणं ।
पिंगलस्य[5] मते चेयं महर्षेर्न्यंकुसारिणी ॥
स्कंधोग्रीवी क्रौष्टुकेश्च यास्कस्योरोबृहत्यपि ।

मत्स्यपायि ते महः । इंदुरिति रेफव्यूहेन तृतीयोऽष्टाक्षरः[7] ॥

४. द्वादशक इत्येव ।

आदितस्त्वष्टका यस्यास्त्रयोऽंत्यो द्वादशाक्षरः ।
उपरिष्टाद्बृहत्येषा न तमंह[8] उदाहृतिः ॥

५. चेदित्येव । अष्टास्य संतीत्यष्टी ।

यद्यष्टाक्षरयोर्मध्ये पादौ स्यातां दशाक्षरौ ।
विष्टारबृहती सोक्ता युवं ह्यास्तमुदाहृतिः[9] ॥

६. त्रयो द्वादशका यस्याः सा ह्यूर्ध्वबृहती मता ।

अजीजनो अमृत मर्त्येष्वा[10] दिवः पीयूषं पूर्व्यं यदुक्थ्यं[11] ॥

७. यदि ह्यष्टाक्षरो मध्ये त्रयोदशकयोर्भवेत् ।
सा पिपीलिकमध्योक्ता बृहती द्विस्त्रयोदशात् ॥

अभि वो वीरमंधसो मदेषु गाय[12] ॥

८. नवाक्षरोऽष्टाक्षरश्च तथैवैकादशाक्षरः ।

---

[1] *Rigv.* VII, 32, 22. [2] I, 40, 1. [3] X, 22, 3. [4] X, 22, 1; *Rigv.* Pr. 905. [5] Piṅgala, *Kh*anda*h*-sûtra, III, 26. [6] I, 175, 1. [7] Cp. *Rigv.* Pr. 907 and comm.; Ind. Stud. VIII, 95, 243–4. [8] *Rigv.* X, 126, 1; *Rigv.* Pr. 907. [9] *Rigv.* I, 120, 7; *Rigv.* Pr. 908. [10] *Rigv.* IX, 110, 4. [11] IX, 110, 8; *Rigv.* Pr. 906–7, where this metre is called urob*ri*hatî virâ*t*. [12] *Rigv.* VIII, 46, 14.

चतुर्थोऽष्टाक्षरश्चेति पादा यस्यास्तु सोच्यते ।
बृहत्येषा तु विषमपदेति खलु चक्रुषैः ॥

सनितः सुसनितरुग्र[1] ॥

९. चतुर्भिर्नवकैः पादैर्युक्तापि बृहती मता ॥

तं त्वा वयं पितो वचोभिः[2] ॥

चतुर्थं बृहती तृतीयो द्वादशक[3] इत्यत्र लाघवाय चतुर्नवकाश्चेति वाच्येऽल्पप्रयोगसूचनार्थं गुरुसूत्रकरणमित्याहुः । तथा च सूच्यते हि भगवता पिंगलेन पाणिन्यनुजेन[4] क्वचिन्नवकाश्चत्वार[5] इति । तत्र क्वचिदिति हि प्रयोगाल्पत्वं सूच्यते ।

इति चक्रुषसिंहेन बृहत्यो नव कीर्तिताः[6] ॥

८, १. आ त्रिष्टुभः पंक्त्यधिकारः । अत्र पंचपदेत्युक्तेश्चतुष्पात्त्वं मास्म भूत् ।

अष्टाक्षराः पंचपादा यस्याः सा पंक्तिरुच्यते ।
इंद्रो मदाय वावृधे[8] इत्था हि सोम इन्मदे[9] ॥

२. पंक्तिरुच्यत इति शेषः । अथेत्यधिकारे । तेन विराड् दशकैरित्यादौ चतुर्भिः पादैरिति सिद्धं भवति । असत्यस्मिन्योगेऽनादेशसिद्धचतुष्पात्त्वस्य पंचपदाधिकारेण बाधः स्यात् ॥

३. दशाक्षरैश्चतुर्भिस्तु पादैः पंक्तिर्युता विराट् ॥

ऋतस्य पथि वेधा अपायि[10] ॥

४. तृतीयाद्यौ द्वादशकौ द्वितीयांत्यौ तथाष्टकौ ।
यस्याः सतोबृहत्येषा न त्वावा[11]नित्युदाहृतिः ॥

५. जागतावित्येव । द्वितीयांत्यौ द्वादशकौ तृतीयाद्यौ तथाष्टकौ ।
यस्याः सा विपरीतेति नाम्नोक्ता चक्रुषोत्तमैः ॥

य ऋष्वः श्रावयत्सखा[12] ॥

[1] *Ṛigv.* VIII, 46, 20. [2] I, 187, 11; *Ṛigv.* Pr. 909, where M. M. remarks that this verse is considered an anush*t*ubh by the Sarvânukrama*n*î; all the MSS. however agree, in the sûtra on I, 187, in the statement that it is anush*t*ubh or b*ri*hatî. Sâya*n*a in his quotation of the sûtra omits बृहती वा. [3] Sûtra, § 7, 1. [4] MSS. (W 1, I 2, I 4, P 1, P 2), not पाणिनीयानुजेन as Weber, Ind. Stud. VIII, pp. 160 and 248. [5] Piṅgala, *Kh.*-sûtra, III, 33. [6] Identical with the nine forms in *Ṛigv.* Pr. 904–912. [7] °क्लि° MSS. [8] *Ṛigv.* I, 81, 1. [9] I, 80, 1. [10] VI, 44, 8; in the sûtra on this hymn (q. v.) this verse is stated to be virâ*g* or trish*t*ubh. *Ṛigv.* Pr. (922) gives another example (VIII, 96, 4). [11] *Ṛigv.* VII, 32, 23; *Ṛigv.* Pr. 922 has I, 84, 20. [12] *Ṛigv.* VIII, 46, 12.

६. जागताविल्येव । आद्यौ द्वादशकौ पादावष्टकौ च परौ यदि ।
प्रस्तारपंक्तिः सा प्रोक्तोक्षुंचस्तेत्याद्युदाहृतिः[1] ॥
७. जागताविल्येव । आद्यावष्टाक्षरौ पादौ ततो द्वादकौ परौ ।
यस्याः सास्तारपंक्तिः स्यादग्निं नेत्याद्युदाहृतिः[2] ॥
८. जागताविल्येव । द्वादशाक्षरयोर्मध्ये पादावष्टाक्षरौ यदि ।
यस्याः संस्तारपंक्तिः स्यात् पितुभृतो न तंतुमित्[3] ॥

मनु च । आ याहि वनसा सहेति द्विपदाः शंसति[5] आ याहि वनसा सहेमा नु कं[6] वभ्रुरेक[7] इति द्विपदासूक्तानीति[8] ब्राह्मणसूत्राभ्याम् आ याहि संवर्त उपस्यं द्वैपदमिति[9] सर्वानुक्रमण्यां च द्विपदासूक्ते पितुभृत इत्येषा पठ्यते । तत्कथमियं चतुष्पदोदाह्रियते । उच्यते । द्विर्द्विपदा ऋचः समामनंतीति[10] द्वयोर्द्विपदयोरध्ययन एकर्चत्वमत्रैव वक्ष्यते । तेन चतुष्पात्त्वमित्यदोषः ॥

९. जागताविल्येव । यस्यास्त्वष्टकयोर्मध्ये भवेतां द्वादशाक्षरौ ।
विष्टारपंक्तिः सा प्रोक्ता अग्ने तव श्रवो वयः[11] ॥
इति पंक्तय उद्दिष्टा अष्टौ[12] शिष्टेष्टपुष्टिदाः ।
वक्रूचार्यसिंहेन कात्यायनमहर्षिणा ॥

९, १. आ जगत्यास्त्रिष्टुबधिकारः । त्रैष्टुभमित्यनादेशाष्टाक्षरनिवृत्त्यर्थं । पादाश्च चत्वारोऽनादेशात् । चत्वार एकादशकास्तु पादा यस्याः सोक्ता त्रिष्टुबाचार्यविशिष्टैः । कस्य नूनं[13] ॥

२. यस्या द्वादशकौ पादावंत्यावेकादशाक्षरौ ।
त्रिष्टुब् जागतसूक्तस्था सोच्यते जगतीति वै ॥
इमं स्तोममिदं सूक्तं जागतं त्वियमत्र च ।
यस्मै त्वमायजसे[15] ॥

३. सैव त्रैष्टुभसूक्तस्था त्रिष्टुबित्युच्यते यथा ।
यूपव्रस्का[16] ये वाजिनम्[17] इत्येतत्सूक्तं हि त्रैष्टुभं ॥

४. यस्या दशाक्षरौ पादौ ततो वै द्वादशाक्षरौ ।
सोक्ताभिसारिणी त्रिष्टुब् यो याचा वीत्युदाहृतिः[18] ॥

[1] *Rigv.* X, 18, 11; *Rigv.* Pr. gives X, 93, 1. [2] *Rigv.* X, 21, 1; नेत्यादिसूक्तकं W 1, I 4. [3] X, 172, 3; cp. *Rigv.* Pr. 922, note. [4] *Rigv.* X, 172, 1. [5] Ait. Br. V, xvii, 10; cp. Ait. Âr. V, ii, 2, 9. [6] X, 157, 1. [7] VIII, 29, 1. [8] Âsv. Sr.-sûtra, VIII, ii, 24; cp. Sâyana on X, 172. [9] See sûtra on X, 172 and comm. [10] § 12, 10. [11] *Rigv.* X, 140, 1. [12] The eight forms of paṅkti are identical with those given in the *Rigv.* Pr., 913-921. [13] *Rigv.* VIII, 84, 7. [14] I, 94. [15] I, 94, 2. This metre, in *Rigv.* Pr. 924, is called upa*g*agatî, a name not occurring in the Sarvânukramanî. [16] I, 162, 6: in the sûtra on this hymn verse 6 is said to be *g*agatî; it is not quoted in the *Rigv.* Pr. [17] Ibid., ver. 12. [18] *Rigv.* X, 23, 5; *Rigv.* Pr. 925.

५. यस्या नवाक्षरौ पादौ तृतीयो दशकस्तथा ।
एकादशाक्षरोऽंत्यश्च विराट्स्थाना तु सा मता ॥

स्वस्ति न इंद्रो वृद्धश्रवाः[1] ॥

यस्या दशाक्षरावाद्यौ तृतीयश्च नवाक्षरः ।
एकादशाक्षरश्चांत्यो विराट्स्थानैव सापि च ॥

श्रुधी हवमिंद्र मा रिषण्यः[2] ॥ वेति प्रकारविकल्पार्थं ॥

६. एकादशाक्षरा यस्याः पादाः स्युस्त्रय आदितः ।
चतुर्थश्चाष्टकः सोक्ता विराड्रूपेति बह्वृचैः[3] ॥

तुभ्यं श्चोतंत्यध्रिगो शचीवः[4] श्रुतं मे मित्रावरुणा हवेमेति[5] च ॥ नात्र[6] क्रमादर आ यो रुवर्युर्मित्यृचि तृतीयस्याष्टकत्वदर्शनात्[6] । बहुवचनस्य त्रित्वाद्यनेकविषयत्वेऽपि कपिंजलाधिकरणन्यायेनानादेशे चतुष्पदाश्चर्च इति[8] परिभाषया चैकादशाक्षरपादत्रित्वे सिद्धे त्रय इति न्यायप्राप्तानुवादः । श्रुत्यनुकरणं वा ॥

७. यस्या द्वादशकाः पादास्त्रयः क्वाप्यस्ति चाष्टकः ।
एषा ज्योतिष्मती[9] त्रिष्टुबुक्तात्र ह्युदाहृतिः ॥

८. यत इति सप्तम्यर्थे तसिल् । तत इत्यनुकरणे । पुरस्ताद्वा मध्ये वोपरिष्टाद्वा यत्राष्टकोऽष्टाक्षरः पादस्तेन युक्तो ज्योतिःशब्दो नाम भवेत् । पुरस्ताज्ज्योतिर्मध्येज्योतिरुपरिष्टाज्ज्योतिरित्येताः संज्ञाः पैंगलेऽपि शास्त्रे दृष्टा हि । तद्यथा । पुरस्ताज्ज्योतिः प्रथमेन । मध्येज्योतिर्मध्यमेन । उपरिष्टाज्ज्योतिरंत्येन[10] । तत्र पुरस्ताज्ज्योतिरुदाहरणं वेदांतरे । इमे त इंद्र ते वयं ये त्वारभ्य चरामसीति[11] । अस्माकं त्वियम् इमे त इंद्र ते वयं पुरुष्टुतेति[12] पाठाज्जगत्येव । मध्येज्योतिः । यद्वा यज्ञं मनवे संमिमिक्षथुः[13] ताभिरा यातं वृषणोप मे हवमिति[14] च । तृतीयाष्टकेन पादेन मध्येज्योतिर्वेदांतरे ।

तदश्विना भिषजा रुद्रवर्तनी सरस्वती वयति पेशो अंतरं ।
अस्थि मज्जानं मासरैः कारोतरेण दधतो गवां त्वचि[15] ॥

[1] *Rigv*. I, 89, 6. [2] II, 11, 1; *Rigv*. Pr. 926. [3] Cp. *Rigv*. Pr. 928, which does not prescribe the order of the pâdas. [4] *Rigv*. III, 21, 4. [5] I, 122, 6. [6] W 1 alone adds this remark, which, though apparently contradicting Shadg.'s own words above (एकादशाक्षरास्त्रय आदितः), agrees both with the vagueness of the *Rigv*. Pr. and with the actual facts; cp. the third pâda in I, 122, 5, and the first in V, 19, 5 (quoted in *Rigv*. Pr.). [7] *Rigv*. I, 122, 5. [8] § 3, 12. [9] *Rigv*. Pr. 929. [10] Piṅgala, III, 52-54; Ind. Stud. VIII, pp. 250, 251. [11] This verse (= the following with पुरुष्टुत omitted) does not occur in the text of any of our recensions of the other three Vedas; it must be the reading of another Sâkhâ. [12] *Rigv*. I, 57, 4; Sâma-v. I, iv, 2, 4, 4. [13] VIII, 10, 2. [14] VIII, 22, 12. [15] Vâg. Samh. XIX, 82.

इति । उपरिष्टाज्ज्योतिः । अग्निनेंद्रेण वरुणेन विष्णुनेत्याद्याः । ऋतावानं महिषं विश्वदर्शतमिति[2] च । पूर्वत्र[3] तु क्रमाविवक्षयेह त्वनेकसंज्ञार्थोऽयमारंभः[4] । एतदेव ज्ञापकं भवत्यन्यत्रोक्तक्रमविवक्षेति[5] ॥

९. चत्वारोऽष्टाक्षराः पादाः कश्चाप्यन्यो द्वादशाक्षरः ।
यस्यास्तु प्रोच्यते नाम्ना सा महाबृहतीति वै ॥

अत्रापि क्रमो न विवक्षितः । तेनादितो द्वादशकोऽंततो द्वादशकः सिध्यति । तत्रादितो द्वादशकः । नमोवाके प्रस्थिते अध्वरे नरा[6] । अंततो द्वादशकः । नवानां नवतीनामिति[7] व्यूहेत् ॥

१०. जागत इत्येष ।
आद्यावष्टाक्षरौ यस्यास्तृतीयो द्वादशाक्षरः ।
पुनर्द्वावष्टकौ चेत्सा यवमध्या प्रकीर्तिता ॥

सं मा तपंत्यभितः[8] ॥

११. आद्यौ दशाक्षरौ यस्यास्त्रयश्चाष्टाक्षराः परे ।
पंक्त्युत्तरा विराट्पूर्वा तस्या द्वे नामनी इमे[9] ॥
द्विनामत्वं ब्राह्मणेषु[10] चोक्तिद्वैधोपलंभनात्[11] ।

एषेंद्राग्निभ्यामहावि हव्यं[12] ।
इति त्रिष्टुभ उद्दिष्टा दश[13] कात्यायनर्षिणा[14] ॥

१०, १. आ प्रगाथाज्जगत्यधिकारः । जागतेत्यष्टाक्षरनिवृत्त्यर्थं । अनादेशे चतुष्पात्त्वं ।
यस्याः पादास्तु चत्वारो द्वादशाक्षरसंयुताः ।
जगती नाम सा प्रोक्ता इमं स्तोमम्[15] उदाहृतिः ।

[1] *Rigv.* VIII, 35, 1; *Rigv.* Pr. 929. [2] *Rigv.* X, 140, 6. [3] Sûtra 7.
[4] W 1, I 4 (omits इह); पूर्वेक्रमाविवक्षयाद्या त्वेक° I 2, P 2; पूर्वेच क्रमाविवक्षाद्या त्वेक° P 1.
[5] W 1; विवक्षितः I 4; अन्यथा उक्तक्रम वेति जपति I 2, P 2; अन्यतोक्तक्रमं वेव जयति (sic) P 1. Cp. with this statement sûtra 6 and comm. (note 6). [6] *Rigv.* VIII, 35, 23; *Rigv.* Pr. 932. [7] *Rigv.* I, 191, 13. Uvata in his comm. on *Rigv.* Pr. (972) calls this verse a paṅkti. [8] *Rigv.* I, 105, 8; W 1 alone adds मूषो न शिश्ना (apparently to indicate that X, 33, 2 is not meant). The *Rigv.* Pr. (931) quotes VI, 48, 7, which in the text of the Sarvânukr. is simply called a mahâbṛihatî. [9] द्वे सार्त्त्री इमे I 2, P 1, P 2. [10] W 1, P 1; ब्राह्मणे तु I 4; च P 2, I 2. [11] तस्माद्वेदोपलंभनात् W 1, I 4; उक्तिद्वेधापलंभनात् I 2, P 2; कृतं द्वेधोपलंभनात् P 1. [12] *Rigv.* V, 86, 6; in *Rigv.* Pr. 1028 called mahâsatomukhâ. [13] Identical with those given in *Rigv.* Pr. 922-31. [14] I 4; °महर्षिणा the rest. [15] *Rigv.* I, 94, 1.

यस्यास्त्वष्टाक्षराः पादास्त्रयो द्वौ द्वादशाक्षरौ ।
महासतोबृहत्युक्ता सा नात्रोक्तक्रमादरः ॥
आ यः पप्रौ भानुनेति[1] तृतीयाद्यौ हि जागतौ[2] ।

तत्र स्वावित्यात्मीयौ जागतावित्यर्थः । कुतः । प्रकृतत्वाज्जगत्याः ॥

३. वेति प्रकारविकल्पे ।

आदावष्टाक्षरौ यस्याः सप्तकोऽथ षडक्षरः ।
दशाक्षरोऽथ नवकः सा महापंक्तिरुच्यते ॥

सूर्ये विषमा सजामीति[3] तिस्रः[4] ।

अष्टाक्षरा वा यस्याः षट् सा महापंक्तिरेव हि ।
अव द्रुके अव त्रिका[5] उभे यदिंद्र रोदसी[6] ॥
तिस्रो[7] जगत्यस्तु प्रोक्ता कात्यायनमहर्षिणा ॥
इति छंदांसि सर्वेह व्याख्यातानि विभागशः ।
एषु छंदोद्वयंयुताः[8] संज्ञा वक्तुं विजृंभते ॥

११, १. अथशब्दोऽधिकारार्थः । सूक्तसंख्यानुवर्तत इत्यतः प्राक् प्रगाथा अधिक्रियंत इत्यर्थः । प्रगाथ्यते संमेल्यते[9] छंदसा छंद इति प्रगाथः ॥

२. प्रगाथ इत्येव । बार्हतः प्रगाथ इत्युक्तः । आदौ बृहती ततः सतोबृहती । छंदोद्वयं मिलितं विद्यात् । चतुर्थं बृहती तृतीयो द्वादशको[10]ऽयुजौ जागतौ सतोबृहतीत्युक्ते[11] । अयं दश प्रागाघर्मित्यादावयं[12] वामिति[13] बृहती त्रिवंधुरेणेति[14] सतोबृहतीत्येवमादि[15] । बार्हत इति सोऽस्यादिरितिच्छंदसः प्रगाथेष्विंत्यण्[16] । एवं काकुभादिष्वपि द्रष्टव्यं ॥

३. बृहतीस्थाने ककुप् चेत् काकुभः प्रगाथः । मध्यमश्चेत्ककुबित्युक्तं[17] । उत्तरा सतोबृहत्येव पूर्ववत् । वयमु त्वा[18] काकुभः प्रगाथ इत्यादौ वयमु त्वा ककुभम् उप त्वा कर्मन्निति[19] सतोबृहतीं विद्यात् ॥

४. प्रगाथ इत्येव । एते चत्वारोऽष्टका जागतश्च महाबृहत्यष्टिनस्त्रयः[20] स्वौ च द्वौ महा-

[1] *Rigv.* VI, 48, 6; *Rigv.* Pr. 937. [2] Cp. *Rigv.* Pr. 937, note 3. [3] *Rigv.* I, 191, 10. [4] I.e. the three verses 10-12. [5] *Rigv.* X, 59, 9; *Rigv.* Pr. 935 (cp. also 975, comm.) quotes VIII, 37, 2 and VIII, 41, 1. [6] *Rigv.* X, 134, 1; *Rigv.* Pr. 937. [7] Identical with those given in *Rigv.* Pr. 933–7. [8] I 2, P 2; छंदोऽन्वय° W 1, P 1; छंदस्त्वय I 4. [9] W 1; प्रगाथ्यंते समेल्यंते ... प्रगाथाः I 4; प्रगाथ्यंते संमिलति I 2, P 2; प्रगाथांते संमेलंवे (sic) P 1. [10] § 7, 1. [11] § 8, 4. [12] See sûtra on I, 47. [13] *Rigv.* I, 47, 1. [14] I, 47, 2. [15] *Rigv.* Pr. 1003 gives four examples, not the above. [16] Pâ*n*. IV, ii, 55. [17] § 5, 3. [18] *Rigv.* VIII, 21, 1. [19] VIII, 21, 2; *Rigv.* Pr. 1003 quotes this and VIII, 19, 1-2. [20] § 9, 9.

सतोबृहतीत्युक्ते[1]। उत्तरपदवृद्धिश्छांदसी। अन्यथा माहाबृहत[2] इति हि प्राप्नोति। यज्ञायज्ञीये[3] महाबार्हतबार्हतौ प्रगाथावित्यत्र बृहद्भिरग्न[4] इति द्वौ ॥

५. प्रगाथ इत्येव। बृहती विपरीता सतोबृहती च। ताभ्यां विपरीतोत्तरः प्रगाथो भवति। युजौ चेद्विपरीतेत्युक्तं[5]। त्वावतीये[6] विपरीतोत्तरः प्रगाथ इत्यत्र नहि ते शूरेति द्वे[7] ॥

६. अत्र शास्त्रेऽस्माभिरनुष्टुम्मुखास्तृचा इत्युक्त आनुष्टुभः प्रगाथः प्रत्येतव्यः। अत्र चाद्यानुष्टुब् द्वे गायत्र्याविति विद्यात्। अत्रानुष्टुप् च गायत्री चेत्यनुष्टुब्गायत्र्याविति द्वंद्वो मा विज्ञायीति। द्वंद्वे ह्येकानुष्टुबेका गायत्री स्यात्। आ त्वेकोना प्रियमेध आदावनुष्टुम्मुखास्तृचाश्चत्वार[8] इत्या त्वा रथमित्यनुष्टुप्[9] तुविशुष्मेति[10] द्वे गायत्र्यावित्यादि। अनुष्टुम्मुखास्तृचा इत्युक्त इति वचनं गायंति त्वादशानुष्टुभमित्यनुष्टुबेका[11] गायत्रीद्वयं चेति मा भूदिति। अथ छंदांसीत्युपाक्रमचतुर्दशछंदःसु गायत्र्यादिजगत्यंताद्यसप्तवर्गे भेदा उक्ताः[12]। उत्तरसप्तवर्गेऽतिजगत्याद्यातिधृत्यंतेऽक्षरसंख्यैव न पादविशेषात्संज्ञाविशेषाः। पादाश्चानुक्रमण्यंतरसिद्धा[13] उच्यंते।

पादा अतिजगत्यां तु त्रयो द्वादशकाः परौ।
अष्टकौ शक्करीपादाः सप्तैवाष्टाक्षरास्तु ते[14] ॥
अतिशाक्करपादौ द्वावादितः षोडशाक्षरौ।
जागतोऽप्यष्टकावष्टिपादाः षोडशकास्त्रयः ॥
अष्टकौ चात्यष्टिपादौ जागतौ चाष्टकास्त्रयः।
जागतश्चाष्टकश्चाथ धृतिपादास्तु[15] जागतौ ॥
पादास्त्रयोऽष्टकाश्चाथ[16] षोडशाक्षर[17] एव च।
अष्टकश्चाथातिधृतौ द्वौ पादौ जागतौ ततः[18] ॥
त्रयोऽष्टका जागतश्च तथाष्टाक्षरकावपि[19]।
पूर्वसप्तकपादास्तु प्रसंगात्स्वयमीरिताः ॥

[1] § 10, 2. [2] माहाबार्हत W 1, P 2; महाबार्हत P 1, I 2; महाबृहत I 4. [3] *Rigv.* VI, 48. [4] VI, 48, 7–10; *Rigv.* Pr. 1015. [5] § 8, 5. [6] *Rigv.* VIII, 46. [7] VIII, 46, 11–12; *Rigv.* Pr. 1016, where this metre is called विपरीतांत. [8] Sûtra on VIII, 68. [9] Ver. 1. [10] Ver. 2. [11] Sûtra on I, 10. [12] W 1, I 4; अत्र अथ छंदांस्युच्यमानेषु चतुर्दशछंदसु गायत्र्यादिजगत्यंते आद्ये सप्तके भेदो वर्गे उक्ते P 2, I 2; P 1 also except छंदांस्युसीषात्वे (sic) and °जगत्यंताद्य°. Besides these four, the *Rigv.* Pr. specifies 23 other pragâthas; cp. sûtras 1002 to 1030. [13] Pâdânukramanî, § 1 (MS. B). [14] B; °क्षराश्च ते P 1, P 2, I 2; °क्षराः स्मृताः W 1, I 4. [15] पादौ तु W 1, I 4. [16] °श्चात्राथ B. [17] W 1, I 4; षोळशक एव च B; चतुर्दशक एव च P 2, I 2; त्रयोदशक एव च P 1. [18] Marginal correction by the same hand in W 1; जागतः षोडशाक्षरः all the MSS. [19] Marginal correction by the same hand in W 1; द्वावष्टकौ जागतश्चतष्टाक्षर-

तत्रातिजगत्याद्यतिधृत्यंतोदाहरणानि प्रदर्श्यंते। अतिजगती। प्र वो महे मतयो यंतु[1]। शक्वरी। प्रो ष्वस्मै पुरोरथं[2]। अतिशक्वरी। साकं जातः क्रतुना[3]। अष्टिः। त्रिकद्रुकेषु महिषो यवाशिरं[4]। अत्यष्टिः। अग्निं होतारं मन्ये[5]। धृतिः। अवर्मह इंद्र दादृहि श्रुधी नः[6]। अतिधृतिः। स हि शर्धो न मारुतं[7]। इत्येतस्यां शाकल्यसंहितायामेतावंति चतुर्दश छंदांस्येव संतीति पुरस्तान्नोक्तादिपंचकस्य परस्ताच्च कृत्याद्युत्कृत्यंतस्य सप्तकस्य चानुक्तिरिति वेदितव्यं[8]। तत्र च। उक्तम्[9] अत्युक्तं मध्यं प्रतिष्ठा सुप्रतिष्ठेति[10] चतुरुत्तरवृद्ध्या चतुरक्षरादिविंशत्यक्षरांतं पुरस्ताच्छंदःपंचकं परस्ताच्छंदःसप्तकं तु कृतिः प्रकृतिराकृतिर्विकृतिः संकृतिरभिकृतिरुत्कृतिरित्यशीत्यक्षरादि चतुरुत्तरवृद्ध्या चतुरधिकशतांतं। एतान्यपि भगवता[10] पिंगलनागेन[11] सूत्र्यंते। उक्तं। साति[12]। मध्यं[13]। प्रतिष्ठा। सु च[14]। चतुःशतमुत्कृतिः। चतुरश्चतुरस्त्यजेदुत्कृतेः। तान्यभिसंख्याप्रेभ्यः कृतिः। प्रकृत्या चेति[15]। अथोक्तादिद्वादशकस्योदाहरणानि प्रदर्श्यंते। तत्रोक्तं नाम छंदः। नूनम[16]येत्येकपदा। तथा हि चतुर्थारण्यके सूच्यते। नूनमयेत्येक[17]पदेति। अत्युक्तं। अग्निर्ज्योतिर्ज्योतिरग्नि[18]रिति द्विपदा। मध्यं। अग्निर्ज्योतिः सूर्यो ज्योतिः प्रजा ज्योतिरिति त्रिपदा। प्रतिष्ठा। अग्ना३इ पत्नीवंत्सजूर्देवेन त्वष्ट्रा सोमं पि[19]बेति त्रिपदा। सुप्रतिष्ठा। पुरूतमं पुरूणां स्तोतॄणां विवाचि वाजेभिर्वाजयतामि[20]ति त्रिपदा। मध्यमः षट्कश्छेदतिनिचृद्गा[21]यत्रीमिमां वयं ब्रूमः।

कावपि (sic) I 4; तथैवाष्टक इत्यपि all the other MSS. The reading of all the MSS. (except the marginal corr. in W 1) gives only 72 syllables instead of 76 for atidh*r*iti; cp. M. M., *R*igv. Pr. pp. cclviii and cccxxv. [1] *R*igv. V, 87, 1; यंतु omitted in B; *R*igv. Pr. 950 quotes VIII, 97, 13. [2] *R*igv. X, 133, 1; पुरोरथं omitted in B. [3] *R*igv. II, 22, 3; *R*igv. Pr. gives I, 137, 1. [4] *R*igv. II, 22, 1; यवाशिरं omitted in B. [5] *R*igv. I, 127, 1; *R*igv. Pr. gives IX, 111, 1. [6] *R*igv. I, 133, 6; श्रुधी नः omitted in B; *R*igv. Pr. gives IV, 1, 3. [7] *R*igv. I, 127, 6; here ends the quotation from the Pâdânukrama*n*î. [8] W 1 (which however reads पुरस्तान्नो° and परस्तान्न); पुरस्तान्नोक्तानि। उक्तादिपंचकं नोक्तं पुरस्तात्कृत्याद्युत्कृत्यंतस्य च सप्तकस्यानवत्तिरिति वेदितव्यं P 2, I 2; पुरस्तान्नोक्तानि पंचकस्य पुरस्तान्न कृत्याद्युत्कृत्यंनंतस्य च सप्तकस्यानवत्तिरिति वेदितव्यं P 1; पुरास्तान्नोक्तादि पंचकस्याश्ननं कृत्याद्युत्कृतिपर्यंतस्य च सप्तकस्य चानुक्तिरिति वेदितव्य I 4. [9] Cp. Ind. Stud. VIII, pp. 113, 283. [10] W 1, I 4; the intervening words are omitted in P 1, P 2, I 2. [11] W 1, I 4; °महर्षिणा P 1, P 2, I 2. [12] साति only in P 1, P 2, I 2; साति। सति W 1, I 4. [13] W 1; मध्यां I 4; मध्यमं P 1, P 2, I 2. [14] P 1, P 2, I 2; सुवा W 1; युवा I 4; cp. Ind. Stud. VIII, 283. [15] Piṅgala, IV, 1–4; Ind. Stud. VIII, p. 281. [16] *R*igv. VIII, 46, 11. [17] Ait. Âr. V, ii, 5. [18] Vâg. Sa*m*h. III, 9; Sâma-v. II, 1, 1, 8, 1; Sâṅkh. *S*r.-sûtra, II, 9. [19] Vâg. Sa*m*h. VIII, 10. [20] *R*igv. VI, 45, 29. [21] Cp. comm. to § 4, 5, and sûtra on VI, 45.

उक्तादि पंचकं कैश्चिद्गायत्रीत्येव कथ्यते ।
यथा ह्यतिजगत्यादि त्वतिच्छंदः प्रवर्ण्यते[1] ॥
उक्तादिपंचकस्योक्तं कृतीनामथ वक्ष्यते ॥

तत्र कृतिः । त्रिशुग्घर्मो विभातु मे । आकूत्या मनसा सह । विराजा ज्योतिषा सह । यज्ञेन पयसा सह । ब्रह्मणा तेजसा सह । क्षत्रेण यशसा सह । सत्येन तपसा सह । तस्य दोहमशीमहि । तस्य सुम्नमशीमहि । तस्य भक्षमशीमहि[2] ॥

प्रकृतिः । भगो अनु प्रयुंक्तामिंद्रो यातु पुरोगवः । यस्याः सदो हविर्धाने । यूपो यस्यानुमीयते । ब्राह्मणा यस्यामर्चंति । ऋग्भिः साम्ना यजुर्विदः । युध्यंते यस्यामृत्विजः । सोममिंद्राय पातवे । सा नो भूतिर्दक्षिणाया सुशेवा यज्ञे ददातु सुमनस्यमानेति पंचावसाना ॥

आकृतिः । तच्चक्षुर्देवहितं पुरस्ताच्छुक्रमुच्चरत् । पश्येम शरदः शतं । जीवेम शरदः शतं । नंदाम शरदः शतं । मोदाम शरदः शतं । भवाम शरदः शतं । शृणवाम शरदः शतं । प्रब्रवाम शरदः शतं । अजीताः स्याम शरदः शतं । ज्योक् च सूर्यं दृश[3] इति ॥

विकृतिः । इमे सोमाः सुरामाणः । छागैर्न मेषैर्ऋषभैः । सुताः शष्पैर्न तोक्मभिः । लाजैर्महस्वंतो मदा । मासरेण परिष्कृताः । शुक्राः पयस्वंतोऽमृताः । प्रस्थिता वो मधुश्चुतः । तानश्विना सरस्वती । इंद्रः सुत्रामा वृत्रहा । जुषंतां सोम्यं मधु । पिबंतु मदंतु व्यंतु सोमं[4] । इति दशाष्टाक्षराः पादा एक एकादशाक्षरः ॥

संकृतिः । देवो अग्निः स्विष्टकृत् । सुद्रविणा मंद्रः कविः । सत्यमन्मा यजी होता । होतुर्होतुरायजीयान् । अग्ने यान्देवानयाट् यानपिप्रेः । ये ते होत्रे अमत्सत । तां ससनुषीं होत्रां देवंगमां । दिवि देवेषु यज्ञमेरयेमं । स्विष्टकृच्चाग्ने होताभूः । वसुवने वसुधेयस्य नमोवाके वीहीति[5] ॥

अभिकृतिः । देवो अग्निः स्विष्टकृद्देवान्यक्षद्यथायथं होताराविंद्रमश्विना वाचा वाचं सरस्वतीं अग्निं सोमं स्विष्टकृत् स्विष्ट इंद्रः सुत्रामा सविता वरुणोऽभिषग्गिष्टो देवो वनस्पतिः स्विष्टा देवा आज्यपाः स्विष्टो अग्निरग्निना होता होत्रे स्विष्टकृद्यशो न दधदिंद्रियमूर्जमपचितिं स्वधां[6] । इति त्रयोदश गायत्रपादाः ॥

उत्कृतिः । छागस्य हविष आत्तामद्य मध्यतो मेद उद्भृतं पुरा द्वेषोभ्यः पुरा पौरुषेय्या गृभो घस्तां नूनं घासे अज्राणां यवसप्रथमानां सुमत्क्षराणां शतरुद्रियाणामग्निष्वात्तानां पीवोपवसनानां पार्श्वतः श्रोणितः शितामत उत्सादतो अंगादंगादवत्तानां करत एवेंद्राग्नी[7] जुषेतां हविरिति ॥

॥ इति च्छंदांसि संप्रोच्य त्वथायं परिभाषते ॥

१२, १. सूक्त ऋचां संख्या सूक्तसंख्या । सा पूर्वमुक्तान्यस्याः सूक्तैकसंख्याया आ अधिक्रियत

[1] W 1, I 4; प्रवर्त्स्यते P 2, I 2; प्रवर्ण्यर्त्स्यते (sic) P 1. [2] Taitt. Âr. IV, xxi, 1. [3] Taitt. Âr. IV, xliv, 32; cp. Vâg. Samh. XXXVI, 24. [4] Vâg. Samh. XXI, 42, where the text reads होतर्यज instead of सोमम् (all the MSS.). [5] Taitt. Br. III, v, 9, 1. [6] Vâg. Samh. XXI, 58. [7] MSS.; text एवाश्विना. [8] Vâg. Samh. XXI, 43.

इति वेदितव्यं । आङ् मर्यादायां । वायो वायव्यैंद्रवायवमैत्रावरुणास्तृचा[1] इत्यत्राग्निं नवेत्यतो[2] नवेत्यनुवर्तत इत्यर्थः । इह यत्र[3] सूक्तग्रहणमसूक्तगतर्क्संख्याया[4] अवधित्वमधिकारश्च मा भूदिति । तेनादहेत्येताः पण्माहत्य[5] इति षट्संख्याया नाधिकारो नाप्यवधित्वमिति । सुरूपकृत्नुं दशैंद्रमिति[6] दशसंख्यैवानुवर्तत इति सिद्धं ॥

२. अनुवर्तत इत्यनुवर्तते । अन्यस्माद्भेरा[7] प्राक् प्रकृतर्षिश्चाप्यनुवर्तते । स चेद्वाविशिष्टो न भवति । वाशब्देन विशेषो यदुक्तौ वाशब्दोऽस्ति यथाप्त्यस्त्रितो वेति[8] स इत्यर्थः[9] । इंद्रं विश्वा अवीवृधन्नित्यतः[10] प्राग् वायवा याहीत्यादौ[11] मधुच्छंदा इत्यादि निदर्शनं । अवाविशिष्ट इति वचनं । चंद्रमा एकोनाप्त्यस्त्रितो वेति[12] वाविशिष्टस्त्रितः । इंद्रं मित्रं वरुणमग्निमूतय[13] इति नास्यानुवृत्तिरिति[14] । अथ निपातविशेषान्वयेन तत्परिभाष्यते[15] ॥

३. तु हि ह वै तद् इति पंचभिः शब्दैर्विशिष्टानि संबद्धान्यृषिदैवतच्छंदांसि यथासंख्यं द्वित्रिचतुःपंचषट्सूक्तभांजि सूक्तान्वयवंति भवंति । कदा नरस्तु[16] देवरातो वारुणं तु[17] गायंति द्वादशानुष्टुभं त्विति[18] तुशब्दोक्तावृषिदैवतच्छंदोभिर्द्विसूक्तान्वयं विद्यात् । एवं हिशब्दयोगे त्रित्वं । हयोगे चतुष्कं । वैयोगे पंचतां । तच्छब्दयोगे षट्कमिति द्रष्टव्यं । तत्र भांजीति । भजो ण्विः[19] । अत उपधायाः[20] । शौ नुं[21] ॥

४. स्वरूपेणोक्ता निरुक्ता पंच नवेत्यादि । पंचोना पंचाधिकेत्यादि विशेषणरूपेणोक्ता स्वरूपेणानुक्तानिरुक्ता संख्या विंशतिरिति वेदितव्यं । यथा । कस्य पंचोनेति[22] पंचोनविंशतिः पंचदशेति । एवं च निरुक्तशब्दः[23] । इदं विंशतिरूषस्यम्[24] इत्यादिषु विंशतिग्रहणानि चार्थवंति[25] भवंति । अन्यथानुवृत्तिसंख्यानिरुक्तसंख्याविंशत्योर्विषयविभागोऽपि न ज्ञायेत । किं च । एवं चानादेशे त्विंद्रो देवतेत्युत्तरत्र[26] अनादेशग्रहणं चार्थवद्भवति । इतरथात एवानिरुक्तेत्येवानुवर्तिष्यत इति ॥

५. देवानामनुक्तौ तु ज्ञेय इंद्रो देवता । तेना तु[27] युंजंतीत्यादाविंद्र[28] एवेति सिद्धं भवति । तुशब्दोऽवधारणे । सुरूपकृत्नुं दशैंद्रम्[29] इत्यादावनुक्तेरैवेंद्रत्वे सिद्धे मंडलादिष्वाग्नेयमैंद्रादित्याग्नेयावद्व्यर्थमैंद्रग्रहणं[30][31] । एवमुत्तराण्यपि दशेंद्रग्रहणानि वेदितव्यानि ॥

[1] Sûtra on I, 2. [2] I, 1. [3] P 1, I 2, I 4; यत्र P 2; उभयत्र W 1. [4] W 1, I 4; °ख्यायां P 1, P 2, I 2. [5] Sûtra on I, 6. [6] I, 4. [7] P 1, P 2, I 2; आ omitted in W 1, I 4. [8] Sûtra on I, 105. [9] W 1, I 4; वाविशिष्टो (न P 1) वाशब्देन विशेषितः यद्युक्तो (ौ I 2) वाशब्दोऽस्ति यथा अप्त्यस्त्रितो वा । त्रितो वा भवति स इत्यर्थः P 1, P 2, I 2. [10] Sûtra on I, 11. [11] I, 2. [12] I, 105. [13] I, 106. [14] W 1; इति मास्मानुवर्तत इति I 2, I 4, P 1; इत्यादिषु कुत्स एव P 2. [15] W 1, I 2, I 4; °न्वयेन परिभाषते P 1, P 2. [16] Sûtra on VI, 35. [17] In sûtra I, 24. [18] I, 10. [19] Pân. III, ii, 62. [20] Pân. VII, ii, 116. [21] Cp. Pân. VII, i, 72. [22] Sûtra on I, 24. [23] W 1, I 4; एवं विंशतिशब्दः P 2, I 2; एवं च तिशब्दः P 1. [24] Sûtra on I, 113. [25] चार्थवद् W 1, I 4. [26] § 12, 5. [27] Sûtra on I, 5. [28] I, 6. [29] I, 4. [30] § 12, 12. [31] P 1, P 2; °व्यर्थं I 4; °पवादा° W 1, I 2.

६. अनादेश इत्येव । छंदोऽनुक्तौ त्रिष्टुप् छंदो भवति । तेनेंद्रस्य पंचोनेत्यादौ छंदोऽनुक्तौ त्रिष्टुप् छंद इति सिद्धं । देवरातो वारुणं तु त्रैष्टुभम्[2] इत्यत्रानुक्तेरेव त्रैष्टुभत्वे सिद्धे त्रैष्टुभमित्यादौ गायत्रं प्राग्धैरण्यस्तूपीयादि[3]ति गायत्रत्वापवादः ॥

७. अनादेश इत्येव । अयं दश प्रागाथम्[4] इत्यत्र[5] विशेषानुक्तौ बृहतीसतोबृहत्यौ बार्हत[6] इत्युक्तो बार्हत एव प्रगाथो भवति । तेन युजः सतोबृहत्योऽयुजो बृहत्य इति सिद्धं ॥

८. द्विपदा विंशत्यक्षराः परिमाणतश्छंदस्तो विराज इति विद्यात् । यथा । पश्वा दश पराशरः शाक्त्यो द्वैपदमित्यादौ ॥

९. या एकपदा[8]स्ता दशाक्षराः परिमाणतश्छंदस्तः पूर्ववद्विराज इत्येव विद्यात् । यथा । अंत्यैकप[9]देति । तदर्धं विंशत्यर्धमित्यर्थः । अथ प्रसंगाद्द्विपदास्व[10]ध्ययनकाले विशेषमाह ॥

१०. ऋचोऽध्ययने त्वध्येतारो द्वे द्वे द्विपदे एकैकामृचं कृत्वा समामनंति समामनेयुः । अधीयीरन् । आम्यासे[11] । लिङर्थे लेट्[12] । पाघ्रादिना[13] शपि मनादेशः । द्वे द्विपदे यासां ता ऋचो द्विर्द्विपदाः । समामनंतीति वचनाच्छंसनादौ न भवंति[14] । तेन पश्वा न तायु[15]मिति द्वैपदमिति शंसने दशर्चत्वम् आसां चाध्ययने तु पंचत्वं भवति ॥

११. समामनंतीत्येव । अयुक्ष्वेकादशादिषु द्विपदास्वंत्यैव द्विपदा भवेन्नान्यथा[16] । यथा । वनेमेकादशेत्य[17]त्र साधुर्न गृध्नु[18]रित्यादि ॥

१२. आ ऐंद्राद् ऐंद्रसंशब्दना[19]त्प्राङ् मंडलादिष्वाग्नेयं विद्यात् । यथा । अग्निं नर मधुच्छंदा[20]स्त्वमग्ने जागतं त्वि[21]त्यादिषु ॥

१३. यस्य सूक्तस्यांते त्रिष्टुबित्युच्यते तस्य सूक्तस्य तद्वर्जं शिष्टा अन्या ऋचो जगत्यो वेदितव्याः । यथा । आग्नेयं त्रिष्टुबंत्याष्टमीषोळश्यौ चेति[22] ॥

१४. संहितादौ त्वमग्ने द्यूना हिरण्यस्तूप[23] इति हिरण्यस्तूपसंशब्दनात्प्राक् छंदो गायत्रीति विद्यात् । छंदसः प्रत्ययविधाने नपुंसके स्वार्थे उपसंख्यानमिति गायत्र्येव गायत्रं । संहितापेक्षमादित्वं । अन्यत्र हिरण्यस्तूपस्यानुलंभात् संहितायाः परमप्रकृतत्वाच्च ॥

॥ इति द्वादशखंडी[24] तु परिभाषा प्रवर्णिता[25] ॥

[1] Sûtra on I, 32. [2] In sûtra on I, 24. [3] § 12, 14. [4] Sûtra on I, 47. [5] P 1, P 2, I 2; इत्यादौ W 1, I 4. [6] § 11, 2. [7] Sûtra on I, 65. [8] For Yâska's view of the ekapadâ, cp. *Rig*v. Pr. 993 and Ind. Stud. VIII, pp. 133, 144, foot-notes. [9] Sûtra on V, 41. [10] W 1, I 4; ॰पदाध्ययनकाले I 2, P 1, P 2. [11] W 1, I 4; नाभ्यासे P 1; omitted in P 2, I 2. [12] Pâ*n*. III, iv, 7; छंदसां लिङर्थे लेट् P 2, I 2. [13] Cp. Pâ*n*. VII, iii, 78. [14] I 2; भवति W 1, I 4. [15] Sûtra on I, 65. [16] W 1; नान्या I 4; नान्याः P 1, P 2, I 2. [17] Sûtra on I, 70. [18] Ver. 11. [19] संशब्दत्वात् W 1. [20] Sûtra on I, 1. [21] II, 1. [22] I, 31. [23] I, 31. [24] I 4, P 1, P 2; कंडी W 1; खंडेषु I 2. [25] W 1, I 4; प्रवर्णिताः P 1, P 2, I 2.

अग्निमीळे इत्यादि खिलरहितसप्तदशाधिकसूक्तसहस्रस्य प्रतिसूक्तमादिसूक्तप्रतिज्ञानमृष्यादिकं दर्शयितुमुपक्रमते। अत्र च सूत्रेष्वनुक्तं परिभाषातो गृहीतव्यं। अत्र शास्त्रे सर्वत्र नवार्था ज्ञातव्याः। सूक्तादिः। ऋक्संख्या। छंदः। पादः। अक्षराणि। देवतं। ऋषेर्नाम। गोत्रं च। क्वचित्कथेति च॥

१, १. अग्निमिति सूक्तादिः। ईळे पुरोहितं। नवेति सूक्तस्य ऋक्संख्या। मधुच्छंदा इत्यृषेर्नाम। वैश्वामित्र इति तस्य गोत्रं। अत इञो[1]ऽपवादः। ऋष्यण्[2]। आदौ गायत्रं प्राग्घैरण्यस्तूपीयादिति गायत्री छंदः। मंडलादिष्वाग्नेयमैंद्रादित्यग्निर्देवता सुरूपकृत्नुं दशैंद्र[3]मित्यतः प्राक्। त्रिपदा गायत्री पादाश्चाष्टाक्षराः। प्रथमं छंदस्त्रिपदा गायत्र्य[4]नादेशेऽष्टाक्षराः पादा[5] इति। एवमुत्तरत्रापि सर्वत्रोक्तादन्यत्परिभाषातो ग्राह्यं[6]। सूक्तादिरेव सर्वत्र स्थिरः[7]। अन्यद्विचार्यं। अत्राग्निः पूर्वेभिर्ऋषिभि[8]रेकोनत्वान्निचृद्गायत्री वेदितव्या। एवमुत्तरत्राप्युष्णिगादा[9]वेकोनत्वे निचृत्त्वम् एकाधिक्ये[10] भुरिक्त्वं द्व्यूनत्वे विराट्त्वं द्व्याधिक्ये[11] स्वराट्त्वं च। ततश्छंदःसु स्वयमेव[12] वेदितव्यमित्याचार्यवच[13]नद्वयमपि नाभिदध्मः॥

२. नवेत्येव। ऋषिः स एव। छंदश्च तदेव। वायव्यं। वाय्वृतुपित्रुषसो यत्[14]। ओर्गुणः[15]। वांतो यि प्रत्यय[16] इति वांतादेशः। इंद्रवायुमित्रावरुणाभ्यामण्यादिवृद्धिः[17]। देवताद्वंद्वे चे[18]त्यानङ्। उभयत्र वायोः प्रतिषेधः[19]। दीर्घाच्च वरुणस्य[20]। ऐंद्रवायवः। मैत्रावरुणः। ऋचि त्रेरुत्तरपदादिलोप इति संप्रसारणं[21]। ऋक्पूरि[22]त्यप्रत्ययस्तृचः। देवतानिर्देश आग्नेयत्वापवादः। एवमुत्तरत्रापि॥

३. तृचा इत्येष। मधुच्छंदाः। गायत्रं। अश्वद्वंद्वा[23]ज्जातत्वाद[24]श्वावश्विनौ। अत इञ्[25]। देवतानाम्नीनण्यनपत्य[26] इति प्रकृतिभाव आश्विनः। सरस्वत्या अण् सारस्वतः। एता वाय्वाद्याः सरस्वत्यंता वायवायाह्यश्विनेति सूक्तद्वयवर्तितृचसप्तकस्तुत्याः प्रउगस्य देवताः। प्रउगं नाम होतुः प्रातःसवनिकं द्वितीयं शस्त्रं। एता इत्येतावत्संख्याः संनिहिता वाय्वादय एव स्युः। वायो सैका गायत्रमुक्ता देवताः प्रउगेऽ[27]ध्येतत्क्रमोक्तदेवतासप्तकज्ञानार्थमिदं॥

[1] Cp. Pân. IV, i, 95. [2] Cp. Pân. IV, i, 114. [3] Sûtra on I, 4. [4] Introd. § 4, 1. [5] Ibid. § 3, 11. [6] ज्ञातव्यं W 1. [7] सुस्थिरः W 1. [8] *Rigv.* I, 1, 2; cp. comm. on Introd. § 3, 4. [9] °ष्णिहाद् W 1; °ष्णिहादौ न्यूनत्वे I 2 (corr.); °त्राप्यांताद् P 1, P 2, I 2, I 4. [10] एकाधिके W 1, I 2. [11] °धिके W 1. [12] W 1, I 2 (तत्र I 2); तत्रछंदः सुखत एव P 1; तत्रछंदः सुखत्रातं इति (sic) P 2; तत्रछंदोमुखत एव I 4. [13] P 1, P 2, I 2; °चार्यवचनद्वयमपि I 4, W 1 (वचन corr. W 1). [14] Pân. IV, ii, 31. [15] Pân. VI, iv, 146. [16] Pân. VI, i, 79. [17] Cp. Pân. VII, iii, 21. [18] Pân. VI, iii, 26. [19] Cp. Vârt. on Pân. VI, iii, 26. [20] Pân. VII, iii, 23. [21] Cp. Vârt. to Pân. VI, i, 37. [22] Cp. Pân. V, iv, 74; °त्यकारः। तृचः P 1, P 2, I 2. [23] I 4; अत्र ज्ञातत्वाद् P 2; अस्तद्वंद्वाज्जातत्वाद् P 1; अत्र द्वंद्वजातत्वाद् I 2; अश्वद्वंद्वाज्ञातत्वाद् W 1 (corr. to °जात). [24] P 2, I 2; अस्याव् P 1; अवस्याव् I 4; दृष्टाव् W 1. [25] Cp. Pân. V, ii, 115. [26] Pân. VI, iv, 164. [27] Sûtra on II, 41.

४. मधुच्छंदाः । गायत्रं । अवध्यर्थमैंद्रपदमित्युक्तं ॥

६. दशेत्येव । आदह स्वधामन्वित्याद्याः षडृचो मरुद्देवत्याः । आसु च वीळु चिदारुजत्नुभिरिंद्रेण सं हीत्येते ऐंद्र्यौ चकारान्माहत्यौ च । षट्सु द्वितीयाचतुर्थ्यौ हि ते । शिष्टा ऐंद्र्यः ॥

१०. तुशब्दो द्विरुक्तभावीति परिभाषासिद्धं । तेनेदं चोत्तरं च द्वे सूक्ते आनुष्टुभे अनुष्टुप्छंदस्के । गायत्रत्वापवादः ॥

११. मधुच्छंदःसुतो जेता नामर्षिः ॥

१२. मेधातिथिर्नामर्षिः काण्वगोत्रः । अत इञो[1]ऽपवाद ऋष्यण्[2] । आग्नेयं । अग्नेर्ढक्[3] । अग्निदेवत्यं सूक्तं । अग्निनाग्निः समिध्यत[4] इति पादो द्व्यग्निदैवतः । द्वावग्नी देवते यस्य सः । कौ द्वौ । निर्मथ्य आहवनीयश्च । निर्मथनेन प्राप्तव्योऽरणीभ्यां[5] सोऽग्निरित्युच्यते । एत्य[6] हूयते यस्मिन् स[7] आहवनीयः । हु दानादानयोः । अधिकरणेऽनीयर् । सोऽग्निरित्युक्तः ॥

१३. अत्र सूक्त आद्याया इध्मोऽग्निर्देवता समिद्धोऽग्निर्वा । अथ तनूनपात् । अथ नराशंसः । अथेडः (जस्) । अथ बर्हिः । अथ देवीर्द्वारः । जस्द्वयं । अथोषासानक्तौ । अथ दैव्यौ होतारौ । एतदेव व्याचष्टे प्रचेतसाविति प्रकृष्टज्ञानबलाविति । तौ चाग्न्यादित्यावग्नीवरुणौ वरुणादित्यौ वा । अथ तिस्रो देव्यः । तास्तिस्रः स्वयमाह सरस्वतीळाभारत्यः । सरस्वती ब्रह्मपत्नी । इडा विष्णुपत्नी पृथिवीत्यर्थः । भरतस्यादित्यस्य पत्नी भारती । अथ त्वष्टा । अथ वनस्पतिः । अथ स्वाहाकृतयः । का एताः । विश्वे देवाः । तथा हि ब्राह्मणं । तदाहुः का देवताः स्वाहाकृतय इति विश्वे देवा इति ब्रूयादिति[8] । इत्येवं प्रत्यृचम् ऋचमृचं प्रति देवताः । यथासंख्यमन्वयो हि लौकिकः । यथा ।

पद्मेंदुमृगमातंगपुंस्कोकिलकलापिनः ।
वक्त्रकांतीक्षणगतिस्वरकेशैस्त्वया जिताः ॥

इति लक्ष्मीं प्रति नारदस्तोत्रे दर्शनात् । एतत्सूक्तमाप्रीसंज्ञकं भवति । आप्रीभिराप्रीणाति[9] होता यजत्याप्रीभिरिति[10] ब्राह्मणसूत्रविनियोगस्यान्वयार्थमिदं ॥

एतेनान्यान्युक्तदैवतानि । अस्मिञ्छास्त्रे समिद्ध आप्रिय इत्याद्याप्रमित्युक्तान्[11]यन्यान्याप्रीसूक्तान्येतेन सूक्तेन प्रतिपादितदेवतानि भवंति । एतत्क्रमकैतद्देवतानीत्यर्थः[12] ॥

एकादशकानीत्यादि । अस्मिञ्छास्त्रेऽस्माभिराप्रमित्युक्तानि सूक्तानि नराशंसयुक्तानि तनूनपाद्वर्जितान्येकादशर्चानि भवंति । यथा । समिद्ध एकादशाप्रमित्यादावाप्रशब्दोक्तान्यतनूनपांतीति[13] सिद्धेरन्यद्विस्पष्टार्थं । तत्र तत्र त्वुक्तेरेकादशत्वं सिद्धं परिशेषाच्च नाराशंसतेति ॥

[1] Pân. IV, i, 95. [2] Cp. Pân. IV, i, 114. [3] Pân. IV, ii, 33. [4] Ver. 6.
[5] P 1, P 2, I 2, I 4; रणिजः W 1, I 2 (corr.). [6] W 1, I 2 (corr.); इत्य P 1, P 2; omitted in I 4. [7] W 1; यस्मिन्नित्या° P 1; ऽस्मिन्नित्या° P 1, P 2. [8] Ait. Br. II, xiii, 3–4. [9] Ait. Br. II, iv, 1. [10] Âsv. Sr.-sûtra, III, ii, 5. [11] W 1; आप्रिय इत्याद्या इत्युक्तान्य° I 2, I 4, P 1, P 2. [12] W 1; एतत्क्रमदेवतानीत्यर्थः I 4; °क्रमकैतदेव° P 1· °क्रमके दे° P 2, I 2. [13] Sûtra on II, 3.

१५. ऋतव्यं । वाय्वृतुपित्रुषसो यत्[1] । ऋतुदेवत्यं । ऋतवो वसंताद्याः । तत्रर्तुदेवत्ये सूक्त आद्यैंद्रदेवत्या । अथ मारुती । अथ त्वाष्ट्री । अथाग्नेयी । अथैंद्री । अथ मैत्रावरुणी । दीर्घाश्च वरुणस्येत्युत्तरपदवृद्धिनिषेधः[2] । अथ चतस्रो द्रविणोदसे । एतन्नामकदेवताभिधायिन्यः[3] । द्रविणोदस इति तादर्थ्ये ङे[4] । अथाश्विनी । अथाग्नेयी ॥

इत्यृतुदेवताः सर्वत्र । ऐंद्रीत्याद्याग्नेयीपर्यंता द्वादश देवता एतत्क्रमका ऋतुदेवत्ययुक्तदेवा इति वेदितव्याः । सर्वत्र चैवं भवंति । तत्र तुभ्यं चकृतव्यं तु जागतं तु मंदसेत्यत्रोपतिष्ठंते[6] । सूत्रे च । ऋतुयाजैश्चरंतीति[7] ॥

१७. युवाकु हि शचीनामिति त्रिःसप्तके द्वे ऋचौ । शिष्टा गायत्र्यः । इंद्रावरुणदेवत्यं ॥

१८. अत्र नवर्चसूक्त आदितः पंचर्चो ब्रह्मणस्पतिदेवत्याः । चतुर्थ्यामृचींद्रश्च सोमश्च चकाराद्ब्रह्मणस्पतिश्च देवतात्वेन स्थिताः[9] । पंचम्यामृचि दक्षिणा चकाराद्ब्रह्मणस्पतिश्च[10] । अन्याः शिष्टाश्चतस्रः सादसस्पत्याः । सदसस्पतिदेवत्याः । नाराशंसी वांत्या । नवम्याः सदसस्पतिर्नराशंसो वा देवता विकल्प्यते ॥

१९. अग्निश्च मरुतश्च देवता अस्येति ॥१॥

२०. ऋभुदेवत्यं ॥

२२. सैका । एकया सहिता विंशतिः । अनिरुक्ता संख्या विंशतिरित्युक्तं[11] । आदितश्चतस्रोऽश्विदेवत्याः । तथा चतस्रः सावित्र्यः । अथ द्वे अग्निदेवत्ये । अथैका देवीनां संबंधिनी[12] स्तुतित्वेन । अथैकेंद्राणीवरुणान्यग्नायीनां । इहेंद्राणीर्मित्येषा[13] तिस्रो देवताः स्तौति । इंद्राणी वरुणानी । इंद्रवरुणेत्यादिना[14] स्त्रियां पुंयोगे ङीपानुकौ । अग्नायीति वृषाकप्यग्नीति[15] ङीप् ऐत्वं । अथ मही द्यौरिति[16] द्वे द्यावापृथिवीदेवत्ये । द्यावापृथिवीसुनासीरेति[17] यत् । अथ पृथिवीदेवत्या पार्थिवी । अथ षडृचो विष्णुदेवत्या वैष्णव्यः । विष्णोर्देवताख्योर्गुणः[18] । अतो देवा अवंतु न[19] इत्यृग्दैवी देवदेवत्या वैष्णवी वा ।

अतो देवा इति दैवी सूक्तशेषं तु वैष्णवं ॥

[1] Pân. IV, ii, 31. [2] Pân. VII, iii, 23. [3] W 1; चतस्रो द्रविणोदोनामकदेवताभिधायिन्यः I 4. [4] तादर्थे ङे W 1, I 2, P 2; तादर्थ्ये ङ P 1; तादर्थे चतुर्थी I 4. [5] Sûtra on II, 36, 37. [6] °त्यशयं [शेषं] तिष्ठते I 4. [7] Sâṅkh. Sr.-sûtra, VII, viii, 1; Ait. Br. II, xxix, 1; Schol. Pân. VII, iii, 62; Âsv. Sr.-sûtra, V, viii, 1. [8] Verses 4 and 5. [9] P 1, P 2, I 2, I 4; स्थितिः W 1. [10] A marginal note in W 1 adds इंद्रसोमौ च. [11] Introd. § 12, 4. [12] °धिन्या W 1; अ – – – ग्निदेवत्यौ अथ द्वे देवीनां देवसंबंधिन्यौ । स्तुतित्वेन P 1; अग्निदेवत्यौ द्वे देवीनां देवसंबंधिन्यौ स्वस्तिनत्वेन (sic) P 2, I 2; अथ द्वे अग्निदेवत्ये । अथ देवीनामेका I 4. [13] Ver. 12. [14] Cp. Pân. IV, i, 49. [15] Cp. Pân. IV, i, 37. [16] Ver. 13. [17] Pân. IV, ii, 32. [18] Pân. VI, iv, 146. [19] Ver. 16.

इति देवतानुक्रमण्यां। आपश्चतो[1] देवा अवंतु न इति जपेदपि वान्यां वैष्णवीमिति सूत्राच्च विकल्पः। तत्र ह्यन्यामित्यनेन पूर्वस्या अपि वैष्णवीत्वं साध्यते ॥

२३. पूर्वत्र सैकेतिवच्चतुरधिकेति वाच्ये चतुर्विंशतिरित्युक्तेरविशेषाल्लघुत्वे विस्पष्टत्वाच्चास्य लाघवार्थं हि परिभाषणं। तर्हि सचतुष्केति वाच्यमिति चेद् वैचित्र्यमेव प्रयोजनं। आद्या वायुदेवत्या। एकेति द्वंद्वभ्रमनिवृत्त्यर्थं। वायव्यैंद्रवायव्याविति द्वंद्वेऽनादेशावृत्तौ ऐंद्री हि स्यात्। अथ द्वे ऐंद्रवायव्याविंद्रवायुदेवत्ये। अथ मित्रावरुणदेवत्य एकस्तृचः। अथ मरुत्वज्जुषेंद्रदेवत्य इति। कुत एतद् मरुत्वतीयस्तृच इत्युक्ते मरुत्वज्जुषेंद्रदेवत्य इति। मरुत्वांस्त्विंद्रो देवतेति[2] वक्ष्यमाणत्वात्। मरुद्भिस्तद्वानिति गम्यते। मरुत्वतीय इति मृङ् प्राणत्यागे। मृत्रोरुदिति मरुत्[3] झय[4] इति मतुपो वत्वं। तसौ मत्वर्थे[5] इति भत्वं। द्यावापृथिवीशुनासीरेत्यादिना[6] छः। अथ वैश्वदेव एकस्तृचः। विश्वेदेवदेवत्य इत्यर्थः। अथ पूषदेवत्य एकस्तृचः। अथ शेषा आप्यः। उक्तपंचदशकादन्या अब्देवत्याः। अंत्याध्यर्धाग्नेयी। पयस्वानित्यर्धर्चयुक्ता सं माग्ने वर्चसेत्येषाग्निदेवत्येत्यर्थः। तत्राप्स्वंतः[7] पुरउष्णिक्। सांहितिकः कंप ऐकश्रुत्ये नास्ति[8]। पराप्सु मे सोमो अब्रवीदित्याद्यापश्च विश्वभेषजीरित्यंतानुष्टुप्। अनुष्टुप्छंदोयुक्तेत्यर्थः। तिस्रश्चांत्याः। अनुष्टुबित्यनुवृत्तमनुष्टुभ इति विपरिणम्यते। एकविंशी प्रतिष्ठा। शिष्टा गायत्र्यः ॥

२४. आजीगर्तिः। अजीगर्तशब्दाद् अत इञो[9]ऽपवाद ऋष्यणि[10] प्राप्ते बाह्वादित्वादिञ्। अजीगर्तपुत्रो जन्मना शुनःशेपो नाम। शेपपुच्छलांगूलेषु शुनः संज्ञायां। षष्ठ्या अलुक्। शुनःशेपः कृत्रिमः क्रियया निर्वृत्तः[11]। डुकृञ् करणे। ड्वितः क्त्रिः[12]। त्रेर्मम्नित्यं[13]। वैश्वामित्रः। दत्तपुत्रतया[14] विश्वामित्रपुत्रो देवरातो नाम। देवै रातो दत्तः[15]। रा दाने। श्रूयते हि। देवा वा इमं मह्यमरासतेति स ह देवरात[16] इति। इदं चोत्तरं च द्वे सूक्ते वरुणदेवत्ये। त्रैष्टुभमिदं सूक्तं। प्राग्घिरण्यस्तूपाद्[17]यथाप्राप्तगायत्रत्वापवादः। अत्र चादौ कायी कदेवत्या। कशब्दात्प्रजापतिवचनाद्देवतायां कस्येदितीत्वे[18] वृद्धिः। अण् ङीप्। अणो यस्येति चेति[19] लोपः। ननु ब्राह्मणे[20] स प्रजापतिमेव

[1] W 1; आपदि omitted in the other MSS.; cp. Sây. on ver. 16. [2] See sûtra on I, 165. [3] W 1; मृत्योरिति मरुत्व इति I 4; मृत्योरिति मरुत्य इति P 1; मृत्योरिति मरुत्वत्य इति P 2, I 2. [4] Pân. VIII, ii, 10. [5] Pân. I, iv, 19. [6] Cp. Pân. IV, ii, 32. [7] Ver. 19. [8] W 1; एकश्रुत्ये नास्ति I 2; नास्ति I 4; एव नास्ति P 1; एव स्वास्य (sic) नास्ति P 2. [9] Pân. IV, i, 95. [10] Cp. Pân. IV, i, 114. [11] W 1; क्रियया निवृत्तः I 4; क्रियाया निवृत्तः P 1; क्रियायो निवृत्तः P 2, I 2. [12] Pân. III, iii, 88. [13] Pân. IV, iv, 20. [14] P 2, I 2; यत् त्वपुत्रतया W 1; यदपुत्रतया I 4; यदत्र पुत्रतया P 1. [15] देवरातः। देवदत्तः W 1. [16] Ait. Br. VII, xvii, 3. [17] °घैरण्यस्तूपाद् W 1; see sûtra on I, 31; Introd. § 12, 14. [18] Pân. IV, ii, 25. [19] Pân. VI, iv, 148. [20] कल्पसूत्रे I 4; all except W 1 omit ननु.

प्रथमं देवानामुपससारेति[1] प्रजापतिदर्शनात्प्राजापत्येयं भवितुमर्हति कस्य नूनमिति न तु कायी। उच्यते। प्रजानां पतिरित्यर्थः। क एव तत्राप्युक्तः। अथ द्वितीयाग्नेयी। अथ सावित्रस्तृचो गायत्रः। अभि त्वा देव सवितरिति तृचः सवितृदेवत्यो गायत्रीछंदस्कश्च। गायत्र इत्यत्र विहित-त्रैष्टुभत्वापवादः। अस्य सावित्रस्य तृचस्यांत्या भगभक्तस्येत्येषा भगदेवत्या सावित्री वा। शिष्टा दश वारुण्यः।

अत्रेतिहासः श्रुत्युक्तः[2] सम्यगेव प्रवर्ण्यते[3]।
हरिश्चंद्रो ह वैधस इत्यादि ब्राह्मणेरितः[4]।
राजसूये कृतावेष शौनःशेप[5] इति श्रुतः[6] ॥१॥
शतभार्यो हरिश्चंद्र ऐक्ष्वाकः पुत्रकाम्यया।
नारद[7]श्रुतपुत्रार्थो वरुणात्सुतमाप्तवान् ॥२॥
जाते पुत्रे त्वामनेन यक्ष्येऽहमि[8]ति चोक्तवान्।
वरुणस्तनये जाते निर्देशे[9] जातदंतके ॥३॥
च्युतदंते पुनर्जातदंते वर्मभरे[10] तथा।
मेध्यस्ये[11] तदवस्थोऽसाविति राज्ञा[12] प्रतारितः ॥४॥
निर्बंध्य स नृपं प्रोचे पुत्रेणाद्यैव मां यज।
इत्युक्तो[13] वरुणेनोचे[14] स्वपुत्रं रोहितं नृपः[15] ॥५॥
एनं यक्ष्ये त्वयाद्येति नेति सोऽभ्यद्रवद्वनं।
वनस्थो रोहितः श्रुत्वा नृपं जातमहोदरं ॥६॥
दिदृक्षुः पंचवर्षेषु[16] विप्ररूपेंद्रवारितः।
षष्ठे[17]ऽजीगर्तनामानं त्रिपुत्रं बाधितं क्षुधा ॥७॥
आसाद्यास्य शुनःशेपं मध्यमं जगृहे सुतं।
गवां शतेन पितरं पुरस्यं दृष्टवान्सुतः ॥८॥

[1] Ait. Br. VII, xvi, 3. [2] Ait. Br. VII, iii. This story is quoted from Shadg. by the Nîtimañgarî (N). [3] W 1, I 2; °वर्त्यते P 1; वक्ष्यते I 4; °वर्त्तिते P 2; प्रवर्तते N. [4] इति ब्राह्मण ईरितः W 1; इति कल्पसूत्र ईरितः I 4, i.e. in the Sâṅkh.-sûtra; cp. M. M., A. S. L., p. 408 and App. [5] शुनःशेप W 1. [6] श्रुतेः P 2, I 2. [7] °दाश्रुत° W 1, I 4; °दशत° P 1; °दःशत° P 2, I 2; नारदोक्ताद्धि पुत्रार्थे N. [8] यक्ष्यैनमिति I 4, P 1; यक्ष्येनम् P 2, I 2. [9] निर्हशे I 4; निर्देशे W 1, C, P 2, I 2; निर्दशे P 1. [10] P 1, N, I 4; चर्मभरे W 1, C; वर्मभटी P 2, I 2. [11] W 1; मध्य° the rest. [12] W 1, P 1; राजा I 4, P 2, I 2. [13] °क्ते W 1. [14] °णेनासौ I 4; °णेनात्र P 2, I 2. [15] देहि तं नृपं P 1, P 2, I 2, I 4. [16] षड्वर्षेषु N. [17] सप्तमे N.

मया कार्यमनेन त्वं कुरु तातेति चाब्रवीत् ।
वरुणोऽपि नृपेणोक्तः[1] शुनःशेपपशुं[2] क्रतुं[3] ॥९॥
राजसूयं सोऽनुमेने तेनायष्ट च भूमिपः ।
तदाभिषेचनीयेऽह्नि[4] शुनःशेपनियोजने ॥१०॥
अन्याभावाद्गोशतार्थी त्वजीगर्तो युयोज तं ।
पुनर्विशसनं कर्तुं पिता जग्राह गोशतं ॥११॥
यूपे बद्धः शुनःशेपो जिघांसुं पितरं ततः ।
ऊचे तिष्ठाहमेवान्या[5] उपधावामि देवताः ॥१२॥
अस्तौत्क्रमादावग्निं[6] च सवितारं भगं च सः ।
वरुणं पुनरप्यग्निं विश्वान्देवानथो खलु ॥१३॥
इंद्रं च पूर्वव्यापारसंप्राप्तस्तुतिसुप्रियं ।
हिरण्मयरथस्यापि स्वस्मै[7] दातारमेव च ॥१४॥
अश्विना उषसं[8] चापि तृचाभ्यामंततस्तदा ।
अतिप्रीतियुतैर्देवैस्तैर्यूपान्मोचि[9]तस्तदा ॥१५॥
ऋत्विग्गणैः[10] प्रार्थितोऽसावंजःसवमकारयत् ।
गतरोगं हरिश्चंद्रं यत्र ग्रावेति[11] सूक्ततः[12] ॥१६॥
अंजःसवो राजसूये प्रयोगः[13] पश्विष्टिद्रव्यादि[14]विहीन एकः ।
यतोऽंजसाभिष्टुवतेऽत्र साम्ना[15] यच्चांजसा देवतास्तं भजंते ॥१७॥
स पित्रा प्रार्थितस्त्यक्त्वा तातं गाधिसुतं गतः[16] ।
पुत्रत्वेन गृहीतश्च विश्वामित्रेण धीमता ॥१८॥
देवरात इति प्रोक्तो[17] देवैर्दत्तो यतः स्वयं[18] ।
दत्तपुत्रविधेर्योगा[19]द्वैश्वामित्रः स कृत्रिमः ॥१९॥

[1] W 1; °क्तं the rest. [2] शुनःशेपं पशुं W 1, P 1, I 4; °शेपं पशु P 2, I 2. [3] क्रतौ I 4. Slokas 10 and 11 are omitted in P 1, P 2, I 2, I 4, and N, which also omits 9. [4] तदाभि° W 1. [5] °हमत्रैव सुप° W 1; दृष्ट्वासिमहमेवान्या N. [6] क्रमाद् P 2, I 2. [7] तस्मै P 2, I 2, I 4. [8] उषसश्च W 1. [9] तद्यूपान्मो° P 1, P 2, I 2, I 4. [10] I 4; °णः प्रा° P 1, P 2, I 2; °णप्रा° W 1. [11] *Rigv.* I, 28. [12] N quotes no further. [13] W 1 omits. [14] W 1; द्रव्यादि P 1, P 2, I 2; °ष्टिरित्यादि° I 4. [15] W 1; °भिष्टुतो ऽत्र सोमो I 4, P 1; °भिष्टुतो ऽत्र सो P 2, I 2. [16] W 1; ततः the others. [17] ख्यातो W 1. [18] P 1, I 4; यतस्त्वयं W 1; ततः स्वयं P 2, I 2. [19] W 1; °विधियोंगात् the rest.

आर्षानुक्रमणे चोक्तं कस्य नूनं शुनःशेपः ।
आजीगर्तिः[1] कृत्रिमस्तु वैश्वामित्रो देवरातः ॥२०॥
इति कृत्रिमपुत्रत्वं देवरातत्वमेव च ।
अजीगर्तसुतत्वं च वैश्वामित्रत्वमेव च ॥२१॥
शुनःशेपमहर्षेस्तु सम्यगत्र प्रवर्णितं[2] ।
बंधक्षयकरी पाशमोचनीयं[3] कथेरिता ॥२२॥

२५. त्वमग्ने प्रथमोऽंगिरा[4] इत्यतः प्राक् शुनःशेपार्षं वेदितव्यं ॥

२७. सप्तभिरूना विंशतिः । त्रयोदशेत्यर्थः । गायत्रे सूक्तेऽंत्या त्रयोदशी दैवी देवदेवत्या छंदसा त्रिष्टुप् । गायत्र इत्यनुवादः । त्रिष्टुबंतस्य सूक्तस्य शिष्टा जगत्य[5] इति जगतीत्वनिवृत्तये[6] । ननु । स विश्वान्देवांस्तुष्टाव नमो महद्भ्यो नमो अर्भकेभ्य इत्येतयर्चेति[7] ब्राह्मण[8]दर्शनाद्वै[9]श्वदेवीयं स्यान्न तु दैवी । उच्यते । तत्र विश्व इति[10] सर्वशब्द इति पर्यायः । न तु विश्वेदेवगणोऽभिप्रेतः ॥

२८. षडनुष्टुभ आदौ यस्य तत्सूक्तं षडनुष्टुबादि अत्र

मध्यमस्य[11]डकारस्य ळकारं बह्वृचा विदुः ।
मध्यमस्यढकारस्य[12] ळ्हकारं[13] वै यथा खलु ।
ईळे[14] मृळ[15] पुरोळाशं इळा[16] साळ्हा निदर्शनं[17] ॥

अन्यथा तु षडनुष्टुबादि स्यात्[18] । अस्य सूक्तस्यानादेश इंद्रो देवता । यच्चिद्धि गृहेगृह इति द्वे[19] उलूखलदेवत्ये । उलूखलादयो ङीप्यौयणौ । परे मुसलदेवत्ये । चकारादुलूखल्यौ च । अंत्या प्रजापतेः प्रजानां पत्युर्हरिश्चंद्रस्य क्षत्रियस्य स्तुतिरधिषवणचर्मप्रशंसा वा । इयं सोमस्य चर्मणो वा स्तुतिः । हरिश्चंद्रः प्रजापतिर्[20]धर्मसोमौ चेति बृहद्देवताविदः । तत्र हि ।

चर्माधिषवनीयं वा सोमं वांत्या प्रशंसति[21] ।

[1] W 1; the others insert स. [2] प्रवर्त्तितं P 1, P 2, I 2. [3] °नेयं W 1. [4] Sûtra on I, 31. [5] Introd. §§ 12, 13. [6] W 1; इत्यनुवर्त्तते the others. [7] इत्येतयर्चा omitted in W 1. [8] Ait. Br. VII, xvi, 8. [9] कल्पसूत्रे दर्शनात् I 4. [10] विश्वानिति हि W 1. [11] मध्यमस्य W 1; अंतर्ममध्यस्य° P 1, P 2, I 2, I 4. [12] मध्यमस्यडकारस्य W 1; अंतर्मध्यस्यडकारस्य P 1, P 2, I 2; अंतर्मध्यडकारस्य I 4. [13] हकारं corr. to लकारं W 1; लकारं P 1; ळकारं P 2, I 2; नकारं I 4. [14] W 1; इडा I 4; इमे P 1; इम P 2, I 2. [15] W 1, I 4; मृडु P 1, P 2, I 2. [16] W 1; ल्हा P 1, P 2, I 2; omitted in I 4. [17] Cp. *Rig*v. Pr. 53. [18] P 1, P 2, I 2; विद्यात् W 1; षळनुष्टुबादि न स्यात् I 4. [19] Vers. 5–6. [20] °पतिरिति corr. on margin to °पतिर्धर्मसोमौ चेति W 1; हरिश्चंद्रस्य प्रजापतेरिति P 1; हरिश्चंद्रस्य प्रजापतिरिति P 2, I 2; हरिश्चंद्रस्य प्रजापतित्वं बृ° I 4. [21] MSS. of Bri. Dev., Adhyâya III, sloka 411 (M 1), 383 (M 2 and M 3).

इत्युक्तं । अथैनं द्रोणकलशमित्यादिना ब्राह्मणेन[2] सोमस्तुतित्वमेवास्या लक्ष्यते । इयं तु देवतानुक्रमणीस्थां देवतामनुवदति[3] । तत्र ह्येवं ।

प्रजापतिं हरिश्चंद्रं चर्म वांत्या प्रशंसति ।

हरिश्चंद्रस्य प्रजापतिरिति विशेषणं । प्रस्कण्वहरिश्चंद्रावृषी[4] इति निपाततः[5] सुट् प्रस्कण्वो ब्रह्मर्षिर्मा भूदिति । [6]आद्यास्तस्र इंद्रदेवत्याः । अंत्यास्तिस्रो गायत्र्यः ॥

२९. पंक्तेरिदं पांक्तं । तस्येदमित्यण्[7] । आदिवृद्धिः ॥

३०. अस्माकं शिप्रिणीनामित्येषा पादनिचृत्त्रिसप्ताक्षरपादयुक्ता । शश्वदिंद्र इति त्रिष्टुप् । प्राग्घिरण्यस्तूपगायत्रत्वापवादस्त्रिष्टुबिति । इंद्रो देवता । तत आश्विनस्तृचः । ततः परस्तृच उषस्य उषोदेवत्यः । गायत्राधिकारस्यावधिः पूर्णः ॥

३१. ऊना विंशतिः । अष्टादशर्चं । हिरण्यस्तूप इत्यृषिनाम । आंगिरसोऽयं गोत्रतोऽनुक्रगोत्रत्वात् । सूक्तमग्निदेवत्यं । अंत्याष्टादशी त्रिष्टुप् । अष्टमीषोडश्यौ च त्रिष्टुभौ । शिष्टाः पंचदश जगत्यः । त्रिष्टुबंतस्य सूक्तस्य शिष्टा जगत्य[8] इति परिभाषातः सिद्धं ॥

३२. पंचदशर्चं । त्रिष्टुप् । अनादेशे त्विंद्रो देवता त्रिष्टुप् छंद[9] इति चैंद्रः । आंगिरसो हिरण्यस्तूपः ॥२॥

३४. अश्विदेवत्यं । हिरण्यस्तूपः । नवमी त्रिष्टुबंत्या च त्रिष्टुप् । शिष्टा जगत्यः ॥

३५. सवितृदेवत्यं सूक्तं । नवमी जगत्याद्या च जगती । सा लिंगोक्तदैवतपादा । लिंगेनाभिधानसामर्थ्येनोक्ताः प्रतिपादिता अग्निमित्रावरुणरात्रिसवित्राख्या देवताः पादेषु यस्याः सा ॥

३६. कण्वो नामर्षिर्घोरपुत्रः । अग्निदेवत्यं सूक्तं । प्रागाथं । प्रगाथा बार्हता इति । ऊर्ध्व ऊ षु ण ऊतय ऊर्ध्वो नः पाह्यंहस इत्येते द्वे यूपदेवत्ये ॥

४०. ब्रह्मणस्पतिदेवत्यं । पर्यंताद्यक्[10] ॥

४१. वरुणमित्रार्यम्णां स्तुतित्वेन संबंधीदं सूक्तं[11] । मध्ये तृचश्चतुर्थ्यादिरादित्येभ्यः । तादर्थ्ये भ्यः । आदित्यानां स्तावकं ॥

४३. रुद्रदेवत्यं । तृतीया मित्रावरुणदेवत्या । च[12]कारादौद्री । अंत्यस्तृचः सोमदेवत्यः । सोमाट्ट्यण्[13] ॥

४४. प्रस्कण्वो नाम काण्वः । कण्वपुत्रः । प्रगतः कण्वादिति[14] । प्रस्कण्वहरिश्चंद्रेति[15] सुण्

[1] अभ्यवनिनाय added in P 2, I 2. [2] Ait. Br. VII, xvii, 1. [3] W 1; देवतानुक्रमणीमनुसरति the rest. [4] Pân. VI, i, 153. [5] W 1; निपातित: the rest. [6] The following in I 4 only. [7] Pân. IV, iii, 120. [8] Introd. § 12, 13. [9] Ibid. § 12, 5–6. [10] Cp. Pân. V, i, 128. [11] W 1; संबंधि सूक्तं the rest. [12] This च is overlooked in M. M.'s Index. [13] Pân. IV, ii, 30. [14] W 1; प्रस्कण्व: I 4; प्रशस्त: P 1; प्रशास्ते P 2, I 2. [15] W 1, I 4; °श्चंद्रात्वे सुण् P 1, P 2, I 2; cp. Pân. VI, i, 153.

निपात्यते । आद्यो तृचः । द्वे स्तृचौ । स्तुकपूर्वित्यकारः । ऋचि त्रेरुत्तरपदादिलोप[2] इति संप्रसारणविधौ त्रेरित्युपलक्षणमुक्ता तृचवद्द्वृचशब्दं प्रयुंजते । यथा तृचाः प्रतिपदनुचरा द्वृचाः प्रगाथा इति[3] तद्वदत्राप्याद्यो द्वृच इति । स चाश्विनोरुभयत्र चकारादग्नेः स्तावकः ॥

४९. चतुष्कं चतुर्थं ॥

५०. सौर्यं सूर्यदेवत्यं । सूर्यागस्त्ययोश्छे च ङ्यां चेति[4] नियमात् सूर्यतिष्यागस्त्येति यलोपो न भवति । आद्या नव गायत्र्यः । आनुष्टुभत्वापवादः । अंत्यस्तृचो रोगघ्नो रोगशांतिकरः[5] । उपनिषत् । एकस्मै शुश्रूषव एकेन वक्तव्यमिति गुह्यमुपनिषदित्युच्यते । सूत्र्यते हि चतुर्थारण्यके । द्वयोरेवैक एकस्मै प्रब्रूयादिति ह स्माह जातूकर्ण्यो न वत्से च न तृतीय इति[6] । उपनिषत्संज्ञायामारण्यकधर्मः प्राप्यते तर्हि दिवारण्येऽस्याध्ययनं प्राप्नोति[7] । इष्टमेवैतत्संगृहीतं । सूर्यत्वादेवास्याध्ययनं दिवैव । उक्तं हि सौर्याणि प्रतिपद्यते सूर्यो नो दिव[8] इत्यादौ सूक्ते । सूत्रकृतो सूर्यत्वे लिंगतः[9] सिद्धेऽप्यत्र सौर्याणीति शब्दत एषां[10] दिवैवाध्ययनं यथा स्यादिति वै कृतमिति । उक्तरत्राप्युपनिषदित्युक्तेरेतदेव प्रयोजनं । यथा । आद्या गर्भस्राविण्युपनिषदि[11]त्यादि । उपेत्य नियमयुक्ताय सद्यत[12] उपदिश्यत इत्युपनिषत् । निपूर्वात् षद्लृ विशरणगत्यवसादनेष्वित्यस्मात्संपदादि[13]त्वात्कर्मणि क्विप् । सदिरप्रतेरिति[14] षत्वमिति ह्युपनिषच्छब्दो निरूप्यते । अस्त्युपनिषत्स्व

एकः श्रोता दक्षिणतो निषीदेद्द्वौ वा भूयांसस्तु यथावकाशं[15] ।

इति प्रातिशाख्ये दर्शनादध्ययने यथाकामिता[16] प्राप्नोति न त्वेकस्मा एकेनैव वाच्यं स्यात् ॥

५१. सव्यः । व्यञ् संवरणे[17] । सर्वमात्मीयं तेजसा संवृणोतीति । पृषोदरादिः । गोत्रत आंगिरसः ऋषिस्तत्पर्यंचिदिति सूक्ताः[18] । अंते द्वे चतुर्दशीपंचदश्यौ त्रिष्टुभौ यस्य सूक्तस्य तद्धि त्रिष्टुबंतं । शिष्टास्त्रयोदश जगत्यः । अनादेशादैंद्रं । अत्रेतिहासमाह । अभ्यध्यादिति[19] प्राप्ते लुङि शब्भावश्छांदसः[20] । तपसा युक्तो देवताश्चिंतितवान् । सव्य इति नाम्ना स्वयमेवेंद्रोऽन्यो मत्तुल्यो जगति

[1] Cp. Pân. V, iv, 74. [2] Vârt. to Pân. VI, 1, 37. [3] I 4; तथा । तृचाः प्रतिपदनुचराः । द्वृचाः प्रगाथ इति W 1; यथा । तृचा प्रतिपदानुचराः द्वृचाः प्रगाथ इति P 1; यथात्र चारु प्रतिपदनुचरा द्वृचाः प्रगाथा इति P 2, I 2. [4] Cp. Pân. VI, iv, 149. [5] W 1; सर्वशांतिकरः P 1, I 4, P 2, I 2; द्विषंतं मह्यमर्धेयं जपेच्छत्रुनिवारणं added by I 4 only. [6] Ait. Âr. V, iii, 3. [7] तद्वारण्ये दिवाध्ययनं प्राप्नोति P 1, I 4, P 2. [8] Âsv. Sr.-sûtra, VI, v, 17–18. [9] W 1; लिंगतः omitted in the rest. [10] W 1; एषां omitted in the rest. [11] Sûtra on I, 101. [12] W 1; °युक्ता प्रसज्यते P 1, P 2, I 2, I 4 (उपेत्य being omitted by I 4). [13] W 1, I 4; सदादित्वात् P 1; संपदेदादित्वात् P 2, I 2. [14] Pân. VIII, iii, 66. [15] *Rig*v. Pr. 830. [16] W 1; यथाकाममिति the rest. [17] सव्यः सव्यनामाप्येतत्संवरणे P 1; °सचरणे P 2, I 2; सव्येनाथे तत्संवत्सरेण I 4. [18] Introd. § 2, 3. [19] P 1; अभ्यध्यायदिति P 2, I 2; अभ्यधावदिति W 1. [20] लुङि शभावः W 1; लुङि शब्भाव [शप्लुग्भाव ?] छांदसः P 1, P 2, I 2; लुङि शप्लुक् भाव छांदसः I 4.

मा भूदित्यस्यांगिरसः पुत्रत्वेनाजायत प्रादुर्भूतवान् । तथा[1] चास्य सव्यस्यर्षेरांगिरसत्वं सम्य-गुपपन्नं ॥

५३. सांहितिकः कंप एकश्रुत्ये नास्ति । उपांत्याप्यंत्यासादृश्यार्थादंत्या । यथा प्रथमयोः पूर्वसवर्णः[2] इति द्वितीयापि प्रथमा ॥

५८. नोधा नामर्षिः । गौतमः । गोतमादृष्यण् । अंते चतस्रस्त्रिष्टुभो यस्य तत्सूक्तं चतुस्त्रिष्टुबंतं ॥

५९. वैश्वानरीयं । वैश्वानर इत्यग्नेर्गुणः । वृद्धाच्छः[3] ॥

६१. नोधाः । श्रूयते हि । अस्मा इदु प्र तवसे तुरायेति नोधास्त एते प्रातःसवन[4] इति ॥४॥

६४. अत्र परिभाषते । इत्या षोळशैंद्र[6]मित्यत ऐंद्रसंशब्दनात्प्रागतः परमग्निदेवत्यं । असत्यस्मिन्सू-त्रेऽनादेशादैंद्रं हि स्यात् । पंचदशकृत्व आग्नेयग्रहणं कर्तव्यं स्यात् । पराणि पंचदशाग्नेयानीत्युक्तौ च गुरुत्वं स्यात् । तर्हि लाघवादेवं सूत्रं । इत्या षोळशेत्यत्रावध्यर्थमैंद्रपदमकृत्वा पश्वा दश पराशरः शाक्त्यो द्वैपदं तदा[6]ग्नेयं तद्धि तदिति वाच्यं स्यात् । तद्धि तदिति पंचदशेत्यर्थः । सत्यं । सुखप्रतिपत्तये तथा न कृतं ॥

६५. पराशरो नामर्षिः । शाक्त्यः । शक्तिपुत्रः । शक्तेर्गर्गादित्वाद् यञ्[7] । अनंतरस्य गोत्रत्वो-पचारः[8] । जामदग्न्यः परशुराम इतिवत् । अन्यथानंतरत्वादृष्यणि[9] शाक्त इति स्यात् । पराशरस्य शक्त्यनंतरापत्यत्वं पुराणेषु स्मर्यते हि ।

वसिष्ठस्य सुतः शक्तिः शक्तेः पुत्रः पराशरः ।
पराशरस्य दायादः कृष्णद्वैपायनो मुनिः ॥

द्वैपदं द्विपदासूक्तं । विंशतिका द्विपदा विराज[10] इति ह्युक्तं । अतो विंशत्यक्षराश्छंदस्तो[11] विराजः स्युः । द्विर्द्विपदास्त्वृचः समाममंती[12]पुक्तत्वादध्ययने द्वे द्वे[13] द्विपदे एकर्ग्भवति । शंसने तु यथा-प्राप्तं । सूच्यते । पश्वा न तायुमिति द्वैपदमि[14]ति । तदिति षडित्यर्थः । अतः परं षट् सूक्तानि द्वैपदानि तु[15]भ्यादिसूत्रतः । अग्निदेवत्यं ॥

७०. अयुक्संत्या द्विपदैवेति साधुर्न गृभुरिति[16] द्विपदैवाध्ययने । पूर्वास्तु दशार्चो भवंति । इति षट् द्वैपदानि सूक्तानि ॥

७९. आद्यस्तृचस्त्रैष्टुभः । द्वितीय औष्णिहः । पूर्वस्तृचस्त्रैष्टुभो मध्यमस्थानाय वैद्युताग्नये

[1] न तथा P 1, P 2, I 2. [2] Pân. VI, i, 102. [3] Ibid. IV, ii, 114. [4] Ait. Br. VI, xviii, 4–5. [5] Sûtra on I, 80. [6] P 1, I 4 omit the rest. [7] Cp. Pân. IV, i, 105. [8] W 1; अनंतरस्या गोत्रोपचारः P 1; आनंतरस्य गोत्रापवादः I 4; अनंतपरस्य गोत्रापवादः P 2; अनंतरस्य गोत्रोपचारः I 2. [9] अन्यथा अनंतरत्वा ऋष्यणि W 1; अन्यथातत्वाद् I 4; अन्यथाननार्ष्यणि P 2, I 2; अन्यथांननात्वाद् P 1. [10] Introd. § 12, 8. [11] °ते corr. to °तो W 1; °त्वेति P 1, P 2, I 2, I 4. [12] Introd. § 12, 10. [13] W 1, I 4; द्वे (once) P 1, P 2, I 2. [14] Âsv. Sr.-sûtra, VIII, xii, 24. [15] Introd. § 12, 3. [16] Ver. 6.

शुद्धाग्नये वा । तादर्थ्ये ङे । मध्यमो धामच्छद्गुणोऽग्निरित्येके । हिरण्यकेशो रजसो विसार इति सूत्रे[1] धामच्छद्गुणेऽग्नौ[2] विनियोगदर्शनादिति[3] तदनुपपन्नं[4] । तत्र हि धामच्छदग्नौ त्वं त्या चिद्[5] धामन्[6] इति द्वे याज्यानुवाक्ये[7] उक्ते[8] हिरण्यकेश इति वृषस्तु शुद्धाग्नेरेव । न हि धामच्छदे[9] याज्यानुवाक्याद्वयं[10] विकल्प्यते[8] । किं तु तत्र[8] शुद्धोऽग्निरग्निर्वा[8] धामच्छदिति विकल्प्यते । तस्माद्विगुत एव मध्यमः[11] ॥

आग्नेयाधिकारस्य पूर्णोऽवधिः ॥

८८. ऐंद्रमित्याग्नेयावध्यर्थं । अन्यथानादेशादैंद्रत्वं सिध्यति ॥५॥

८९. आदितोऽनुष्टुभः षट् । अथौष्णिहस्तृचः । अथ पांक्तस्तृचः । अथ गायत्रस्तृचः । अथ त्रैष्टुभस्तृचः । अथ बृहती । अथ सतोबृहती ॥

९०. विराट्स्थान[12] ऋजुनीतीति । ऋत्यक[13] इति ह्रस्वप्रकृतिभावौ । यथा । पर ऋणा सावीरिति[14] । अष्टौ पिंडान्कृत्वा ऋतमग्र[15] इति गृह्ये ॥

९१. पंचमीप्रभृतिद्वादशर्चो गायत्र्यः । अथोष्णिक् सप्तदशी । चेतयेत्यर्थः ॥

९२. चतस्रो जगत्य आदौ यस्य तच्चतुर्जगत्यादि । षडुष्णिहोऽंते यस्य तत्षडुष्णिगंतं । अंत्यस्तृचोऽश्विदेवत्यः ॥

९३. अग्निश्च सोमश्च । ईदग्नेः सोमवरुणयोः[16] । अग्नेः स्तुत्स्तोमसोमा[17] इति षत्वं । द्यावापृथिवीत्यादिना[18] छः । आदितोऽनुष्टुभस्तिस्रः । नवम्याद्यास्तिस्रो गायत्र्योऽष्टमी जगती वा त्रिष्टुब्वा । यो अग्निषोमा हविषा सपर्यादिति कथं जगतीत्वं । आद्यैकादशपादद्वयव्यूहेन । असत्यस्मिन् द्वाभ्यां विराट्स्वराजावीति[19] द्व्यक्षराधिक्यात् स्वराट्त्रिष्टुप्त्वं स्यात् । शिष्टाः पंच त्रिष्टुभः ॥

९४. कुत्सः । अनुक्तगोत्रत्वादांगिरसोऽयम् । तदिति षडित्युक्तं । अत्र सूक्ते पूर्वो देवा भवतु सुन्वतो रथ[20] इति त्रयः पादा देवदेवत्याः । तन्नो मित्रो वरुणो मामहंतामित्यर्धर्चो[21] लिंगेनाभिधानसामर्थ्येन प्रतिपादितमित्रादिमद्देवत्यः । यद्देवत्यं वा सूक्तं तद्देवत्यो वायमर्धर्चः । तेनात्राग्नेः प्राधान्यं मित्रादीनां निपातभाक्त्वेनाप्राधान्यं[22] । अंत्योऽर्धर्च इति वाच्ये तन्नो मित्रो ग्रहणमुत्तरत्राप्य-

[1] Âsv. *S*r.-sûtra, II, xiii, 7. [2] W 1; °गुणे कौ P 1; °गुणकाविति I 4; °छद्वैगुणको P 2, I 2. [3] W 1, P 1; वियोग° P 2, I 2; यागे द° I 4. [4] P 1, P 2, I 2; तदुपपन्नं W 1, I 4. [5] *Rig*v. VI, 2, 9. [6] IV, 58, 11. [7] द्वे याज्या पुरो नुवाक्ये I 4. [8] W 1; उक्ते, विकल्प्यते, तत्र, वा omitted in the rest. [9] W 1, P 1; °छदो P 2, I 2. [10] °युगद्वयं W 1. [11] Cp. Sâya*n*a on I, 79, introd. [12] If sûtras 89 and 90 are written without an intervening pause. [13] Pâ*n*. VI, i, 128. [14] *Rig*v. II, 28, 9. [15] Âsv. G*r*ih.-sûtra, I, v, 4. [16] Pâ*n*. VI, iii, 27. [17] Pâ*n*. VIII, iii, 82. [18] Cp. Pâ*n*. IV, ii, 32. [19] Introd. § 3, 5. [20] Ver. 8. [21] Ver. 16, 3–4. [22] W 1; निपातत्वे न प्राधान्यं I 4; निपातने न प्राधान्यं P 1, P 2.

स्यैवमिति वक्तुं । यद्देवत्यं वेतीदमिति वाच्ये[1] सूक्तग्रहणं चास्यैवार्थस्य पोषाय[2]। तेन नासत्याभ्यामित्यतः[3] प्राक् तत्तत्सूक्तदेवत्यो[4]ऽप्ययमर्धर्चो वा भवति[5] ॥६॥

९५. ईदूदेद्द्विवचनं प्रगृह्यमि[6]ति प्रगृह्यत्वं । ननु लाघवाय नवोनेति वाच्यं नैकादशेति ।·न ह्यत्र त्र्यम्येकादशे[7]त्यादिवत्संधितः समाक्षरत्वं । सत्यं । शैलीयमाचार्यस्य सर्वत्रैकादशेत्येवेति । औषसाय[8]। उषसिभवाय प्रातराहुतिभोजिनेऽग्नये शुद्धाय वेदं सूक्तं स्तावकं । अग्नय इत्यौषसत्वगुणविशेषितत्वात्[9]। यथा पूर्वोऽग्नये वा मध्यमाये[10]त्यत्र मध्यमगुणविशेषितायाग्नय इति । अयं चाग्निरुत्तरत्र गुणविशेषितत्वायानुवर्तते[11]। तेन स प्रत्नथा नव द्रविणोदस[12] इत्यादावग्नय इति सिद्धं भवति । तदित्युक्तेर्वानुवृत्तेश्च यावत्तयोवृषीयं[13] शुद्धाग्नेयत्वं च वा भवति । औषसायेति । उषःशब्दाद्भवार्थेऽण् ॥

९६. द्रविणोदस्त्वगुणयुक्तायाग्नय इदं स्तावकं शुद्धाय वा ॥

९७. अग्नय इत्येव । वेति च । तादर्थ्ये के । शुचिगुणाग्न्यर्थमिदं शुद्धाय वा ॥

९८. तिस्र ऋचो यत्र सूक्ते तत्तृचं । तच्च वैश्वानरगुणाग्निदेवत्यं । शुद्धाय वा ॥

९९. एकर्चमिदं सूक्तं । जातवेदोगुणाग्निदेवत्यं शुद्धाग्निदेवत्यं वा । जातवेदःस्तावकत्वेन भवं । भवे छंदसीति[14] यत् । मारीचः कश्यप ऋषिः । कुतः । कश्यपार्षमिति वक्ष्यमाणत्वात् । एतज्जातवेदस इत्येकर्चमादिर्येषां तान्येतदादीनि सूक्तान्येकभूयांस्येकर्चबहुतराणि द्व्यृचं तृचं चतुर्ऋचं पंचर्चमित्यादि सहस्रर्चातान्यत्र संति । तान्येतावंतीत्याह । सूक्तसहस्रमिति । एतत्सूक्तसहस्रं कश्यपार्षमिति । आर्षं दर्शनं कश्यपस्य यत्र तत्कश्यपार्षं । अयं च कश्यपो मरीचिपुत्र इति वक्ष्यते । मारीचः कश्यप[15] इति ।

> खिलसूक्तानि चैतानि त्वाद्यै[16]कर्चमधीमहे ।
> शौनकेन स्वयं चोक्तमृष्यनुक्रमणे त्विदं[17] ॥
> पूर्वात्पूर्वासहस्रस्य सूक्तानामेकभूयसां ।
> जातवेदस इत्याद्यं कश्यपार्षस्य[18] शुश्रुम ॥ इति ॥

[1] P 1, I 4; वाच्य° P 2, I 2; °दमपि सूक्त° W 1. [2] W 1; पौष्याय P 1, P 2, I 2; पौष्णाय I 4. [3] Sûtra on I, 116. [4] W 1; प्राक्तनसूक्तदेवत्योप्य° P 1, P 2, I 2, I 4 (प्रातान° I 4). [5] This ardhar*k*a is repeated at the end of each sûkta from 94 to 115, except 97, 99, ar l 104. [6] Pâ*n*. I, i, 11. [7] Sûtra on I, 34. [8] उषसाय P 1, P 2, I 2, W 1; ओषसाय I 4. [9] °विशेषित्वाय W 1. [10] Sûtra on I, 79. [11] P 2, I 4; °शेषितयानुवर्तते W 1; °दोषिवायानु° P 1. [12] Sûtra on I, 96. [13] I, 100. [14] Pâ*n*. IV, iv, 110. [15] See sûtra on VIII, 29. [16] W 1, P 1; त्वायै° I 4; भूत्वायै° P 2, I 2. [17] I 4, W 1 (corr. on margin to इत्यनुक्रम°); इत्यनुक्रमणीस्त्वयं P 2; °णी त्वियं I 2; इत्यनुक्रमणोस्त्वियं P 1. [18] P 1, I 4; कश्यार्षं W 1; कश्यपार्षं स P 2, I 2.

सयोवृषीयांता वेदमध्यास्त्वखिलसूक्तगाः[2] ।
ऋचस्तु पंच लक्षाः स्युः सैकोनशतपंचकं[3] ॥
आद्यंतपादार्धहृतमि[4]त्यार्यभट्ट[5]संख्यया ।
यथै[6]कादिदशांते च पंचपंचाशदुच्यते ॥

आम्नायोक्तेरेव च्युतत्वेऽपि खिलस्य कश्यपर्षैरनेकसूक्तदर्शनेन माहात्म्यज्ञानार्थोऽयमुपदेशः प्रासंगिकः । इतरथैकर्षसूक्तदर्शित्वं स्यात् ॥

१००. वार्षागिरा वृषागिरो नाम महाराजस्यापत्यभूताः । ऋज्राश्वः । अंबरीषः । सहदेवः । भयमानः । सुराधाः । इति पंच राजर्षयःसहद्रष्टारः । अत्रैव सूक्त एतत्स्य इंद्रे[7]त्यत्रोक्ताः । उक्तं ह्यार्षानुक्रमण्यां ।

सूक्तं स यो वृषेत्येतत् पंच वार्षागिरा विदुः ।
नियुक्ता[8] नामधेयैः स्वैरपि चैतत्स्यदित्यृषि ॥ इति ॥

१०१. कुत्सो नामांगिरसोऽयं । आद्या गर्भस्राविणी । अस्या जपात्सुखं गर्भाः स्रवंतीत्यर्थः । उपनिषदित्युक्तार्थो[9] ॥

१०५. आप्त्यः । अप्त्यपुत्रः । ऋष्यण् । यस्येति च[10] । त्रितो नाम । वेत्युक्तेः[11] कुत्सेन[12] विकल्पो भवति । एष चाप्त्यस्त्रितो वाविशिष्टत्वादुत्तरत्रानुवर्तितुं नेष्टः[13] । कुत्स एवानुवर्तते नासत्याभ्यामतः[14] प्राक् । त्रितः कूपेऽवहितो देवान्हवत इति[15] त्रितोक्तौ कुत्सोक्तौ च संगतत्वाद्विकल्पः । उक्तं चार्षानुक्रमण्यां ।

चंद्रमाःसूक्तमाप्त्यं च[16] त्रितं प्रतिबभावृषिं[17] ।

पंक्तिश्छंदः । अंत्या त्रिष्टुप् । पांक्तमिति शिष्टा जगत्य इत्यपवादः[18] । अष्टमी महाबृहती यवमध्या । चत्वारोऽष्टका जागतश्च महाबृहतीत्युक्ता मध्ये चेद्यवमध्ये[19]त्युक्तेत्यर्थः । तेन दशकश्चेद्यवमध्येत्याद्यंन्यासां यवमध्यानां निवृत्तिः ॥

१०७. तिस्र ऋचो यस्मिन्सूक्ते तत्तृचं ॥

११२. आश्विनमिदं सूक्तं । आद्यः पादो द्यावापृथिवीदेवत्यः । द्वितीयोऽग्निदेवत्यः । उक्तं हि देवतानुक्रमण्यां ।

[1] स यो वृषा MSS. [2] जातवेदे मध्यमस्थलसूत्रगाः W 1; जातवेदमध्यस्त्वस्तिलैसूक्तगाः I 4; जातवेदमध्यस्त्वषिलसूक्तगाः P 1; जातवेदमध्यास्त्वखिलसूक्तशः P 2, I 2. [3] °कां P 2, I 2. [4] W 1; आद्यंतपदार्थैर्हतम् I 4, P 1; आद्यंतं पडार्थैहनं P 2, °हतम् I 2. [5] °भट MSS. [6] W 1; यद्येक° P 2, I 2; पद्येका° P 1; दोद्येका° I 4. [7] Ver. 17. [8] P 1, P 2, I 4; वियुक्ता I 2; निरुक्तना° W 1. [9] °र्थं MSS. Cp. comm. to I, 50. [10] Pân. VI, iv, 148. [11] P 1; °क्ते P 2, I 2; °क्तो I 4. [12] कुत्सो न P 1, P 2, I 2; कुत्सेत I 4. [13] W 1; नेष्ट P 1, I 4; °त्र तु न निवर्तते P 2, I 2. [14] I, 116. [15] Ver. 17. [16] वा P 1. [17] Cp. Nirukta, IV, 6. [18] जगत्यपवादः MSS. [19] Introd. § 9, 10.

ईळे द्यावापृथिव्योराद्यःपादः परोऽग्नय आश्विनं तच्च सूक्तं[1] ॥
अंत्ये द्वे त्रिष्टुभौ । शिष्टास्त्रयोविंशतिर्जगत्यः । आंगिरसः कुत्सः ॥ ७ ॥

११६. दीर्घतमस ऋषेः पुत्रः कक्षीवान्नामर्षिः । स उशिक्प्रसूतः । अंगराजस्य या महिषी तस्या या प्रधानदासी सोशिङ्नाम । उशिग् वष्टेः कांतिकर्मणः । पृषोदरादिः । पुरा किल गंगायामंगराजो युवतिभिः स्वपत्नीभिः सह जले चिक्रीड । तत्समीपं स्रोतसा वृद्धोऽंधो दुर्बलो दुर्गंधो[2]ऽशक्तो[3]ऽयमिति पतिद्वेषिण्या भार्यया पुत्रैर्दासैश्च प्लवे बद्धो गंगायां मध्ये प्रक्षिप्तः सर्वज्ञो महर्षिर्दीर्घतमा आजगाम[4] । तं दृष्ट्वांगराजोऽपि बंधादुन्मुच्य स्थानं चास्मै कल्पयित्वा हे भगवन्नपुत्रस्य मम ज्येष्ठ-महिष्यां पुत्रोत्पत्तिं कुर्विति ययाचे । स च तथेति प्रतिपेदे । अथ राजापि महिषीमुवाच । ऋषिं गच्छेति । सा चायमृषिर्वृद्धोऽंधो दुर्बलः[5] सुगंधेतरगंधाढ्य[6] इति मत्वा राज्ञश्च भीता[7]स्मै स्वदासीं प्राहिणोत् । सा चांगराजमहिष्या प्रेरिता सर्वज्ञेन दीर्घतमसा दासीति ज्ञात्वा मंत्रपूतजलाभिषिक्ता[8] महातेजस्विन्यृषिपत्न्यभूत् । स तस्यां कक्षीवंतमुत्पादयामास । स एवार्थः समाम्नायते । कक्षीवंतं य औशिज[9] इति तदेतदाह । उशिक्प्रसूत इति ॥ आश्विनं वै । इदमादीनि पंच सूक्तान्यश्विदेवत्यानि । तुह्यादिसूक्ते वैशब्दः पंचेत्यर्थ इत्युक्तं ॥

१२०. अश्विदेवत्यं । कक्षीवान् । अथ स्वप्नस्य निर्विद इत्यंत्या दुःस्वप्ननाशिनी दुःस्वप्नजनितदोष-दुःखं नाशयति परिहरतीत्यर्थः । अत्राद्या गायत्री त्रिपदा । द्वितीया ककुबुष्णिक् । तृतीयाचतुर्थ्यौ द्वे क्रमेण काविराण्नष्टरूप्यौ । पंचमी तनुशिरा । षष्ठ्यक्षरैरुष्णिक् । षष्ठ्यृगष्टाविंशत्यक्षरसंख्ययोष्णिक्त्वं संपादनीयं न तु पादभेदात् । अथ सप्तमी व्यूहेन विष्टारबृहती । अथाष्टमी कृतिरनुष्टुप् । अथ नवमी विराट् । अथ दशम्याद्यास्तिस्रो गायत्र्यः[10] । [आदितो द्वे गायत्र्यौ । अथ द्वे अनुष्टुभौ । अथोष्णिहौ । द्वृचा इति यज्ञताः । अथवा विद्वांसाविहुर इत्येषोष्णिक् । ननु च । चतुर्विंशतिर्गा-यत्र्यष्टाविंशतिरुष्णिगिति लक्षणमुक्तं । तत्किं विद्वांसाविहुर इत्यस्य गायत्रीत्वमुष्णिक्त्वं वोच्यते । इयं हि पंचविंशत्यक्षरा । किं च । ऊनाधिकेनैकेनेति[11] सूत्रे भुरिग्गायत्र्युदाहरणं चैषेत्युक्तं । उच्यते । ब्राह्मणद्वयदर्शनादेवमुक्तं । व्यूहेन चाक्षरसंपत्तिः । सर्वश्रुतिदर्शी ह्ययमाचार्यः । आसां तृतीयादितिसृणां

[1] ईळे द्यावापृथिवी आद्यः पादः परो ग्नयः आंश्विनं चैव सूक्तं P 1, P 2, I 2; ईळे द्यावा-पृथिवी पूर्वचित्तये द्यावापृथिव्योराद्यः पादः परोऽग्नये आश्विनं तच्च सूक्तं W 1; ईळे द्यावापृथिवी यु आद्यः पादः परो ग्नं यः (sic) I 4, omitting the rest.

[2] दुर्धरो W 1.

[3] दुरितासक्तो P 1, P 2, I 2, I 4.

[4] W 1; जगाम P 1, P 2, I 2, I 4.

[5] W 1; वृद्धौ जन्य इति P 2; वृद्धोऽंधो दुर्बलः जन्य इति I 2; वृद्धो धोऽजन्य इति I 4, P 1.

[6] W 1; दुर्गंधतरगंधाढ्यः I 4, P 2, I 2.

[7] W 1; भीत्वा I 4; भाषा° P 1, P 2, I 2.

[8] °क्ता W 1; °भिक्षिक्ता I 2; °भ्युदिता P 1; °भ्युता I 4; °भ्युक्षिता P 2.

[9] *Rigv.* I, 18, 1.

[10] P 2, I 2, I 4; the whole of the comm. on this hymn is omitted in P 1.

[11] Introd. § 3, 4, and comm.

ताननुक्रमंत एवोदाहरिष्याम[1] इति वचनात्कविराडादिविशेषण एव वाच्ये पूर्वविकल्पेन गायत्रा-
नुष्टुभौष्णिहा वृथा इति वचनं सामान्यसंज्ञाविज्ञाता अदृष्टफलप्रदा इति वक्तुं] ॥[2]

१२१. पंचदश । इंद्रो वा विश्वे देवा वा तत्र देवताः । चेत्यनादेशसिद्धेंद्रत्वार्थं नाश्विनविकल्पार्थं । आश्विनं वा[3] इति पंचसूक्तान्वयस्य पूर्वेणैव पूर्णत्वान्निवृत्तौ हि तौ ॥८॥

१२२. आ वो रुवण्युमिति विराड्रूपे । प्र वश्चेति विश्वेदेवानुकर्षणं चकारेण न कृतं । चेत्यनुवृत्तिर्मा भूदिति ॥

१२५. राज्ञां च दानस्तुतय[4] इति स्वनयस्य राजत्वं । तस्येंद्रसखस्य दानं प्रस्तूयते कक्षीवता । उप क्षरंति सिंधव इति द्वे जगत्यौ ॥

१२६. इतिशब्द आश्चर्ये । दानेन तुष्टः कक्षीवान् भावयव्यं स्वनयं पंचभिर्ऋग्भिस्तुष्टाव । भावयव्य इति स्वनय[5] एवोच्यते तत्पुत्रत्वात् । यथा । आ रुद्रास[6] इति रुद्रपुत्रा मरुतः । उप मा श्यावाः स्वनयेन दत्ता[7] इति दर्शनात् । अयमेव हि तत्र सूक्ते सिंधावधि क्षियतो भाव्यस्येति[8] प्रस्तुतः । लाघवाय तमस्तौदिति वाच्ये भावयव्यं तुष्टावग्रहणमनुक्रमण्यंतरानुकरणं[9] । तथैव कक्षीवान्ग्रहणं । प्रकृतत्वात्तस्यैव हि कर्तृत्वं सिद्धं भवति । ते च भावयव्यरोमशयोर्दंपत्योर्जायापत्योः संवादः सरसवाक्यप्रबंधः[10] । रोमशेति स्वनयभार्याया हि नाम । या तेनोच्यते सा देवतेति[11] संवादेषु सर्वत्र वक्तृप्रतिसंबंधिनोर्देवतात्वमिति । यस्य वाक्यं स ऋषिरिति[12] वक्त्रोरनयोरेवर्षित्वं ॥

१२७. दिवोदासस्य राज्ञः पुत्रो दैवोदासिः । परुच्छेपो नामर्षिः । पारुच्छेपं परुच्छेपराजर्षिदृष्टं सर्वं प्राग्वेदिषद[13] इत्यस्मादात्यष्टम् अत्यष्टिच्छंदसा व्याप्तं । तत्र पारुच्छेपेऽतिधृतिः षष्ठी । पारुच्छेपमात्यष्टमित्यस्मिन्नसत्यनादेशे त्रिष्टुप्त्वं स्यात् । बहुश उक्तौ च गुरुत्वं स्यात् । सर्वमित्यसति प्र सु स्म मैत्रावरुणं त्वंत्ये लिंगोक्तदेवत्ये अंत्या त्रिष्टुबिति[14] शिष्टानां जगतीत्वं स्यात् ॥

१२९. षष्ठींदुदेवत्या । इंदोर्देवताख्योर्गुणो ङीप् । प्रप्रा वो अस्मे स्वयशोभिरिति द्वे अतिशक्वर्यौ । अष्टेः सर्वतोऽक्तिन्नर्थादित्येक इति न ङीप् । अंत्येंद्र याहीत्यादि पररूपं[15] । समिधाग्निं दुवस्यतेत्यू षु ब्रवाणि त[16] इति सूक्ते दर्शनात् ॥

१३२. युवं तमिंद्रापर्वतेत्यर्धर्च ऐंद्रापर्वतदेवत्यः । इंद्रश्च पर्वतश्चेति देवताद्वंद्वे[17] चेत्यानङ् । अस्यादिवृद्धिः । उत्तरपदवृद्धिर्न[18] छंदोवत्वाभावात् ॥

[1] Introd. § 3, 8. [2] The comm. enclosed in brackets is that of W 1, corresponding to the various reading in the text of that MS. It will appear that the only practical difference in the two readings is that verse 2 is stated in W 1 to be ushnih or gâyatrî. [3] See sûtra on I, 116. [4] Introd. § 2, 23. [5] Cp. Sâyana on *Rigv.* I, 125, 1; *Sâṅkh.* Sr.-sûtra, XVI, xi, 5. [6] *Rigv.* V, 57, 1. [7] I, 126, 3. [8] Ver. 1. [9] Cp. comm. on III, 43. [10] W 1, P 1; प्रतिबंधः I 4; संबंधः P 2, I 2. [11] Introd. § 2, 5. [12] Introd. § 2, 4. [13] Sûtra on I, 140. [14] I, 136. [15] Referring to the Sandhi between sûtras 129 and 130. [16] Âsv. Sr.-sûtra, II, viii, 7. [17] Pân. VI, iii, 26. [18] W 1, I 4;

१३३. आदौ त्रिष्टुबेका । अथ तिस्रोऽनुष्टुभः । अथ गायत्री । अवर्मह इंद्रेतीयं धृतिः । अंत्यात्यष्टिः । प्रथमातिक्रमे हेत्वभावादादाविति विस्पष्टार्थं ॥

१३५. चतुर्थ्याद्या अष्टम्यंताः पंचैंद्रदेवत्याः । चकाराद्वायव्यश्च[1] । उपांत्ये सप्तम्यष्टम्यावष्टी । शिष्टा अत्यष्टयः । आदितस्तिस्रोऽंत्या च शुद्धवायव्याः ॥

१३६. अंत्ये षष्ठीसप्तम्यौ स्वसामर्थ्यप्रतिपादितदेवतायुक्ते । सप्तमी त्रिष्टुप् । शिष्टा अत्यष्टयः । पारुच्छेपं सर्वमात्यष्टमित्यत्र सर्वग्रहणाभावात्र शिष्टानां जगतीत्वमाशंकनीयं ॥९॥

१३७. षष्ट्यक्षरातिशक्वरी । तस्येदम[3]भ्युत्तरपदवृद्धिश्छांदसी ॥

१३८. चतुर्भ्र्यंचं । संख्याया अतिशदंतायाः कन्[4] ॥

१३९. आद्या वैश्वदेवी । अथ मैत्रावरुणी । अथ तिस्रोऽश्विदेवत्याः । ऐंद्री षष्ठी । सप्तम्याग्नेयी । अष्टमी मारुती । नवम्यैंद्राग्नी । दशमी बार्हस्पत्या । एकादशी वैश्वदेवी । अंत्या त्रिष्टुप् । पंचमी बृहती । अन्या अत्यष्टयः ॥

एतत्सूक्तं वैश्वदेवं । तर्हि मैत्रावरुण्यादिबार्हस्पत्यांतः प्रत्यृचं देवतानिर्देशः किमर्थमित्याशंक्य परिहारत्वेन[5] पुरस्ताद्यैभिर्वैश्वदेवम्[6] अग्निरुक्थे मनुर्वैवस्वतो वैश्वदेवं हेति[7] च प्रोच्यमानवैश्वदेवशब्दस्यार्थमाह ॥

अन्यासामन्यदेवतासंबंधिनीनामप्यृचां सूक्तप्रयोगे सूक्तरूपविनियोगे सत्यन्यत्राप्येवं वैश्वदेवत्वं वेदितव्यं । सूक्तभेदप्रयोग ऋग्रूपविनियोगे यल्लिंगं विनियुक्ताया ऋचोऽर्थेन यत्प्रतिपादितं सा तस्या देवता । अत ऐभिरग्ने दुव इति वैश्वदेवमि[8]ति सूत्रितं । सूक्तविनियोगे[9] वैश्वदेवमिदं । अत्रैव विश्वेभिः सोम्यं मध्व[10]ग्नीति याज्येत्यृ[11]ग्रूपविनियोगेऽस्या अग्निदेवतात्वं भवति । यथा बभ्रुरेक[12] इति द्विपदासूक्तानी[13]त्यत्र वैश्वदेवत्वं । अस्या एव[14] बभ्रुरित्यनुक्रमण्यामृग्रूपे विनियोगे[15] सोमदेवत्वं । ऐभिर्वैश्वदेवमित्यादित एवास्मिन्नर्थे वाच्येऽप्यत्र वचनं बहुदेवतासंभवा[16]दनुक्रमण्यंतरानुकरणार्थं[17] चेत्याहुः[18] । अत्यष्ट्यधिकारो निवृत्तः ॥

उभयपदवृद्धिर्न P 1; उभयपदवृद्धिश्छंदोवद्भावात् P 2, I 2. Of all the MSS. only I 4 has °पर्वत in the text; W 1 has a *caret* mark below the â. Shad*g*. must have read ऐंद्रापर्वतो.

[1] This च is overlooked by M. M. in his Index.
[2] Sûtra on I, 127.
[3] Pâ*n*. IV, iii, 120.
[4] Pâ*n*. V, i, 22.
[5] P 1, P 2, I 2, I 4; °शंक्याह परिहारत्वेन W 1.
[6] Sûtra on I, 14.
[7] VIII, 27.
[8] Âsv. *Sr*.-sûtra, VIII, x, 5.
[9] W 1; वैश्वदेवमिति सूक्ते त्र विहिते सूक्तविनियोगे सोमदेवत्वं the rest; all that intervenes between सूक्तविनियोगे[9] and विनियोगे[15] being omitted by them.
[10] *Rig*v. I, 14, 10.
[11] Âsv. *Sr*.-sûtra, V, x, 10.
[12] *Rig*v. VIII, 29.
[13] Âsv. *Sr*.-sûtra, VIII, vii, 24.
[14] अस्या एव स बभ्रु° W 1.
[16] W 1; बहुदेवतासत्वाद् I 4; बह्वन्यदेवतासहावाद् P 1; बह्वन्यदेवतासाहचर्याद् P 2, I 2.
[17] W 1; °णां I 4; °नुक्रमण्यनुकरणां P 1, P 2, I 2.
[18] W 1; चेत्याह P 1, P 2, I 2, I 4.

१४०. दीर्घतमा नामौचथ्य उचथपुत्रः[1] । अनंतरापत्ये गोत्रत्वारोपाद् गर्गादि[2] यञ् । शाक्त्यः पराशरः । पाराशर्यो व्यासः । जामदग्न्यो राम इति[3] । उचथ्यादृष्यंधेत्यण् वा[4] । द्वित्रिष्टुबंतं तु । द्वे त्रिष्टुभावंते ययोः सूक्तयोस्ते इमे इदं चोत्तरं च । त्रिष्टुब्दशमी वा पक्षे । शिष्टा जगत्य इत्यपवादः । शिष्टा दश नित्यं जगत्यः ॥

१४२. एतेनान्यान्युक्तदेवतानीत्युक्तत्वाद् इध्माद्या देवताः[6] । इंद्रदेवत्या त्रयोदशी । नाराशंसतनूनपाद्युक्तमिदं सूक्तमाप्रिय इत्युक्तेः । आप्रशब्दोक्तौ हि तनूनपाद्वर्ज[7] ॥

१४३. तुह्यादिसूत्रेण[8] तु द्वे तत् षडिति तु तदित्यष्ट । इदमादीन्यष्टसूक्तान्यग्निदेवत्यानि । अष्टाविति वाच्ये लाघवाय तु तदित्युक्तं । द्व्यक्षरत्वे समेऽपि मात्राधिक्यात् । तु तदिति हि मात्राः सार्धास्तिस्रः । अष्टेति चतस्रः । अष्टाविति पंच । किंच । तु तदित्यसत्याग्नेयानीति स्यात् । तच्च गुरु ॥

१५५. अत्रादितस्तिस्र ऐंद्र्यः । चकाराद्वैष्णव्यश्च । उत्तरस्तृचो वैष्णव एव ॥

१५८. ऊदिति प्रगृह्यत्वं ॥

१६२. अनेनोत्तरेण च सूक्तेनाश्वमेधिकोऽश्वः स्तूयते । कुतः । चतुस्त्रिंशद्वाजिनो वंक्रय इति वा मा नो मित्र इत्यावपेत[9] तमवस्थितमुपाकरणाय यदक्रंद[10] इत्येकादशभिः स्तौतीति[11] च सूत्रे दर्शनात् ॥

१६४. द्विपंचाशत् । द्वे पंचाशच्च । विभाषा चत्वारिंशत्प्रभृतौ सर्वेषामित्यात्वं[12] विकल्प्यते । अल्पा स्तुतिः स्तवो यस्मिन्नेतत्सूक्तमल्पस्तवं । अन्येष्वसत्स्वल्पस्तुतिविशेषस्तुशब्देन द्योत्यते न द्वित्वं । तस्यर्ष्यादिभिरयोगात् । अत्र सूक्ते प्रायेण बाहुल्येन संशयोत्थापनप्रश्नप्रतिवाक्यानि संति । संशय उत्थाप्यते येन तत्संशयोत्थापनम् अचिकित्वाञ्चिकितुष[13] इत्यादि । प्रश्नः । पृच्छामि त्वा परमंतं पृथिव्या[14] इत्यादि । प्रतिवाक्यं । इयं वेदिः परो अंतः पृथिव्या[15] इत्यादि । ज्ञानमोक्षाक्षरप्रशंसा च प्रायेणास्ति । ज्ञानमोक्षाक्षराणां प्रशंसा चात्र क्वचिदस्तीत्यर्थः । तत्र ज्ञानप्रशंसा । य ईं चकार न सो अस्येत्यादि[16] । मोक्षो ब्रह्मसाक्षात्कारः । तस्य प्रशंसा । अपश्यं गोपामित्यादि[17] । अक्षरं ब्रह्म न क्षरतीति ।

क्षरः सर्वाणि भूतानि कूटस्थोऽक्षर उच्यते ।
अक्षरं ब्रह्म परमिति[18] गीतोपनिषच्छ्रुतेः[19] ॥

तस्य प्रशंसा द्वा सुपर्णेत्यादि[20] । पंचपादं पितरं[21] साकंजानां सप्तथमाहुरेकजं[22] यत्रे अधि[23] अयं स

[1] उचथ्य MSS.; उचथ marg. corr. by the same hand in W 1. [2] For उक्थ read उचथ in the Gana गर्गादि (Böhtlingk's Pân., vol. ii). [3] W 1 only; अनंतरा° .... राम इति omitted in all the rest. [4] W 1; उचथ्यादृष्यण् P 1, P 2, I 2; ऋष्यण् I 4. [5] Paribhâshâ to I, 13. [6] °द्युक्तदेवताः W 1. [7] Cp. Paribhâshâ to I, 13. [8] Introd. § 12, 3. [9] Âsv. Sr.-sûtra, X, viii, 7. [10] Rigv. I, 163. [11] Âsv. Sr.-sûtra, X, viii, 5. [12] Pân. VI, iii, 49. [13] Ver. 6. [14] Ver. 34. [15] Ver. 35. [16] Ver. 32. [17] Ver. 31. [18] W 1, I 4; परमम् P 1, P 2, I 2. [19] Bhagavadgîtâ, VIII, 3, which reads परमम्. [20] Ver. 20. [21] Ver. 12. [22] Ver. 15. [23] Ver. 23.

शिंक्ते येन गौः[1] सप्तार्द्धगर्भा भुवनस्य रेतो[2] गौरीर्मिमाय सलिलानीति[3] जगत्यः। शिष्टास्त्रिष्टुभः। एतदंतं। गौरीर्मिमाय सलिलानि तक्षतीत्येतदंतं वैश्वदेवमिति। श्रूयते ह्यारण्यके। अस्य वामस्य पलितस्य होतुरिति वैश्वदेवं[4] बहुरूपं बहुरूपं वा एतदहरेतस्याह्नो रूपं[4] गौरीर्मिमाय सलिलानीत्येतदंतमिति[5] सूच्यते[6]। वैश्वदेवाभिधिज्ञानादस्य वामस्य पलितस्य होतुरिति सलिलस्य दैर्घतमस एकचत्वारिंशतमिति[7]। अथ तस्याः समुद्रा[8] इत्यादिना व्याचक्षाणो देवता दर्शयति। अधि वि क्षरंति[8] ॥

इतिशब्दो[9]ऽत्रेत्यर्थे। समुद्रा इत्युक्ता वाचः। वाचो जलं। आपोऽक्षरं। ततः क्षरत्यक्षरमित्यक्षरशब्देनाप उच्यंत इत्यर्थः। तेनाद्योऽर्धर्चो वाग्देवत्यः। द्वितीयोऽब्देवत्यः। सा तस्या[10] इत्यादिकर्क् प्रस्तारपंक्तिः। शकमयं धूममारादपश्यमित्यर्धर्चेन[11] शकधूमः। शकधूम इत्युच्यते। उक्षाणं पृश्निमपचंतेत्यर्धर्चेन सोम इत्युच्यते। तेन शकमयमित्यस्या ऋचः शकधूमसोमौ देवते। त्रयः केशिन ऋतुथेत्य[12]त्राग्निः सूर्यो वायुश्च केशिन इत्युक्ताः। एतेनास्या देवता अग्निः सूर्यो वायुश्चेत्येव सिद्धे पुनः केशिन इति वचनमेषां केशिसंज्ञार्थं। संज्ञा चैकर्चाः केशिन[13] इत्याद्यर्था। चत्वारि वाग्वाच इति चत्वारि वाक्परिमिते[14]त्येषा वाचं स्तौति। तादर्थ्ये ङे। तेनैषा वाग्देवत्या। इंद्रं मित्रं सौर्यौ। इंद्रं मित्रं वरुणमग्निमाहुः कृष्णं नियानमि[15]त्येते सूर्यदेवत्ये। द्वादशेति संवत्सरसंस्त्यं। द्वादश प्रधयश्चक्रमेकमि[16]त्यनया संवत्सरात्मा संयक्स्यतः कल्पः कालरूपचक्रेण[17] वर्ण्यते[18]। संस्त्य इति। आतश्चोपसर्गे[19] इति। यस्ते सरस्वत्यै। यस्ते स्तनः शशय[20] इत्यनया सरस्वती स्तूयते। तादर्थ्ये ङे। यज्ञेन साध्येभ्यः। यज्ञेन यज्ञमयजंत देवा[21] इत्यनया साध्याः स्तूयंते। पूर्ववत्साध्येभ्यस्तादर्थ्ये। परानुष्टुप् सौरी। समानमेतदुदकमि[22]त्येषानुष्टुप् सूर्यदेवत्या। पर्जन्याग्निदेवता वा। पर्जन्यश्चाग्निश्च पर्जन्याग्नी तौ देवते यस्या सा वा। अंत्या सरस्वते सूर्याय वा। दिव्यं सुपर्णमित्येषा सरस्वंतं देवं स्तौति सूर्यं वा। तादर्थ्ये ङेद्वयं। तत्रानुक्तछंदस्काः शिष्टाश्चतुश्चत्वारिंशत्त्रिष्टुभः ॥

१६५. संवादः। केषां। अगस्त्येंद्रमरुतां। संवादः संभूयभाषणं। तत्र तृतीयापंचमीसप्तमीनवम्यो मरुतां वाक्यं। त्रयोदश्याद्यास्तिस्रोऽगस्त्यस्य वाक्यं। शिष्टा युज आद्या चैकादशी चेंद्रस्य वाक्यं।

संवादेषु च सर्वेषु स ऋषिर्यस्य वाक्यं तत्।
आत्मस्तवेषु य ऋषिर्देवता स एवोच्यते[23] ॥

[1] Ver. 29. [2] Ver. 36. [3] Ver. 41. [4] W 1 only has the intervening words; I 4 reads simply वैश्वदेवमित्यारभ्य; P 2, I 2 °देवं चारभ्य; P 1 °देवश्चारभ्य. [5] Ait. Âr. I, v, 3, 7–8. [6] P 1, P 2, I 4; सूत्रे I 2; omitted in W 1. [7] Ait. Âr. V, iii, 2, 14. [8] Ver. 42. [9] P 2, I 2, I 4; अतिशब्दो P 1; क्षरंतीति अधिशब्दो W 1. [10] Ver. 42. [11] Ver. 43. [12] Ver. 44. [13] कैशिनं W 1. [14] Ver. 45. [15] Vers. 46–7. [16] Ver. 48. [17] W 1; संवत्सरात्मना समकृतः काल[:] चक्ररूपेण P 1, P 2, I 2; समाकृतकालचक्ररूपेण I 4. [18] W 1, I 4; वर्ण्यते P 1; वर्ण्यते P 2, I 2. [19] Pân. III, i, 136. [20] Ver. 49. [21] Ver. 50. [22] Ver. 51. [23] सैवोच्यते P 1, P 2, I 2, I 4; सैव उच्यते W 1.

तेन[1] वाक्येन यः प्रतिपाद्यते[2] स स्यादेवता[3]।

तत्रेति देवतानुक्रमण्युपदेशात्। या तेनोच्यते सा देवतेति[4] स्वयमुक्तेष्वागस्त्येंद्रमरुतां सर्वेषां देवतात्वे प्राप्त आह मरुत्वांस्त्विंद्रो देवतेति। मरुद्भिस्तद्वानिंद्रो देवतास्य सूक्तस्य। तृतीयादीत्ययुगुक्तिराद्यायां मा भूदिति। एकादशी चेत्युक्तत्वान्मरुतां वाक्यमस्या मा भूदिति। तुशब्दो विशेषार्थः। गुणाद्धि परः श्रूयते। मरुदगस्त्यदेवतानिवृत्तिरूपश्च[5] विशेषः। त्रिष्टुप् छंदः। यस्य वाक्यं स ऋषिरिति[6] परिभाषया पूर्वोक्तदेवतानुक्रमण्या च वक्तार एव सर्वेऽत्रर्षयः॥११॥

१६६. अगस्त्यो नाम मैत्रावरुणिः। कुतः। वक्ष्यमाणत्वात्। अथागस्त्यस्य गोत्रं वक्तुमिच्छति[7]। यज्ञार्थं दीक्षणीयेष्टिं कृत्वा स्थितयोः। उर्वशीं। उरुणा सृष्टा। अशूङ् व्याप्तौ[8] व्याप्तिश्चात्र सृष्टिरूपा। पृषोदरादिः। बदर्याश्रमवासिना भगवता नारायणेन समाधिभेदार्थमिंद्रप्रेषिताप्सरसां क्रीडार्थमात्मीयोरुप्रदेशात्सृष्टा हि सेतीतिहासविद आहुः। अप्सरसं स्वर्गलोकवारयोषितं यदृच्छयागतां दृष्ट्वा सभायामवलोक्य स्थितयो रेतः शुक्लं वासतीवराख्यजलाधारे कुंभेऽपतत्। ततः कुंभान्महाघटादगस्त्यवसिष्ठावजायेतां प्रादुरभूतां। इयेजायीर्यसूक्ते[9] तु कथैषा संप्रपद्यते। तेनागस्त्यस्य मैत्रावरुणित्वं सिद्धं। तथा सप्तममंडलस्य[10] द्रष्टुर्वसिष्ठस्य प्रसंगान्मैत्रावरुणित्वं सिद्धं॥

१६९. द्वितीया विराड् दशकचतुष्टययुक्ता॥

१७०. यजमानेनागस्त्यर्षिणैंद्रे हविषींद्राय निरुप्ते हविषि मरुतामर्थे मरुद्भ्य इत्यर्थः। उद्यते होतुमुद्यिते सतींद्रागस्त्ययोः संवादः। इंद्रपरिदेवनातच्छमनार्थोऽगस्त्यवाक्यरूपः। तदुक्तं निरुक्ते। अगस्त्य इंद्राय हविर्निरुप्य मरुद्भ्यः संप्रदित्सांचकार स इंद्र एत्य परिदेवयांचक्रे[11]। न नूनमस्तिनो श्व इति[12]। ऐंद्रः। इंद्रदेवत्यः। इंद्रवाक्यस्यागस्त्यदेवतानिवृत्त्यर्थमिदं। अथ विषादशांतये कया शुभीयमभूत्[13]। श्रूयते हि। यत्कया शुभीयमेतेन ह वा इंद्रोऽगस्त्यो मरुतस्ते समजानतेति[14]॥

अत्र संवाद आद्या तृतीया चेंद्रस्य वाक्यं। चतुर्थींद्रस्य वागस्त्यस्य वा[15]। आदौ बृहती तिस्रोऽनुष्टुभः। अनुक्तेरंत्या त्रिष्टुप्। अगस्त्यः स्ववाक्य ऋषिः। इंद्रश्च स्ववाक्ये। सर्वत्र चेंद्रो देवता॥

१७१. अंत्याश्चतस्रो मरुत्वदिंद्रदेवत्या मरुत्वांस्त्विंद्रो देवतेति[16] दर्शनात् प्रायेणैंद्रे मरुत[17] इति च। आदितो द्वे मारुत्यौ॥

१७५. इदमादिद्वे सूक्ते आनुष्टुभे ते च त्रिष्टुबंते। आनुष्टुभं त्विति शिष्टा जगत्य इत्यपवादः[18]।

[1] येन W 1. [2] Omitted by P 1, P 2, I 2, I 4. [3] P 1; सा स्या W 1; शस्या I 4; शंस्याद् P 2, I 2. [4] Introd. § 2, 5; cp. Ind. Stud. vol. i, p. 116. [5] W 1; मरुदगस्त्यदेवतात्वं मा भून्निवृत्तिरूपश्च the rest. [6] Introd. § 2, 4. [7] I 4, P 2, I 2; वक्तुमिति P 1; वक्तुमितिहासयति W 1. [8] Cp. Naigh. II, 18. [9] *Rigv.* X, 95. [10] Cp. VII, 33. [11] Nirukta, I, 5. [12] Ibid. Naigama, I, 6. [13] *Rigv.* I, 165. [14] Ait. Br. V, xvi, 14. [15] W 1, P 1, I 4; आद्या तृतीया चतुर्थी इंद्रस्य वाक्यं अगस्त्यस्येतन्याः P 2, I 2; चतुर्थ्यामिंद्रो वागस्त्यो वा I 3. [16] See sûtra on I, 165. [17] Introd. § 2, 22. [18] Introd. § 12, 13; जगत्यपवादः MSS.

आद्या स्कंधोग्रीवी । द्वितीयो द्वादशक इतरे त्रयोऽष्टकाः । तत्रेंदुरिति व्यूहेन रेफेण तृतीयस्याष्टाक्षरत्वं[1] ॥

१७९. जायापत्योः । जायायाः पत्युश्च । कयोः । लोपामुद्राया अगस्त्यस्य च । संवादमाद्यं तृचद्वयं संपन्नरतिप्रयोजनं । अंतेवासी । अगस्त्यशिष्यो ब्रह्मचारी श्रुत्वांत्यं तृचमपश्यत् । तत्राद्यो तृचोऽगस्त्यभार्याया लोपामुद्रायाः । द्वितीयोऽगस्त्यस्य । तृतीयो ब्रह्मचारिणः । रतिर्देवता । सा हि पद्सूच्यते ॥

१८०. इदमादिद्वे सूक्ते गायत्रच्छंदस्के । आद्यानुष्टुब्गर्भा ।

तृतीया पंचमी षष्ठी सप्तम्येकादशी तथा ।
अनुष्टुभस्तु पंचैता बृहत्यंत्यापि[2] वा भवेत् ॥

अन्नस्तुतिः । सप्तमस्य देवतेत्यर्थः ॥

१८८. आप्रीसूक्तस्य देवता[3] अत्र ॥

१९१. उपनिषदिंत्युक्तार्थो[5] । अमृणसोर्यं । आपस्तृणानि सूर्यश्च देवताः कीर्तिताः । आमृण[6]सूर्यमिति प्राप्त उत्तरपदवृद्धिश्छांदसी । विषशंकावान् । शंका भयं । शंका वितर्कभययोरिति निघंटुः[7] । विषभीतोऽगस्त्यः प्राब्रवीत् । उच्चैरुच्चारणं कृतवान् । विषदोषनिवृत्त्यर्थं । न केवलमदर्शीदेव । दशम्याद्यास्तिस्रो महापंक्तयः । अथ त्रयोदशी महाबृहती । चत्वारोऽष्टका जागतश्च महाबृहतीत्युक्तं[8] । इति पंचमो द्वादशकः । आद्यानां चतुर्णां पादानामष्टाक्षरत्वं व्यूहेन । शिष्टा द्वादशानुष्टुभः । चेत्ययेत्यर्थः ॥

॥ शतर्चिनां मंडलं तु समाप्तं प्रथमं त्विति ॥

२. द्वितीयं मंडलं व्याख्यातुं तदृषेर्जन्मविवक्षयेतिहासमाह । आंगिरसकुले शुनहोत्रपुत्रो भूत्वा यज्ञेऽसुरैर्गृहीतो मुक्तः[9] । पश्चादिंद्रेणोक्तगृत्समदनामा भृगुकुले शौनकः शुनकपुत्रोऽभवत् स द्वितीयं मंडलमपश्यत् । शौनकेनापीदमुक्तमृष्यनुक्रमणे हि ।

त्वमग्ने तु[10] गृत्समदः शौनको भृगुतां गतः ।
शौनहोत्रः प्रकृत्या तु स आंगिरस उच्यते ॥
व्याख्यातेयं कथा पूर्वं शौनकाचार्यवर्णने[11] ॥

एतच्च सूत्रमगस्त्यापवादस्य गृत्समदस्यैवर्षित्वाय ॥

[1] Cp. comm. on Introd. § 7, 3. [2] Cp. comm. on Introd. § 7, 9. [3] Cp. comm. on I, 142. [4] Cp. comm. on I, 50. [5] I 4; °र्थं the rest. [6] W 1; अमृण° the rest. [7] Not in Yâska's Nigha*ntu*. [8] See Introd. § 9, 9. [9] इंद्रेण मोचितः marg. corr. by the same hand in W 1. [10] त्वमग्न इति P 1, P 2, I 2, I 4; त्वमग्ने W 1 (no particle). [11] At the beginning of Sha*dg*.'s Introd. quoted by M. M., A. S. L., pp. 230–9.

१. मंडलादिष्वाग्नेयमैंद्रादित्या[1] श्रुधीहवीया[2]दग्निर्दैवता ॥

३. आप्रमिति वचनात्सनराशंसं तनूनपाद्वर्जितमिदं[3] । एकादशकानि तु नाराशंसान्यःप्रश-
व्दोक्तान्यतनूनपांतीति[4] सूक्तं । सप्तमी जगती । शिष्टास्त्रिष्टुभः[5] ॥

४. सोमाहुतिर्भार्गवो भृगुवंश्य इदमादीनि चत्वारि सूक्तानि ददर्श ॥

११. सैका विंशतिः । ऐंद्रमित्याग्नेयनिवृत्त्यर्थं । विराट्स्थानाछंदस्कं । अंत्यैकादशी त्रिष्टुप् । सूते
विना ।

ङ्सेरम् व्यत्ययाच्छंदोवद्भावाच्छंद एव च[6] ।
अन्यारादितृतेयोगे[7] पंचमी सूच्यते[8] खलु ॥

२०. स नो युवेंद्र इत्येषा विराड्रूपा[9] ॥

२२. अष्ट्यादि । अष्टिरादिः प्रथमा यस्मिंस्तत् । अतिशाक्वरं । अतिशक्वरीछंदस्कं । उत्तरपदवृद्धि-
रपि छांदसी । चतुर्थ्यष्टिरतिशक्वरी वा । व्यूहेनाष्टित्वं । श्रुतिदर्शनाद्विकल्पः ॥

२३. ब्राह्मणस्पत्यं ह । इदमादीनि चत्वारि सूक्तानि ब्रह्मणस्पतिदेवत्यानि । तत्र बृहस्पते देव-
निद[10] इत्यादि दृष्टबृहस्पतिशब्दाद्बृहस्पतिदेवत्याः ॥१४॥

२४. अंत्या त्रिष्टुप् द्वादशी च त्रिष्टुप् । सा द्वादशींद्रदेवत्या ब्रह्मणस्पतिदेवत्या च ॥

२७. गृत्समदः कूर्मो नाम्नेदमादिषु त्रिषु वाशब्देन गृत्समदेन सह विकल्प्यते । अयं तु वावि-
शिष्टत्वादुत्तरत्रानुवर्तितुं नेष्टः । गृत्समद इष्ट एव[11] ॥

३०. षष्ठींद्रासोमदेवत्या । देवताद्वंद्वे चेत्यानङ्[12] । उभयपदवृद्धिः । सरस्वति त्वमस्मानिति[13]
सरस्वतिदेवत्योऽर्धर्चः । यो नः सनुत्य[14] इत्येषा बृहस्पतिस्तवः । तं वः शर्धमित्येषा[15] मारुती ॥

३२. द्यावापृथिव्यैका । आद्या द्यावापृथिवीदेवत्या । तत्रैकशब्दः प्रथमपर्यायः । एकेऽल्पप्राणा[16]
एको गोत्र[17] इति यथा । यथा य एक इद्धव्यश्चर्षणीनामिति[18] । द्वे द्वितीयातृतीये इंद्रदेवत्ये
त्वष्टृदेवत्ये वा । ततः सिद्धेऽप्येका द्वे इति पदद्वयं द्वंद्वशंकानिवृत्त्यर्थं । तदन्यतरेण सिद्धं चेदनुक्रम-

[1] Introd. § 12, 12. [2] *Rig*v. II, 11. [3] See sûtra on I, 13. [4] Paribhâshâ to I, 13. [5] I 2, P 2; षष्ठीप्रभृति षड् जगत्यः । आदौ पंच त्रिष्टुभः P 1, I 4, W 1; a marg. note by the same hand in W 1 says: षष्ठ्यादि जगत्यौ इति केचित् सुपाठः । सप्तमी जगतीत्यन्ये । षष्ठ्यादि जगत्य इति तु चिंत्यः । cp. Aufrecht, note on this hymn in his Index. [6] W 1; वा the rest. [7] W 1; अन्यारादितरर्ते इति P 1, P 2, I 2, I 4; cp. Pâ*n*. II, iii, 29. [8] पंचमी सूच्यते omitted in all but W 1. [9] The words स नो विराड्रूपा are omitted in the text and there is no comm. in P 1, P 2, I 2; no comm. in I 4. [10] Ver. 8. [11] P 2 reads उपांत्या दुःस्वप्ननाशिनी in the text, but has no comment, nor have P 1, I 4; यो मे राजन्निति दुःस्वप्ननाशिनी I 3. [12] Pâ*n*. VI, iii, 26. [13] Ver. 8 a. [14] Ver. 9. [15] Ver. 11. [16] Cp. Schol. on Pâ*n*. I, i, 9. [17] Pâ*n*. IV, i, 93. [18] *Rig*v. VI, 22, 1.

ध्यंतरानुकरणं। द्वे द्वे राकासिनीवाल्योः। कुचाविति शेषः। चतुर्थीपंचम्यौ राकास्तुतिः। षष्ठीसप्तम्यौ सिनीवाल्याः स्तुतिः। अंत्या गुंग्वादिषड्देवत्या॥

३३. अश्वादिमोक्षांतफलप्रसिद्धै तुष्टो मुनिर्गृत्समदाभिधानः।
त्रिष्टुप्छंदःपंचदशार्चकेन भिषक्तमं रुद्रमस्तौन्महात्मा ॥१॥
आतेपितीयं[1] यदि रुद्रसूक्तं मरुद्गणाः कीर्त्यते त्रिः किमत्र।
त्रयोदशयामाद्यमंत्रे च रुद्रः सर्वत्र वा मारुते स्तूयते किं ॥२॥
निपातभाजो मरुतो न चात्र प्रायेणैंद्रे मरुतः सूक्तदृष्टेः।
नैतद्ध रुद्रो मरुतां यत्पितासीन्निपातभाजो मरुतस्ततोऽत्र ॥३॥
निपातभाङ् मारुते न तु रुद्रः प्रायेणैंद्रेत्यादि सूक्तं च तत्र।
इंद्रेण सख्यातिशयादनुक्तं तेषां च तस्यापि च सख्यमेतत् ॥४॥
हनिष्यंतं वृत्रमन्ये[2] पुरेंद्रं[3] हित्वा[4] जहुर्मरुतोऽवर्धयंस्तं[5]।
प्रायेणैंद्रेत्यादिसूक्तेऽपि वाच्यं रौद्रे चेति[6] खलु किं तत्र नोक्तं ॥५॥
प्रायग्रहो बहुलार्थे यतोऽत्र तस्मादैंद्रे बहुशो योग एषां।
अनैंद्रेषु त्वल्पशो योग एषामित्येषोऽर्थो वेदितव्यो हि तत्र ॥६॥
कथं त्वभून्मरुतां वै पितृत्वं जगद्गुरोर्देवदेवस्य शंभोः।
यथा रुद्रो मरुतां वै पितासीत्तथेतिहासः प्रतिदर्श्यतेऽत्र[7] ॥७॥
शतक्रतोरसुरारेर्वधार्थं दितिस्तु गर्भं लभते स्म भर्तुः।
शुश्रूषमाणः किल तामथेंद्रो मायाविदामग्रणी रंध्रदर्शी ॥८॥
प्रकीर्णकेशीं च दितिं[8] प्रसुप्तामालक्ष्य[9] वज्री ह्यणुमात्ररूपः।
प्रविश्य कुक्षिं प्रबिभेद गर्भं मा रोद रोदेति वदंस्तु गर्भं ॥९॥
भित्त्वा गर्भं निर्गते वै महेंद्रे प्रबुध्य[10] सा रोदिति स्मार्तरूपा।
अत्रांतरे त्वंतरिक्षे तदासीज्जगज्जनित्री[11] ह्यखिलेशपत्नी ॥१०॥
वृषेंद्रमारुह्य गिरींद्रपुत्री सुरेंद्रवृंदैरभिवंद्यमाना।
नद्याहृतैः पंकजकुंडलाद्यैर्हारेण संभूषितसर्वदेहा ॥११॥
संसारवृक्षस्य कुठारकेण शशांकचूडामणिमंडितेन।

[1] W 1, P 1; °तर्यं P 2, I 2; पित्तरिकं I 4. [2] P 1, W 1, I 4; अन्यैः P 2, I 4. [3] सुरेंद्रं W 1. [4] W 1, I 4; हित्या P 1; हत्वा P 2, I 2. [5] W 1, P 1; वर्धयंस्ते P 2, I 2; वृद्धयस्ते I 4. [6] I 4; रुद्रे चेति P 1; रुद्रं चेति P 2; रौद्रे वै खलु W 1. [7] प्रतिदर्श्यतेऽधुना W 1; प्रदर्श्यतेऽधुना (◡ – !); प्रदर्श्यते only, P 1, P 2, I 2. [8] P 2, I 2, I 4; °केशीरुदितिं W 1; °केशीं रुदितिं P 1. [9] W 1; अवेक्ष्य P 1; °मवेक्ष्य I 4; °मवैक्ष्य P 2, I 2. [10] W 1; °बुद्धा the rest. [11] °भूज° W 1.

देवेन सार्धं सुरसिद्धसंघैः स्त्रीणां गणैश्चाप्यभिपूज्यमाना[2] ॥१२॥[1]
गर्भस्य मातुश्च तदार्तनादं शुश्राव आकाशगता यदृच्छया[3] ।
सुरांगनानामवलोक्य वृंदं कृपापरा साथ हरं ययाचे ॥१३॥
वज्रेण भिन्नानि तु यानि[4] देवखंडानि गर्भस्य तनूनि चापि ।
समात्मके सप्तकभेदने न बहूनि खंडानि बहूनि संति ॥१४॥
एकैकमेषां लभतां शरीरं मदर्थमेतत्क्रियतां महेश ।
स्युश्चैव सर्वे तरुणाः सदैव स्वलंकृतास्तव पुत्रा भवंतु ॥१५॥
मा रोद वादान्मृतियोगतो वाख्याताश्च लोके मरुतश्च नाम्ना ।
सख्यं च तैरस्तु सुरेश्वरस्य सुरैरतुल्यं नियतं[5] महेश ॥१६॥
न ज्येष्ठता नापि कनिष्ठतैषां वेषो वयश्चैव[6] समानमेषां[7] ।
घृणाश्रित्वं व्यक्त[8]मेवं तव स्यान्मयि प्रीतिश्चातुला वै महेश ॥१७॥
पादादिकेशांतमलंकृताश्च भवंत्वेते सर्वमेतन्ममास्तु ।
तथेति देवः प्रतिपन्नवाक्यो देव्या यथोक्तं प्रचकार सर्वं ॥१८॥
इत्थं तु सिद्धं मरुतां पितृत्वं जगद्गुरोर्देवदेवस्य शंभोः ।
अथापरे वर्णयंतीतिहासं यथा रुद्रो मरुतां वै पितासीत् ॥१९॥
इमां हि[9] गोरूपधरां तु[9] पृश्निं वृषोऽथ भूत्वा रमयन्महेशः ।
अजीजनन्मरुतः पृश्निपुत्रा रुद्रस्य पुत्रा अपि ते बभूवुः ॥२०॥
रौद्रेषु[10] सूक्तेष्वथ मारुतेषु कथाद्वयं श्रूयते तत्र तत्र ॥

३५. अपोनप्त्रियं । अपोनप्तृपांनप्तृभ्यां घः । छ च[11] । अपांनपाद्देवत्यं । वरुणवाचिनोऽपांनपाच्छब्दस्यापोनप्तृभावः प्रत्ययसंनियोगेन हि निपात्यते ॥

३६. इदमादिद्वे सूक्ते ऋतुदेवत्ये जगतीछंदस्के च । ऋतुदेवताः सर्वत्रेत्युक्ते[12]रिंद्रादिमित्रावरुणांताः षट् प्रत्यृचं देवताः ॥१५॥

३७. ऋतव्यं । तत्र द्रविणोदसश्चतस्रः । अश्विनोः पंचमी । अग्नेः षष्ठी । इंद्राद्यग्न्यंतद्वादशकस्य प्रतिसूक्तमृतव्यत्वप्राप्तौ सत्यां सामर्थ्यादृयोः सूक्तयोर्द्वादशस्वृक्षु निवेशः । ऐंद्रीत्या[12]दिदेवताशब्दानामृगन्वयित्वदर्शनात् । अर्धर्चपादान्वयश्च दुर्घटः । तथा च सूत्रकारोऽपि । ऋतुयाजेषु द्वादशेति सूत्रयति । तुभ्यं हिन्वानो वसिष्ठ गा अप इति द्वादशेति[13] ॥

[1] W 1; स्त्रीगणैश्च the rest. [2] ०सेव्यमाना W 1. [3] MSS.; hypermetric by one syllable (identical in scansion with the last pâda of ver. 7 in the var. lect. of W 1). [4] रूपाणि P 1, P 2, I 2. [5] W 1; महेश्वरस्य सुरैश्च तुल्यं महतां the rest. [6] वेषो वयस्येव I 4. [7] समानतैषां P 1. [8] W 1; युक्तम् the rest. [9] हि—हि W 1; तु—तु the rest. [10] रौद्रेयसूक्तेष्व० W 1. [11] Pân. IV, ii, 27–8. [12] Sûtra on I, 15. [13] Âsv. Sr.-sûtra, VIII, i, 8.

४०. सोमपौष्णं । देवताद्वंद्वादुभयपदवृद्धौ प्राप्तायां पूर्वपदवृद्ध्यभावश्छांदसः[1] । अंत्योऽर्धर्चः सोमापूष्णोरदितेश्च ॥

४१. एकविंशतिः । उक्ता देवताः प्रउगेण[2] । वायुरिंद्रवायू मित्रावरुणावश्विनाविंद्रो विश्वे देवाः सरस्वतीति प्रउगदेवताः सप्त क्रमेण देवता भवंतीत्यर्थः । तत्राद्यदेवतायास्तृचभाक्त्वा[3]पवादमाह । आद्ये तु तृचेऽस्त्वैंद्रवायवीति । तुशब्दो विशेषार्थः । आद्ये तृचे वायुदेवत्ये प्राप्तेऽयं विशेषः । आदितो द्वे वायुदेवत्ये । तृतीयैंद्रवायवी । मित्रावरुणादिसरस्वत्यंताः पंच देवता अयं वां मित्रावरुणेत्या[4]दिपंचतृचभाज एव । इत्यष्टादश गताः । अंत्यस्तृचो द्यावापृथिवीदेवत्यो हविर्धानाख्य एकदेवत्यो वा । प्रेतां यज्ञस्य शंभुवे[5]त्यादि ब्राह्मणे सूत्रे चोभयत्र विनियोगो दृश्यते । प्रेतां यज्ञस्य शंभुवेति द्यावापृथिवीयमिति[6] प्रेतां यज्ञस्येति तृचं द्यावापृथिवीयमन्वाह । तदाहुर्यद्धविर्धानाभ्यामि[7]त्यादि च । अभि त्वा देव सवितः[8] प्रेतां यज्ञस्य शंभुवाऽयं देवाय जन्मन[9] इति तृचा[10] इति द्यावापृथिव्याः । युजे वां ब्रह्म पूर्व्यं नमोभिः[11] प्रेतां यज्ञस्य शंभुवा यमे इव यतमाने यदैत[12]मिति[13] हविर्धानयोरिति । अत्र तृतीयः पादोऽग्निं च हव्यवाहनमित्यग्निदेवत्यो वा । तत्रांबितमे नदीतम[14] इति सारस्वते तृचे षष्ठे छंदोविशेषमाह । आदितोऽनुष्टुभौ तृतीया बृहती चेत्यर्थः ॥ नन्वेवं कस्मान्न व्याख्यायते । आद्यो द्वृचो वायव्यः । तृतीयाद्यास्तिस्र इंद्रवायुदेवत्याः । अथ मित्रावरुणावश्विनाविंद्रो विश्वे देवा इति चतस्रो देवतास्तृचभाजः । सप्तमतृचस्य देवतांतरदृष्टत्वात्सरस्वतीति निवर्ततामिति[15] । उच्यते । वायो ये ते सहस्रिण इति प्रउग[16]मिति ब्राह्मणं व्याचक्षाणेन सूत्रकारेणैंद्रवायव्योरेकर्चत्वस्य सारस्वततृचसंभवस्य चात्र दर्शित्वात् तथा हि सूत्र्यते । वायो[17] ये ते सहस्रिण इति द्वे तीव्राः सोमास आ गही[18]त्येकोभा देवा दिविस्पृशे[19]ति द्वे शुक्रस्याद्य गवाशिर इत्येकाऽयं वां मित्रावरुणेति पंच तृचा गार्त्समदं प्रउगमित्येतदाचक्षत[20] इत्येष हि तृचभाग्भ्यः सप्तभ्यः प्रउगदेवताभ्यस्तृचं प्रयच्छन्नयं वां मित्रावरुणेति पंच तृचा इति मित्रावरुणादिसरस्वत्यंते[21]भ्यश्चतुर्थ्याद्यष्टादश्यंतान् पंच तृचान्दत्त्वे[22]वात्मैकर्चाय हि वायवे लब्धैकर्चाभ्यां द्वाभ्यामिंद्रवायुभ्यां च तीव्रा इति वायव्यामुभेत्यैंद्रवायव्यौ[22] च यथाक्रमं ददाति । मंत्रे लिंगं[23] चेत्येवमनुस्मृतं भवति ॥

[1] This comment in W 1 only. [2] See sûtra on I, 3. [3] तृचत्वोक्ताव° W 1. [4] Ver. 4. [5] Ver. 19. [6] Ait. Br. V, xvii, 9. [7] Ibid. I, xxix, 3–4. [8] *Rig*v. I, 24, 3. [9] I, 20, 1. [10] Âsv. *Sr.*-sûtra, VIII, ix, 5. [11] *Rig*v. X, 13, 1. [12] X, 13, 2. [13] Âsv. *Sr.*-sûtra, IV, ix, 4. [14] Ver. 16. [15] W 1; सप्तमस्तृचः यद्देवतांतरावदृष्टत्वात् सरस्वती निवर्त्ततामिति P 1, P 2, I 2. [16] Ait. Br. IV, xxxi, 6. [17] There is a lacuna in W 1 between उच्यते and वायो. [18] *Rig*v. I, 23, 1. [19] Ibid. ver. 3. [20] Âsv. *Sr.*-sûtra, VII, vi, 2–3. [21] W 1; °सरस्वत्यंताः P 1, P 2, I 2, I 4, all of which omit the rest of the comm. on this hymn. [22] W 1, which is corrupt in this passage, reads: तृचां दत्वा इव आत्मा एकभावे हि वायवै तब्धैकर्चाभ्यां वार्यमिंद्रवायुभ्यां च तीव्रा इति वायव्यादुभयत्यैंद्रवायव्यौ (sic). [23] लिंगे W 1.

४३. गृणमित्येव । द्वितीयातिशक्वर्येष्टिर्वा । कनिक्रददित्यादिसूक्तद्वयस्य देवतामाह । एताभ्यां प्रदक्षिणित् कनिक्रददित्येताभ्यां सूक्ताभ्यामृषिर्गृत्समदोऽध्वनि मार्गे वाश्यमानं (वाशृ शब्दे । दिवादि । अनुदात्तेत्) शकुंतं कपिंजलाख्यं पक्षिरूपिणमिंद्रं तुष्टाव । अस्तौदिति लाघवेन वाच्ये तुष्टावेत्युपदेशप्रत्यभिज्ञानार्थं । उक्तं हि बृहद्देवतायां व्यक्तं ।

स्तुतिं तु पुनरेवेच्छन्निंद्रो भूत्वा कपिंजलः ।
ऋषेर्जिगमिषोराशां ववाशास्याय[1] दक्षिणां ॥
स तमार्षेण संप्रेक्ष्य[2] चक्षुषा पक्षिरूपिणं ।
एताभ्याम[3]भि[4]तुष्टाव सूक्ताभ्यां तु कनिक्रदत् ॥

इति[5] । एताभ्यामिति योगविभागेन भगवानपीमां कथामसूचयत् । सूक्तद्वयं स्वस्त्ययनमित्याहुर्ब्रह्मवादिनः । तथा च सूत्र्यते गृह्ये । वयसाममनोज्ञा वाचः श्रुत्वा कनिक्रदज्जनुषं प्रब्रुवाण इति सूक्ते जपेदिति[6] ॥

॥ गार्त्समदं द्वितीयं मंडलं समाप्तं ॥

३. अथ तृतीयमंडले[7]ऽसत्यपवादे स्वयमृषित्वमनुभवतो विश्वामित्रस्य गोत्रविषक्षयेतिहासमाह[8] ।

इषीरथसुतस्त्वासीत्कुशिको नाम नामतः ।
इंद्रतुल्यः सुतो मे स्यादितीच्छन्सकरोत्तपः ॥१॥
ब्रह्मचर्यं तु चरतस्तस्मादिंद्रोऽभ्यजायत ।
मत्समोऽन्यो न चैव स्यादहमेवास्य पुत्रतां ॥२॥
गच्छामि सम्यगेवं स्यादिति मत्वा[9] शतक्रतुः ।
स गाथी नाम कुशिकादिषीरथसुतादभूत् ॥३॥
इंद्ररूपाद्गाथिनस्तु विश्वामित्रोऽपि[10] जज्ञिवान् ।
तृतीयं मंडलमिदं तपसा सोऽथ दृष्टवान् ॥४॥

इषीरथाद्बाह्वादित्वादिञ् । गाथिन इतीर्णताद्दण् । कुतः । तस्मात्तत इति चानुक्तेः । गाथिशब्दादणि गाथिविदथीति[11] प्रकृतिभावः ॥

१. अग्निः । मंडलादिष्वाग्नेयमैंद्रादिति[12] ॥

४. इध्मादिस्वाहाकृत्यंता आप्रीदेवताः ॥

५–६. इत्याग्नेययोः । प्रत्यग्निः प्र कारव इत्यग्निदेवत्ययोः सूक्तयोरन्यासामपि देवतानां

[1] M 1–3; वाचा संस्थाय W 1; ववाश स्थाप्य P 1; प्राय [प्राप्य] I 4; ययाशे दर्प्येण (sic) P 2. [2] तत्र स तमृषिः प्रेक्ष्य W 1. [3] पराभ्याम् M 1–3. [4] ०मपि W 1. [5] Bri. Dev. IV, 501–2 (M 2–3), 470–1, M 1. [6] Âsv. Grihya-sûtra, III, x, 9. [7] W 1; तृतीयं मंडलं दर्शिनो the rest. [8] Cp. M. M., vol. ii, p. xl. [9] W 1; गत्वा the rest. [10] च W 1. [11] Pân. VI, iv, 165. [12] Introd. § 12, 12.

द्यावापृथिव्याद्देवपितृमित्राख्यानां निपातोऽभ्यागतभोजनभाक्त्वं दृश्यत उपलक्ष्यते । उक्तं हि बृहद्देवतायां ।

द्वे आग्नय[1] उत्तरे त्वस्य[2] सूक्ते ।
द्यावापृथिव्यौ तु निपातभाजा[3]वापोऽथ देवाः पितरश्च मित्रः[4] ॥ इति ॥१६॥

८. यूपः स्तूयते[5] । षष्ठ्याद्याभिर्बहवो यूपाः स्तूयंते । किमर्थमिदं षष्ठ्याद्याभिर्बहव इति । यूपस्तुतेरेव सिद्धत्वाद्यूपदेवतात्वस्य षष्ठ्यादेर्विनियोगो यूपैकादशिन्यां नैकयूप इति । यत्रैकतंत्रे बहवो सपशवोऽंत्यं परिधाय संस्तुयादनभिहिंकृत्य यान्वो नरो देवयंतो निमिम्युरिति षड्भिः पंचभिर्वेति[6] सूत्रोक्तप्रयोगविशेषदर्शनार्थं । अंत्या व्रश्चिनी । अधिकरणे ल्युट् । यत्र स्थाणौ यूपो वृक्णः[7] स स्थाणुः स्तूयते । देवताण्यादिवृद्ध्यभावश्छांदसः । ङीप् । अष्टमी वैश्वदेवी वा यौपी वा ॥

१३–१४. इदमादिद्वे सूक्ते ऋषभो ददर्श स च वैश्वामित्रः । वक्ष्यति । ऋषभस्तौ वैश्वामित्राविति[8] ॥

१५. उत्कीलो[9] नाम कात्यः । कतगोत्रः । गर्गादिभ्यो यञ् । अयमिदमादिद्वे सूक्ते अपश्यत् ॥

१९. गाथी नामायं कौशिक इदमादीनि चत्वारि सूक्तानि ददर्श ॥

२०. द्वितीयाद्यास्तिस्र आग्नेय्यः । प्रथमपंचम्यौ विश्वेदेवत्ये ॥

२१. आद्याचतुर्थ्यौ त्रिष्टुभौ । द्वितीयातृतीये अनुष्टुभौ । पंचमी विराड्रूपा सतोबृहती च । एकादशिनस्त्रयोऽष्टकश्च विराड्रूपेति[10] लक्षणाभावेऽपि श्रुतिदर्शनाद्विराड्रूपेत्युक्तं । सर्वश्रुतिदर्शी ह्ययमाचार्यः । एषा हि लक्षणतः सतोबृहत्येव । अयुजौ जागतौ सतोबृहतीति[11] । छंदोनुक्रमण्यामपि सतोबृहत्येषा । तथा चोक्तं ।

सतोबृहत्यौ तत्र द्वे[12] ओजिष्ठं ते दश क्षिप[13] ॥ इति ॥

२२. पुरीष्येभ्यः । पुरीष्यनामकाग्नीनामर्थाय । पुरीष्यसंज्ञका[14] अग्नयो देवता इत्यर्थः । पुरीषमिति चयनस्याभिधानं । भवार्थे यत् ॥

२३. भरतगोत्रे देवश्रवा देववातश्चेत्युभावृषी ॥

२५. विराट् छंदः । उपांत्याग्न इंद्रश्चेत्यैंद्राग्निदेवत्या । आनङ् । अण्यादिवृद्धिः । नेंद्रस्य परस्येति[15] नोत्तरपदवृद्धिः । आद्गुणः[16] । शिष्टा आग्नेय्यः ॥

[1] आग्नेये M 1-3. [2] त्वत्र M 1-3. [3] द्यावापृथिव्या उपस्यौ निपाताद्यौ निपातभाजाविति P 2, I 2; द्यावापृथिव्यावुपसो निपाता M 1-3. [4] *Bri.* Dev. IV, 504 (M 2-3). [5] W 1; यूपस्तुतये the rest. [6] Âsv. *Sr.*-sûtra, III, i, 10-11. [7] W 1; यूपवृक्षः P 2, I 2; यूपो वृक्षः I 4; रूपो वृविक्णः (sic) P 1. [8] Sûtra on IX, 71. [9] P 1 and P 2 read कात्योत्कीलस्तु in the text. [10] Introd. § 9, 6. [11] Ibid. § 8, 4. [12] MS. of *Kh*ando'nukrama*n*î; सतोबृहत्यावत्र W 1; सतोबृहत्यौ त – – – P 1; सतोबृहत्यतः P 2, I 2; सतोबृहत्यंत (lacuna) I 4. [13] *Rig*v. II, 23, 3. [14] W 1 adds तिस्रः. [15] Pâ*n*. VII, iii, 22. [16] Ibid. VI, i, 87.

२८. आद्यौ तृचौ जागतौ । प्रथमस्य वैश्वानरोऽग्निर्देवता । द्वितीयस्य मारुतोऽग्निः । शिष्टास्त्रिष्टुभः । अग्निरस्मीति ब्रूपस्याग्निः परं ब्रह्म वा । नवम्या उपाध्यायस्तुतिः । सप्तमीवर्जस्य सूक्तस्य विश्वामित्र ऋषिः । सप्तम्या अथवाक्यत्वाद्यस्य वाक्यमिति[1] न्यायेन ब्रह्मर्षिः ॥

२९. पंचम्यृत्विग्देवत्या वा ॥१७॥

३०. ऐंद्रमिति मंडलादिष्वाग्नेयमैंद्रादित्यपवादः ॥

३१. ऐषीरथिः कुशिकः । स हेक्षांचक्रे विश्वामित्र इत्यादि । अभि तष्टेव दीधया मनीषामित्यादि[2] ब्राह्मणश्रुतिदर्शनादधिकृत एव गाथिपुत्रो विश्वामित्रो वा । सर्वत्र श्रुतिमूलत्वेऽप्यत्र श्रुतिरिति प्रत्यक्षश्रुतिरिति वक्तुं[4] । एवेति पौनर्वचयीयको[5] वाविशिष्टत्वादस्योत्तरत्र[6] निवृत्तिर्मा भूदिति । मांडलिको ह्ययं । उक्तं चार्षानुक्रमण्यां ।

कुशिकं शासदित्याहुर्विश्वामित्रं[7] यथाश्रुति[8] ॥ इति ॥

३३. उपितीर्षोर्विश्वामित्रस्य नदीभिः सह संवादोऽस्मिन् सूक्ते प्रतिपाद्यते । तत्र संवादे चतुर्थी षष्ठ्यष्टमी दशमी चेति चतस्रो नदीनां वाक्यं । शिष्टा विश्वामित्रस्य । षष्ठ्यां सप्तम्यां चेंद्रः स्तूयते । षष्ठीसप्तम्योस्त्विंद्रस्तुतिरिति षष्ठ्यां विश्वामित्रदेवत्वं सप्तम्यां नदीदेवत्वं च मा भूदिति ॥

३६. उपांत्यां दशमीं घोर आंगिरसोऽपश्यत् । सा च दशम्यृक् शस्यमाना यज्ञेषु निर्दहेत्सर्वमिति हि श्रूयते श्रुतिषु । उक्तं चार्षानुक्रमण्यां ।

ऋगेकास्मै[9] प्र यंधीति घोरस्यांगिरसस्य तु[10] ।
निर्दहेच्छस्यमानेति श्रूयते सा न शस्यते ॥ इति ।

सूच्यतेऽच्छावाकशस्त्रे । इमामू ष्वित्युपोत्तमामुद्धरेत्सर्वत्रेति[11] । सर्वत्र श्रौते कर्मणीत्यर्थः । सापि निर्दहेदिति श्रुतिदर्शनादेवं सुद्धारं विदधाति[12] । शस्यमानेति विशेषणं गृह्ये जातकर्मण्यंसाभिमर्शे इंद्र श्रेष्ठानि द्रविणानि धेह्यस्मे प्र यंधि मघवन्नृजीषिन्निति[13] चेत्यत्र[14] निर्दहो नास्तीति वक्तुं । न ह्यत्रांसाभिमर्शनं शंसतीति चोदितं ॥

३८. प्रजापतिर्नामर्षिः । स वैश्वामित्रो वाच्यो वा । वाच्योऽपत्यं वा । वाङ्मतिपितृमतामिति[15] ण्यः । द्वौ वा तौ । वाच्यवैश्वामित्रप्रजापती सहापश्येतां वा । न वैकोऽपि । एनयोर्मध्य एकोऽपि नापश्यदिति वा । अत्र पक्षे गाथिपुत्रो विश्वामित्र ऋषिः । उक्तं चार्षानुक्रमण्यां ।

[1] Introd. § 2, 4. [2] Ait. Br. VI, xviii, 2. [3] W 1; °रि–त्यक्षश्रु° P 1; °ति त्यक्षश्रु° I 4; °रित्यक्षरश्रु° P 2, I 2. [4] W 1; अत्र मूलमिति वक्तुं the rest. [5] W 1; पौनर्वाचिको P 2, I 2; पौनर्वचनिको P 1, I 4. [6] W 1; °त्तरनि° the rest. [7] W 1; °त्रो the rest. [8] W 1; °श्रुतेरिति the rest. [9] W 1; ऋगस्मै the rest. [10] W 1; °गिरसोऽपश्यत् I 4, P 2, I 2; °गिरस्यत् P 1. [11] Âsv. Sr.-sûtra, V, xvi, 2. [12] W 1; देषत्पद्धारं विदधाति P 1, P 2, I 2; अन्यत्रैतामृचं विदधाति I 4. [13] *Rigv.* II, xxi, 6. [14] Âsv. Grihya-sûtra, I, xv, 3. [15] Vârt. on Pân. IV, i, 85.

इमं त्रीण्यभितष्टीयं वैश्वामित्रः[1] प्रजापतिः ।
वाच्यः प्रजापतिर्वा स चतुर्थमुभयोर्न वा[2] ॥

इति । तत्रेमं मह[3] इत्यादि त्रीणि सूक्तानि चतुर्थमभितष्टीयमित्यर्थः ॥

५१. आदितस्तृचो जागतः । अंत्यास्तिस्रो गायत्र्यः । मध्ये षट् त्रिष्टुभः ॥

५२. आदितश्चतस्रो गायत्र्यः । षष्ठी जगती । शिष्टास्त्रिष्टुभः ॥

५३. सचतुष्केत्यनुक्तेर्वैश्विम्याय । आद्यैंद्रापार्वतदेवत्या । पंचदश्यादिके वाचे ससर्पर्यै । ससर्परी नाम वाक् । तादर्थ्ये ङे ।

ससर्परीमृचे प्राहुरितिहासं पुराविदः ।
सौदासनृपयज्ञे[4] वै वसिष्ठात्मजशक्तिना ॥१॥
विश्वामित्रस्याभिभूतं बलं वाक् च[5] समंततः ।
वासिष्ठेनाभिभूतः स सवासीदत्र[6] गाथिजः[7] ॥२॥
तस्मै[8] ब्राह्मीं तु सौरीं वा नाम्ना वाचं ससर्परीं ।
सूर्यवेश्मन[9] आहृत्य ददुर्वै[10] जमदग्नयः ॥३॥
कुशिकानां ततः[11] सा वागमतिं[12] तामपानुदत्[13] ।
उप प्रेतेति[14] कुशिकान् विश्वामित्रोऽन्वयोजयत्[15] ॥४॥
लब्ध्वा वाचं च हृष्टात्मा जमदग्नीनपूजयत्[16] ।
ससर्परीरिति द्वाभ्यामृग्भ्यां वाचं स्तुवन्स्वयं[17] ॥५॥ इति ।

अथ चतस्रो रथांगस्तुतयः । रथांगानि रथावयवा इत्यर्थः । अंत्याश्चतस्रोऽभिशापार्थाः । अभिशापोऽप्रियशंशनमर्थो यासां ताः । ताश्च वसिष्ठद्वेषिण्यो[18] नाम । प्रयोजनं शौनकोपदेशे च ।

[1] W 1; विश्वामित्रः the rest. [2] च W 1. [3] *Rig*v. III, 54. [4] नृपतेर्यज्ञे W 1. [5] W 1; वाक्च I 4; वाक् स P 2, I 2; च omitted in P 1. [6] W 1, P 1; सवासीदय P 2, I 2; °भूतश्च सत्यवाचीद गाधिजः (sic) I 4. [7] The preceding three lines are adapted from Bṛ*h*. Dev. 517: सुदासश्च महायज्ञे शक्तिना गाधिसूनवे । निगृहीतं बलाच्चेतः सोऽवासीदद्विचेतनः ॥ [8] The following three *s*lokas are quoted from the BD. (518–20); तस्या M 1-3. [9] सूर्यक्षयादिह M 1-3. [10] ददुस्ते M 1-3. [11] W 1, M 1-3; मति I 4; मतिं P 1, P 2, I 2. [12] W 1, M 1-3; सा वागामति I 4; सा वाममतिं P 1, P 2, I 2. [13] W 1, P 1; तामुपानुदत् P 2, I 2, I 4; अपाहनत् M 1-3. [14] उपेति चास्यां M 3; उपेति चाख्यां M 1-2. [15] P 1, I 4; न्ववोजयत् W 1; त्वयोजयत् P 2, I 2; बुबोधयत् M 1-3. [16] तानृषीन्प्रत्यपूजयत् M 1-3. [17] Cp. Ind. Stud. vol. i, pp. 119–20. [18] Cp. BD. 522: पराश्चतस्रो यास्तत्र वसिष्ठद्वेषिण्यः स्मृताः । विश्वामित्रेण याः प्रोक्ता अभिशापा इति स्मृताः ॥

वसिष्ठद्वेषिणो: पठन्तीत्यादि। ताश्च न वसिष्ठाः शृण्वंति। लिङर्थे लट्। यदि शृणुयुः शिरः शतधा भिद्येत। तथा बृहद्देवतायां।

शतधा भिद्यते मूर्धा कीर्तितेन[2] श्रुतेन वा।
तेषां बालाः प्रमीयंते तस्मात्तास्तु न कीर्तयेत्[3]॥ इति॥

५४. प्रजापतिर्ऋषिः। स चाभितष्टीयसूक्ते[4] प्रतिपादितगोत्रद्वयः। वैश्वामित्रो वाच्यो वेति। ननु च क्वचित्कर्थचिदिति सिद्धेरुक्तगोत्र इत्येतन्न वक्तव्यं। वक्तव्यमवश्यं। किं। नियमार्थं[5]। नासत्तत्र प्रजापतिः परमेष्ठी भाववृत्तं त्विति परमेष्ठिगुणस्य[7] वक्ष्यमाणस्य प्रजापतेर्वैश्वामित्रत्वं वाच्यत्वं च मा भूदयमेवोक्तगोत्रो यथा स्यादिति॥

६२. मित्रावरुणदेवत्यस्तृचो जमदग्न्यार्षो वैश्वामित्रो वा। आर्षं इति तस्येदमण्। जमदग्निर्ऋषिर्वेत्यर्थः। जमदग्न्यार्षं इति वचनं देवताभ्रांतिनिवृत्त्यर्थं॥

॥ तृतीयं मंडलं समाप्तं॥

अथासत्यपवादे चतुर्थमंडले वामदेवस्यर्षित्वायाह[10] वामदेवो गौतमश्चतुर्थं मंडलमपश्यत्॥

४, १. आद्याष्टिः। चतुःषष्ट्यक्षरा द्व्यर्धर्चा। द्वितीयातिजगती द्विपंचाशदक्षरा। तृतीया धृतिर्द्विसप्तत्यक्षरा त्र्यर्धर्चा। चतुर्थ्याद्याः सप्तदश त्रिष्टुभः। उपाद्या द्वितीयाद्याश्च तस्रो वरुणदेवत्याश्च वा। अग्निवरुणदेवत्याः शुद्धाग्निदेवत्या वेत्यर्थः[11]। पुरस्ताच्च परस्ताच्च षोडश शुद्धाग्निदेवत्या एव। मंडलादिष्वाग्नेयमैंद्रादिति सूक्तं॥

३. अग्निः। अत्राद्या वो राजानमित्येषा यजुर्वेदेऽग्नये रुद्रवत[12] इत्यारभ्य दर्शनाद्रुद्रगुणाग्निदेवत्या। अस्माकं तु बह्वृचानामियं शुद्धाग्निदेवत्या। अग्नेरेव विशेषणं रुद्र इति। रोरूयमाणत्वाद्रुद्र[13] इति निर्वचनमिति नैरुक्ताः। युद्धेषु शत्रून् रोदयंतीत्यैतिहासिकाः[14][15]। सामवेदे[16] त्वियं भगवतो रुद्रस्यैव प्रतिपादिका। सैषा रौद्री संहितेति[17] सामगाः समामनंति। तत्र हीयमन्यथाम्नायते[18]।

[1] *Rigvidhâna*, II, iv, 2. [2] W 1, P 1; कीर्तिता च P 2, I 2; कीर्तनेन I 4, M 2; कीर्तीनेन M 1; कीर्तिस्तेन गुणेन वा M 3. [3] तस्मात्तास्तु न कीर्तयेत् omitted in W 1, P 1, I 4; BD. 524. [4] See sûtra on III, 38. [5] किमर्थं W 1. [6] Sûtra on X, 129. [7] °गुणविशिष्टस्य W 1. [8] Pâ*n*. IV, iii, 120. [9] जमदग्निदृष्टो W 1. [10] W 1, P 1; °त्वमाह I 4, P 2, I 2. [11] Cp. M. M., *Rig*v. vol. vi, p. xxii. [12] Taitt. Sa*m*h. II, ii, 2, 3; cp. ibid. I, iii, 14, 1; Taitt. Br. II, viii, 6, 9. [13] Cp. Nir. X, 5. [14] I 4; युद्धेषु शत्रुं नादयंती° W 1; शुद्धेषु - - - न्ये दयती° P 1; शुद्धेषु अन्ये दयती° P 2, I 2; cp. Sâmavidhâna Br. I, viii, 14; also Ârsheya Br. I, 69. [15] W 1, I 4; °तिहासिकाः P 1; °तिहासिकार: P 2, I 2. [16] Sâma-v. I, i, 2, 2, 7. [17] Sâmavidh. Br. I, iv, 16. [18] I 4; °मपराम्नायते W 1; °प्याम्नायते P 1; गीयमानमप्याम्नायते P 2, I 2. What follows is omitted in P 1, P 2, I 4 up to यथा गाव° etc.

आ वो राजा तह्वोवर्ग[1] इति[2]। एकस्यैव हि मंत्रस्य वेदभेदेन देवताभेदो[3] दृश्यते। यथा। गावश्चिद्घा समन्यव[4] इति बहृचानां माहती सैव[5] सामवेदविदां[6] गोदेवत्या गवां तृणमुष्टि[7]दानदर्शनात् ॥

४. राक्षोघ्नं। रक्षोहेत्यग्नेर्गुणः। देवताणि चपूर्वेहर्[8]त्यलोपः। हो हंतेरिति[9] कुत्वं घकारः। आदिवृद्धिः ॥२०॥

५. वैश्वानर इत्यग्नेर्गुणः। वैश्वानरोऽग्निः ॥

१०. पदपंक्तिच्छंदस्कं। पंचमी महापदपंक्तिः। अंत्योष्णिक्। चतुर्थी षष्ठी सप्तमी वेति विकल्पेनोष्णिहस्तिस्रः। सप्तम्यष्टम्योः पंक्तित्व उष्णिक्त्वे चानु[10]क्तरूपत्वादवश्यं[11] ज्ञेयत्वाच्च पादव्यवस्थामाह। सप्तम्या इत्यादि। सप्तम्या मुख्यौ प्रथमद्वितीयौ पादौ पंचाक्षरौ। तृतीयः सप्ताक्षरः। चतुर्थो नवाक्षरः। अष्टम्याः प्रथमः पादः पंचाक्षरो द्वितीयश्चतुरक्षरस्तृतीयः सप्ताक्षरश्चतुर्थ एकादशाक्षरः। तद्यथा। कृतं चिद्धि ष्मा। सनेमि द्वेषः। अग्न इनोषि मर्तात्। इत्था यजमानादृतावः॥ शिवा नः सख्या। संतु भ्राता। अग्ने देवेषु युष्मे। सा नो नाभिः सदने सस्मिन्नूधन् ॥ असति पादव्यवस्थावचने सप्तम्याः पदपंक्तित्वे पंचकाश्चत्वारः षट्कश्चैकश्चतुर्थ[12] इति पादव्यवस्था स्यात्। अस्या एवोष्णिक्त्वेऽष्टकौ दशाक्षर इति स्याद् विराडुष्णिगिति[13] कृत्वा। अष्टम्यास्तूष्णिक्त्वादष्टकौ द्वादशक[14] इति स्यात् ॥

१३–१४. इदमुत्तरं च द्वे सूक्ते लिंगोक्तदेवते। स्वसामर्थ्यप्रतिपादितोषःप्रभृतिदेवत्यमेके वदंति। अपरे तु सिद्धाग्निदेवत्यमेव ॥

१५. ऋषिर्वामदेवः। बोधन्मना हरिभ्यामि[15]त्याभ्यामृग्भ्यां सहदेवस्य पुत्रकं सोमकं राजानमभ्यवदद् आशीर्भिरपूरयत्। पराभ्यामेष वां देवावश्विनेत्याभ्यामृग्भ्यामस्य सोमस्य राज्ञ आयुर्जीवनं शतसंवत्सरलक्षणमश्विनौ देवते प्रार्थयांचक्रे। सोमको हि राजा वामदेवस्य याज्यत्वादिनातिबंधुः[16]। सोमकस्य राजत्वं ब्राह्मणे[17] स्पष्टमीरितं। एतमु हैव प्रोचतुः पर्वतनारदौ सोमकाये[18]त्यादिना सर्वं हैव

[1] Sâmavidh. Br. I, iv, 16. [2] W 1 here adds in the text, and I 2 on the margin, the following quotation, which is evidently corrupt, and to which I have been unable to find any clue either in the Brâhma*n*as of the Sâma-veda or elsewhere: एतदभिप्रायं च पुराणवचनं। मंत्रा ऊचुः सुरा यूयं (सुरापितं I 2) तमोऽपहर चेतसः (पहरेत सः W 1)। येनाध्वरस्य राजानं न ये सध्वे महेश्वरं (°र I 2) ॥ इति। [3] I 2; देवता। भेदेन W 1. [4] *Rigv.* VIII, 20, 21. [5] सैव omitted in W 1. [6] सामविदां W 1; Sâma-v. I, v, 1, 2, 6; cp. Sâmavidh. Br. III, ii, 6. [7] W 1; तृणमग्नि° P 1, P 2, I 2, I 4. [8] Cp. Pâ*n*. VI, iv, 135. [9] Ibid. VII, iii, 54. [10] चानूक्त° W 1; चानुक्तरूपत्वाद° I 4; वानुक्त° P 1; चानुरुक्त° P 2. [11] W 1; °श्यज्ञे° P 1, I 4; °श्याग्ने° P 2. [12] Introd. § 4, 2. [13] Cp. ibid. § 5, 1. [14] Ibid. [15] Vers. 6 and 7. [16] W 1; °नातिस्तिक्यबं° P 1; °नास्तिक्यं बं° P 2; °नातितरां बंधुः I 4. [17] °णेन P 1. [18] Ait. Br. VII, xxxiv, 9.

महाराजा आसुरित्यनेन । बोधदिति द्वृचेन सोमकः स्तूयत एव वामिति द्वृचेनाश्विनौ स्तूयेते शिष्टाभिः षड्भिरग्निः स्तूयते ॥

१६. ऐंद्रमिति मंडलादिष्वाग्नेयावध्यर्थं ॥

१७. असिक्न्यां यजमान इत्येकपदा दशाक्षरा । विंशतिका द्विपदा विराजस्तदर्धमेकपदे[2]त्युक्तं ॥

१८. अत्र । गर्भस्थो ज्ञानसंपन्नो[3] वामदेवो महामुनिः ।
मतिं चक्रे न जायेयं योनिदेशात्तु मातृतः ॥१॥
किंतु पार्श्वादितश्चेति[4] ज्ञात्वास्य[5] जननी त्विदं ।
दध्यौ शांत्यै शचीं देवीमदितिं त्विंद्रमातरं ॥२॥
अदितिस्त्विंद्रसहिता गर्भिणीमभ्यगाद्वने ।
अदितींद्रवामदेवाः संवादमथ चक्रिरे ॥३॥
संवाद इति सूत्रेण[6] कथा सैषात्र[7] सूच्यते ।
नोक्तो वक्तृविशेषोऽत्र ह्युपदेशेष्वनुक्तितः ॥
अर्थतस्त्ववगंतव्यो वक्तृभेद इति स्थितिः ॥४॥
इंद्रोऽदितिर्ऋषिश्चास्मिन्मिथः सूक्ते समूदिरे ।
गर्भे शयानं सुचिरं मातुर्गर्भादनिर्गतं[8] ॥५॥
वामदेवं[9] प्रति ब्रूत आद्ययर्चा शतक्रतुः ।
द्वितीयादिभिरर्धर्चैर्ऋषिरत्राह पंचभिः[10] ॥६॥
न ही न्वस्येति सप्त स्युरर्धर्चा अदितेर्वचः ।
ममच्चन त्वा युवतिरित्यृचः पंच वै मुनेः ॥७॥
दौर्गत्यशांतिमत्राह वामदेवस्तथांत्यया ।
एवमर्थाद्वक्तृभेद इति वक्तृवशासनं ॥८॥
अर्थो[11] विवेकस्पष्टत्वादुपदेशेषु नेरितः[12] ।
ऋषिदैवतसिद्ध्यर्थं विवेकात्वेऽर्थ[13] ईरितः[14] ॥९॥२१॥

[1] Ait. Br. VII, xxxiv, 9. [2] Introd. § 12, 9. [3] °पूर्णो W 1. [4] W 1; पश्चादितश्चेति I 4; पार्श्वादितिश्चेति P 1, P 2, I 2. [5] W 1; ज्ञात्वा तु the rest [6] P 1, P 2, I 2; सूक्तेन I 4; वाक्येन W 1. [7] W 1, I 4; °नुसू° P 2, I 2; °वसूच्यते P 1. [8] In place of this sloka W 1 and P 1 have the following half sloka: आद्यैंद्रवाक्यं द्वितीयाद्यर्धर्चाः पंच वै मुनेः; I 4 has it as well. [9] W 1 omits the three slokas 6-8. [10] Sloka 6 is omitted by P 1. [11] अयं I 2. [12] W 1, I 4; निरितः P 1; नोदितः P 2, I 2. [13] विवेकत्वे त्वर्थे P 1; विवेकादर्थे P 2, I 2; विवेकस्त्वर्थे W 1. [14] Sâyana quotes this story in his introduction to *Rig*v. IV, 18.

२३. उपांत्यास्तिस्र ऋतस्य हीत्याद्या[1] ऋताख्यदेव्यो[2] वा । ऋतस्य देवे[3]ऽभिधायकत्वेन साधना[4] वैंद्र्यो वा । भवे छंदसीति यत्[5] तत्र साधुरिति[6] वा ॥

२६. ऋषिर्वामदेव आद्याभिस्तिसृभिरात्मानं स्वयमिंद्रमिव स्तुतवान् । स्वयं वेंद्र आत्मानं तुष्टाव । ततश्चाद्ये तृच इंद्रवामदेवयोर्ऋषित्वं विकल्प्यते । इंद्रवामदेवात्मनोर्दैवतात्वं च । परा नव । चतुर्थ्याद्याश्चतस्रः पंचर्चोत्तरसूक्तं च श्येनस्तुतिः । श्येन इति सुपर्णात्मनो ब्रह्मणो नाम । स आभिः स्तूयते । अथ नव श्येनस्तुतिः । किंत्वंत्यौ । अत्र पक्ष उत्तरसूक्तस्यांत्या श्येनस्तुतिरैंद्री वा । उत्तरसूक्तस्याप्यत्रैव देवताभिधानं लाघवार्थं । तथा हि । परा नवेत्यादिके त्वसति वचनेऽत्रैव पराः श्येनस्तुतिरित्युक्त उत्तरसूक्तेऽपि गर्भो नु पंचांत्या शक्वरीत्यस्यानंतरमाद्याश्चतस्रः श्येनस्तुतिः सर्वा वेति वाच्यं स्यात् । समापि त्रिष्टुभः । चतुर्थ्यादिचतुष्कं नित्यं वामदेवार्षं ॥

२८. ऐंद्रासौमं सूक्तं । इंद्रश्च सोमश्च । आनङ् । अण्यादिवृद्धिः । उत्तरपदवृद्ध्यभावश्छांदसः । शुद्धेंद्रदेवत्यं वा ॥

३०. चतुर्विंशतिरित्युक्तौ चोक्तं तीव्राश्चतुर्विंशतिरित्युक्तं[8] परिहृतं च । दिवश्चिद्घैव इत्युषोदेवत्यश्चकारादैंद्रश्च ॥

३१. अभी षु णः सखीनामिति[10] पादनिचृत् ॥

३२. त्रयोविंशीचतुर्विंशीभ्यामैंद्र्योरश्वयोः स्तुतिः क्रियते ॥२२॥

३३–३४. इदमादीनि पंच सूक्तान्यृभुदेवत्यानि । आर्भवं वा ऋभुर्विभ्वेति सूत्रयोः संधावायादेशे[11] शाकल्यलोपे[12] प्र ऋभुभ्य[13] इत्यृत्यक[14] इति ह्रस्वप्रकृतिभावौ ॥

३८. इदमादीनि त्रीणि सूक्तानि दधिक्राख्यदेवताया अभिधायकानि ॥

४२. पुरुकुत्सस्य पुत्रस्त्रसदस्यू राजर्षिः । त्र्यरुणत्रसदस्यू राजानाविति[15] वक्ष्यति । स आदितः षड्भिरात्मानं तुष्टाव । शिष्टा ऐंद्रावरुण्यः । पुरुकुत्सो गर्गादिः[16] ॥

४३. सुहोत्रपुत्रौ पुरुमीळ्हाजमीळ्हौ द्वावृषी सूक्तस्य चोत्तरस्य च ॥

४६. आद्या वायुदेवत्या । इदमाद्यावर्जमुत्तरं चेंद्रवायुदेवत्यं ॥

४७. आद्या वायव्या । ऐंद्रवायवं तु सूक्तं । एवं तर्ह्याद्या वायव्येत्यनुक्त्वा पूर्वसूत्र एव वायव्यादि

[1] Verses 8-10. [2] W 1; ऋतदेव्यो the rest. [3] P 1; ऋतस्य देव P 2, I 2; स्योपदेशे I 4; omitted by W 1. [4] W 1; अभिधायकत्वेन भावः । साधा वा P 1; अभिधायत्वेन भावः । साधु वा P 2, I 2; भिधायकत्वेनेछभावः । साधवो I 4. [5] Pân. IV, iv, 110. [6] Pân. IV, iv, 98. [7] वा in W 1 only. [8] Sûtra on I, 23. [9] Verses 9-11. [10] Cp. Introd. § 4, 4, comm. [11] W 1, I 4; °वयादेशे P 1, P 2, I 2. [12] Cp. Pân. VIII, iii, 19. [13] प्र ऋभुभ्यः omitted in W 1, P 1, I 4; ऋत्यक इति omitted in P 2, I 2. [14] Pân. VI, i, 128. [15] Sûtra on V, 27. [16] For पुरुकात read पुरुकुत्स in the Gana गर्गादि (Böhtlingk's Pân., vol. ii).

त्विंद्रवायवं त्विति वाच्यं लाघवं भविष्यतीति कृत्वा । सत्यं । तथा तु न कृतं । किं कुर्मः । प्रति-पत्तारो हि वयं न कर्तारः ॥

५०. दशम्येकादश्यावैंद्रदेवत्ये चकाराद्बृहस्पतिदेवत्ये च ॥२३॥

५५. अहम्याद्यास्तिस्रो गायत्र्यः । उत्तरं च सूक्तं त्रिगायत्र्यंतं ॥

५७. क्षेत्रपतिर्देवत्या आदितस्तिस्रः । क्षेत्रपतिशब्दात्पत्युत्तरपदाख्यापवादे श्वपत्यादित्वादणि[1] ङीप् । जसि यण्[2] । अथैका चतुर्थी शुनाख्यदेवतार्था । शुन इति वायोरभिधानं । आहुर्बृहद्देव-ताविदः ।

वायुः शुनः सूर्य उक्तश्च[3] सीरः शुनासीरौ वायुसूर्यौ वदंति ।
शुनासीरमिंद्रं यास्कस्तु[4] मेने सूर्येंद्रौ तु मन्यते शाकपूणिः ॥

इति । परा पंचमी पुरउष्णिक् । सा पंचम्यष्टमी च शुनासीराभ्यां शुनासीरदेवतार्थे स्तुतित्वेन । उपांत्ये षष्ठी सप्तमी च सीतास्तुत्यर्थे । सीता लांगलपद्धतिः । ते उपांत्ये अनुष्टुभौ । प्रथमाचतुर्थ्यौ चानुष्टुभौ ॥

५८. अग्निदेवत्यं सूर्यदेवत्यं वाब्देवत्यं वा घृतं वा स्तूयते ॥

॥ इति चतुर्थं मंडलं समाप्तं ॥

५. नमोऽत्रिभ्यः । अत्रिशब्दात्पूजायां बहुवचनं । नमः स्वस्तीति[5] चतुर्थी । अत्रये भगवते नमस्कुर्मः । अथवा[6] बहुवचनेनात्रिवंश्या गृह्यंते । कथं । इतश्चानिञ[7] इत्यत्रेर्ढकि तस्यात्रिभृगुकुत्स-वसिष्ठगोतमांगिरोभ्यश्चेति बहुषु लुग् अत्रयः । अत्रिश्चात्रिश्चेत्येकशेषोऽत्रयः । तेभ्यो नमस्कुर्म इति । अत्र पुरस्ताच्च[9] कृतेनानेन नमस्कारेण श्रुतिमहाभारतानुक्रमण्याद्युक्तमत्रिमाहात्म्यं सूचयति भग-वान् कात्यायनः । श्रूयते हि ।

यं वै सूर्यं स्वर्भानुस्तमसाविध्यदासुरः ।
अत्रयस्तमन्वविंदन्नह्यन्ये अशक्नुवन्[10] ॥ इति ।

महाभारते चात्रिमाहात्म्यमुक्तमर्जुनजन्मनि ।

[1] Cp. Pân. IV, i, 84; °त्यादित्वणि W 1. [2] W 1; क्षेत्रपशिब्दात्पत्युत्तरपदाख्यः । तदपवादो श्वपत्यादित्वादणि ङीप् जस् यण् I 4; °पत्युत्तरपदाख्युः । पदस्यपवादश्वपत्यंताद्यपि ङीप् जस् । यण् P 1; पत्युत्तरपदात् स्यः पदस्यवापदश्च पत्यंतार्थेत्वापीति ङीप् । जस् । यण् P 2, I 2; according to this Shadg. must have read क्षैत्रपत्यः, though *all* the MSS. read क्षैत्रपत्याः in the text. W 1 in a marginal note referring to क्षैत्रपत्याः remarks, दीर्घश्चिंत्यः. [3] M 1-3; वायुः शुनः सीरः सूर्यः W 1; वायुः शुनः सूर्यः च सीरः P 1, I 4; सूर्य नुः सीरः P 2; सीरः सूर्यः I 2. [4] शुनासीरं यास्क इंद्रं तु M 1-3. [5] W 1; स्वस्तीत्यादि P 1; स्वस्तीत्यादिना I 4; नमस्कारो-तीत्यादि चतुर्थी P 2, I 2. [6] W 1; अथ P 1, I 2, I 4; अत्र च P 2. [7] Pân. IV, i, 122. [8] Ibid. II, iv, 65. [9] W 1; पुरस्ताच्च वचनेन I 4; पुरस्तात्परस्ताच्च P 1, P 2, I 2. [10] *Rigv.* V, 40, 9.

भरद्वाजः कश्यपो गोतमश्च विश्वामित्रो जमदग्निर्वसिष्ठः ।
यश्चोदितो भास्करोऽभूत्प्रतिष्ठः[1] सोऽप्यत्राचिर्भगवान्[2] संबभूव ॥ इति ।

नमस्कार एवार्षानुक्रमण्यां प्रयुक्तः[3] । नमोऽत्रिभ्यस्त्वबोधीति । अत्रशब्दयोगादत्रिनामेति बृहद्देवताविदः । तथा हि ।

त्रिसांवत्सरिकं सत्रं प्रजाकामः प्रजापतिः ।
आहरत्सहितः साध्यैर्विश्वैश्चैवेति नः श्रुतं ॥१॥
तत्र वाग्दीक्षणीयायाम्[4]आजगाम शरीरिणी ।
तां दृष्ट्वा युगपत्तत्र कस्याथ वरुणस्य च ॥२॥
शुक्रं चस्कंद तद्वायुरग्नौ प्रास्यद्यदृच्छया ।
ततोऽर्चिभ्यो[5] भृगुर्जज्ञेऽंगारेष्वंगिरा[6] ऋषिः ॥३॥
प्रजापतिं सुतौ दृष्ट्वा तुष्टा[7] वागभ्यभाषत ।
आभ्यामृषिस्तृतीयोऽपि भवत्वत्रैव मे सुतः ॥४॥
प्रजापतिस्तथेत्याह भाषमाणां तु भारतीं ।
ऋषिरत्रिस्ततो जज्ञे सूर्यानलसमद्युतिः ॥५॥ इति[8] ।

अत्रशब्दोऽस्यास्तीत्यत्रिः । पृषोदरादित्वाद् अत इनि[9] नलोपे[10] चात्रिः । अथात्रेर्गोत्रमाह । भौमोऽत्रिः । भूम्या अत्रेति निर्दिष्टे प्रदेशे जात एष हि । अथ पंचममंडलवर्तिनामनिर्दिष्टगोत्राणां क्वचित्क्वचिदित्यादिपरिभाषोक्तमांगिरसत्वं निरस्यन्[11] गोत्रमाह । पंचमे मंडलेऽनुक्तगोत्रमात्रेयं विद्यात् । पंचम इति प्रथमादौ मा भूत् । अतश्चेमं षोडश कुत्स[12] इत्यांगिरसत्वमेव भवति । मंडल इति विशेष्यत्वाय[13] । पंचमे मंडल इत्युत्तरत्राप्य[14]नुवर्तते । किमर्थं । तं गूर्धय यो यजात्यग्निनेंद्रेणेति सूक्तत्रयस्य[15] पंक्त्यंतत्वेऽप्यपंचममंडलवर्तित्वाच्छेषमानुष्टुभं मा भूदिति वक्तुं । अनुक्तगोत्रमिति वृशो वा जान[16] इत्युक्तगोत्रस्य वृशस्यात्रेयत्वं मा भूदिति विद्यात् अवगच्छेत्सर्वानुक्रमणीजिज्ञासुः ।

[1] W 1; प्रनष्टः P 1, P 2, I 2; omitted in I 4. [2] W 1; प्यत्रिरत्र P 1, P 2, I 2. [3] W 1; प्रत्युक्तः P 1, P 2, I 2. [4] W 1, P 2, I 2; वार्मीक्षणांया P 1; वर्षीक्षणायाम् I 4. [5] P 1; त्रिभ्यो W 1, I 4, P 2, I 2. [6] W 1, I 4; आंगिरेष्वं° P 1; संतरेष्वं° P 2, I 2. [7] W 1; दृष्ट P 2, I 2; omitted in I 4, P 1. [8] This story is not to be found in the passage in the BD. referring to this hymn. [9] Cp. Pân. V, ii, 115. [10] अत इन् अलोपे W 1; अत इति नलोपे P 1; अत इति न लोपे P 2, I 2; अत इत्रि नलोपे I 4. Cp. U*n*âdi-sûtra, IV, 68. [11] W 1; निरस्यन्नांगिरसं । अनुक्तगोत्रमाह I 4; निरस्यन् आंगिरसः उक्तं च गोत्रमाह P 1, P 2, I 2. [12] Sûtra on I, 94. [13] P 1, I 4; विशेषत्वाय W 1; विशेष्यत्वात् P 2, I 2. [14] W 1; °त्र चानु° the rest. [15] *Rigv.* VIII, 19, 31, and 35. [16] See sûtra on V, 2.

पंक्त्यंतस्य च सूक्तस्य शेषमानुष्टुभं । विद्यादित्येव । अस्मिन् पंचमे मंडले सखाय इयः पंक्त्यंतम्[1] इत्यादौ शिष्टा ऋचोऽनुष्टुभो विद्यात् । इति परिभाष्यारभते ॥

१. बुधश्च गविष्ठिरश्च द्वावृषी आत्रेयौ । मंडलादित्वादाग्नेयमैंद्रादित्यग्निर्देवता ॥

२. कुमार इत्यृषेर्नामात्रेयो जननाम्न ऋषेः पुत्रो वृशो वा । उभौ वा वृशकुमारौ सह वेत्यर्थः । क्रमेतं त्वं चि ज्योतिमेत्यृचौ वृश एवापश्यत् । न कुमारो न चोभौ ॥

५. आप्रमित्युक्तेर्नात्र तनूनपात् । अत्राप्रीसूक्तदेवताः ॥

९. गयो नामात्रेयः पंचमे मंडलेऽनुक्तगोत्रत्वात् । ननु क्वचित्कथंचिदित्यादेरयमपवादः पंचमे मंडलेऽनुक्तगोत्रत्वमिति ततश्च तस्यांगिरसत्वं नास्ति परावतस्प्लुता गयः प्लात[4] इति प्लातस्य[5] वक्ष्यमाणत्वादस्य प्लातत्वमेव नात्रेयत्वमिति । नैवं[6] । तस्मात्प्रयादयमन्यो गयः । तत्र[7] च हेतुरत्र प्लातत्वानुक्तिः । न चोत्तरत्र प्लातत्वोक्तावृषभस्तौ वैश्वामित्राविति[8] परत्र वैश्वामित्रत्वोक्तावित्र लाघवं[9] भवतीत्यात्रेयोऽयं गयोऽत्रान्यस्मादृषेः । अत्र मंडले त्वेकस्य दर्शितत्वाभावात्पूर्वोक्तैव परिभाषा ऋषिश्चान्यस्मादिति[10] । न प्लात इति सिद्धं ॥

१०. चकारः[11] पंक्त्यनुकर्षणार्थः । अंत्या सप्तमी चतुर्थी च द्वे पंक्ती ॥

१५. आंगिरस इत्यात्रेयनिवृत्त्यर्थं ॥

१९. मृक्तवाहा इति विशेषणमात्रेयत्वसिद्ध्यर्थं द्वितस्य । गोत्रतोऽयमात्रेय एव । मृक्तवाहोविशेषणमन्यथ प्र पुनानाय चढ् द्वित आप्त्य[12] इति वक्ष्यमाणस्य द्वितादन्यस्मादन्यत्वार्थं । असत्यस्मिन्नयमाप्त्य एव स्यान्नात्रेयः । क्वचित्कथंचिदविशेषितविषयांगिरसत्वापवादेनात्रेयविधानादस्य चोत्तरत्राप्त्य इति विशेषितत्वात् । एवं तर्हि गयस्योत्तरत्र प्लातत्वोक्तेरिहात्रेयत्ववदेतस्याप्युत्तरत्राप्त्योक्तेरस्याप्यात्रेयत्वं सिद्धमिति चेद् अनुक्रमण्यंतरानुकरणं ब्रूमः । उक्तं ह्यार्षानुक्रमण्यां ।

मृक्तवाहा द्वितः प्लातः प्र पुनानाय चाप्त्यजः । इति ।

मृक्तः । गतः । परिचरणेन प्राप्तो वाह्रो वह्निर्येन[13] स मृक्तवाहा इति विशेषणार्थः । वहसो वा वाहा गताविति[14] नैघंटुकाः ॥

२०. प्रयस्वंत इति जसंतं प्रयस्वंतो हवामहे[15] इति मंत्रलिंगाद् एतदृषेर्नाम । प्रयस्वंत ऋषय आत्रेयाः संभूयापश्यन्[16] ॥

[1] Sûtra on V, 7. [2] Verses 2 and 9. [3] Introd. § 2, 3; cp. comm. on V, 28. [4] Sûtra on X, 63. [5] प्लातत्वस्य W 1. [6] नाशंका W 1. [7] अत्र W 1. [8] Sûtra on IX, 71; cp. III, 13. [9] MSS.; प्लातत्वं marg. corr. in the same hand in W 1. [10] Introd. § 12, 2. [11] W 1; चेति the rest. [12] Sûtra on IX, 103. [13] ग्निर्येन W 1; प्राप्नोति चरणेन प्राप्तो वह्निर्येन P 1; प्राप्नोति चरणो न प्राप्तो वह्नित्वेन I 4; प्राप्नोति चरणाम प्राप्तो विह्निर्येन P 2, I 2. [14] W 1; वहसौ वहा जगराविति P 1; वहसो वा जगराविति I 4; वहा सौ वहा जगराविति I 2; वाहा सौ वहा जगराविति P 2. Yâska's explanation, Nirukta, IV, 16, is different. [15] Ver. 3. [16] This comm. is omitted in P 1, P 2, I 2, I 4.

२२. प्रमाणमेव सूक्तादि[1] प्र समोनेति[2] वै यथा ।
विश्वसामेत्यृषेर्नाम स चात्रेयो हि गोत्रतः ॥

२३. शुस्रो नामात्रेयः । विश्वचर्षणिरिति विशेषणमनुक्रमण्यंतरानुकरणमेव सूक्तवाहोवत्[3] । विश्वे सर्वे चर्षणयो मनुष्या बंधवो यस्य स विश्वचर्षणिरिति विशेषणार्थः ॥

२४. बंध्वादयश्चत्वार ऋषयो यथाक्रममेकर्चाः[5] । एक ऋग्दृश्या यस्य स एकर्चः[6] ॥

२५. वसूयव इति जस्त्वम्[7] एवां अग्निं वसूयवः सहसानं ववंदिमेति[8] मंत्रलिंगात् । वसूयवो नामर्षेय आत्रेयाः संभूयापश्यन् ॥

२६. नवेत्येव । वसूयवः । गायत्री । अग्निः[9] ॥

२७. त्रिवृष्णपुत्रस्त्रैवृष्णः स च त्र्यरुणाभिधानः पुरुकुत्सपुत्रस्त्रसदस्युर्नाम राजानो च भरत-पुत्रोऽश्वमेधश्च राजेति त्रयोऽपि संभूयैतत्सूक्तमपश्यन् । चेति राजत्वानुकर्षणार्थः । राजानाविति द्विवचनादेव सिद्धेर्द्वावित्यनुक्रमण्यंतरानुकरणं । सर्वास्त्वृचस्त्रिमेवर्षिं मन्यंते केचित् । कुत इत्याह । नात्मने दद्यादिति । न ह्यात्मा स्वयमात्मने स्वस्मै ददातीत्यस्माद्धेतोः । तथा हि । यो मे शता चेत्यादौ[10] त्र्यरुणाय मे त्र्यरुणो ददाति तस्मै त्र्यरुणाय शर्माग्ने देहीत्यर्थोऽनुपपन्नः । अतोऽत्रिरेव सर्वास्वृषी राजानो दातारस्त्र्यरुणादयः । तेभ्यः शर्माग्ने प्रयच्छेत्यत्रिरग्निं प्रत्याह । अत्रिर्भौम इति । पूर्वस्मिंस्तु पक्ष आत्मकृतपुण्यपापयोरात्मन्यध्यारोपात् ।

आत्मैव ह्यात्मनो बंधुरात्मैव रिपुरात्मनः[11] ।

इत्यादावात्मानमेव प्रत्यात्मनो बंधुरिपुत्वोक्तिवद्यापि गवादिलाभहेतुभूतकर्मणार्जकोपायमात्मने गवादि ददाति । तस्मै त्र्यरुणाय मह्यमग्ने शर्म देहीति संबंधोपपन्निवर्तित्वात्[12] त्रीणामेवर्षित्वमुक्त-मित्याहुः ॥

२८. विश्ववारा नामात्रेय्यृषिका । आत्रेयी । अत्रिगोत्रजा । गोत्रोक्तिः पंचमे मंडल इत्यस्य ऋषिकार्षंचित्सू[13]त्रविषयत्वात् तत्र चा[14]स्त्रियमित्युक्तेः ॥

२९. ऐंद्रमित्याग्नेयावध्यर्धं । अत्र सूक्त उशना यत्सहस्यैरयातमिति[15] पाद उशनोदेवत्यः ॥

---

[1] This comm. (all MSS.) shows that Shaḍg. read प्र विश्वसामा only in the text, though all the MSS. (P 1, P 2, I 4 also) have the fuller pratîka. [2] Sûtra on I, 62. [3] °वाहावत् W 1; °वाहस्त्ववद्भितः I 4; °वाहास्त्ववत् त्रितः P 1; °वाहाः स च त्रितः P 2, I 2. [4] As to the Gaupâyanas and Laupâyanas, see comm. on X, 57–60. [5] यथाक्रमेकर्चाः W 1. [6] Only in W 1. [7] जसंतं W 1. [8] Ver. 9. [9] P 1, P 2, I 4 read in the text अग्ने गायत्रं only, and the above is the whole of the comm. on this hymn in all the MSS. [10] Ver. 2. [11] Mahâbhârata, XI, 80; XIII, 321 (quoted in Indische Sprüche); cp. Manu, VIII, 84. [12] W 1; °पन्नित्वाद् I 4; °पन्निमत्वाद् P 1, P 2; °पन्निं मत्वा I 2. [13] °चिदेतात्सू° W 1. [14] तत्रा च W 1; तथा the rest. [15] Ver. 9 a.

३०. अत्र सूक्ते ऋणंचयो नाम राजर्षिरपि बभ्रुणा स्तुतः । न हि केवलमिंद्र एव ॥

३१. उग्रमयातमवहो ह कुत्समिति[1] पादः कुत्सदेवत्य ऐंद्रो वा । सं ह यद्वामिति पाद औशनस ऐंद्रो वा । पर ऋगिंद्राकुत्सदेवत्या ॥

३२. दृशि चेत्तु[3]त्वेनादर्दो द्वादशेति प्राप्ते प्रातिशाख्ये

दीधरभारवरीवरदर्दर्दर्दरदर्धरजागरजीगः ।

वारपुनः पुनर्[4] ।

इति रेफित्वाद् अदर्द्वादशेत्युक्तं प्रकृतिवदनुकरणं भवतीति ॥२५॥

४०. अस्य सूक्तस्य नवम्यनुष्टुम्मध्ये वर्तमाना या सा चानुष्टुप् । यस्या सूर्येत्येषा[5] । किंच सौरी सूर्यदेवत्या । सौरीत्यनंतरं तदादीत्युक्तत्वादत्रिदेवत्यत्वं मा भूदिति । पंचम्यनुष्टुप्सूर्यदेवत्येति यावत् । तदादीतिहासः । अत्रिर्देवः । कुतः । अत्रेः स्तुतिं प्रति कर्मत्वात् । अत्रिर्ह्यत्र स्तूयत एवेति[6] कर्मार्थे । षष्ठ्यादिचतुर्ऋचमत्रिदेवत्यं । अत्र्यार्षेयमेवेति यथाप्राप्तमेवोक्तं । षष्ठ्याद्यत्रिदेवत्यमिति वाच्येऽन्यासर्वं विस्पष्टार्थं । न ह्यन्यत्रेतिहासो देवतात्वहेतुश्च वर्ण्यते ॥

४१. वै तत् । एकादशेत्यर्थः । तुभ्यादिसूत्रे[7] वै पंच तत् षडित्येवमीरितं । एतदादीन्येकादश सूक्तानि वैश्वदेवानि ॥

४२. एकादशी रौद्रीति वचनं सूक्तरूपविनियोगेऽप्येवमन्यासामपि वैश्वदेवत्वमिति प्राप्तस्य वैश्वदेवत्वस्य निवृत्त्यर्थं । ऋग्रूपविनियोगे हि सूक्तभेदप्रयोग[8] इत्येव रौद्रत्वं सिद्धं ॥

४२–४३. एतयोरुपांत्यैकपदा । एतयोः सूक्तयोर्यथाक्रममुपांत्या सप्तदशी षोडशी चैकपदे । लाघवार्थमिदं । अन्यथा प्र शंतमा ध्रुनैकादशी रौद्री सप्तदश्येकपदा धेनवस्त्रूना षोळश्येकपदेति वाच्यं स्यात् । द्वयोरुपांत्यैकपदेति । तर्हि सूत्रमिदमंतिममकृत्वा प्र शंतमा ध्रुनैकादशी रौद्र्युपांत्यैकपदा त्विति[9] सूच्यतां ।

एवं न सूचितं येन पृच्छ कात्यायनं तु तं ॥

४४. अत्र सूक्ते ये दृष्टलिंगका अधीतस्तनामकाः सदापृणयजतबाहुवृक्तश्रुतविद्वयादयस्ते वर्जित्वे[10]ऽधासारेण समुच्चीयंते स्तनामवतीष्वृक्ष्वित्यर्थः ॥

४६. अंत्यो वृचो देवपत्नीस्तवः । देवपत्न्यः स्तूयंत इत्यर्थः ॥२६॥

४७. अंत्या तृणपाणिः । पंचमीमधीयानः पाणौ तृणं गृह्णातीत्यध्ययनद्वारेणेयं तृणपाणिर्भवति । अतोऽत्रार्थादध्येतुस्तृणपाणित्वं विधीयते । किमर्थं । रक्षसां हननाय । अधीत्यांते तच्च तृणमग्नावप्सूदरे[11] वा प्रक्षिपेत्[12] । नान्यत्र । यज्ञायज्ञीये[13] तृणपाणिसूक्त ऋग्विधाने तथा दर्शनात् । उपदेशस्तूपदेशमुपोद्बलयतीत्यंतः ।

[1] Ver. 8 c. [2] Ver. 8 d. [3] Pân. VI, i, 114. [4] *Rigv.* Pr. 104. [5] Ver. 5.
[6] W 1; एव omitted in the rest. [7] Introd: § 12, 3. [8] Cp. Paribhâshâ to I, 139.
[9] W 1; °पदेति the rest. [10] च ऋणचयो W 1. [11] °प्सूषिरे P 1, P 2, I 2, I 4; °प्सु रे W 1.
[12] क्षिपेत् W 1. [13] *Rigv.* VI, 48. [14] W 1, P 2, I 2; °द्बलायती° I 4; °द्बयति° P 1.

तथा हि । तृणपाणिर्जपेत्[1] सूक्तं रक्षोघ्नं दस्युभिर्वृतः ।
न भयं विद्यते[2] किंचिद्[3] रक्षोभ्योऽरिभ्य एव च ॥
पाणिना तृणमादाय यक्षायक्षेति योऽभ्यसेत्[4] ।
सोऽधीतस्यास्य सूक्तस्य फलं प्राप्नोति पुष्कलं[5] ॥
सूक्तांते च तृणं त्वग्नाविरिणे[6] वोदकेऽपि वा ।
निक्षिपेत्[7] तत्प्रयत्नेन त्यक्त्वा[8] न्यत्र भयावहं[9] ॥ इति[10] ॥

५०. स्वस्त्यात्रेयो नामात्रेयः ॥

५१. एकादश्याद्यास्तिस्रो व्यूहेन जगत्यस्त्रिष्टुभो वाव्यूहेन । वैश्वदेवत्वस्य पूर्णोऽवधिः । अंत्ये इति विस्पष्टार्थं पारिशेष्यादेव सिद्धेः ॥

५२. ह तद् दश । षष्ठी षोडशी सप्तदशी च पंक्तयः[11] । शिष्टाश्चतुर्दशानुष्टुभः[12] ॥

५३. चतुर्दशी विष्टारपंक्तिरिति केचित् । तत्र पाठे गायत्री सतोबृहती विष्टारपंक्तिः ककुप् सतोबृहती । एवं ककुबादिसतोबृहत्यंतानीत्युक्तं[13] । आद्यापंचमीदशम्येकादशीपंचदश्यः ककुभः षष्ठीसप्तमीनवमीत्रयोदशीचतुर्दशीषोडश्यः सतोबृहत्योऽष्टमीद्वादश्यौ गायत्र्यौ द्वितीया बृहती तृतीयानुष्टुप् चतुर्थी पुरउष्णिगित्युक्तावन्यथा[14] समुच्चितग्रंथच्छंदःकथनेन[15] ग्रंथगौरवमक्षरकृतं प्रतिपत्तिकृतं च ग्रंथगौरवं[16] स्यादित्युभय[17]लाघवाय यथाक्रमं छंदोऽभिधानं ॥

६०. आग्नेयं च वा । आग्निमारुतं वेदं[18] सूक्तं केवलं मारुतं वा । चेत्यसति केवलाग्निदेवत्यं पक्षे स्यात् । वेत्यसति शुद्धमारुतं पक्षे न स्यादित्याग्नेयं च वेत्युक्तं ॥

६१. अत्र सूक्ते श्यावाश्व ऋषिः । विददश्वस्य राज्ञः पुत्रौ वैददश्वी तरंताख्यं राजानं पुरुमीळ्हाख्यं च राजानं दल्भस्य राज्ञः[19] पुत्रं रथवीतिनामानं च तृतीयं[20] मरुतश्चात्मनो दत्तरुक्माभरणान्दानतुष्टः[21] स्तुतवान् । तरंतस्य वैददश्वेर्महिषीमधिराज्ये सहाभिषिक्तां च शशीयसीं नाम

[1] P 1, P 2; जपन् Rigvidhâna. [2] विंदते Rigvidh. [3] क्वचिद् Rigvidh. [4] भ्यस्येत् W 1; omitted in I 4, in which the rest of the quotation is corrupt. [5] नातृणः Rigvidh. [6] °चरण्ये P 2. [7] W 1, Rigvidh.; प्रक्षिपेत् P 1, P 2, I 2. [8] P 1, P 2, Rigvidh.; त्यक्ते W 1. [9] Rigvidh.; भयावहं । भवेदिति P 1, P 2, I 2, I 4; भयं भवेदिति W 1. [10] Meyer, Rigvidhâna II, xxii, 2–4. [11] °दश्यश्च पंक्तयः W 1; °दश्यश्च पंक्तिः I 4; षष्ठी सप्तदशी च पंक्तिः P 1, P 2, I 2, which read अंते च in the text; षष्ठीसप्तदश्यौ पंक्ती I 3 (Gagannâtha). [12] W 1, I 4; पंचदश P 1, P 2, I 2. [13] °तादिति । उक्तं P 1; °तादित्युक्तं P 1, I 2; °ताद्रत्युक्तं I 4; W 1 omits this passage (from केचित्). [14] W 1 omits from अन्यथा to च ग्रंथ° (incl.). [15] ग्रंथनेन added in P 1. [16] महत्स्यात् W 1. [17] W 1; उभर° the rest. [18] चेदं I 4; देवं P 1, P 2, I 2; पक्षे W 1. [19] दाल्भ्यस्य W 1; दल्भराजपुत्रं P 1; दत्तराजपुत्रं P 2, I 2. [20] W 1; नृपं the rest. [21] W 1; दत्तरुक्माभरणं दानं तुष्टावात्मानं P 1, P 2, I 2; दत्तरुक्माभरणदानं तुष्टाग्य । आत्मन I 4.

पूर्वं विस्मृत्य पुनर्बुद्ध्वा स्तुतवान् । शशीयसी हि श्यावाश्वाय बहु वसु दत्तवती । प्रकृते श्यावाश्व इतिहाससूचनार्थं (वैददश्वी इति । विददश्वशब्दादत इञ्[1] । दल्भाद्यञ्[2] ण्यो वा[3]) श्यावाश्वस्येतिहासोऽयं वैशद्याय प्रदर्श्यते ॥

राजर्षिरभवद्दाल्भ्यो रथवीतिरिति श्रुतः ।
स यक्ष्यमाणो राजार्षिमभिगम्य प्रसाद्य च ॥१॥
आत्मानं कार्यमर्थं[5] च ख्यापयन्प्रांजलिः[6] स्थितः ।
अवृणीतार्षिमात्रेयमार्त्विज्यायार्चनानसं ॥२॥
स सपुत्रोऽभ्यगच्छत्तं राजानं यज्ञसिद्धये ।
श्यावाश्वस्त्वत्रिपुत्रस्य[8] पुत्रः स्वल्वर्चनानसः ॥३॥
सांगोपांगात्सर्ववेदान् यः पित्राध्यापितो[9] मुदा ।
अर्चनानाः[10] सपुत्रोऽथ गत्वा[11] नृपमयाजयत् ॥४॥
यज्ञेऽथ[12] विततेऽपश्यद्राजपुत्रीं यशस्विनीं ।
स्नुषा मे राजपुत्री स्यादिति तस्य मनोऽभवत् ॥५॥
श्यावाश्वस्य च तस्यां वै सक्तमासीत्तदा मनः ।
संयुज्यस्व मया राजन्निति याज्यं[13] च सोऽब्रवीत् ॥६॥
श्यावाश्वाय सुतां दित्सुर्महिषीं स्वां नृपोऽब्रवीत् ।
किं ते मतमहं कन्यां श्यावाश्वाय ददामि हि ॥७॥
अत्रिपौत्रो[14]ऽदुर्बलो हि जामाता त्वावयोरिति ।
राजानमब्रवीत्सापि नृपर्षिकुलजा ह्यहं ॥८॥
नानृषिर्नौ तु जामाता नैष मंत्रान् हि[15] दृष्टवान् ।
ऋषये दीयतां कन्या वेदस्यांबा[16] भवेद्यथा[17] ॥९॥

[1] Pân. IV, i, 95. [2] Cp. Pân. IV, i, 105. [3] P 1; दाभ्यं इति दाभ्यादयः W 1; दलभाद्यञ् । ण्यो वा I 4; दाल्भ्याद्यञ् ⁻ ण्यो वा P 2, I 2. [4] राजर्षि N. [5] अर्थे P 1, P 2, I 2, I 4. [6] च ख्यापयत्प्रांजलिः I 4; च ख्यापयत्प्रांजलि° the rest. [7] अव-रिहार्षि P 1, P 2, I 2, I 4. [8] श्यावाश्वस्यात्रि° P 1, P 2, I 2, I 4. [9] पुत्रानध्या° P 2, I 2, I 4; यः पुत्रानध्या° P 1. [10] अर्चनानसपुत्रो P 1, P 2, I 2, I 4. [11] W 1; मत्वा P 1, P 2, I 2, I 4. [12] च W 1. [13] M 1-3, N, I 2; राजन् ⁻ ⁻ ⁻ राजमब्रवीत् P 1; राजन् निति याराज सोमब्रवीत् P 2; निविज्याज्यं C, W 1 (°वि° corr. to °रूप° on margin); I 4 omits this sloka. [14] °पुत्रो दु° MSS. [15] M 1; नैष मंताभि P 1; नैष मंताभिद् P 2; नैषमंत्राग्निद् I 2; मंत्रानपि च I 4; नैष मित्रापि C. [16] वेदस्यां वा M 1, W 1, P 1, I 4; देवस्यां वा P 2, I 2; वेदस्यां C. [17] P 1, P 2, I 2, I 4; तथा M 1, W 1; भावयेत्तथा C.

[1]ऋषिर्नैवदृशं वेदपितरं[2] मन्यते यतः[3] ।
इति तद्वचनं श्रुत्वा[4] प्रत्याचष्ट मुनिं नृपः[5] ॥१०॥
अनृषिर्नैव जामाता कश्चिद्भवितुमर्हति[6] ।
प्रत्याख्यात ऋषिस्तेन वृत्ते यज्ञे न्यवर्तत ॥११॥
श्यावाश्वस्य तु कन्यायां[7] मनो नैव न्यवर्तत ।
तेन स्वस्थो वसेत्युक्तो नृपोऽगान्मंदिरं[8] प्रति ॥१२॥
अर्चनानाः सपुत्रोऽथ याज्यावस्य[9] नृपौ पथि[10] ।
तरंतपुरुमीळ्हाख्यौ[11] प्राप्य पुत्रमदर्शयत्[12] ॥१३॥
तौ चक्रतुस्तयोः पुजां विददश्वसुतौ नृपौ[13] ।
तरंतमहिषी तत्र नाम्नाख्याता शशीयसी[14] ॥१४॥
तस्यै स[15] दर्शयामास त्वृषिपुत्रं[16] महानृपः[17] ।
तरंतानुमता सास्मै[18] प्रादाद्[19]बहुविधं वसु ॥१५॥
अजाविकं गवाश्वं च महिषी सा शशीयसी[20] ।
[21]अत्रिं याज्यार्चितौ गत्वा पितापुत्रौ स्वमाश्रमं ॥१६॥
अभ्यवादयतामत्रिं महर्षिं दीप्ततेजसं ।
श्यावाश्वस्य मनस्यासीन्मंत्रस्यादर्शनादहं ॥१७॥
न लब्धवांस्तु तां[22] कन्यां हंत सर्वांगसुंदरीं[23] ।

[1] P 2, I 2; ऋषिं W 1, P 1, I 4. [2] M 1; वेदः पितरं W 1, C, I 4; वेदं पितरं P 1, P 2, I 2; cp. var. lect., p. 58, note 11. [3] M 2 and M 3 omit slokas 7-10 a. M 3 has the marg. note: अस्य सर्वानु . . वृत्तावन्यथा पाठः. [4] P 1, I 4; °नं राजा P 2, I 2; °नाद्राजा W 1. [5] तदा W 1; प्रत्याचष्टे स तं राजा सह संमंत्र्य भार्यया M 1-3; प्रावोचस्तथ तं राजा सह सामंत्र्य भार्यया N. [6] P 1, P 2, I 2, I 4 omit this line. [7] कन्याया M 1, M 3. [8] P 1, P 2, I 2, I 4; स्वपुरं W 1. This line does not occur in the MSS. of BD. [9] W 1; अत्रिर्नृपौ I 4; अर्श्विनृपौ P 1; अर्श्विनृपो P 2, I 2. [10] ततस्तौ तु निवर्त्याशु तावेतावभिजग्मतुः M 1-3. [11] °ळ्हौ तु M 2-3, N. [12] राजानौ वैददश्विनौ M 2-3; राजानौ वैददश्व्यृषी N; शशीयसीं तरंतं च पुरुमीळ्हं च पार्थिवं M 1. [13] ताभ्यां तौ चक्रतुः पूजामृषिभ्यां नृपती स्वयं M 1-3, N. [14] This line is omitted in M 1-3. [15] W 1; च P 1, I 4; व P 2, I 2. [16] W 1; अत्रिपौत्रं P 1, P 2, I 2; अत्रिपुत्रं I 4. [17] महातपाः W 1; ऋषिपुत्रं महिष्याश्च दर्शयामास तं नृपः M 1-3, N (वै नृपः N). [18] चैव M 1-3, N. [19] अदाद् M 2-3. [20] श्यावाश्वाय M 1-3, N. [21] 16 b-18 omitted in M 1-2, N. [22] लब्धवा सुतां P 1, P 2, I 2; लब्धवान्सुतां I 4; लब्धवानहं M 1, W 1. [23] P 1, P 2, I 2, I 4; °शोभनां W 1, M 1.

अप्यहं[1] मंत्रदर्शी स्यां भवेद्वार्यो[2] महात्मन ॥१८॥
इत्यरण्ये[3] चिंतयतः प्रादुरासीन्मरुद्गणः ।
ददर्श संस्थितान्पार्श्वे तुल्यरूपान्महात्मनः[4] ॥१९॥
समानवयसो रुक्मवक्षसः पुरुषाकृतीन्[5] ।
श्यावाश्वोऽविस्मितो[6]ऽपश्यत्केष्ठानरश्चतुष्कातः[7] ॥२०॥
ततः स मरुतो देवान् रुद्रपुत्रानबुध्यत[9] ।
य ईं वहंतेत्यादिभि[10]र्बुद्धा तुष्टाव तानृषिः[11] ॥२१॥
अतिक्रमं हि तं मेन[12] ऋषिर्विपुलमात्मनः ।
यत्र[13] दृष्ट्वैव तुष्टाव यत्र[14] के ष्ठेति पृष्टवान्[15] ॥२२॥
अथास्य मरुतो रुक्मान् स्ववक्षोभ्योऽवमुच्य ते[16] ।
कंठे व्यासज्य[17] त्रिदिवं प्रययुस्तस्य पश्यतः[18] ॥२३॥
मरुत्सु तु[19] प्रयातेषु श्यावाश्वः सुमहायशाः[20] ।
रथवीतेर्दुहितरमग[21]च्छन्मनसा तदा[22] ॥२४॥
ऋषित्वमात्मनस्तत्र[23] विवक्षू[24] रथवीतये ।
एतं मे स्तोममित्याभ्यां दूत्ये रात्रिं न्यवेदयत्[25] ॥२५॥

[1] अथाहं I 4, M 1. [2] M 1, W 1; भवेदर्यो P 2, I 2; न वेदर्यो P 1; नावेदर्योर्महात्मने I 4. [3] इत्यारण्यके P 1, P 2, I 2. [4] इवात्मनः M 1-3. [5] समानवयसश्चैव मरुतो रुक्मवक्षसः । तांस्तुल्यवयसान्दृष्ट्वा देवान् पुरुषविग्रहान् M 1-3, N. [6] W 1, M 1-3, N; विस्मितो P 1, P 2, I 2, I 4. [7] पृच्छत्के ष्ठेति मरुतस्तदा M 1-3, N. [8] सुनून् M 1-3, N. [9] अबोध्यत P 1, I 4; अबाध्यत P 2, °त I 2. [10] य ईं वहंत इत्याभिः M 1-3; this line is omitted in N, P 1, P 2, I 2, I 4. [11] तथा M 1-3. [12] M 2-3, P 1, I 4; तन्मेने M 1; ते मेने P 2, I 2; वै मेने W 1. [13] W 1; यत्र I 4, M 1-3; येन P 2, I 2; यंन P 1. [14] W 1; यांश्च M 1-3; दृष्टाय यस् P 2, I 2; दृष्ट्वा यःस्के I 4; यष्टाय यस् P 1. [15] M 1-3 and N add the line स्तुताः स्तुत्या तया प्रीता गच्छंतः पृश्निमातरः । [16] वमुच्यत W 1; वमुंचत P 1, P 2, I 2, I 4. [17] W 1; वसति P 1; वसतिं I 4; वसवस् P 2, I 2. [18] Instead of this sloka, M 1-3 have the line अवमुच्य स्ववक्षोभ्यो रुक्मं तस्मै तदा ददुः । N, अवमुच्य स्वकंठेभ्यो रुक्मं तस्मै ददुस्तदा, with which words the story ends in the Nîtima*ñgarî*. [19] च P 1, P 2, I 2, I 4. [20] *S*lokas 24-25, 28-33 are quoted by Sâya*n*a (*Ri*gv. V, 61, 18). [21] आगच्छन् P 1, P 2, I 2, I 4. [22] कृतां P 1, I 4. [23] P 1, P 2, I 2, I 4; स तत्र ऋषिरात्मानं W 1, M 1-3. [24] W 1, C; °क्षा P 1, P 2, I 2, I 4; प्रवक्ष्यन् M 1-3. [25] न्ययोजयत् M 1-3.

रात्रावनिद्रां जानासि[1] मम रात्रि महाद्युते ।
रथवीतिमहिष्या मां मंत्रयुक्तं निवेदय[2] ॥२६॥
रथवीतिम[3]पश्यंतं संप्रेक्ष्यार्धेण चक्षुषा ।
रम्ये हिमवतः पृष्ठ एष क्षेतीति चाब्रवीत् ॥२७॥
ऋषेर्नियोगमाज्ञाय[4] देव्या राज्ञ्या प्रचोदितः ।
आदाय कन्यां तां दाल्भ्य उपेया[5]र्चनानसं ॥२८॥
पादौ तस्योपसंगृह्य स्थित्वा[6] प्रह्वः कृतांजलिः ।
रथवीतिरहं दाल्भ्य इति स्वं नाम चाब्रवीत्[7] ॥२९॥
मया [8]संगतिमिच्छंतं त्वां प्रत्याचक्षि[9] यत्पुरा ।
तत्क्षमस्व नमस्तेऽस्तु मा च मे भगवन् क्रुधः[10] ॥३०॥
ऋषेः पुत्रः स्वयमृषिः पितासि भगवन्नृषेः ।
हंत प्रतिगृहाणेमां स्नुषामित्येवमब्रवीत् ॥३१॥
पाद्यार्घ्ये[11] मधुपर्कं च शुक्लमश्वशतं तथा[12] ।
पूर्वं दत्त्वात्रिपुत्राय श्यावाश्वाय ददौ सुतां[13] ॥३२॥
रुक्माभरणयुक्तं तु सोऽत्रिर्दृष्ट्वा स्वपौत्रकं[14] ।
महान् प्रसादो[15] महता[16]मिति हृष्टो[17] बभूव ह ॥३३॥
अथात्रिः पुत्र[18]मित्येव श्यावाश्वं बह्वमन्यत ।
श्यावाश्वः कृतदारोऽस्तौत्स्वो[19]पकारकरान् बहून् ॥३४॥
अतः प्र[20]ष्ठ्यैरूपेण वाच्यत्वे[21] मरुतां स्तुतेः[22] ।

[1] °मि W 1, C. [2] W 1; रथवीतिर्महिमानं च युक्तमत्र निवेदयत् P 1, P 2, I 2; I 4 and M 1-3 omit this *sloka*. [3] W 1; °तिं न प° the rest. [4] आस्थाय P 2, I 2. [5] I 4, M 1-3; उपेयाद् W 1, C, P 1; उपादाय P 2, I 2. [6] स्थितः M 1-3. [7] P 2, I 2; चाब्रुवान् P 1; स्वं नाम चोक्तवान् W 1, C, I 4; नाम शशंस च M 1-3. [8] W 1, M 1-3; संयोगम् the rest. [9] प्रत्याचक्ष M 1-2; °चक्षिम M 1; प्रत्याचक्षीय P 1, P 2, I 2, I 4; प्रत्याचिक्षिपत्पुरा W 1, C. [10] क्रुधाः M 1-3; क्रुधीः S. [11] पादार्घ्ये° W 1; पाद्यमर्घ्यं I 4; पाद्यार्घे P 1, P 2, I 2. [12] पुरा W 1, C. [13] पाद्यार्घ्यमधुपर्कैश्च पूजयित्वा स्वयं नृपः । शुक्लमश्वशतं दत्त्वानुजज्ञे गृहान् प्रति ॥ M 1-3, which have the following *sloka* in conclusion: शशीयसीं तरंतं च पुरुमीळ्हं च पार्थिवं। मद्भिः सनादिति स्तुत्वा जगामर्षिरपि क्षयं ॥ [14] W 1; स्वपुत्रकं P 1, P 2, I 2, I 4. [15] P 1; महाप्रसादो W 1, P 2, I 2; मह्यं प्रादात्स I 4. [16] महत W 1. [17] W 1; हृष्टा P 1; दृष्ट्वा P 2, I 2; च I 4. [18] पौत्रम् W 1. [19] W 1; स्तोत्स्व° P 1; सौ स्व° P 2, I 2; सी सू° I 4. [20] W 1, I 4; पृष्ठ्य° P 1; प्रपृष्ठ° P 2, I 2. [21] W 1; वाच्यत्वान् P 1, I 4; वाच्यातां P 2, I 2. [22] W 1; स्तुते P 1; स्तुतौ I 4; तु मे P 2, I 2.

चतुष्के देवताः के ह य ई मद्रे च[1] ते स्तुताः ॥३५॥
सनात्साम्नांचतुष्के च तरंतमहिषी स्तुता ।
उत मे पुरुमीळ्हस्तु स्तुतो यो मे तरंतकः ॥३६॥
शतं मे तमृचे[3] दाल्भ्यो रथवीतिः स्तुतस्तथा ।
उक्ता बृहद्देवतायां शौनकेन कथा त्वियं[4] ॥३७॥

७३. पुरादयं पौरः । न पौरोऽयं बाहुवृक्तो यथा नाम्ना[5] बाहुवृक्तः । पुरास्यर्षी[6] न स्तः । ऋषि[7]नामापि नोच्यते ॥

७६. अत्रिर्नाम भौमः । भौमोऽत्रिरिति[8] सूक्तं । ननु पंचमे मंडलेऽनुक्तगोत्रत्वादात्रेयत्वं यदि हि स्याद्[10] भौमोऽत्रिरिति सूत्रमनर्थकं स्यात् । तर्हि पंचमे मंडलेऽत्रेरात्रेयत्वं मंडलांतर आंगिरसत्वं च मा भूदित्येवमर्थं । मंडलांतरस्थात्रेर्भौमत्वार्थं तच्चेदत्र वचनमसंगतं[11] । परिभाषात्वेन तत्रैव भौमत्वं वाच्यमित्यत्रा[12]प्यत्रेर्भौमत्वं भविष्यतीत्येतच्च नास्ति । तत्रोक्तावप्यत्रेः क्वचित्कथंचिदिति भौमत्वमन्यत्र स्यादेव । किंच । न ह्यत्रिरात्रेयोऽप्यपत्यं भवति विरोधाच्च च ह्यावत्री स्तो[13]ऽन्यायश्चानेकार्थत्वमिति[14] । तर्हि सर्वत्रात्रेर्भौमत्वमेवेति । ननु भौमोऽत्रिरिति सूत्रमकृत्वा सर्वास्वत्रिमिति[15] केचिदित्यत्र[16] भौममित्यु[17]क्त्वा क्वचित्कथंचिदित्यादिना सर्वत्रात्रेर्भौमत्वं साध्यं । एवं चैकमं[18]त्रिग्रहणं न कार्यं स्यात् । सत्यं । तथा तु न कृतं । किं कुर्मो वयं ॥ अत्रिस्त्रिष्टुबश्विनौ । सूच्यते हि । आ भात्यग्निरित्यारभ्य तदु त्रैष्टुभमिति[19] ॥

७८. अंत्याः पंचानुष्टुभः । वि जिहीष्वेत्याद्याः । ता एव गर्भस्राविण्युपनिषच्च[20] । पंचर्चसमुदायोपदे[21]ष्टत्वा[22]द्वेदाः[23] प्रमाणामितिवदेकत्वं । एतासां हि जपात्सुखप्रसवो भवति । अथानुष्टुभो गर्भस्राविण्युपनिषदिति सिद्धे पंचांत्या इति शक्यमकर्तुं[24] । इहापक्रामंतु गर्भिण्य इत्युक्ता पंचैता

[1] W 1; चः स्तव I 4; च ― च P 1; चहंते च P 2, I 2. [2] W 1; °म्नां the rest. [3] P 2; मे त्ये तमृचे P 1, I 4; तमृचो W 1; तदृचे I 2. [4] BD. V, 580-604. [5] W 1; यथा मिना P 1, P 2, I 2, I 4. [6] P 1; पुरास्यामी P 2, I 2; पुरास्यार्षे ॥ I 4; पुरार्षी W 1. [7] न स्तो चिना° MSS. [8] Introd. to Mand. V. [9] W 1; °त्वम् the rest. [10] °त्रेय विद्याद् I 4. [11] W 1; वचनं संगतार्थं P 2, I 4; वचनसंगतार्थं P 1. [12] W 1; °त्यत्रेयोक्तेरत्रा° P 1; °त्यत्रोक्तेरत्रा° P 2; °क्ते त्रा° I 4. [13] See, however, sûtra on X, 143, where the author is stated to be अत्रिः सांख्यः. [14] W 1, P 1, I 4; °र्थं इति P 2, I 2. [15] P 1, I 4; °त्रिं P 2, I 2, W 1. [16] °त्यन्यत्र W 1. [17] भौम इति I 4. [18] W 1, P 1; चैवम् P 2, I 2; चैकत्रा° I 4, C. [19] Âsv. Sr.-sûtra, IV, xv, 2. [20] According to Sâyana, only the last three verses. [21] °स्योप° P 1, P 2. [22] W 1, P 1, P 2, I 2; °दिष्टत्वाद् I 4. [23] W 1; वेधा P 1, P 2, I 2; वेधो I 4. [24] W 1; सकृद्वाक्यमकर्तुं I 4; सकृति दाक्यमधर्तुं P 1; सकृति वाक्यमकर्तुं P 2; प्रकृतिवाक्यमकर्तुं I 2.

अधीयते[1] श्रवणमात्रेण किल गर्भध्वंसं मन्यमानाः । न चैतत्सुष्ठु । न ह्येताः श्रवणमात्रेण गर्भिणीर्बाधंते । किंत्वेतदनुमंत्रितजल[2]पानेन[3] सुखप्रसवकारिण्यः प्रसववेदनानां[4] । उक्तं ह्यृग्विधाने ।

वि जिहीष्व वनस्पते तदिदं च्यावनं[5] स्मृतं ।
यं च्याव[6]यितुकामः स्याच्च्यावये[7]त्तमिदं[8] जपन्[9] ॥१॥
क्षिपंतं वा पदाक्रम्य[10] भूमौ पांशुमयीं कृतिं[11] ।
निष्पे[12]ष्यन्निव संग्रामाच्च्यवते[13] नात्र संशयः[14] ॥२॥
स्त्रियं गर्भप्रमूढां वा पाययेदनुमंत्रितं ।
उदकं च्यावनेनैव[15] गर्भः प्रच्यवते[16] सुखं[17] ॥३॥ इति[18] ॥

किंच । यत्र हि श्रवणं नेच्छंति तत्र ब्रवीति । यथा न वसिष्ठाः शृण्वंतीति[19] । न चैवमत्रोक्तं न हि गर्भिण्यः शृण्वंतीति[20] । अत्र च गर्भस्राविण्युक्तेरुपांशुत्वमिच्छतः प्रजापते न त्वदि[21]त्येतस्याः क्रियमाणामुपांशुत्वं न घटते[22] । [23]उपनिषदुक्तेरुपांशुत्वं चेदु[24]द्यन्नृ[25]चस्यात्मो[26]पनिषत्संहितोपनिषदात्मकस्याप्युपांशुत्वं स्यात्[27] । एतेन प्र मंदिन[28] इत्येषा व्याख्याता ॥

८७. अतिजागतं । अतिजगतीछंदस्कं । अत्युत्तरपदवृद्धिश्छांदसी ॥

॥ इति पंचमं मंडलं समाप्तं ॥

६. भरद्वाजः । अपवादानुक्तावयमेवर्षिः । षष्ठे मंडले वाविशिष्टत्वं[29] चास्य न बाधकमित्यर्थः ॥

[1] P1, P2, I2; °यंते W1, I4. [2] °तोदक° W1. [3] W1, I4; प्राशनेन P2, I2; पायसेन P1. [4] °दनां P1, I4; °दिनां P2, I2; °दनामधिते: W1, C. [5] स्यापनं P1, P2, I2. [6] यः स्याप° P2, I2. [7] स्यापयेत् P2, I2. [8] तमिमं W1, C; तदिदं P2, I2. [9] W1; जपेत् P2, I2. [10] W1; चापदं क्रम्य P2, I2. [11] W1; पांसुमधीकृतं P2, I2; मपीकृतं P1, which omits the rest of this line as well as 1 b. [12] निःपीषंनिव संग्रामाच् W1; निष्पेषंनिव सग्रामान् P1; निधेष्येदनिष संग्रामान् P2; निशेषंनिव संग्रामान् I2. [13] W1, C; मुच्यते P1; मुत P2, I2. [14] W1, C, P1; नामा प्रसंशयः P2, I2. [15] W1; च्याव C (after which follows a great lacuna extending into Mand. IX); चवनेनैव P1; वधनेनैव P2, I2. [16] धच्यवते I4. [17] W1, I4; स्वयं । सुखमिति. P1, P2, I2. I4 has only the beginning and tho end of this quotation: वि जिहीष्व वनस्पते तदिदं ॥ गर्भो धच्यवते सखं. [18] Meyer, *Ṛig*vidhâna II, xvii, 1–4. [19] See sûtra on III, 53. [20] W1, P2, I2; this sentence is omitted in P1, I4. [21] *Ṛig*v. X, 121, 10. [22] W1, P1, P2, I2; °त्वं स्यात् I4 (which reads: वसिष्ठाः शृण्वंतीत्युक्तेरुपांशुत्वं भवति ॥ प्रजापते etc.). [23] W1; तदुप° P1, P2, I2. [24] W1, P1; चेत्र P2, I2. [25] *Ṛig*v. I, 50, 11-13. [26] °चस्यास्य W1; °चस्यात्मौ° P1; °चस्यांत्यो र्थो° P2, I2. [27] I4 omits this sentence. [28] *Ṛig*v. I, 101. [29] W1, I4; अवाविशिष्टत्वं P1, P2, I2; cp. Introd. § 12, 2.

१. पिबासोममभीयात्प्राङ् मंडलादिष्वाग्नेयमैंद्रादित्याग्नेयत्वं ॥२८॥

७. वैश्वानर इत्यग्नेर्गुणः । इदमादिषु त्रिषु ह्यग्निर्वैश्वानरोऽस्ति ॥

१५. वीतहव्यो नामांगिरसोऽयमर्षिः प्रकृतो भरद्वाजः । ननु वीतहव्यो वेत्येतदेवास्तु । तस्मिन्विकल्पिते मांडलिको भरद्वाजः स्वयमेव संपत्स्यते । किमृषिरिति । विस्पष्टार्थं । तर्हि वाविशिष्टत्वाद्भरद्वाजस्योत्तरत्रानुवृत्तिर्न स्यात् । नैतत् । वाविशिष्टत्वं चास्य न बाधकमिति सुक्तं । किंचारण्यकेऽपि पिबा सोममिति द्वे तदु[2] भारद्वाजीय[3]मामनंति[4] ॥ बृहत्या उपांत्ये इत्यावादेशे शाकल्यवल्लोपे[5] पूर्व[6]त्रासिद्धमित्यात्गुणाभावः । यथा । उभा उ नूनमिति[7] ॥

१६. सप्तविंश्यनुष्टुप् । ते ते अग्न इत्यनुष्टुप् । आ ते अग्ने अग्निं देवास इति द्वे च । तयोः पूर्वा त्रिष्टुप् । त्रिष्टुप्पूर्वे । वीती यो देवमिति त्रिष्टुप्ययोः पूर्वा ते इत्यर्थः । मंडलाद्यग्नेः पूर्णोऽवधिः ॥२९॥

१७. ऐंद्रमित्याग्नेयापवर्ग्यं । पंचदश्यया वाजमिति द्विपदा । [8]नन्वनादेशपरिभाषया त्रिष्टुभि प्राप्तायां त्रैष्टुभग्रहणं व्यर्थमिति चेद् द्विपदांतमित्युक्तेऽनादिष्टत्वेनाया वाजमिति द्विपदाया विंशतिका द्विपदा विराज इति विंशत्यक्षरविराट्त्वं मा भूदित्येतदर्थं त्रैष्टुभमिति । तथा चांत्यैकादशाक्षरा त्रिष्टुब्द्विपदेति सिद्धं भवति[8] । तर्ह्यंत्या द्विपदा त्रिष्टुब् द्विपदांत्या त्रिष्टुप् कस्मान्नोक्ता । शृणु । श्यमुक्तादितश्चतुर्दश जगत्यः स्युः । त्रिष्टुबंतस्य सूक्तस्य शिष्टा जगत्यः परिभाषिताः ॥

२०. वि पिप्रोरहिमायस्येति दशकचतुष्कयुक्ता विराट् । सप्तमी विराडित्यनुक्तिलाघवे विशेषाभावाद्विस्पष्टाच्च ॥

२७. द्वयाँ अग्न रथिन इत्यष्टम्यां चायमाननाम्नो युद्धेऽभिमुखगमनात्प्राभ्[9]यावर्तित्वगुणस्य चायमानस्य राज्ञो दानं स्तौति । अभ्यावर्त्युक्तिरभ्यावर्ती चायमानो ददातीति दर्शनात्प्रशंसार्था ॥

२८. गव्यं गोदेवत्यं । द्वितीया गव्या । ऐंद्री वा । सूक्तांत्यपादश्चैंद्रः । द्वितीयाया ऋचोऽंत्य इति संबंधे कृते कृतकरकत्वाद्वैयर्थ्यं स्यात् ॥३०॥

३१. सुहोत्रो नाम भारद्वाजोऽयं । कुत एतत् । वक्ष्यति हि । सुहोत्रादयोऽनुक्तगोत्रा भारद्वाजा इति[10] । सत्यपि लाघवे शाक्ययुंपांत्येत्यनुक्तौ प्रयोजनं चिंत्यं ॥

४४. तिस्रश्च विराजः । अथ तिस्रो विराजः । अयार्ये चेति । आसां तिसृणां मध्यमैव[11]

[1] *Rig*v. VI, 17. [2] W 1, P 1, P 2, I 2; तदुभे I 4. [3] W 1, P 1, I 2, I 4; भारद्वाजं । यमा° P 2. [4] Cp. Ait. Âr. I, ii, 6, 6-8. [5] Cp. Pân. VIII, vi, 19. [6] Ibid. VIII, ii, 1. [7] *Rig*v. X, 106, 1. [8] W 1; अनादेशादेव त्रैष्टुभत्वे सिद्धे त्रैष्टुभत्वमिति । अया वाजमित्यंत्याया द्विपदाया विंशतिका द्विपदा विराज इति विंशत्यक्षरविराट्त्वं च मा भूदिति । किं तर्हि । द्व्येकादशाक्षरत्रिष्टुप्त्वं च यथा स्यादिति the rest. [9] प्राप्राव° W 1 (with a stroke over व to indicate its omission); °प्राप्राभ्याम° P 1, P 2, I 2; युद्धाभिगमनात्प्राप्राभ्याम° I 4. [10] Paribhâshâ to VI, 53. [11] W 1; the rest add वा.

सूक्तस्याष्टम्यृतस्य यथेत्येषैव[1] विराट् । न सप्तमीनवम्यौ । ते त्रिष्टुभावेव[2] । शिष्टाः पंचदश त्रिष्टुभ इत्यर्थः ॥

४५. पुरूतमं पुरूणां स्तोतॄणामित्यतिनिचृत्[3] । अंत्ये तृचेऽधि बृबुः पणीनामित्यत्र बृबुर्नाम तक्षा दैवतं देवता । अयं हि[4] बृबुस्तक्षेंद्रभक्तः शंयोर्बेधुरिति श्रूयते[5] ॥

४७. अगव्यूति क्षेत्रमागन्मेत्यर्धर्चो[6] लिंगोक्तदेवतः । देवान् भूमिं च स्तौतीत्यर्थः । उक्तं हि बृहद्देवतायां ।

अगव्यूति स्तौति देवान् पादो भूमिमथोत्तरः । इति[7] ।

लिंगोक्तदेवतवचनं लाघवाय । अगव्यूतीत्यर्धर्चे पादौ देवभूमिदेवत्याविति हि गुरु स्यात् । अगव्यूत्यर्धर्चो दैवभौम[8] इत्युक्तावपि पादद्वयस्यापि द्विदेवत्यत्वं स्यात् । अर्धर्च इत्यकृत्वागव्यूतिपादौ दैवभौमावि[9]त्यस्तु । अत्रापि पूर्वोक्त एव दोषो यथासंख्यमिति नियमाभावात् । तत्रैंद्री मारुती त्वाष्ट्रीत्या[10]दित उक्तेरेव क्रमसिद्धिरिति चेद् विस्पष्टार्थं । प्रस्तोक इन्नु राधसस्त इंद्रेति[11] त्रिष्टुप् । अनुवादोऽयं । न त्वनुष्टुबादिवद्विधिरनुक्तसिद्धेः । असत्यस्मिन् प्रस्तोक इत्यस्या अनुष्टुप्त्वमित्यादिदोषः[12] स्यात् । दशाश्वानि[13]त्यनुष्टुबित्याद्युक्तौ दानस्तुत्यादि प्रस्तोक इति नोक्तं स्यात् । ततो दशाश्वानित्यनुष्टुप् । दश रथान्प्रष्टिमत[14] इति गायत्री । महि राध[15] इति द्विपदा द्व्येकादशिका । कुतः । वक्ष्यति हि त्रिष्टुब्द्विपदेति । इतिशब्द आद्यर्थः । प्रस्तोक इन्न्वित्याद्युक्तच्छंदस्कश्चतुर्ऋचः[16] संजयपुत्रस्य प्रस्तोकनाम्नो राज्ञो दानस्तुतिः । परौ तृचौ वनस्पते वीड्वंग[17] उप श्वासय पृथिवीमि[18]ति यथाक्रमं रथदुंदुभिदेवत्यौ । श्रूयते हि । वनस्पते वीड्वंगो हि भूया इत्यस्य रथोपस्थमभिमृशेदिति[19] । गृह्ये सूच्यते । उप श्वासय पृथिवीमुत द्यामिति तृचेन दुंदुभिमभिमृशेदिति[20] । समश्वपर्णाश्चरंतीति दुंदुभितृचस्यांत्योऽर्धर्च इंद्रदेवत्यः । यजानो हरिता रथ[21] इति बृहती । त्रिष्टुब्द्विपदा पूर्वमुक्ता महि राध इति द्विपदा त्रिष्टुब्द्व्येकादशका न तु विंशतिका द्विपदा विराज[22] इति विंशत्यक्षरा विराट् । तर्हि तत्रैव द्विपदा त्रिष्टुप् त्रिष्टुब्द्विपदेति वास्तु । नैतत् । त्रिष्टुब्द्विपदेत्युक्तौ महि राध

[1] W 1; the rest add वा. [2] Sâyana (introd. to this hymn) interprets the words of the Sarvânukr. as meaning, 'verses 7-9 are virât, verse 8 virât or trishtubh,' instead of 'verses 7-9 are virât, or only verse 8 is virât, 7 and 9 being trishtubh.' [3] Cp. comm. on Introd. § 4, 5. [4] P 1, P 2, I 2, I 4; बृहद्देवतायां हि W 1. [5] The BD. merely says: स आनयदिति त्वस्य तृचोऽधीति बृबुस्तुतिः । V, 617. [6] Ver. 20. [7] BD. V, 620. [8] W 1; देवभूमीत्यु° P 1, I 4; देवभूमिरित्यु° P 2. [9] W 1; देवभूमाव् the rest. [10] Paribh. to I, 15. [11] Ver. 22. [12] W 1; शेष the rest. [13] Ver. 23. [14] Ver. 24. [15] Ver. 25. [16] W 1; उक्तछंदस्काश्चतुर्ऋच: I 4; उक्तछंदसः चतुर्ऋचः P 1; उक्तं छंदसः चतुर्ऋचं P 2, I 2. [17] Ver. 26. [18] Ver. 29. [19] °ति च P 1, I 4. Ait. Br. VII, ix, 2; cp. Âsv. Gri.-sûtra, II, vi, 5, 7. [20] Âsv. Gri.-sûtra, III, xii, 17. [21] Ver. 19. [22] Introd. § 12, 8.

इत्यस्यास्त्रिष्टुप्त्वं वनस्पत इत्यस्या द्विपदात्वं पंचानां दानस्तुतित्वं च स्यात् । द्विपदा त्रिष्टुबित्युक्तौ वनस्पत इत्यस्यास्त्रिष्टुभः प्रस्तोकस्य दानस्तुतित्वं स्यात् । नैष दोषः । प्रस्तोकादिपंचर्चस्य दानस्तुतित्वे परौ तृचावित्युक्तिर्नोपपद्यते दानस्तुतिपंचर्चात्परस्य तृचद्वयस्य[1] सूक्तेऽभावात् । अतो वनस्पत इत्यस्या न दानस्तुतित्वं नाप्यस्या द्विपदात्वं सरूपादेव । न हि चतुश्चत्वारिंशदक्षरा चतुष्पदा द्विपदा भवति । तत्किं त्रिष्टुब्द्विपदेति पृथगुक्तं । सत्यं । पृच्छ कात्यायनं येन द्विः कृतं द्विपदेति ह । वयं हि प्रतिपत्तारो न कर्तारोऽस्य चांजसा[2] । एकत्र त्रिष्टुब्द्विपदाशब्दयोः पृथगर्थत्वावबोधनोदार्थमिति ब्रूमः ॥ दिवस्पृथिव्या इत्येषा जगती । सप्तविंशत्यनुक्तिः प्रतिपत्तिलाघवाय ॥ ३१ ॥

४८. यदत्र तृणपाणित्वे वाच्यं तस्य तत्पूर्वमीरितं । प्र ये वसुभ्य[4] इत्यस्यास्तृणपाणित्वं वर्तते । पृश्निसूक्तं पृश्निदेवत्यं । पृश्निर्नाम मरुतां माता । सा देवता ॥ आसामिति सूक्तांतत्वनिवृत्त्यर्थं । अथ काकुभः प्रगाथः । अत्र पूर्वेत्र च प्रगाथमिति शक्यमकर्तुं । काकुभ इत्येव प्रगाथप्रतीतेः । अत्र त्रयोऽपीतिकरणाः समाप्त्यर्थाः । दश पंच चतस्र[5] इति वाच्यत्वार्थाः[6] । अंत्या द्वाविंशत्यनुष्टुप्सती[7] द्यावाभूम्योर्वा पृश्नेर्वा स्तुतिः । पृश्नेर्वा बृहती महाबृहती यवमध्या[8] । ननु चादौ पृश्निसूक्तमित्युक्ता बृहती महाबृहती यवमध्यानुष्टुबिति पृश्नेरंत्या[9] द्यावाभूम्योर्वेति कस्मान्नोक्तं लाघवाय[10] । विशेषाभावात् । किंच । अनुक्रमण्यंतरानुकरणार्थं च ॥

४९. पंचोन ऋजिश्वा हेति । ऋतयक[11] इति ह्रस्वप्रकृतिभावौ ॥

५१. व्युष्णिगनुष्टुबंतमिति कर्मधारयद्वंद्वबहुव्रीहिः । तिस्र उष्णिह एकानुष्टुबंते[12] यस्येति विग्रहः ॥

५२. ऋजिश्वा । विश्वे देवाः । अस्यैषां च पूर्वोऽवधिः । अथाभूरेकः सुहोत्रस्त्वित्यत्रेयमंतो[13][14]क्तानां सुहोत्रादीनामनुक्तगोत्राणां गोत्रादिविशेषणमाह । सुहोत्रशुनहोत्रनरगर्गऋजिश्वान इत्येते सुहोत्रादयः । अनुक्तगोत्रा इति शंयोर्बार्हस्पत्योक्तगोत्रस्य[15] भारद्वाजनिवृत्त्यर्थं । भारद्वाजा भरद्वाजपुत्रा इत्यर्थः । विदादिभ्यो[16] बहुषु लुक् । एते च बृहस्पतेः पौत्राः । दुःष्यंतनृपपुत्रस्य भरतस्य वा पौत्राः । भारद्वाजा इत्येव गोत्रज्ञाने सिद्धे पौत्रत्वविकल्पोपदेशोऽदृष्टार्थो रोगघ्नोपनिषदित्यादिवत् । एतत्पौत्रा एत इति ज्ञाने[17]ऽपि महदभ्युदयरूपं फलमस्तीति कथमेतान्प्रति द्वयोः पितामहत्वं विकल्पेनोपपद्यते । द्वैमातुरा हि दृष्टा न द्विपितृकाः ।

[1] W 1; पञ्चर्चस्य परस्य P 1, P 2, I 2; पञ्चर्चस्य परस्य I 4. [2] P 1, P 2, I 2, I 4; स्य चांजसा omitted by W 1. [3] पृथक्त्वा° W 1. [4] *Rigv.* V, 49, 5; cp. comm. [5] दश कपिंजल (!) I 4. [6] W 1; वाच्यार्थाः the rest. [7] W 1; सा the rest. [8] W 1; यवमध्यावत् P 1, P 2, I 2; °ध्यात् I 4. [9] W 1; पृश्ने त्या P 1; पृश्नेर्द्यावा° I 4; पृश्नेर्वा द्या° P 2, I 2. [10] W 1; लाघवं P 1, P 2, I 2; लाघवाविशेषभावात् I 4. [11] Pâ*n*. VI, i, 128. [12] अंत्ये I 4; अर्वाते P 1, P 2. [13] Sûtra on VI, 31. [14] W 1; °यमंतमुक्ता° P 1, I 4; °येमंत उक्ता° P 2, I 2. [15] Sûtra on VI, 44. [16] W 1; विदाद्यंतोऽपवादः । P 1; विदाद्यातो पवादः P 2; विदाद्यचोपनादः I 4; cp. Pâ*n*. IV, i, 104 and II, iv, 65. [17] W 1, P 2, I 2; ज्ञाते P 1, I 4.

सुहोत्रादिमहर्षीणां पौत्रत्वस्य विकल्पनात्[1] ।
इतिहासो हेतुभूतो विस्पष्टार्थं[2] प्रवर्ण्यते[3] ॥१॥
प्रजापतेः पुत्र आसीदंगिरा नाम वै मुनिः ।
तस्य पुत्रास्त्रयस्त्वासंस्त्रेताग्निसमतेजसः ॥२॥
उचथ्यो ज्येष्ठ इत्येव[4] मध्यमस्तु बृहस्पतिः ।
संवर्तस्तु कनिष्ठोऽथ[5] ज्येष्ठो गुणगणैर्भुवि ॥३॥
यः संवर्तो मत इति[6] प्रथितो भारते भृशं[7] ।
उचथ्यभार्या ममता[8] नाम्नासीद्[9]वरवर्णिनी ॥४॥
उचथ्याहितगर्भां तां[10] चकमेऽथ बृहस्पतिः ।
उचथ्यपुत्रो[11] ममतागर्भ[12]स्थोऽथोचदुस्तरं[13] ॥५॥
ज्येष्ठपत्नीं मातृतुल्यां मैनां गंतुं मनः कृथाः ।
अहो कामस्य दौरात्म्यं यदि मां त्वमिहागतः ॥६॥
किं चाहमत्र प्रविष्टः क्व ते[14] गर्भो निधीयताम् ।
अमोघरेतास्त्वं चासि न द्वयोरिह संभवः ॥७॥
द्वितीयस्तात मा[15] मैवमकार्ये च कृथा महत् ।
इति गर्भवचः श्रुत्वा शशापैनं बृहस्पतिः ॥८॥
दीर्घं तमस्त्वं प्रविश मद्वाक्यादंध एव च ।
ततो दीर्घतमा नाम ह्यु[16]चथ्यतनयोऽभवत् ॥९॥
शप्त्वा गर्भं ममतया[17] संबभूव बृहस्पतिः ।
ततो बृहस्पतेर्गर्भो ममतायामभूत्तथा[18] ॥१०॥
पूर्वगर्भो दीर्घतमास्तद[19]र्थाच्च्यावयद्[20]बलात् ।
स्वमातुरुदराद्गर्भः स्वयं च निरगात्ततः ॥११॥

[1] W1; °त्वं विकल्प्यते I4; °त्वस्य विकल्पः P1, P2. [2] W1; °ष्टाय I4, P1; °ष्टार्थः P2. [3] प्रकीर्त्यते I4. [4] एतेषां W1. [5] च W1. [6] I4; मत्त W1; मत्तीये P1; स्ति मत्तीये I2; स्ति मर्त्तीये P2. [7] भवत् I4. [8] महता P2. [9] भूद् I4. [10] °र्भा तां W1. [11] °गर्भो W1. [12] °जठर° W1. [13] अथोचत्तु तं W1. [14] W1, P1; कुतो I4; केन P2, I2. [15] W1; मे the rest. [16] W1; नाम उच° the rest. [17] P1, P2, I2; ममतायां W1; °तायाः I4. [18] W1; तदा the rest. [19] W1, P1, P2; तदृष्या° I2, I4. [20] W1; °च्यापयद् P1; °च्यावयद् P2, I2; °च्यावर्धद् I4.

बृहस्पतेः स[1] पुत्रो[2] वै भरद्वाज इति श्रुतः ।
अत्रांतरे तु भरतो दौःषंतिश्चक्रवर्त्यभूत् ॥१२॥
स पुत्रेषु मृतेष्वार्तो बृहस्पत्युपदेशतः ।
दत्तपुत्रविधानेन भरद्वाजं गृहीतवान् ॥१३॥
दौःषंतेर्भरतस्यासीद्भरद्वाजः सुतस्ततः[6] ।
स्वपत्न्यां पुष्करिण्यां च पंच पुत्रानजीजनत् ॥१४॥
सुहोत्रं शुनहोत्रं च नरं गर्गमृजिश्वनं ।
इति सिद्धं सुहोत्रादेः पौत्रत्वस्य विकल्पनं ॥१५॥

५३. यां पूषन्ब्रह्मचोदनीमित्येषानुष्टुप् । अष्टम्यनुष्टुबित्युक्तौ प्रतिपत्तिगौरवं स्यात् ॥

५७. चकारात्पौष्णं च । इंद्रापूष[7]देवत्यमित्यर्थः ॥

६१. सारस्वतं सरस्वतीदेवत्यं सरस्वतीमा विवासेमेति[8] लिंगात् ॥३२॥

६३. सांहितिकः कंपो नैकश्रुत्य इति क्व१त्येति नोक्तं[9] । न ह्यन्यं[10] व्युषा आव[11] इति च सूत्रे
यथा । आ वां सुम्न इत्येकादशी त्रिष्टुबेकपदा । कुतः । त्रैष्टुभमित्युक्तेः । तद्धि[12] तदर्धमेकपदेति[13]
दशाक्षर[14]विराट्त्वं मा भूदिति । सूक्तं[15] ह्यनुक्तेरेव त्रैष्टुभं भविष्यति[16] ॥

६९. ऐंद्रावैष्णवं । देवताया । ओर्गुणः[17] इति च । देवताद्वंद्वे चे[18]त्यानङ् । उभयपदवृद्धिः ॥

७२. ऐंद्रासोमं पूर्ववत् । वृद्ध्यानङ् ॥

७४. सोमरौद्रमिति पूर्वपदादिवृद्ध्यनुक्तिश्छांदसी[19] । सोमरौद्रं तु चर्वेना इति मानवे शास्त्रे[20]
यथा[21] ॥

७५. भरद्वाजपुत्रः पायुर्नामर्षिः । पा रक्षणे । कृवापाजीत्युण् युक्[22] । सूक्त[23]दर्शनेन सर्वा[24]न्द्वाज्ञो
युद्धेषु[25] पाति[26] रक्षतीति पायुः । एवं हि श्रूयते । पुरा खलु[27] भरद्वाजस्य[28] याज्यभूतो चाय-

[1] °तेस्तु I 4. [2] गर्भो W 1. [3] दौष्यंति° W 1. [4] I 4, P 1; स्वपुत्रे तु मृतेष्व° W 1; स पुत्रे यं मृते त्व° P 2, I 2. [5] दौष्यंते° W 1. [6] P 2, I 2, I 4; ततः सुतः W 1; सुतस्तुतः P 1. [7] इदमैंद्रापौष्ण° I 4, P 1. [8] Ver. 2. [9] क्व त्येतुक्तौ I 4. [10] I 4; न ह्यष्टौ P 1, P 2; न ह्यन्यं षळाकरमित्यष्टौ W 1. See sûtra on VIII, 80. [11] Sûtra on VII, 75 (व्युषा अष्टा). The word अष्टौ is apparently transposed from this quotation to the previous one in P 1, P 2, W 1. [12] W 1, P 1, I 4; तर्हि P 2, I 2. [13] Cp. Introd. § 12, 9. [14] W 1; °क्षराधि° P 1, P 2, I 2. [15] W 1; सूक्ते P 1, P 2, I 2. [16] P 2, I 2 (as well as Gagannâtha, I 3) add आद्या विराट्. [17] Pân. VI, iv, 146. [18] Ibid. VI, iii, 26. [19] W 1; पूर्वपदादिश्छंदोनुकृतिः P 1, P 2, I 2. [20] Manu, XI, 254. [21] I 4 omits the whole of this comm. [22] Cp. comm. on Pân. III, iii, 1. [23] एतत्सूक्त° W 1. [24] सर्वदा° I 4. [25] युद्धे W 1. [26] पाति in W 1 only. [27] किल W 1. [28] भरद्वाजपुत्रस्य W 1.

मानप्रस्तोकाख्यौ पारशिखाख्यैः[1] प्रबलैः[2] शत्रुभिर्युद्धे[3] जितौ भरद्वाजं सगुरुमुपेत्योचतुः । भगवन्नावां भवत्पुरोहितौ संतौ पारशिखैर्युद्धे[3] जितौ । ततश्च यथावां[5] जयेव तथा कुर्विति । भरद्वाजोऽपि स्वपुत्रं पायुमुवाच[6] । एतौ[7] विजयिनौ कुर्विति । ततः[8] पायुस्तदर्थमेतत्सूक्तदर्शी सन्[9] संग्रामांगानि कवचादीन्यृग्भि[10]स्तुष्टाव तौ चैतत्सूक्ताभिमंत्रितैः[11] संग्रामांगैस्ताञ्जित्वा सपुत्रं[12] भरद्वाजमुपेत्य[13] महद्धनं ददतुरिति । तदेतदाह संग्रामांगान्यृक्शोऽभितुष्टावेत्यादि[14] । संग्रामांगानि युद्धोपकरणानि वर्मादीनि । ऋक्श एकैकया[15] ऋग्भिः । अस्तौदिति वाच्ये तुष्टावेत्यनुक्रमण्यंतरानुकरणं[16] । अंगानि तानीमानी[17]त्याह । वर्मेत्यादि । वर्म कवचमाद्ययास्तौत् । धनुश्चापि[18] द्वितीययास्तौत् । ज्यां मौर्वीं तृतीयया । आर्त्नी ज्याबंधकौ द्वौ चतुर्थ्या । इषुधिं शरकोशं[19] पंचम्या । एताः पंच त्रिष्टुभः । उत्तरा षष्ठी रथे तिष्ठन्नित्येषा[20] जगती । तस्या जगत्याः पूर्वार्धे सारथिमस्तौत् । उत्तरार्धे रश्मीन् अभीशून् । अथ सप्तम्याद्याभिस्तिसृभिस्त्रिष्टुब्भिर्यथाक्रममश्वान् रथं च[21] रथगोपान् रथरक्षितॄंश्च[22] । इति नव गताः । अथ दशमी ब्राह्मणासः पितर इति जगती । तया[23] लिंगोक्तदेवता अस्तौत् । ब्राह्मणपितृसोम्यद्यावापृथिवीपूष्णो[24]ऽस्तौत् । अथ द्वाभ्यामेकादशीद्वादशीभ्यामिषून्शरान्[25]स्तौत् । अथ त्रयोदश्या प्रतोदमश्वप्रेरकं । अथ चतुर्दश्या हस्तघ्नं[26] । अथ द्वाभ्यां पंचदशीषोडशीभ्यामिषून्शरानस्तौत् । अतः परा यत्र बाणाः संपतंतीति पंक्त्यादयः[27] सप्तदश्याद्यास्तिस्रो लिंगोक्तदेवताः । युद्धभूमिकवचबंधनब्रह्मणस्पत्यदितिसोमवरुणदेवब्रह्मदेवत्याः । संग्रामाशिषश्च योधानामा[28]शीर्भिः पूरयिष्यश्च रोगघ्नप्रायश्चित्तादिवत्[29] । संग्रामाशीरूपमपि[30] ज्ञेयमित्युच्यते । अंत्या सूक्तस्यांत्या यो नः स्वो अरण इत्येषानुष्टुप् । ऋजीते परि वृङ्धि न[31] आ

[1] W 1; पारशिकाख्यौ P 1, P 2, I 2; पाशराख्यौ I 4. [2] W 1; प्रबंध° P 1; प्रवध° P 2, I 2; प्रवद्धै I 4. [3] W 1; युद्धेषु the rest. [4] P 1; °शिखाख्यै° W 1; पारिशेयै° P 2, I 2; पाशरकाख्यौ° I 4. [5] W 1; भवानावां P 1; भगवावावा P 2, I 2; भगवान्ना I 4. [6] °माचष्ट W 1. [7] W 1 omits एतौ. [8] P 2, I 2; तव P 1, I 4; स च W 1. [9] P 1, P 2, I 2; दर्शयन् I 4; ददर्श W 1. [10] W 1; ऋक्शो भि° P 1, P 2, I 2; ऋक्सौभि° I 4. [11] W 1; °त° P 1; °तः P 2, I 2; °मंत्रि° I 4. [12] W 1; स्वपुत्रं the rest. [13] W 1; °मेत्य the rest. [14] This sentence in W 1 only. [15] W 1; ऋच एकाभिर्ऋ° the rest. [16] W 1, I 4; °नुक्रमण्यनुकरणं P 1, P 2, I 2. [17] W 1; कानीमानी° P 1, I 4; कानि नामानी° P 2, I 2. [18] W 1; चापं the rest. [19] W 1; °चापं P 2, I 2; °वापं P 1; शरधिं I 4. [20] W 1, I 4; °त्येव P 1, P 2, I 2; °त्ये च I 2. [21] च omitted in W 1. [22] W 1; रथरक्षितॄन् omitted in the rest. [23] W 1; पितर इति या लिं° P 1, I 4; इति या लिं° P 2, I 2. [24] °पूषणम° P 1, P 2; °पूषणो I 4; °रूपेण W 1. [25] W 1; शरान् omitted in the rest. [26] W 1 has the marginal note: अत्र धन्विनः प्रकोष्ठे बंधनीयस्य हस्तघ्नस्य स्तुतिः । [27] W 1; पंक्तिः P 1, I 4; omitted in P 2, I 2. [28] योधुनाम् P 1. [29] P 1, P 2, I 2, I 4; °चित्तवत् W 1. [30] °मपि° P 1. [31] Ver. 12.

मंथंति सान्वेषामिति[1] च द्वे अनुष्टुभौ । आलाक्ता या रुरुशीर्ष्णी[2] अवसृष्टा परा पतेति[3] च[4] द्वे अनुष्टुभौ । द्वे द्वे इति[5] वचनं प्रतिप्रतीकं द्वित्वार्थं[6] । शिष्टास्त्रिष्टुभः ॥

॥ इति षष्ठं मंडलं समाप्तं ॥

७. अथ सप्तमस्य प्राधान्येन द्रष्टारमाह । सप्तमं मंडलं वसिष्ठोऽपश्यत् । मैत्रावरुणिर्वसिष्ठ इत्युक्तं मित्रावरुणयोर्दीक्षितयोरित्यत्र[7] ॥

१. अत्र सूक्त आदितोऽष्टादश विराजः । ताश्च द्व्येकादशकाः । शिष्टास्त्रिष्टुभः । अस्य सूक्तस्य नानाछंदस्त्वमस्मद्ग्रंथयो सूत्रे च सूच्यते[8] । ता उ विच्छंदसः संति विराजः संति त्रिष्टुभः[9] । अष्टादशोत्तमे विराज[10] इति च । तत्र सुत्तम इत्यग्निर्नरीयमुच्यते । मंडलादित्वादग्निः ॥३३॥

२. आप्रमित्युक्तेर्द्वितीयात्र नाराशंसी न तानूनपाती[11] ॥

१७. सप्तापि द्विपदा द्व्येकादशकाः । त्रैष्टुभमिति विंशतिका द्विपदा विराज इति मा भूदिति । आग्नेयाधिकारस्य पूर्णोऽवधिः ॥

१८. सवध्र्यैंद्रमित्युक्तं । अस्यांत्याभिश्चतसृभिर्द्वाविंश्यादिभिः पिजवनपुत्रस्य[12] राज्ञः सुदानाम्नो दानं स्तूयते ॥

२२. आदितोऽष्टौ विराजः । दशकास्त्रयः । अंत्यामृते । ऊसेरम् व्यत्ययाच्छंदोवद्भावाच्छंद एव वा[13] । सा त्रिष्टुप् । ऋतेऽंत्यामिति लाघवात् । त्रिष्टुबंतम् अंत्या त्रिष्टुबिति हि गुरुः ॥

३१. दशम्याद्यास्तिस्रो विराजोऽंते यस्य तत्सूक्तं त्रिविराडंतं । ताश्च द्व्येकादशकाः ॥

३२. तृतीयाया बृहतीत्वे चतुर्थ्याः सतोबृहतीत्वे च क्रमात्सप्तविंश्याश्चानादेशात्त्रिष्टुप्त्वे एकपुरोडाशेष्वु[14]पांशुयाजन्यायेनाद्योपादानांत्यलोपन्यायेन वा बृहतीत्वे प्राप्त आह तृतीया द्विपदेति । विंशत्यक्षरा विराट् ॥ इंद्र क्रतुं न आ भरेति षड्विंश्यादिप्रगाथे कथामृषिविकल्पायाह सौदासैरित्यादिना । पुरा किल ।

वसिष्ठस्य सुतः[15] शक्तिः पुष्पार्थं ययौ वनं ।
राज्ञः सुदासो दासास्तु[16] वासिष्ठं ददृशुश्च तं ॥१॥
विश्वामित्रप्रयुक्तैस्तु रक्षोभिर्वेष्टिताश्च[17] ते ।
वनाग्नौ प्राक्षिपंश्चैनं देवभक्तोऽयमित्युत ॥२॥

[1] Ver. 13. [2] Ver. 15. [3] Ver. 16. [4] W 1, I 4; एते च P 1, P 2, I 2. [5] च added in P 1, P 2, I 2. [6] W 1; द्वित्वं विस्पष्टार्थं P 1, P 2, I 2; प्रतिप्रतीकं स्पष्टार्थं I 4. [7] See sûtra on I, 166. [8] W 1; श्रूयते हि P 1, P 2, I 2; श्रूयते I 4. [9] Ait. Br. V, v, 17. [10] Âsv. Sr.-sûtra, VIII, viii, 4. [11] तनूनपाती W 1; तनूनपात् P 1, I 4; omitted in P 2, I 2. [12] Cp. Nir. II, 24. [13] Cp. comm. on II, 11. [14] W 1; एके पुरोडाशेष्वु° P 1, P 2, I 2; एकपुरोडाशे ष्वु° I 4. [15] वसिष्ठपुत्रः W 1. [16] W 1; च the rest. [17] W 1, I 4; वेष्टिताश्च P 1; विधिताश्च P 2, I 2.

आस्तिकोऽयं वसिष्ठस्य पुत्र इत्येव च क्रुधा ।
प्रक्षिप्यमाणः सोऽपश्यदिंद्र क्रतुमिति तृचं[1] ॥३॥
अर्धर्चमुक्तवानाद्यं ततोऽदह्यत सोऽग्निना ।
चिरायमाणे पुत्रे तु पुत्रस्नेहपरिप्लुतः ॥४॥
मार्गविक्षिप्तनयनो[2] वसिष्ठोऽभ्यागमद्वनं ।
दग्धं सुतमथ श्रुत्वा भूतेभ्यः शोककर्शितः ॥५॥
ज्ञात्वा तु दृष्टशिष्टं[3] तु शिक्षा णादि समापयत् ।
[4]यद्यर्धर्चत्रयं शिष्टमद्रक्ष्य[5]न्मम वै सुतः ॥६॥
अजीविष्यदयं संयक् सुखी च[6] शरदां[7] शतं ।
इत्युक्त्वा धृतिमालंब्य प्रययावाश्रमं पुनः ॥७॥
एवं तु शाट्यायनकं वदंति ब्राह्मणं किल ।
आद्यार्धर्चमेव[8] शक्तिर्दृष्टवान्दग्ध एव सः ॥८॥
तृचं सर्वं वसिष्ठस्तु दृष्टवानिति तांडकं ।
इति ब्राह्मणवैमत्यं[9] विकल्पाय प्रदर्शितं ॥९॥
अतश्च[10] । इंद्रक्रतुं[11]तृचे शक्तिराद्येऽर्धर्चे विकल्पितः[12] ।
ऋषिर्वसिष्ठः सूक्तस्य देवता त्विंद्र एव हि[13] ॥१०॥

अन्वारेभ इति रभ राभस्ये आङ्पूर्वः । अत्र पश्यतिकर्मा धातुर्द्रष्टुमिति वा शेषः[14] । ततो लिट् । तस्यात एकहल्मध्य[15] इत्येत्वाभ्यासलोपौ । प्रक्षिप्यमाणः । कर्मणि लटि यकि शानचि मुक् । अदह्यत कर्मणि लङ् । समापयत । आंपॢ व्याप्तौ संपूर्वः । हेतुकर्मणि णिच् । लङि णिचश्चे[16]त्यात्मनेपदं लङः[17] । तृचो हि समाप्तिं गच्छति । तमसौ गमयतीति । शाट्यात् फक् वुम् च[18] शाट्यायनकं[19] । तांडिनामाम्नाय[20]स्तांडकं ॥

[1] शक्तिरिंद्र क्रतुं तृचं W 1. [2] मार्गे P 2, I 2. [3] W 1, P 1; दग्धशिष्टं I 4; शिक्षितुं शिष्यं I 2; P 2, the same corr. for दृष्ट तु शिष्यं. [4] W 1; यच्चार्ध° the rest. [5] W 1, I 4; °दृक्षन् P 1, P 2, I 2. [6] W 1; स सुखी the rest. [7] शरदः W 1. [8] I 4; आद्यार्धर्चांत्यैव P 1, P 2, I 2; आद्यार्धार्चोऽन्यैव corr. to आद्यार्धार्चांत्यैव W 1. [9] P 2, I 2; ब्राह्मणद्वौ यथ्यं I 4; ब्राह्मणं वै सत्यं P 1, W 1. [10] W 1 only. [11] W 1, I 4; क्रतु° P 1, P 2, I 2. [12] W 1; आद्यऽर्धर्चविकल्पतः the rest. [13] In all the MSS., except W 1, this sloka comes after 7 a. [14] पश्यतिकर्मा । द्रष्टुमिति वा शेषः W 1; पश्यतिकर्मा धातुर्द्रष्टुमित्येकशेषः P 1, P 2, I 2, I 4. [15] Pân. VI, iv, 120. [16] Ibid. I, iii, 74. [17] लटुः W 1. [18] शाट्यः फक् आयनि धुम च W 1. The comm. beginning शानचि मुक् and ending with वुम् च in W 1 only. [19] W 1; शाट्यायनमतं शाट्यायनकं the rest. [20] तांडिनाम्नायस्तांडकं W 1; तांडिनो मतं तांडकं the rest.

३३. वसिष्ठस्य सपुत्रस्य संस्तवः सहस्तुतिः परस्परस्तुतिरित्यर्थः । आदितो नवभिर्वसिष्ठः स्वान्पुत्रपौत्रान्[1] स्तुतवान् । विद्युतो ज्योतिरित्यादिपंचभिस्ते वसिष्ठं स्तुतवंतः । अथवा वसिष्ठस्येंद्रेण सह संवादः । स्वान्पुत्रपौत्रानादितो नवभिः स्तुतवान् वसिष्ठो विद्युतो ज्योतिरित्यादिभिः पंचभिरिंद्रेण स्तूयते स्मेत्यर्थः । संवादः परस्परसंभाषणं । संवादे वक्तृविवेकानुक्रम उपदेशोऽप्यनुक्तः ॥

३४. आद्या एकविंशतिर्द्विपदाः । आदित एकविंशतिर्ऋचो विंशत्यक्षरा विराज इत्यर्थः । द्वाविंश्याद्यास्ततस्त्रिष्टुभः । श्रूयते हि ब्राह्मणसूत्रयोः प्र शुक्रेत्यारभ्य ता उ[3] विच्छंदसः संति द्विपदाः संति चतुष्पदा[4] इत्येकविंशतिर्वैश्वदेवसूक्त[5] इति च । अत्र[6] हि द्विपदा इति वर्तते द्विपदा एकादश मारुत इत्यतः[7] । अत्र चाब्जामुक्थैरहिं गृणीष[8] इत्यर्धर्चोऽहिनाम्नो दैवतस्य[9] स्तुतिः । मा नोऽहिर्बुध्न्य इत्यर्धर्चो[10]ऽहिर्बुध्न्यनाम्नो दैवतस्य[9] । वैश्वदेवत्वादेव ऋग्रूपविनियोगोक्तदेवतात्वे[11] सिद्धेऽनयोर्दे[12]वतयोरुपदेशः सूक्त[13]विनियोगेऽपि स्मरणार्थः ॥

३५. सर्वशांतिकरं सूक्तं रोगघ्नत्वादिवदयमपि गुणो ज्ञातव्य इत्युक्तं ॥ ३५ ॥

३८. अंत्ये सप्तम्यष्टम्यौ वाजिनां स्तुतिः[14] । वाजिनो वाजिनाख्या[15]हविर्देवताः । केचि[16]द्देवताविशेषाः । भगमुग्रो वस इत्यर्धर्चो भगदेवत्यः । वेत्युक्तेः सावित्रो वा ॥

४१. आद्या जगती लिंगोक्तदेवता । अग्नींद्रमित्रावरुणाश्विभगपूषब्रह्मणस्पतिसोमरुद्रदेवत्येत्यर्थः ॥

४४. आद्या जगती लिंगोक्तदेवता । दधिक्राश्च्युतोऽग्न्यादिस्वसामर्थ्यप्रतिपादितदेवतेत्यर्थः ॥

४८. अंत्या चतुर्थी वैश्वदेव्यार्भवी वा । ऋभुदेवत्यं[17] ॥

५०. चतुर्थी गंगादिसर्वनदीस्तुतिः ॥

५१. आदित्यदेवत्यं । आदित्या नामादितेः पुत्रा आदित्या[18] आदित्यानामिति लिंगात् । आदित्यग्रहेण चरंतीति सूत्रे[19] ॥

५४. वास्तोष्पतिदेवत्यं । पत्यंतात्यः[20] ॥

[1] W 1; पुत्रान्पौत्रान् the rest. [2] °क्रममुप° W 1, I 4, P 2, I 2; °क्रमप° P 1. [3] ता अतिच्छं° W 1. [4] Ait. Br. V, v, 10–11. W 1 omits चतुष्पदाः. [5] Âsv. Sr.-sûtra, VIII, viii, 5. [6] W 1; तत्र the rest. [7] P 1, P 2; °त्यर्थः I 4, W 1; see Âsv. Sr.-sûtra, VIII, viii, 5. [8] Ver. 16. [9] W 1; देवस्य the rest. [10] उत्तरोऽहिर्बुध्न्यायेत्युत्तरोऽर्धर्चो W 1. [11] W 1; वैश्वदेवत्वादेव – – चय (°देवायं वि° P 2, I 2) विनियोगे वैश्वदेवत्वे P 1, P 2, I 2; वैश्वदेवत्वादेवास्य स्तुतिः । उपदेशविनियोगे विश्वेदेवत्व I 4. [12] W 1; तयोः the rest. [13] P 1; सूक्ते W 1; सूक्तं P 2, I 2; omitted in I 4. [14] वाजिनः स्तुती W 1. [15] W 1, P 2, I 2; वाजिनाख्या P 1, I 4. [16] केचन W 1.
[17] W 1; tho rest add आर्भव (ऋभव I 4) इति विधिगर्भानुवादः । आर्भवमंत्येत्यनुक्तिलौकिकार्थे ।
[18] पुत्रः आदित्यः W 1; omitted in the rest. [19] Âsv. Sr.-sûtra, V, xvii, 1. [20] Cp. Pân. IV, i, 85.

५५. आद्या गायत्री वास्तोष्पतिदेवत्या । शेषाः । शिषोऽसर्वोपयोगे कर्मणि षम् । शिष्टा इत्यर्थः । ताः प्रस्तापिन्य उपनिषत् । प्रस्तापिन्यः प्रस्तापिनः स्तुतय उपनिषच्च[1] भवति । ताश्च छंदस्तस्तुपरिष्टाद्बृहत्यादयोऽनुष्टुभः । तिस्र उपरिष्टाद्बृहत्यः सस्तु मातेत्याद्यास्ततस्रोऽनुष्टुभ इत्यर्थः ।

आसां प्रस्तापिनीत्वं तु कथासु परिकल्प्यते[2] ॥
वसिष्ठस्तृषितो[3]ऽन्नार्थी त्रिरात्रालब्धभोजनः ।
चतुर्थरात्रौ चौर्यार्थं वारुणं गृहमेत्य तु ॥१॥
कोष्ठागारप्रवेशाय पालकश्वादिसुप्तये ।
यदर्जुनादि सप्तर्चं ददर्श च जजाप च[5] ॥२॥ इति ॥

५६. अत्र सूक्त आद्या एकादश द्विपदाः । विंशतिका द्विपदा विराजः । अथ चतुर्दश त्रिष्टुभः । श्रूयते हि ब्राह्मणसूत्रयोः । क ईं व्यक्ता इत्यारभ्य ता उ विच्छंदसः संति द्विपदाः संति चतुष्पदा[6] इति द्विपदा एकादश मारुत[7] इति च ॥

५९. अंत्या द्वादश्यनुष्टुप् । एकाक्षराधिकेयं भुरिगनुष्टुब्वेदितव्या[8] । रुद्रदेवत्या । मृत्युविमोचनी । पूर्णो मरुतामवधिः ॥ ३६ ॥

६३. इति । आदौ । अर्धर्चपंचमाः सार्धर्चाः[9] सूर्यदेवत्यास्तिस्रः । चेति सौर्य इत्यनुकर्षणाय[10] । अथ[11] त्रयोऽर्धर्चा मैत्रावरुणाः ॥

६६. चतुर्थ्याद्यास्त्रयोदश्यंत्या दशादित्या आदित्यदेवत्याः[12] ॥

७५. सांहितिकः कंप ऐकश्रुत्ये नास्तीत्युक्तं ॥

७९. कंपाभावः पूर्ववत् ॥

८८. अंत्या पाशविमोचनी ॥

९०. अत्र सूक्ते या ऋचो द्विवदुक्ता वामित्यादिद्विवचनांतपदयुक्तास्ता ऐंद्र्यश्चकाराद्वायव्यश्च । अत एव ब्राह्मणसूत्रयोः प्रउगे वायव्यत्वाय प्र वीरया शुचयो दद्रिरे त[13] इति वामिति द्विवचनस्य स्थाने त इत्येकवचनपाठः कृतः । वामित्युक्तावैंद्रत्वं च स्यादिति । द्विवदुक्ता इति द्वित्वमर्हतीति च द्विवचनं । द्विशब्दो भावप्रधानः । यथा द्व्येकयोरिति[14] तदुक्तं । यास्तु ता द्विवदुक्ता ऐंद्र्यश्च पंचम्याद्यास्तिस्रो द्विवचनयुक्ता[15]द्या च । ते सत्येनेति पंचम्याद्यास्तिस्रश्चैंद्रवायव्या इत्यर्थः ॥

९५. सरस्वत्या अयं न सरस्वच्छब्दात् । अत एव हि तृतीया सरस्वत इत्युक्तं । सरस्वती धरुणमिति[16] लिंगात् । स वावृध इति तृतीया सरस्वते सरस्वदर्थं ॥

[1] ताः प्रस्तापिन्य उपनिषत् omitted in W1; प्रस्तापिन्यः to उपनिषच्च in W1 only. [2] कथासुपरि कल्पते W1. [3] क्षुधितो W1. [4] W1, I4, P1; गोष्ठा° P2, I2. [5] Quoted by Sâyana, Introd. to *Rig*v. VII, 55. [6] Ait. Br. V, v, 13–14. [7] Âsv. *Sr*.-sûtra, VIII, viii, 5. Cp. comm. on VII, 34. [8] This sentence omitted in W1. [9] आदावर्धपंचमाः सार्धचास्तिस्रः W1. [10] °र्चः W1. [11] अत्र W1. [12] Cp. comm. on VIII, 47. [13] Âsv. Sr.-sûtra, VIII, xi, 1. [14] Cp. Pân. I, iv, 22. [15] °युक्ता आद्या च W1. [16] Ver. 1.

९७. बृहस्पतिर्देवत्यमैंद्राग्नादि च । ऐंद्राग्नादियैस्य तासूक्तं । अंत्या दशम्यैंद्री च बार्हस्पत्या च । इंद्राबृहस्पतिदेवत्येति यावत् ॥

९८. अंत्या सप्तम्यैंद्री चेति पूर्वसूक्त एवोक्तदेवता । इंद्राबृहस्पतिदेवत्येत्यर्थः । सैव अत्र पुनराम्नायते ॥

९९. उरुं यज्ञाय चक्रथुरित्याद्यास्तिस्र[1] ऐंद्र्यश्चकाराद्वैष्णव्यश्च । ऐंद्रावैष्णव्य इत्यर्थः ॥

१००. ननु चैतत्[2]सूक्तवर्तिन्योः प्र तत्ते अद्य किमित्[3] इत्यनयोर्विष्णोः शिपिविष्टगुणत्वं किं नोच्यते यथा यथा[4] इत्यत्र वैश्वानरीयैमित्यग्नेर्वैश्वानरत्वं । दृष्टश्चानयोः[5] सूत्रे शिपिविष्टगुणकवि-ष्णोर्विनियोगः । कथं पुरस्ताचंद्रमसेत्यारभ्य वषट् ते विष्णवास आ कृणोमि[6] प्र तत्ते अद्य शिपिविष्ट नामेति[7] चेत्युच्यते[8] । अयं हि[9] मन्त्रयोः[10] गुणविधिर्न सार्वत्रिकः । यथा । उप ते स्तोमान्पशुपा इवाकरमिति[11] द्वे[12] इत्यत्र रुद्रस्य पशुमद्गुणत्वं पशुपतिगुणत्वं चेति मन्यते । किंच । यथोद्देशमि[13]त्युक्तेर्देवतानुक्रमणीबृहद्देवतयोः शिपिविष्टगुणत्वादर्शना[14]च्चैत[15]दादरणीयमिति । नन्वाश्व-लायनोपदेशो वांगीकृत एव[16] । अपि वान्यां वैष्णवीमिति[17] लिंगोक्तता[18] । अतो देवा देवी वेत्यत्र[19] वैष्णवीत्वोक्तेः । सत्यं । अत्र त्वतो देवा अवंतु न इति जपेदित्युक्तेः कर्मविशेषसंबंधात्र[20] सार्वत्रिकमेवेत्यत्रापि वाच्यमेवेति मन्यते । तस्मात्कर्मविशेषादियोगिषु[21] गुणवचनादि तत्कर्माध-धिकमेव न सार्वत्रिकं । यथा हिरण्यगर्भ[22] इति षड्चस्य कदेवत्यस्य हिरण्यगर्भ समवर्तताग्र इति षट् प्राजापत्या[23] इति प्रजापतिदेवतात्वं पश्वधिकमेव । यथा कया नश्चित्र आ भुवदित्यैंद्रीं[24] इंद्राग्नी मरुतो वरुणः क[25] इति कदेवत्यत्वमिति सर्वमनवद्यं[26] ॥३८॥

१०१–२. एते द्वे सूक्ते अग्निपुत्रः कुमारनामा ददर्श वृष्टीच्छाविशिष्टः[27] प्रकृत एव वा[28] वसिष्ठः । नन्विदं सूक्तमकृत्वा तिस्रः षट् पार्जन्यं त्वाग्नेयः कुमारस्तु वसिष्ठ एव वा वृष्टिकाम इति सूच्यतां । एवं हि लघु[29] । सत्यं । तथा न कृतं प्रतिपत्तिसुखाय हि[30] ॥

[1] Verses 4-6. [2] W 1; चात्र the rest. [3] Verses 5-6. [4] Sûtra on I, 59. [5] W 1; वैश्वानरसंदृष्टयोः the rest. [6] Vers. 7 and 99, ver. 7. [7] Ver. 5. [8] See Âsv. Sr.-sûtra, III, xiii, 13-14. [9] च W 1. [10] मन्त्रयोः सूक्ते धर्म्यों गु° P 2, I 2. [11] Rigv. I, 114, 9. [12] Âsv. Sr.-sûtra, IV, xi, 6. [13] Introd. § 1, 1. [14] W 1; °त्वाद° the rest. [15] चैतद° I 4. [16] W 1; नाश्वलायनोऽंगीकृत एव I 4; नत्वाश्वला-यनोऽंगीकृत एव P 1, P 2, I 2. [17] Cp. comm. on I, 22. [18] लिंगोक्त एव P 2, I 2. [19] Sûtra on I, 22. [20] W 1; न omitted in the rest. [21] °योगेषु P 2, I 2. [22] Rigv. X, 121. [23] Âsv. Sr.-sûtra, III, viii, 1. [24] Rigv. IV, 31, 1. [25] Âsv. Sr.-sûtra, II, xvii, 14. [26] W 1, I 4; सर्वमवदानं P 1, P 2, I 2. [27] वृष्टिकामो वा वसिष्ठः W 1. [28] वा omitted in W 1. [29] लाघवं खलु W 1. [30] Neither text nor comm. state ver. 2 to be pâdanikrit.

१०३. तेन पर्जन्यस्तोत्रेण संहृष्टान्[1] अस्माकं वृष्टिर्भविष्यतीति संयुक्तान्[2]मंडूकान् स पर्जन्यस्तुत्यनुमोदकानृषिस्तुष्टाव । कः । वसिष्ठः । वाचिविशिष्टत्वेऽपि मांडलिकत्वादस्यैवानुवृत्तिर्युक्ता । एवं[3]यनेनोत्तरार्थं प्रकृतत्वसूचनाय । अन्यथा वसिष्ठो वा वृष्टिकाम इत्येव वक्तव्यं । अथवा वाचिविशिष्टो[4] मांडलिकवसिष्ठो निवर्तितः । केवल[5]वसिष्ठो मांडलिकोऽनुवर्तिष्यते । यद्वा[6] वेति कुमारेण[7] संबध्यते । वसिष्ठ इति तु वृष्टिकामगुणा[8]विशेषितत्वाय ॥

१०४. रक्षोहेतींद्रासोमयोर्गुणः । राक्षोघ्नमैंद्रासोममिदं । रक्षसां हंतारावींद्रासोमावस्य देवतेत्यर्थः । ऐंद्रासोममित्युभयपदवृद्धौ प्राप्तायामुत्तरपदवृद्ध्यभावश्छांदसः । शाप आक्रोशश्छांदसः । असतो दोषस्याध्यारोपो[9]ऽभिशापः[10] । एतौ शापाभिशापावत्र प्रायो बहुलं[11] भवतः ॥ सप्तमी त्रिष्टुब्जगती वेत्यर्थः । सप्तमी वेति नोक्तं गुरुत्वात् । एकविंशीत्रयोविंश्यौ च जगत्यौ । अष्टादशी मरुद्देवत्या सती च जगती । चकारो जगत्यनुकर्षणार्थः । सप्तदशी ग्राव्णी ग्रावदेवत्या । अणोऽणीति प्रकृतिभावाभावश्छांदसः । ग्राव्ण्यश्मनि दैवते देवतावाच्ये तद्धिते अधंतं न तु क्नीपंतं । प्र वर्तय दिवो अश्मानमिति चतस्र इंद्रदेवत्याः । मा नो रक्षो अभि नडिति त्रयोविंश्या पूर्वार्धर्चो वसिष्ठस्यात्मन आशीः प्रार्थना । उत्तरोऽर्धर्चः पृथिवी नः पार्थिवादिति पृथिव्यंतरिक्षदैवतः ॥

॥ इति वासिष्ठं सप्तमं मंडलं समाप्तं ॥

न चात्राष्टमं मंडलमित्यनुक्तेः सप्तममंडलस्यासमाप्तिराशंकनीया मा चिदन्यदित्यारभ्य स्वादिष्ठयेत्यंतस्याष्टमं मंडलमिति प्रसिद्धेः । किंचानुवाकानुक्रमण्यां मंडलस्यानुवाकसूक्तयोः संख्याने[12] दशाष्टमीमिति[13] द्वे चैव सूक्ते नवतिं च विद्यादथाष्टममिति[14] चोक्तेर्मा चिदित्यादेरष्टमत्वमेव संगच्छते । तथोपाकर्मणि मंडलांत्यानामृचामनुक्रमणे[15] प्रति चक्ष्व विचक्ष्वेत्येषापि[16] गृह्यते । कुसुंभकादिमंडलर्षितर्पणे[17] च वसिष्ठस्य पावमानीनां च[18] मध्ये प्रगाथ इति मंत्र उच्यते । आरण्यके च तस्माद्वसिष्ठस्तस्मात्पावमान्य[19] इति सप्तमनवममंडलस्यप्रशंसामध्ये तस्मात् प्रगाथा[20] इति हि[21] समामनंति । यद्येवमेभिरेव हेतुभिरन्यत्रापि मंडलग्रहणं न कर्तव्यं । सत्यं । यत्र यत्र क्रियते[22] तत्र तत्रान्यत्प्र[23]यो-

[1] W 1; संहृष्टान् P 1, P 2, I 2; I 4 omits both text and comm. to VII, 103. [2] P 1, P 2, I 2; °कांश्च प° W 1. [3] See previous sûtra. [4] वसिष्ठो P 1, P 2, I 2. [5] W 1; °लं P 1, P 2, I 2. [6] W 1; यथा P 1, P 2, I 2. [7] W 1; °णैव P 1, P 2, I 2. [8] °काम इति वि° W 1. [9] W 1, P 1, I 4; अध्याहारो P 2, I 2. [10] Durga (who reads अध्याहारो) in his comm. on Nir. VII, 3, apparently borrows this definition from Shadg. Cp. BR. s. v. अभिशाप. [11] P 1, P 2, I 2, I 4; प्रायेण संभवतः W 1. [12] W 1; संख्या the rest. [13] Anuvâkânukramanî, ver. 32. [14] Ibid., ver. 35. [15] Cp. M. M., A. S. L., p. 218, note. [16] *Rig*v. VII, 104, 25. [17] W 1; तर्पणं P 1, P 2, I 2; तर्पणो I 4. [18] च in W 1 only. [19] Ait. Âr. II, ii, 2, 2 and 4. [20] Ibid. 3. [21] No हि in W 1. [22] W 1; प्रयोजनं the rest. [23] W 1; तत्रान्यदेतत्प्र° I 4; तत्रान्यदेव प्र° P 1, P 2, I 2.

नमस्ति । किं तत् । असत्यपवादे सामान्यर्षित्वादिति[1] । अथोत्तरार्थं परिभाषते । परं गायत्रं प्राग्वत्सप्रेः । प्र देवं दश वत्सप्रीर्भालंदन[2] इति वक्ष्यति । दिवस्परि द्वादश वत्सप्रीराग्नेयं त्रिंति तु[4] न गृह्यतेऽपरत्वात् । अतो वात्सप्रिसंशब्दनात्प्रागतः परं छंदोऽनुक्तो गायत्रं छंद इति वेदितव्यं । तेनेदं वसो त्रिचत्वारिंशदित्यादौ गायत्री[5] छंदः । परमिति शक्यमकर्तुं ॥ ऋषिश्चानुक्तगोत्रः प्राङ् मत्स्यात्काण्वः । त्वामु सैका मत्स्यः सांमद[6] इति वक्ष्यति । अतो मत्स्यसंशब्दनात्प्रागतः परमनुक्तगोत्रोऽप्यर्षिश्च[7] काण्वः कण्वगोत्र इति वेदितव्यं । तेन वक्ष्यमाणमेधातिथ्यादयः काण्वा भवंति । चेति प्रागिति च शक्यमकर्तुं । परमित्यनुकर्षणार्थस्तु चकारो न भवति पूर्वेणैव तस्य व्यर्थत्वात् । प्राक् पंचम्याः प्रत्यासत्त्येव लभ्यते । यथा[8] । स्त्रीपुंसाभ्यां नञ्स्नञौ भवनात्[9] ॥

८, १. मेधातिथिर्मेध्यातिथिश्च द्वावृषी सहापश्यतां तौ च काण्वौ[10] । अत्र मेधातिथेः काण्वत्वं न विधेयम् अग्निं द्वादश मेधातिथिः काण्व[11] इत्युक्तेरेव सिद्धेर्मेध्यातिथेस्तु विधेयमेव । ऐंद्रमिति मंडलाद्याग्नेयत्वनिवृत्त्यर्थं । अत्राद्यं बृचं प्रगाथो नामर्षिरपश्यत् । अपश्यदिति विस्पष्टार्थं । न च प्रगाथशब्दस्य बृहतीसतोबृहतीत्वं निवार्यर्षिनामत्वार्थता[12] द्विप्रगाथादीत्येव तस्योक्तत्वाद् आद्यं बृचं प्रगाथ इत्यनन्वयाच्च ।

आरण्यके तर्पणे च प्रगाथा इति यद्वचः[13] ।
तत्रान्येषामप्यृषीणां प्रगाथत्वमनेन हि ॥
मंडलादेर्दर्शकेन साहचर्यात्कृतर्षिवत् ।
व्याख्यातं हि शतर्चित्वमाद्यमंडलदर्शिनां ॥

अथ प्रगाथस्य घोरपुत्रस्य कण्वभ्रातुः पुत्रत्व[14]मुपपादयति । स गौर इत्यादि । स प्रगाथो घोरपुत्रः सन् भवन्[15] भ्रातुर्ज्येष्ठस्य कण्वस्य पुत्रतां पुत्रत्वं प्राप्तवान् । कथं । अत्रेतिहासः ।

प्रगाथो घोरतनयः कण्वे ज्येष्ठे तु निर्गते ।
प्रविश्य तद्गृहं श्रांत[16]स्तत्पर्यंके निषण्णवान् ॥१॥
सुष्वाप च ततः कण्वः क्षुधितोऽभ्यागतो वनात् ।
पत्नीमपृच्छत्क्रोधांधस्त्वदंके कः स्वपित्ययं ॥२॥
सोवाच[17] त्वत्कनिष्ठोऽयं पुत्रवल्लालितो मया ।
युष्मज्ञनन्यंकमत्या[18] विश्वस्तः स्वपिति प्रभो ॥३॥

[1] °त्वादि W 1. [2] Sûtra on IX, 68. [3] Sûtra on X, 45. [4] W 1; वत्सप्रिरित्ययं तु the rest. [5] °त्रं W 1. [6] Sûtra on VIII, 67. [7] W 1; °श्च ऋषिश्च I 4; °श्चर्षिः P 1, P 2, I 2. [8] W 1 only. [9] Pân. IV, i, 87. [10] W 1; काण्वावित्युक्तं the rest. [11] Sûtra on I, 12. [12] W 1; °हतीत्वर्षिनामत्वार्थं the rest. [13] W 1, P 1, I 4; यद्बृचः P 2, I 2. [14] W 1; काण्वत्वं the rest. [15] भवन् W 1 only. [16] W 1; श्रांतः the rest. [17] W 1, P 2, I 2; साथोच P 1; स्वाथोच I 4. [18] W 1; °न्यंक इव the rest.

नहि कोपं शाम्य मुने पुत्र एवावयोरिति ।
इति पत्न्या वचः श्रुत्वा गतक्रोध उवाच सः ॥४॥
अद्य प्रभृति न भ्राता मम पुत्रो भवत्विति[2] ।
इत्थं भ्रातुस्तु कण्वस्य प्रगाथः पुत्रतामगात्[3] ॥५॥

अथ[4] स्तुहि स्तुहीदेत इति चतुर्दशर्चस्यान्त्यस्य स्थूरमित्यंत्यायाश्चर्षिदैवत[5]विशेषज्ञानार्थ[6]मितिहासमाह । प्रायोगी[7]त्यादि । प्रायोगिः प्रयोग[8]नाम्नः पुत्रश्चासंगो नामासीत् । तं विशिनष्टि । यः स्त्रीत्यादि । [9]य आसंगो देवशापात्पूर्वं स्त्रीभूत्वा[10] पश्चात्तपोबलेन पुमानेवाभूत् । स एवंभूत[11] आसंगो मेधातिथये महर्षये बहु दानं[12] दत्त्वात्मानं स्वांतरात्मानं दत्तदानं स्तुहि स्तुहीति चतसृभिर्ऋग्भिः स्तुतवान् । अस्यासंगस्य पत्नी च भर्तुः स्त्रीत्वेन खिन्ना सती शश्वती नामांगिरस्यंगिरसः[13] पुत्री तपोबलेन लब्धपुंस्त्वं प्रजननमुपलभ्य प्रीतै[14]नमासंगमंत्ययान्त्यस्य स्थूरमित्येतया तुष्टाव स्तुतवती ॥

२. स्वादवः सोमा आ याहीत्येषानुष्टुप् । शिक्षा विभिंदो इत्याभ्यां काण्वो मेधातिथिरेव प्रियमेधरहितो विभिंदोर्महाराजस्य दानं स्तुतवान् । अनयोरयमेवर्षिः । न प्रियमेध इत्यर्थः । सर्वैर्वास्तौदिति वाच्ये तुष्टावेत्यनुक्रमण्यनुकरणमेव ॥

३. एकविंश्यनुष्टुप् । अथ द्वे गायत्र्यौ । अथ बृहती । एताश्चतस्रोऽंत्याः कुरुयाणपुत्रस्य पाकस्थाम्नो राज्ञो दानस्तुतिः ॥

४. स्थूरं राधः शताश्वमित्यंत्यस्तृचः[15] पुरउष्णिगंतः । स एव तृचः कुरुंगस्य राज्ञो दानस्तुतिः । तत्पूर्वाः कुरुंगदानदेवत्यतृचात्पूर्वभूताश्चतस्रः पंचदश्याद्याः पूषदेवत्या इंद्रदेवत्या वा । न चात्र देवतानुक्रमण्यां[16] देवातिथेर्येत्यादौ पूषदेवत्यत्वविकल्पादर्शना[17]दथोपदेशा[18]मिति प्रतिज्ञाबाधः शंकनीयः । बृहद्देवतायां ।

पौष्णौ प्रेति[19] प्रगाथौ द्वौ मन्यते शाकटायनः[20] ।

इत्युपदेशात् ॥३९॥

[1] शांत° I 4. [2] W 1, P 2, I 2; स्वयं त्विति P 1, I 4. [3] This story is similar in substance to that related in the BD. VI, 693-7. [4] W 1 only. [5] देवतविशे° W 1. [6] °ज्ञापनार्थमि° P 2, I 2. [7] P 2, I 2; प्रा° W 1, P 1. All the MSS. (including P 1, P 2) except W 2 read प्रा° in the text. In I 4 the initial of the word is corrupt in both text and comm. [8] P 2, I 2; प्र° W 1, P 1, I 4. [9] The following story is told by Sâyana, VIII, 1, 1, but in other words. [10] °भूत: W 1. [11] W 1; एवं त P 1, P 2; एवं I 2; एव I 4. [12] देयं W 1. [13] आंगिरसपु° W 1. [14] W 1; प्राप्तम् I 4; प्रीतम् P 1, P 2, I 2. [15] °त्याश्चतृच: W 1. [16] W 1; देवतानुक्रम: the rest. [17] °कल्पदर्श° MSS. [18] Introd. § 1, 1. [19] M 1-3; प्रेति omitted in all the rest. [20] BD. VI, 701.

५. आश्विने । अश्विदेवत्ये । द्विबृहत्यनुष्टुबंते । द्वे बृहत्यावनुष्टुप् चांते यस्य तस्मिन्नेव विशिष्टे सूक्तेऽंत्या अर्धर्चाः पंच चैद्यस्य चेदिराजपुत्रस्य कशुनाम्नो नृपस्य दानस्तुतिः । चेदिशब्दाद्वृद्धेत्कोसलाजादाञ्ञ्यङ्[1] चैद्यः ॥

६. अंत्यस्तृचः पर्शुनामराजपुत्रस्य[2] तिरिंदरनाम्नो राज्ञो दानस्तुतिः । पर्शोर्[3]पत्ये ग्रामस्याणो द्व्यः । ओर्गुणः[4] ॥

९. चतुर्दश्याद्ये । चतुर्दशी पंचदशी च ॥

१०. छंदःसांकर्यबाधार्थमपश्यदिति कीर्तितं[6] । प्रगाथशब्दे संदेहश्छंदो वाग्धृचिरिति[7] । अन्यथोत्तरप्रगाथस्याप्यृचिनामत्वमाद्यस्य छंदोवाचित्वं च स्यात् । तत्र द्वितीया सतोबृहती पश्चा-त्तारपंक्तिरिति प्रसज्येत ॥

११. गायत्र इत्यनुवादो[8] न विधिः । स च त्रिष्टुबंतत्वप्राप्तशिष्टाजगतीत्वनिवृत्त्यर्थं ॥४०॥

१४. गोषूक्तिश्चाश्वसूक्तिश्च द्वावृषी । तौ गोत्रतः काण्वायनौ । कण्वशब्दाद्गर्गादित्वाद्यञ् यञि-ञोश्चेति[10] फक् । आपत्यस्य च तद्धितेऽनातीति[11] यलोपाभावः । इदंते नामनी नैव नांते इति विनिर्णयः । गोषूक्तिश्चाश्वसूक्तिश्चेत्येवं सामसु[12] दर्शनात् ॥

१५. उष्णिगक्षरैर्भवति । उष्णिहया सविता सं बभूवेति[13] चाम्नायते ॥

१८. अष्टम्यश्विभ्यामश्विनोरर्थाय । परा नवम्यग्निसूर्यानिलानां स्तुतित्वेन संबंधिनी । तत्रा-निलो वायुः । शिष्टा विंशतिरादित्यदेवत्याः[14] ॥

१९. सूक्तस्यांत्ये षट्त्रिंशीसप्तत्रिंश्यौ यथासंख्यं ककुप्पंक्ती सत्यौ त्रसदस्युनाम्नो राज्ञो दानस्तुतिः । तत्पूर्वे त्रसदस्युदानस्तुतितृचात्पूर्वे चतुस्त्रिंशी पंचत्रिंशी च यथाक्रममुष्णिक्सतोबृहत्यौ सत्यावादि-त्येभ्य आदित्यानामर्थाय ॥

२४. अंत्यस्तृचः सुषामाख्यराजपुत्रस्य वरुनाम्नो राज्ञो दानस्तुतिः । सुषामशब्दादपत्येऽपि न मपूर्वोऽपत्य[15] इति न प्रकृतिभावः ॥

२५. दशम्याद्यास्तिस्रो द्वादश्यंता वैश्वदेव्यः[16] ॥

[1] Pân. IV, i, 171. [2] W 1, P 2; पशुर्ना° I 2; परश्व° P 1; परशु° I 4. [3] W 1; पार्शो: I 2; परशो: P 1, P 2, I 4. [4] Pân. VI, iv, 146. [5] W 1; °साकर्यपश्यदिति I 4; °साकर्यनाधर्यया पश्यदिति P 1; शाकटायनाचार्येण (!) पश्यदिति P 2, I 2. [6] Cp. comm. on VIII, 1. [7] W 1; °चिरित्विति P 1, I 4; °चि P 2, I 2. [8] Cp. Introd. paribhâshâ to Mand. VIII. [9] Introd. § 12, 13. [10] Pân. IV, i, 101. [11] Ibid. VI, iv, 151. [12] Cp. Ârsheya Br. II, 122, and Pañkav. Br. XIX, 4. [13] Rigv. X, 130, 4. [14] This is the comm. in all the MSS. The words चतुर्थ्याद्यास्तस्रोऽदितेः in W 1 are marked with little double horizontal strokes above the line to intimate that they are to be omitted. [15] Pân. VI, iv, 170. [16] W 1; वैश्वदेव्यो वा P 2, I 2; वैश्वदेव्यः omitted in P 1, I 4.

२६. युक्ष्व हीति वायव्यानामादिभूता विंशत्यनुष्टुप्। यद्येवं पूर्वैवैव विंशत्यनुष्टुबाद्या वायव्या इत्युच्यतां। न चाद्यानां तिसृणां वायव्यत्वप्रसंगस्तन्मूर्धा इत्यसंगतेः[3]। सत्यमुक्तं। पुनर्विंशीवच-नार्थोऽत्र विचिंत्यतां॥

२७. मनुर्नाम विवस्वतः सवर्णायां[4] सरण्यूछायायां जातः[5]।

यं सवर्णा मनुं नाम लेभे पुत्रं विवस्वतः[6]।

इति बृहद्देवतादर्शनात्[7]॥

२८. चतुर्थी पुरउष्णिक्। शिष्टास्तिस्रो गायत्र्यः। मनुः। विश्वे देवाः। श्रूयते च। ये त्रिंशति त्रयस्पर इति वैश्वदेवमिति[8]। तानि गायत्राणि गायत्रतृतीयसवन एष त्र्यह इति[8] च॥

२९. मारीचत्वं कश्यपस्य किं नोक्तं जातवेदसि[9]।

तत्रोक्तावत्र कारणत्वं स्यादस्येत्यत्र कथ्यते।

क्वचिदित्यादिनोक्तत्वान्नेति चेत्तर्हि पृच्छ तं॥

दशापि शंसने द्विपदा विंशत्यक्षरा विराजः। श्रूयते च। बभ्रुरेको विषुणः सूनरो युवेति द्विपदाः शंसतीति[10]। अध्ययने चैता द्विर्द्विपदाः पंचर्चः समामनेयुः[11]॥

३०. आद्या गायत्री। द्वितीयाद्याः पुरउष्णिग्बृहत्यनुष्टुभ इत्यनुक्तिर्लाघवाय। अनुवर्तते मनुर्वैव-स्वतो न कश्यपो मारीचो वाविशिष्टत्वात्॥

३१. अत्रादितश्चतुर्ऋचमिज्यास्तवो यज्ञस्तवो यजमानप्रशंसा चास्ति यष्टारश्च स्तूयंते। येत्यादि-पंचम्यारंभादत्रेति तु[12] पूर्वचतुर्ऋचोक्तिः प्रतीयते। या दंपतीत्याद्याः पंचर्चो दंपत्योर्जायापत्योः प्रशंसा। जायाशब्दस्य दंभावः। पतिशब्द उणादिकः[13]। शिष्टा इति वा अंत्या इति वा शक्यमकर्तुं॥४२॥

३४. षोडश्याद्यास्तिस्रो गायत्र्यः। तं गायत्रं तृचं वसुरोचिनामांगिरोगोत्रा ऋषयः सहस्रं संभूयापश्यन्। अंगिरस इति बहुवचनेनांगिरोवंश्या गृह्यंते। कथं। अंगिरःशब्दादृष्यण्। तस्यात्रिभृगुकुत्सवसिष्ठगोतमांगिरोभ्यश्चेति[14] बहुवचने लुक्। तेनांगिरसा इत्यर्थः। अतो गायत्रेऽंत्ये तृचे नीपातिथिरपोद्यते॥

[1] किंचा॰ I 4. [2] तत् in W 1 only. [3] ॰गतः I 4. [4] W 1; सुवर्णायां P 1; सुपर्णाधि P 2; सुवर्णाचां I 4. [5] गतः I 4. [6] W 1; यं सुवर्नाम सुवर्नामा लेभे पुत्रं बृहस्पतेरिति (॰हस्पत इति P 1) P 1, I 4; सुपर्णा नाम मनुर्वचनमालेभे बृहस्पत इति P 2, I 2; M 1–3 read यं सरण्यू मनुर्नाम लेभे पुत्रं विवस्वतः। वैश्वदेवानि पंचैतान्यग्निरुक्थे जगाद सः॥ [7] BD. VI, 719. [8] Ait. Br. V, xxi, 14–15. [9] Cp. comm. on I, 99. [10] Ait. Br. V, xxi, 13. [11] Cp. comm. on Introd. § 12, 10. [12] W 1; ॰रंभा पूर्व॰ P 1, I 4; ॰रभ्य पूर्ववत् P 2, I 2. [13] ॰शब्दो णादिकः W 1; ॰शब्देनोदितः P 1; ॰शब्दे जया आदितः वृद्धिः (!) P 2, I 2. Cp. Uṇâdi-sûtra, IV, 57. [14] Pân. II, iv, 65.

३५. औपरिष्टाज्ज्योतिषं । उपरिष्टाज्ज्योतिश्छंदसा व्याप्तं । उभयपदवृद्धिश्छांदसी ॥

४०. द्वितीया शक्वरी षट्पंचाशदक्षरा । इयं च सप्तपदा । श्रूयते हि । द्वितीया सप्तपदा भवति तां गायत्रीं चानुष्टुभं च करोतीति[2] ॥

४२. आत्रेयोऽर्चनाना ऋषिरिदमपश्यदथवा प्रकृतः काण्वो नाभाकः । अथवास्य सूक्तस्यांत्यं तृचमा वां ग्रावाण इत्यादिकमश्विदेवत्यमनुष्टुप्छंदस्कमेवापश्यदर्चनाना न पूर्वं बाहुर्यां त्रैष्टुभं[3] तृचमपि । प्रथमं वाग्रहणं पक्षे नाभाकप्राप्त्यर्थं । द्वितीयं त्वर्चनानसः पूर्वतृचद्रष्टृत्वबाधनार्थं सदार्चनानसो मुक्तेर्नाभाकत्वप्रदर्शनार्थं[5] ॥

४४. गायत्रमग्निः । सूत्रेऽपि च दृश्यतेऽस्य पूर्वस्य च गायत्राग्नेयत्वमिमे विप्रस्येति सूक्ते इति[6] ॥

४६. वशो नामाश्वपुत्रः । अश्वाद्दृष्यत्यर्थे गर्गादियञ्[7] । वृद्धभावश्छांदसः[8] । अत्र वा स रतु य ईवदेत्यादिभिः कनीतपुत्रस्य पृथुश्रवःसंज्ञकस्य[9] राज्ञो दानस्तुतिः क्रियते । आ स आदीत्यत्र भिसो लुक् छांदसः । आ स आदिभिरित्यर्थः । न हि स्तुतिरादीति संगच्छते । दृश्यते हि बृहद्देवतायां ।

वशायाश्व्याय[10] यत्प्रादात्कानीतस्तु पृथुश्रवाः ।
तदत्र संस्तुतं दानमा स एत्वेवमादिभिः[11][12] ॥ इति ।

त्रयोदशी चतुर्विंशिका चतुर्विंशत्यक्षरा द्विपदा । उत्तरे । द्वे आ स एतु षष्टिं सहस्रेत्येते एकविंशी-द्वाविंश्यौ पंक्ती ॥

४७. त्रितो नामाप्त्यः अप्त्यपुत्रः । ननु चंद्रमा एकोनाप्त्यस्त्रितो वेत्येवं[13] त्रितस्याप्त्यत्वं सिद्धं । असत्याप्त्यवचनेऽत्राधिकारात्काण्वत्वं स्यादिति चेन्न तत् क्वचित्कथंचिन्न्यायेनानुक्तगोत्रविषयत्वात्काण्वत्वस्य । एवं तर्ह्याप्त्य इति विस्पष्टार्थं । आदित्येभ्यः । आदित्यानामर्थायेदं सूक्तं । आदित्यमित्यनुक्तिरदितेः स्यादिति[14] शंकानिवृत्त्यर्थं । तर्ह्यादित्यानां[15] तृचमादित्यमित्यत्र[16] स्वनिर्देशेऽप्यादित्यप्रतीतिवदत्राप्यस्तु । न च तत्रादित्यानामित्यादित्यशब्द[17]श्रवणात् स्पष्टादित्यप्रतीतिरिति वक्तुं युक्तमाप्यादित्या अव हि ख्यतेति[18] श्रवणात् । तर्हि वैचित्र्यार्थं चतुर्थ्या निर्देशः । चतुर्दश्याद्याः पंचोपसेऽपि । उषसोऽप्यर्थाय । महापांक्तं । उत्तरपदवृद्धिश्छांदसी[19] ॥

[1] उत्तर° W 1. [2] Ait. Âr. I, v, 1, 10. [3] W 1; न पूर्वः वा त्रैष्टुभं P 1, P 2, I 2; पूर्वं वा त्रैष्टुभं I 4; न omitted in I 4. [4] °नसमुक्ते° W 1; °नसमित्युक्ते° P 1; °नसमित्युक्ते I 4; सदर्चनानमभ्यासमित्युक्तेर्नाभाकः P 2, I 2. [5] W 1; नाभाकः the rest. Gagannâtha has the comment: अर्चनाना चात्रेयो बाहुयामंत्यस्तृच आश्विनस्तं वै चार्चनाना ऋषिः । [6] Âsv. Sr.-sûtra, IV, xiii, 7. [7] W 1; अपत्याद्दृश्यणादिना यत् P 1; अपत्यवृष्यणादिना यन् I 4; अपत्याद्दृष्यणादिना यत् P 2, I 2. [8] W 1 only. [9] पृथुश्रवसो W 1. [10] W 1; °श्व्याय the rest and M 1-3. [11] स इत्येवेम° M 1-3. [12] BD. VI, 729. [13] Sûtra on I, 105. [14] स्याद् W 1 only. [15] तर्हि W 1 only. [16] Sûtra on VII, 51. [17] W 1; तत्रादित्यानामादित्यास इति श्र° the rest. [18] Ver. 11. [19] P 2 and I 4 omit the Khilas; P 1, however, has both text and comm., omitting only 58.

६४. गायत्रे सूक्ते सत्यंत्या देवदेवत्या सती त्रिष्टुप्। गायत्र इत्यनुवादः। पूर्वं गायत्रमिति शक्यमकर्तुमनुवादेनैव सिद्धेः[1] ॥

६७. मत्स्यो नाम सांमदः। संमदाख्यमहामीनराजपुत्रः। अथवा मित्रावरुणपुत्रो मान्यो नामर्षिः। अथवा बहवो जालनद्धा आनाये[2] बद्धा मत्स्या ऋषय आदित्यान् स्वोपद्रवशांतयेऽस्तुवन् स्तुतवंतः। मत्स्यानां गोत्रं नास्त्यनुपदेशात्। ऋषीणामेव विकल्पो न देवतायाः। तेन सांमदमान्ययोरादित्या एव स्तुत्याः[3] ॥४४॥

६८. सूक्तस्यादितश्चत्वारस्तृचा अनुष्टुम्मुखाः। अनुष्टुब्गायत्र्यौ चानुष्टुभोऽनुष्टुम्मुखास्तृचा[4] इत्युक्तं। उप मा षडित्याद्यंत्याः षडृचश्चतुर्दश्याद्या ऋक्षाश्वमेधयो राज्ञोर्दानस्तुतिः। आद्यावित्ति किं। तृच-चतुष्टयस्यांत्यतृचद्वयस्य च दानस्तुतित्वं मा भूत्। एवमिष्टं चेदंत्या ऋक्षाश्वमेधयोर्दानस्तुतिरित्येवा-वक्ष्यदिति चेत् तर्हि विस्पष्टार्थं। ननु बृहद्देवतायां।

ऐंद्राणि त्रीणि सूक्तानि[5] स्तौत्यृतूनुप[6] मेति षट्।
ऋक्षाश्वमेधयोरत्र पंच दानस्तुतिः पराः[7] ॥

इत्युच्यते। तत्कथमत्र षण्णामपि दानस्तुतित्वमुक्तं। सत्यं। अयं[8] नृक्षस्तुतिमपि राजदानस्तुतिशेषां मन्यते देवतानुक्रमण्यां षट्कस्य दानस्तुतित्वस्यैवोक्तेः। तथा हि।

उप मेत्यासु चेंद्रोऽतोऽश्वमेध ऋक्ष एव च[10]।
प्रीतौ यद्ददतुर्वित्तं प्रियमेधस्तदब्रवीत् ॥ इति पठ्यते ॥

६९. अपादिंद्रो अपादग्निरित्यर्धर्चो[11] वैश्वदेवः। अतः परे वरुण इदिहेत्याद्यास्त्रयोऽर्धर्चा वरुणदेवत्याः ॥

७१. सुदीतिः पुरुमीळ्हश्चेति[12] द्वावांगिरसौ सहापश्यतां। अथवा तयोरन्यतरोऽपश्यत् ॥

७२. अग्निः। अथवा हविषां स्तुतिः ॥

७४. त्रयोदश्याद्यास्तिस्रोऽंत्या अनुष्टुभः सत्य ऋक्ष[13]नामराजपुत्रस्य श्रुतर्वनाम्नो राज्ञो दानस्तुतिः। पारिशेष्यसिद्धेस्तिस्र इति प्राप्तानुवादः। छंदोवचनं गायत्रत्वापवादः। आत्रेयो गोपवनोऽनुवर्तते न तु सप्तवध्रिः। स हि वाविशिष्टः ॥

८०. एकद्यूर्नाम नौधसः पुत्रः। गायत्रे सूक्ते सत्यंत्या देवदेवत्या सती त्रिष्टुप्। गायत्र इत्यनुवादः शिष्टाजगतीत्वापवादः ॥

[1] P 1 reads as W 1 in the text, P 2 and I 4 as I 2. The comm. is the same in all. [2] Omitted in W 1. [3] *Gagannâtha* says: दशम्येकादशीद्वादशीष्वदितिः। [4] Introd. § 11, 6. [5] ऐंद्राख्या त्वा रथं त्रीणि M 1-3. [6] M 1-3; स्तौतनूभृमु° P 1; स्तोतनुभृमु° I 4; स्तुतवतो भृमु° P 2, I 2; सूक्तान्युप मेति षट् W 1. [7] BD. VI, 736. [8] कात्या° marg. corr. in W 1. [9] ऋक्ष° in W 1 only; स्तुतिमपि the rest. [10] W 1; एवेति च the rest. [11] Ver. 11 a. [12] In the text P 1 and I 4 read त्वं नः सुदीतिपुरुमीळ्ह-योर्वान्यतर; P 2 as I 2. [13] आर्क्ष° P 1.

८१. कुसीदी नाम[1] काण्वगोत्रः ॥४५॥

८४. उशना नाम कवेः पुत्रः । गर्गादित्वाद्यम्[2] ॥

८६. विश्वको वा नाम कृष्णपुत्रः । सुप्यव्ययपवादो[3] बाह्वादित्वादिञ्[4] । वेत्युक्तेरांगिरसः कृष्ण
एव वा ॥

८७. द्विर्वेत्युक्तेः प्रकृत आंगिरसः कृष्ण एव वा । वाविशिष्टत्वान्न तु कार्ष्णिर्विश्वकः प्रकृतोऽपि ॥

८८. नोधा गौतमः । नू चित्सव नोधा गौतम[5] इति सूक्तं ॥

८९. नृमेधपुरुमेधौ सहापश्यतां तौ आंगिरसौ ॥

९१. आपाला नामर्षिका कन्यार्षिपुत्रिका[6] । इंद्रमधिकृत्यापाला[7] नाम तपश्चचार सामगा[8]
समामनंति । ऐंद्र इतिहासः । अत्रावगंतव्य[9] इति शेषः । इतिहासश्चायं[10] ।

अपालात्रिसुता त्वासीत्कन्या त्वग्दोषिणी पुरा ।
अत एव दुर्भगेति भर्त्रा त्यक्ता सती पथि ॥१॥
सौम्याद्रसादिंद्रतृप्तिरिति यज्ञस्य वाक्श्रुतेः[11] ।
अन्विच्छंती सोमलतां जलायावतरत्तदा ॥२॥
सोममप्यविदत्कन्यापाभ्यगा[12]त्पितुराश्रमं ।
तामिंद्रश्चकमे दृष्ट्वा विजने पितुराश्रमे ॥३॥
तपसा बुबुधे सा तु सर्वमिंद्रचिकीर्षितं ।
सुषाव स्वमुखे[13] सोमं स्वैर्दंतैर्ग्रावभिस्त्विति[14] ॥४॥
तस्या भक्ष्यतिरेकेण पपाविंद्रश्च तन्मुखात् ।
निरगात्स क्षुधि[15]तः पूर्वं भक्षयित्वा गृहान्मुनेः[16] ॥५॥
उदकुंभं समादाय तेन सार्धं तु[17] साप्यगात् ।

[1] W 1; कुसीदी नामा P 2, I 2; कुसीदिर्नाम P 1; कुसी नाम I 4. Cp. Nirukta, VI, 32.
[2] In Gana गर्गादि read कवि for कपि (Böhtlingk's Pân. vol. ii).
[3] W 1; आतंतपाद P 1, I 4; अनंतया P 2.
[4] बाह्वादिलक्षण इञ् W 1.
[5] Sûtra on I, 58.
[6] कन्या W 1 only.
[7] यामधि° MSS.; यां मधिहृत्य I 2.
[8] माना W 1; साम नाम P 1; सोम नाम P 2, I 2; समा नाम I 4.
[9] W 1; अत्रोच्यते the rest.
[10] Shadg.'s version and that of the BD. (eight lines being almost identical in the two) are printed in M. M.'s *Rigv.* vol. iv, pp. 46–47; cp. also various readings, pp. 43–46. Many expressions are taken verbatim from the *Sâtyâyana* Br. Sâyana quotes the story from the Br.
[11] W 1; यज्ञस्तु – – या – – भूत् P 1; यज्ञस्तुत्युपायो भूत् P 2, I 2; यज्ञस्तुतिः – – या भूत् I 4.
[12] °याागात् W 1; °ह्यागा P 1; °ह्यागाद्यत् P 2; °ह्योगाद्यत् I 2; °ह्यां गा I 4.
[13] W 1; सासुपातमुखे P 1; साश्रुपातमुखे P 2, I 2; सा सुतया मुखे I 4.
[14] W 1; °स्त्विह the rest.
[15] क्षुधित् W 1.
[16] गृहान्मुनः W 1.
[17] W 1; अपामर्थे च P 1; पानार्थे व्ययमप्यगात् P 2, I 2; पानार्थं साप्यगात् I 4.

ऋग्भिः स्तुत्वा जगादेंद्रं कुरु मां सुत्वचं त्विति ॥६॥
रथच्छिद्रे गतामिंद्रः शकटस्य युगस्य च ।
प्रक्षिप्य निष्कर्ष त्रिः सुत्वक् सा तु ततो[1]ऽभवत् ॥७॥
तस्याः पूर्वहता[2] या त्वग्जातिः सा शल्यको[3]ऽभवत् ।
उत्तरा त्वभवद्गोधा कृकलासस्तथोत्तमा[4] ॥८॥ इति[5] ॥

९५. आंगिरस इति शक्यमकर्तुं[6] ॥

९६. तिरश्चीर्नामांगिरसः । अथवा द्युतानो मरुतां[7] पुत्रः ॥

९७. बृहतीछंदस्कं । अत्र चांततः षष्ठीं छंदोविशेषमाह । अंततः । अंत आद्यादित्वात्तसिः[8] ॥४६॥

१००. उपांत्ये दशम्येकादश्यौ वाच्यौ वाग्देवत्ये । वाचो देवताशिष ङीप्यौटि यण् ॥

१०१. अत्र प्र यो वां मित्रावरुणेति तृतीया गायत्री । न यः संपृच्छ इति चतुर्थी सतोबृहती । तृतीयाद्युक्तिश्चतुर्थ्यर्थो[9] । द्वितीयतृचस्य बृहतीस्थाने गायत्रीवचने[10] संयोगशिष्टत्वात्प्रगाथस्य चतुर्थ्याः सतोबृहतीत्वं दुर्लभमिति सतोबृहतीवचनं । स्तोत्रं राजसु गायतेति पूर्वगतपादेन सपादा पादसहिता ते हिन्विरे अरुणमित्यृगादित्यदेवतेत्यर्थः । इत्यनेने[11]त्यध्याहृत्यात्र[12] नेयं । अथ द्वे अश्विदेवत्ये द्वे वायुदेवत्ये द्वे सूर्यदेवत्ये । अथेयं या नीचीति बृहती सत्युमोदेवत्या । अत्र त्रिष्टु-बंतमिति चतुर्दश्यास्त्रिष्टुब्वचनेन प्रगाथस्य निवृत्तत्वात्त्रयोदश्या बृहतीत्वं दुर्लभमिति बृहतीवचनं[13] । अथवा सूर्यप्रभानया स्तूयते । अथ पवमानदेवत्या । माता रुद्राणामिति द्वे गोदेवत्ये ॥

१०२. भृगुगोत्रः प्रयोगो नामर्षिः । अथवा बार्हस्पत्यः पावकविशेषणोऽग्निर्ऋषिः । अथवा सहोनाम्नः पुत्रौ गृहपतियविष्ठसंज्ञा[14]वग्नी सहापश्यतां । अथवा तयोरन्यतरः ॥

१०३. अष्टम्यादि युजः । अष्टमी दशमी द्वादशी चतुर्दशी चेति चतस्रो यथाक्रमं ककुब्गाय-त्री[15]ककुबनुष्टुबिति स्युः । जसो लुगिति स्युरित्यध्याहृत्य नेयं ॥

॥ इत्यष्टमं मंडलं समाप्तं ॥

[1] W 1; सुत्वक् सतो भगवत् P 1, I 4; सुत्वक् सद्यः स वै भवत् P 2, I 2. [2] पूर्वगता I 4. [3] P 1, P 2, I 2; चल्यको I 4; शल्लूको W 1. [4] कृकलासंस्तथोत्तमेति W 1; कृकलस्याथोत्तमे P 1; कृकलासंस्तथोत्तमे P 2, I 2; कलासास्याप्योत्तमे I 4. [5] इति in W 1 only. Cp. BD. VI, 742 b–748 a. [6] W 1; °वक्तुं the rest. A marg. note in W 1: सांहितभाष्ये आ त्वा नव तिरश्चीरानुष्टुभमिति पाठः. [7] I 4, P 2, I 2; माहुतस्य corr. to मरुतां W 1; माहुतिः पुत्रः P 1. [8] W 1; अंते आदिआदित्यादित्वात् P 1, I 4; अंते आदि-त्यादित्वात् P 2, I 2. Cp. Vart. to Pân. V, iv, 44. [9] W 1; चतुर्थीत्यनुक्यर्थो P 1; चतुर्थीत्यनुक्यर्थः P 2, I 2; चतुर्थीत्वस्य I 4. [10] W 1; °नेन च P 1, P 2. [11] W 1; इत्यनेनाध्या° I 4; इत्यनेने ध्या° P 1; इत्यने ध्या° P 2, I 2. [12] अत्र W 1 only. [13] The comm. अत्र त्रि° to बृहतीवचनं in W 1 only. [14] यविष्ठसंज्ञौ W 1; °यविष्ठौ इति संज्ञौ the rest, which in the text read °यविष्ठ°. [15] All the MSS. read गायत्री in the comm.; P 1 reads गायत्री in the text also; P 2 and I 4 हसीयसी in the text.

९. अथ नवमं मंडलमधिकृत्य परिभाषते । नवमं मंडलं पावमानं सौम्यं । वक्ष्यमाणं नवमं मंडलं सोमदेवत्यं । स च सोमः पवमानगुणः । पावमानमिति विशेषणस्य पृथक्करणं क्वचित्सोमापवादभूताग्न्यादेरपि पवमानगुणत्वार्थं । तथा च लिंगं सूक्ते[1]ऽग्नेः पवमानस्य । अग्न आयूंषि पवसे[2]ऽग्ने पवस्वेति[3] द्वे दृष्टे[4] । मंडलमित्यसत्यपवादेऽत्र सौम्यत्वाय । नवममिति द्वितीयादिवद्विस्पष्टार्थमेव ॥

५. असितो नाम काश्यपो गोत्रतः[5] । अथवा देवलो नाम सोऽपि[6] काश्यपः । भवति हि प्रवरः काश्यपासितदैवलेति[7] । विंशतिः सूक्तानि । इदमादीन्यपश्यदिति वाक्यशेषः[8] । अत्राद्यमिदमेकादशर्चं सूक्तमाप्रियं[9] । आप्रिदेवताः समिद्धादिस्वाहाकृत्यंता देवताः । अत्र तनूनपाद्द्वितीयो न तु नराशंस आप्रमित्यनुक्तेः ।

नवमे मंडलेऽनुक्तेरासां न पवमानता ।
इहातिदिष्टा[10] अन्यत्र व्युत्पन्नाः[11] सविशेषणाः[12] ॥१॥
ननु विंशतिः सूक्तानीत्यवाच्यं[13]मनुवृत्तितः ।
न[14] मधुच्छंदसा[15] ह्यादौ दशसूक्तग्रहः कृतः ॥२॥
सत्यं । असितस्यानुवृत्तिः स्याद्वान्वयाद्देवलस्य न ।
इत्यृषिद्वययोगार्थं विंशतिग्रहणं कृतं ॥३॥
तर्हि विंशतिः सूक्तानीत्यनुक्त्वा प्राग्दृढच्युतात् ।
इति वाच्यं लाघवार्थमिति चेत् पृच्छ तं मुनिं ॥४॥

२४. असितदेवलयोः काश्यपयोः पूर्णोऽवधिः ॥

६०. तृतीयेति न तु प्रोक्तं लाघवाद्द्गुणोक्तितः ॥

६५. भृगुर्नाम वारुणिर्वरुणपुत्रः । श्रूयते हि । तस्मात्स भृगुर्वारुणिरिति[17] भृगुर्वै वारुणिरिति श्रुत्यंतरं[18] । तेन वरुणगोत्रो[19] भृगुर्वा जमदग्निर्वेति नैव शंका ॥

६६. वैखानसा ऋषयः शतं संभूयेदं सूक्तमपश्यन् ।

[1] सूत्रे MSS. [2] *Rigv.* IX, 66, 19. [3] Ibid. ver. 21. [4] W 1; °ति दृष्टे P 1, P 2, I 2; °ति दृष्टं I 4. [5] W 1; काश्यपगोत्रः the rest. [6] W 1; देवलनामापि the rest. [7] काश्यपासितो दैवलेति W 1; काश्यपोऽसितो देवलो वेति P 2, I 2, I 4; काश्यपोऽसितो देवलेति P 1. [8] सूक्तान्यपश्यदिति शेषः W 1. See Âsv. *Sr.*-sûtra, XII, x, 8; M. M., A. S. L., p. 385. [9] W 1, P 2, I 2; आप्रियः I 4; आप्रः P 1. [10] W 1; इह चिदिष्टा P 1, I 4; इह चिदृष्टा P 2, I 2. [11] अन्यत्रोत्पन्नाः W 1. [12] W 1 only. [13] W 1; °नीति वाच्यं the rest. [14] न in P 1 only. [15] W 1, I 4; °सो P 1; °दो P 2, I 2. [16] Pâ*n*. VI, i, 87. [17] Ait. Br. III, xxxiv, 1. [18] W 1, P 1, I 4; श्रूयते P 2, I 2; Sat. Br. XI, vi, 1, 1 (where the reading is भृगुर्ह वै). [19] W 1, I 4; °गोत्रे P 1, P 2, I 2.

नैषामांगिरसत्वं स्यादुपदेशेष्वदर्शनात् ।
यथा[1] हि पौरुषे सूक्ते[2] ऋषेर्नारायणस्य तु ॥
यथोपदेशमित्येतत्सर्वैर्नैषानुवर्तते[3] ।
पवस्वेत्यृषयः सूक्तं शतं वैखानसा विदुः ॥

इत्येतावदेव स्वार्षानुक्रमण्यां । तत्राष्टादश्यनुष्टुप् । प्रागगायत्रत्वापवादः । ततः परास्तिस्र एकोनविंशीविंश्येकविंश्योऽग्निदेवत्याः । सोम एव बाध्यते न तु पवमानैर्गुणः । तमग्निर्लभते ॥

६७. आदौ भरद्वाजाद्याः सप्तर्षयः । तृचाः । तिस्र ऋचो दृष्टा यैरिति । आदितः प्रत्येकं[6] क्रमेण तृचदर्शिन इत्यर्थः । इति ह सप्त ऋषयः । इति क्रमतो नामभिः[7] परामृश्यंते । हेति प्रसिद्धौ । एवं नामक्रमका[8] एते सप्तर्षय इह शास्त्रे ग्राह्या इत्यर्थः । एतच्च परीतः षड्विंशतिः सप्तर्षयः[9] प्रागाथम्[10] उत देवाः सप्तर्षय एकर्चा[11] इत्यत्र चैषामेवं नामक्रमकाणामेव ग्रहणार्थं । असत्यस्मिन्सप्त एव तत्र[13] पठितव्याः स्युः । केवलसप्तर्षितः[14] प्रसिद्धेस्तेषामेव ग्रहणेऽप्येष क्रमो दुर्लभः स्यात् । शास्त्रांतरेषु क्रमन्यायेनान्यत्र पददर्शनात्[15] । अत्र तु नास्त्युपयोगः । उक्तिगणनयैव[16] सिद्धेरेक-[17] विंशतिर्गताः । अथ शेष एकादशर्चे पवित्रो नामर्षिरांगिरसो मैत्रावरुणिर्वसिष्ठो वा । अथवा पवित्रवसिष्ठौ सहापश्यतां । शेष इति पूर्वैकविंशत्यृच[18] एतयोरनन्वयार्थं । अत्र च पवस्व सोम मंदयन्नित्याद्यास्तिस्रो गायत्र्यो नित्यद्विपदाः । नित्यमध्ययने द्विर्द्विपदत्वं[19] निवृत्त्यर्थं । गायत्र्य इति विंशतिका विराजो[20] मा भूवन्निति । अविता नो अजाश्व इति तिस्रः पूषदेवत्याः पवमानसोमदेवत्या वा । यत्ते पवित्रमर्चिषीत्याद्याः पंचर्चोऽग्निदेवत्याः । आसां पंचानामंत्यास्तृतीयाद्यास्तिस्र एव साविच्यग्निसावित्री वैश्वदेवी वेति[21] । उभाभ्यां देव सवितरिति सवितृदेवत्या । त्रिभिष्ट्वमित्यग्निसवितृदेवत्या । पुनंतु मामिति वैश्वदेवीत्यर्थः । अत्र त्रिंशी त्रिंशतः पूरणयलाप्यस्येत्येषा पुरउष्णिक् । पुनंतु मां देवजना इति सप्तविंश्यनुष्टुप् । यः पावमानीरध्येति पावमानीर्यो अध्येतीति द्वे एकत्रिंशी द्वात्रिंशी चानुष्टुभौ । ते चांत्ये ऋचौ पावमानीनां नवममंडलवर्तिनीनामृचामध्येतॄणां

[1] W 1, I 4; अथा P 1, P 2, I 2. [2] *Rigv.* X, 90. [3] °वर्त्यते W 1. [4] W 1; अत्र च the rest. [5] पावक° W 1. [6] प्रत्येक° P 1. [7] W 1; इति नामानि P 2, I 2; नाक्रम नामनी परामृश्येते I 4; नाकमनी परामृश्यते P 1. [8] °क्रमतो W 1. [9] इह शास्त्रे to सप्तर्षयः in W 1 only. [10] Sûtra on IX, 107. [11] Sûtra on X, 137. [12] °कानां W 1. [13] एतत्तृचाः I 4. [14] W 1; सप्तयुक्तौ the rest. [15] क्रमनानात्यत्वदर्शनात् P 1; क्रमन्याय्येनान्यत्वपददर्शनात् P 2, I 2; क्रमनामान्यत्वदर्शनात् I 4; शास्त्रांतरेषु to °नात् omitted in W 1. [16] °गणनैव W 1. [17] W 1; °सिद्धेरित्य° the rest. [18] W 1, I 4; °त्यृचेन तयोर° P 1; °तितृचेन तयोरन्वयार्थं P 2, I 2. [19] W 1; °पदेति नि° the rest. Cp. Introd. § 12, 10. [20] Ibid. § 12, 8. [21] W 1; °देवीति the rest.

प्रस्तुतिं[1] कुरुतः। अनुक्तछंदसां[2] गायत्री। अनुक्तदेवतासु सोमः। सोमदेवताः पवमानगुणवत्यः[3]। प्राग्वात्सप्रेर्गायत्रत्वस्य पूर्वो[4]ऽवधिः। अथोत्तरार्थं परिभाषते[5]। जागतमूर्ध्वं प्रागुशनसः। प्र तु नवोशनेति[6] वक्ष्यति। प्रागेतस्मा[7]दुशनःसंशब्दनादि[8]त ऊर्ध्वं यत्सूक्तजातं[9] तत्सर्वमसत्यपवादे जगतीछंदस्कं विद्यात्[10]। तेन हरिं मृजंति[11] सूक्ते द्रप्सस्येत्या[12]दौ जगतीछंदस्त्व[13]मिति सिद्धं। प्र देवमित्यादिसूक्तचतुष्टये त्रिष्टुबंततया शिष्टजगतीत्वसिद्धेर्लेखोदाहृतं[14]। तर्हि तत्र वाच्यं स्यादिति चेद्व अत्र तत्र चोक्तौ न लाघवं। त्रिष्टुबंतसूक्तात्रयोऽपि हि स्तुतिः[15]। ऊर्ध्वं प्रागिति सिद्धे व्यर्थमुभयमिति चोक्तं[16]त्यमेतत्।

आचार्यस्य तु शैलीयं यत्प्रागित्यवधिग्रहः।

प्राग्वात्सप्रेः प्राग्धैरव्यस्तूपादित्यशृणोत्म किं[17]।

विस्पष्टार्थमूर्ध्वमिति प्रोक्तं नान्यत्प्रयोजनं॥

६८. वात्सप्री[18]र्नाम भलंदनस्यापत्यं॥

७०–७१. तौ वैश्वामित्रौ। तावुक्तौ रेणुवृषभौ विश्वामित्रपुत्रौ। श्रूयते हि। अथ ह विश्वामित्रः पुत्रानामंत्रयामास।

मधुच्छंदाः शृणोतन ऋषभो रेणुरष्टकः[19]। इति॥

८२. इति त्रिष्टुबंते। इत्येते प्रकृते प्र सोमस्यासावीति पूर्वे सूक्ते त्रिष्टुबंते न केवलजागते॥

८४. नन्वभि तष्टेवेत्यत्र[20] प्रजापतेर्वाच्यत्वमुक्तमेव किमिति पुनरुच्यते। तत्र हि वैश्वामित्रत्वमप्युक्तं। तन्मा भूदिति॥

८६. दशर्चा ऋषिगणाश्चत्वारोऽपश्यन्। दशर्चो दृष्टा यैस्ते। प्रथमेऽत्र दशर्चे द्रष्टारोऽकृष्टा इति माषा इति च[21] द्विनामानः। द्वितीयदशर्चे सिकता इति निवावरी इति च[22] द्विनामानः। तृतीयदशर्चे पृश्नयोऽजा इति च द्विनामानः। एषां द्विनामत्वं यावच्छ्[23]र्ज्ञेयमदृष्टार्थं। चतुर्थे दशर्चेऽत्रय[24]

[1] W 1; °ध्येतारं प्रति स्तुतिं the rest. [2] °छंदस्सु I 4. [3] सोमपवमानदेवत्याः W 1. [4] W 1, I 4; अत उ° P 1, P 2, I 2. [5] Sûtra on IX, 87. [6] W 1; यं सोमो द्यौ added in the rest. [7] प्रागेव त° W 1. [8] P 1, P 2, I 2; शब्दनाद्व W 1; °शनस प्राक् I 4. [9] W 1; जागतं the rest. [10] W 1; वेदितव्यं the rest. [11] Rigv. IX, 72. [12] Ibid. IX, 73. [13] W 1; °स्क I 4; जगती छंद P 1, P 2, I 2. [14] °जगतीत्वे सिद्धेऽपि P 2, I 2. [15] त्रिष्टुबंतं सूक्तात्रयोपि द स्तुतिम् P 1; त्रिष्टुबतसूक्तत्रयो पि दस्तुतिम् I 4; त्रिष्टुबंतं सूक्तादस्तुतिः P 2, I 2; त्रिष्टुबंतं सूक्तात्रयो पि ह स्तुतिर् C; written on margin in W 1, apparently the same as in C, but partly illegible. [16] W 1; ऊर्ध्वं प्रागिति चेत् the rest. [17] श्रवणान्न किं I 4. [18] W 1, I 4; वात्सप्रिः P 1, P 2, I 2, in both text and comm. Cp. Aufrecht's note in his Index. [19] Ait. Br. VII, xvii, 7. [20] W 1; तदभितष्टीये सूक्ते the rest. Rigv. III, 38. [21] च W 1, C. [22] च in W 1 only. [23] W 1; °श्यं the rest. [24] I 4; दशर्चे अत्रय W 1, C; दशर्चे अत्र P 2, I 2; दशर्चे त्रयो ष्यत ऋषिगणाः पश्यन् P 1.

इतिनामानः । इति चत्वारिंशद्गताः । एषां[1] गोत्रमुपदेशेष्वनुक्तेनोक्तं यथा[2] पूर्वेण वैखानसशतस्य[3] । अथ पंचाग्निर्भौमो ददर्श । अथांत्यास्तिस्रो गृत्समदोऽपश्यत् । स चांगिरसः शौनहोत्रो भूत्वा भार्गवः शौनकोऽभवत्[4] ॥

९६. दिवोदासराजपुत्रः प्रतर्दनो नाम राजर्षिः ॥

९७. आद्यं तृचं मैत्रावरुणिर्वसिष्ठो दृष्टवान् । अथ नव तृचान्वसिष्ठपुत्रा नव पृथगपश्यन् । ते चेंद्रप्रमत्यादिनामानः । पृथगिति नवानामपि नवसु तृचेषु संभूयदर्शित्वं मा भूत् । वसिष्ठा इत्यृष्यण्णोऽत्रिभृग्विति[5] लुक् । एतच्चेंद्रप्रमत्यादीनां गोत्रार्थं ॥

९८. अंबरीषो नाम वृषागीरा[6]जपुत्रः । ऋजिश्वा नाम भरद्वाजपुत्रः । बृहस्पतिपौत्रो वा भरतपौत्रो वे[7]त्युक्तः[8] । चेति[9] सहत्वाय[10] । तौ सहापश्यतामित्यर्थः ॥

९९. रेभसूनु[11]नामानौ द्वावृषी काश्यपौ सहेदमपश्यतां ॥

१०१. अंधीगुर्नाम श्यावाश्वपुत्रः । अत इन्नोऽपवाद ऋष्यण्यपवादत्वाद्बाह्वादीञ् । ययातिर्नाम राजा नहुषपुत्रः । नहुषोऽपि राजा मनुपुत्रः । मनुरपि राजा संवरणपुत्रः । इत्येते चत्वारस्तृचास्तिस्र ऋचो दृष्टा यैः । इति द्वादश गताः । शेषे चतुर्ऋचे प्रजापतिर्ऋषिः । वैश्वामित्रो वाच्यो वेत्युक्तः । शेष इति शक्यमकर्तुं पारिशेष्यादेव सिद्धेः ॥

१०४. पर्वतनारदौ सहापश्यतां । तौ काण्वावित्युक्तौ । अथवा कश्यपपुत्र्यौ शिखंडिनीनाम्या[12]वप्सरसौ सहापश्यतां । द्वे इत्यनुक्रमण्यंतरा[13]नुकरणं[14] ॥

१०५. पर्वतनारदावित्यनुवर्तते । नाप्सरसौ शिखंडिन्यौ । वाविशिष्टे हि ते ॥

१०६. अग्निर्नाम चक्षुर्नाम्नः पुत्रश्चक्षुर्नाम मनुपुत्रो मनुर्नामाप्सुनाम्नः पुत्र इति ते त्रयस्तृचाः । तिस्र ऋचो दृष्टा यैः । इति नवर्चो गताः । अथ पंचर्चोऽग्निर्नामापश्यत् । अयमपि चाक्षुष एव । इदानीमेव सुक्तमग्निश्चाक्षुष इति । पंचेति शक्यमकर्तुं पारिशेष्यादेव सिद्धेः ॥

१०७. सप्तर्षयो भरद्वाजः कश्यपो गोतमोऽत्रिर्विश्वामित्रो जमदग्निर्वसिष्ठ[15] इत्युक्ताः । तत्रैवैतेषां[16] गोत्राणि व्याख्यातानि । एते चेदं सूक्तं संभूयापश्यन् पृथग्दर्शनहेत्वाभावात् । इदं च सूक्तं बार्हतप्रगाथप्रायं । तत्र तृतीयैकविंशत्यक्षरत्वाद्भुरिग्विराड् द्विपदा । षोडशी च विंशत्यक्षरा विराड् द्विपदा । अष्टमीनवम्यौ बृहत्यौ ॥

१०८. गौरिवीतिः शाक्त्यो ऋचमपश्यदिति शेषः । शक्तिरेकां । तृतीयां वासिष्ठः शक्तिरपश्यत् ।

[1] एवं W 1. [2] W 1; तथा the rest. [3] Cp. sûtra on IX, 66. [4] Cp. Introd. to Mand. II. [5] Cp. Pân. II, iv, 65. [6] वृषागिररा° W 1; वृषागीर्नामरा° the rest. [7] Cp. sûtra on VI, 52. [8] क्तं I 4. [9] वेति P 1, I 4. [10] W 1; सहतत्वाय the rest. [11] °सूनौ W 1; °सूनू° the rest. [12] W 1; °न्यौ नाम चा° the rest. [13] W 1; °क्रमण्यनुक° the rest. [14] W 1; °करणमेतत् the rest. [15] Sûtra on IX, 67. [16] W 1; तत्र तेषां the rest.

ऊरुर्नामांगिरस ऋजिश्वा नाम भारद्वाज ऊर्ध्वसद्मा नामांगिरसः कृतयशा नामांगिरस ऋणंचयो नाम राजर्षिरित्येते पंचर्षयो तृचा द्वे ऋचौ दृष्टे यैः। इति त्रयोदश गताः। अथ तिस्रः शक्तिर्वासिष्ठोऽपश्यत्। तिस्र इति शक्यमकर्तुं पारिशेष्यादेव सिद्धेः॥

१०९. अग्नयो नामर्षयो धिष्ण्या यज्ञवेदौ सदसि[1] धिष्ण्यवंतः। ऐश्वरयः[2]। ईश्वरपुत्राः। वाह्लादित्यादिभ्[3]। एते सहापश्यन्[4]। द्वैपदं सूक्तं। विंशतिका द्विपदा विराजः॥

नवमं मंडलं चेदं पावमानं प्रवर्णितं[5]।
इदानीं दशमं सम्यग्वक्ष्यमेव विजृंभते॥

॥ नवमं मंडलं समाप्तं॥

१०.

अग्न इत्यादि दशमं मंडलं तु प्रसिद्धितः।
अनुवाकानुक्रमणीप्रोक्तसंख्यान्वयादपि॥
आचार्यस्तु स्वयं नेदं[6] प्रोक्तवान्निष्फलं ततः[7]।
मंडलाद्याग्नेयतादिसिद्धौ ज्ञेयं तथापि तत्॥

८. तृचोऽंत्य इंद्रदेवत्यः। ऐंद्रवचनं मंडलादिष्वाग्नेयनिवृत्त्यर्थं। अत एवाग्न इत्यादि दशमं मंडलमनुमीमहे। अन्यथाग्न इत्याग्नेय्यः[8] पंचपंचाशदित्यवक्ष्यत्। ऐंद्रत्वमनादेशादेवासाधयिष्यत्॥

९. वेत्युक्तः प्रकृतस्त्वाष्ट्रस्त्रिशिराः। अब्देवत्यं॥

१०. विवस्वत्सुतयोर्यमयम्योः परस्परं संवादः। कथमित्याह। यच्चीत्यादि। वैवस्वती यमी वैवस्वतं भ्रातारं मिथुनार्थं मैथुनार्थं (अण्यादिवृद्ध्यभावश्छांदसः[10]) यच्चर्चान्याभिश्चायुग्भिः प्रोवाच। प्रणयेमोक्तवती। अवश्यं कुरु मास्मानवबाधिष्ठा[11] इति। ततः स च यमस्तां यमीं स्वसारं नवम्यर्चान्याभिश्च युग्भिरनिच्छन्मनसैवाकार्यमिति रतिस्पृहारहितः सन्प्रत्याचष्टे। प्रतिकूलमेवोक्तवान्।

[1] W 1; ये यज्ञसद P 1; ये यज्ञसदसि P 2, I 2; ये यज्ञे सहसि I 4. [2] W 1; अथ आद्य -- ईश्वरपुत्राः P 1; अथ आद्य ईश्वरपुत्रा P 2, I 2; अथाद्याद्वेश्वरपुत्राः I 4. ऐश्वरयो is the reading of P 1, P 2, I 4 in the text. [3] Corr. for वार्हतादित्रा W 1; वार्ध्वेधिवृदिभ् (sic) I 4; वाह्लादिसूत्र – P 1; omitted in P 2, I 2. [4] P 1 here adds एकादशर्षमेके धिष्ण्या नामाग्नयो पश्यन्। (what follows also in P 2 on the margin) कावेरीप्रभृतिषु चोक्तसु नदीषु उत्पन्ना आहवनीयधिष्णिषु व्यभिचारेण। तथा च पुराणकारेणोक्तं (पुराक्त P 1)। व्यभिचारात्स्मृता धिष्ण्यास्तासूत्पन्नास्तु धिष्णियः (तास्तु – न्नास्तु P 1) धिष्णिषु जज्ञिरे यस्मात्ततस्ते धिष्णियः स्मृता इति। P 1, I 2 (marg.): ईश्वर इति गुणतो (°त्ये P 1) विशेषणं. [5] W 1; प्रकीर्तितं I 4; प्रवर्णितं P 1, P 2, I 2. [6] W 1; चेदं P 1, I 4; omitted in P 2, I 2. [7] W 1; °लत्वतः the rest. [8] The comm. तृचोऽंत्य to इत्याग्नेय्यः in W 1 only. [9] W 1; यदि पंच° the rest. [10] °वृद्धिः एव छांदसी W 1. [11] W 1, I 4; °स्मानवताः विष्णा P 1; °स्मानवता यज्ञा P 2, I 2.

मास्म मां बाधिष्ठा[1] अन्यं भजस्वेति । ततश्च षष्ठ्याद्ययुक्षु यमो देवता । यमी चान्यासु देवता । यमो युक्षु नवम्यां चर्षिः । अन्यासु सा यमीति ॥

११. अंगस्यापत्यं । बाह्वादित्वादिञ् ॥

१३. विवस्वान्नामादित्य अदितिपुत्रः । अदितेरर्थः[2] । अथवा प्रकृत एवां[3]गिर्हविर्धानः । हविर्धानाख्ये ये द्वे शकटे तद्देवत्यमिदं ॥

१४. षष्ठी लिंगोक्तदेवता । लिंगोक्ताश्चांगिरःपितृअथर्वभृगवः । अतः पराश्च तिस्रो लिंगोक्तदेवताः । चेति लिंगोक्तदेवत्याः पितृदेवत्या वा । अथ तृचः । श्वानौ सरमापुत्रौ गमनमार्गमभितः स्थितौ [4]स्तौति । [5]श्चभ्यामिति तादर्थ्ये चतुर्थी ॥

१५–१९. अथ परे पंच वक्ष्यमाणा ऋषयो गोत्रतो यामायना वेदितव्याः । यामस्य नडादित्वात्फक्[6] । यामायनशब्दस्य पंचकृत्व उक्तौ गुरुत्वं स्यादिति गुरुत्वाल्लघुत्वार्थमिदं[7] ॥

१७. आदितो द्वे सरण्यूदेवते । सरण्यूनामनी[8] देवता ययोर्ऋचोस्ते । सारण्यौ[9]विति वाच्ये सरण्यूदेवते इति वचनमूकारांतमिदं सूर्यपत्न्यभिधान[10]मिति वक्तुं । तद्धित ओर्गुणे[11] कृते किमिदं ह्रस्वांतमुत दीर्घांतमिति संशेरते । अथ चतस्रः पूषदेवत्याः । अथ तिस्रः सरस्वतीदेवत्याः । सरस्वत्या अण् न सरस्वतः[12] सरस्वीलिंगात्[13] ॥

१८. आदौ चतस्रो मृत्युदेवत्याः । मृत्युर्देवता यासां ता मार्त्य्या इत्यवचनं वैशिष्ट्याय[14] । पितृमेधाः पितृयज्ञाभिधायिन्यः । अंत्या चतुर्दश्यनुष्टुप् सती प्राजापत्या प्रजापतिदेवत्या वा । सा [15]चानिरुक्ता । [16]अप्रका[17]शदेवताभिधाना । यद्य[18]प्रकाशितदेवताभिधायित्वादनिरुक्ता त्र्यंबक[19]मित्यस्यामश्रु[20]तेरुद्रपदायां हंसः शुचिष[21]दित्यदृष्टसूर्यपदायां चानिरुक्तेति वक्तव्यं । न वक्तव्यं । अस्या एवानिरुक्तत्वं ज्ञेयं श्रुतिषु चोदित[22]मिति मन्यते[23] । अत एव शं नः करती[24]त्यस्याः सानिरुक्ता रौद्री शांतेति[25] ब्राह्मणकथिताया

[1] मास्मानवबाधिष्ठा W 1. [2] W 1, I 4; अदितेभ्यः P 1, P 2, I 2. [3] P 2, I 2; एव वर्षि° W 1; एवानुग P 1; omitted in I 4. [4] W 1; तौ the rest. अथ to तौ omitted in I 4. [5] त्रिष्ठभ्यामिति P 1, P 2. [6] W 1 only; याम does not occur in the Gana नडादि in B.'s edition. [7] W 1; the rest merely शंखाद्याः पंच ऋषयो यमपुत्राः । [8] W 1; सरण्यूर्नामन P 1; सरण्यूर्नामना P 2, I 2; सरण्यूर्नाम I 4. [9] सारण्ये W 1; सरण्यायिति the rest. Cp. Pân. VI, iv, 174. [10] W 1; सूर्याभिधानं the rest. [11] Cp. Pân. VI, iv, 146. [12] I 4; न सरस्वत्यं P 1, P 2; सारस्वतः W 1 (no न). [13] W 1; सरस्वतीमिति लिंगात् the rest. [14] W 1; वैस्पष्ट्याय the rest. [15] च omitted in W 1. [16] P 1 here adds तथा चोक्तं । मंत्रेषु ह्यनिरुक्तेषु देवतां कर्मतो वदेत् । मंत्रतः कर्मणा चैव प्रजापतिरसंभवेत् । [17] W 1; अभिप्रकाशित° the rest. [18] W 1; य अप्र° P 1; अप्र° P 2; आप्र° I 4. [19] *Rigv.* VII, 59, 12; W 1, I 4; पंचकम् P 1; वाचकम् P 2. [20] W 1; °श्रमत° P 1, P 2, I 2; दृष्ट° I 4. [21] *Rigv.* IV, 40, 5. [22] °तव्यम् P 2, I 2. [23] मन्यंते P 1. [24] *Rigv.* I, 43, 6; करदिति MSS. [25] Ait. Br. III, xxxiv, 8.

अर्थनिरुक्तत्वमनेन नाभ्यधायि । न हि ब्राह्मणाभिदृष्टमित्येव वा अवश्यं[4] ज्ञेयं । किंतु[5] तयोपदिष्टं[6] तदेवेति[7] ॥५४॥

१९. मथितो नाम यामायनः । अथवा भृगुर्नाम वरुणपुत्रः । यद्वा च्यवनो नाम भार्गवः । क्वचिन्न्यायेन भृगोर्वारुणित्वे सिद्धे वारुणिरित्यनुक्रमण्यनुकरणं । यामायनत्वं हि निवृत्तं ॥

२०–२६. ददर्शेति शेषः । अत उत्तराणि सप्त सूक्तानि वक्ष्यमाणानि विमदो ददर्श । स चैंद्रः प्राजापत्यो वा । वसुकृन्नाम वसुक्रपुत्रो[8] वा ददर्श ॥

२०. आद्यर्गेकपदा । तदर्धमेकपदेति[9] दशाक्षरा विराट् । अथवा नेकपदेयं । किं[10] तर्हि । पाद एव वा । अत्र च पक्षे लिंगं । पादश्च पारणं संप्रकीर्तितं[11] सपादं मुनिभिः पुरेत्या[12]द्यनुक्रमणीव्यवहारः । उभयपक्षे[13] शांत्यर्थः । पुंस्त्वमविवक्षितं । सदा शांतिरत्र प्रयोजनं । न तु शांत्याग्नेयत्वं बाध्यते[14] । न हि शं नः पंचोना शांतिरित्य[15]त्र वैश्वदेवत्वं बाधितं ॥

२१. आस्तारपांक्तं । आस्तारपंक्त्या व्याप्तमिदं । उभयपदवृद्धिश्छांदसी ॥

२२. पुरस्ताद्बार्हतं । पुरस्ताद्बृहत्या व्याप्तमिदं । उत्तरपदवृद्धिश्छांदसी ॥

२४. आस्तारपांक्तमिदमुत्तरं च । पूर्ववत्प्रतिवक्तव्यं[16] । अंत्याश्चतुर्थ्याद्यास्तिस्रोऽश्विदेवत्याः सत्यो ऽनुष्टुभः ॥

२६. तत्र प्रथमाचतुर्थ्यावुष्णिहौ[17] ॥

२८. इंद्रवसुक्रयोः पितापुत्रयोः संवाद ऐंद्रः । इंद्रवाक्यभूता वसुक्राभिधायिन्योऽप्यृच ऐंद्रे कर्मणि विनियोक्तव्या[18] इत्यर्थः । तथा चारण्यकब्राह्मणसूत्रयोः । ऐंद्रे महाव्रते मरुत्वतीये शस्त्रे असत्सु मे जरितः साभिवेगः सत्यध्वृतमिति शंसति[19] । असत्सु मे जरितः साभिवेगः पिबा सोममभीति[20] च विनियोग उपपन्नो भवति[21] । अर्थविज्ञानाय वक्तृविशेषमाह । इंद्रस्नुषा वसुक्रपत्नी । सूक्तस्य प्रथमया विश्वो हीत्यनया संनिहितमेवेंद्रं ज्ञात्वा[22] परोक्षवदसंनिहितवदाह वदति । अनयेति वाच्ये सूक्तस्य प्रथमयेति विस्पष्टार्थं । द्वितीयादियुजश्चतुर्थीवर्जमिंद्रस्य [23]वाक्यमिति शेषः । शिष्टा-

[1] अपि in W 1 only.

[2] न in W 1 only.

[3] W 1; ब्राह्मणादिदृष्टम् the rest.

[4] W 1; इत्यसा – ज्ञेयं P 1; इत्यासा ज्ञेय I 4; इत्यादिना ज्ञेयं P 2, I 2.

[5] W 1 only.

[6] W 1, P 1; तयोपादंष्टं (sic) I 4; ततोपदिष्टं P 2, I 2.

[7] Cp. M. M., note on Sankusuka, *Rigv.* vol. v, p. li.

[8] W 1; वासुक्रो the rest.

[9] Introd. § 12, 9.

[10] W 1; नेयमृ – – P 1; नेयमृक् P 2, I 2, I 4.

[11] Anuvâkânukramanî, ver. 43.

[12] Ibid. ver. 44.

[13] हि added in P 1, P 2, I 2; पि in I 4.

[14] W 1; मध्यतो the rest.

[15] Sûtra on VII, 35.

[16] P 2, I 2; °वर्त्तव्यं P 1; °यत्तव्यं I 4; omitted in W 1.

[17] P 1 and I 4 read आद्या चतुर्थी च in the text.

[18] °युक्तव्या W 1.

[19] Ait. Âr. I, ii, 6, 1. This quotation in W 1 only.

[20] Ait. Âr. V, i, 1, 8.

[21] W 1; भवतीति the rest.

[22] W 1; स्वयमेवेंद्रमाज्ञा I 2; ज्ञामेवेंद्रमज्ञा P 1; ज्ञामद्रयज्ञे I 4.

[23] W 1; पंचेंद्रवा° the rest.

स्तृतीयाद्ययुजश्चतुर्थो चर्षेर्वसुक्रस्य वाक्यं । तेनाद्यायां[1] वसुक्रपत्न्यृषिका । द्वितीयादीनां चतुर्थीवर्जितानां युजामिंद्र ऋषिः । तृतीयादीनां चतुर्थीसहितानामयुजां वसुक्र ऋषिः । सर्वास्त्विंद्रस्त्रिष्टुभः[2] । अत्रेतिहासमाहुः । इंद्रपुत्रे वसुक्रनाम्नि यजमाने सति यज्ञमिंद्रः प्रच्छन्न आजगाम । तदागमनमिंद्र[3]स्नुषा वसुक्रपत्नी नामावबुध्य ततः सा श्वशुरेंद्रागमनकांक्षिणी परिदेवयांचक्रे[4] । अथेंद्रः[5] प्रकाशभूतस्तस्याः प्रीत्यै स्वपुत्रेण वसुक्रेण[6] सह संवादमकरोदिति ॥

३३. अत्र चाद्ययानादेशात्त्रिष्टुभा विश्वे देवा स्तूयंते । अथ द्वितीयादिरिंद्रदेवत्य एकः प्रगाथो बार्हतः । अतः पराश्चतुर्थ्याद्याः षड् गायत्र्यः । तासु चादितो द्वाभ्यां त्रासदस्यवस्य त्रसदस्यवस्य पुत्रस्य कुरुश्रवणनाम्नो महाराजस्य दानं स्तूयते । अथ पराभिस्तिसृभिः षष्ठ्याद्याभिर्ऋग्भिर्ऋषिरैलूषः कवषो मित्रातिथिनाम्नि राज्ञि मृते परलोकं गते शोकाभिभूतमस्य मित्रातिथेः पुत्रमुपमश्रवोनामानं मित्रातिथिस्नेहादुपमश्रवःस्नेहाद्वाभ्येत्य व्यशोकयत् । विगतशोकमकरोत् । तत्करोतीति णिच् । टिलोपः । लङ् । संग्राम युद्ध इति[7] नियमात् । वेः पुरोऽडागमः[8] । उक्तं च ।

यस्येति सूक्तशेषेण[9] मृते मित्रातिथौ नृपे ।
उपमश्रवसः स्नेहादृषिः शोकमपा[10]नुदत् ॥ इति ॥

३४. ऐलूषः कवष ऋषिः । अथवाक्षो नाम मौजवान् मू[11]जवत्पुत्रः । अपत्यानि तस्य लोपेऽप्यादिवृद्धिर्गृह्य[12] सौविष्टकृदिति[13] यथा । अत्र चाक्षकृषिप्रशंसा च क्रियतेऽक्षकितवनिंदा च क्रियते । तत्राक्षान्द्वादशी स्तौति । नवम्याद्या च सप्तमी त्रयोदशी कृषिं स्तौति । कितवं चानुशास्ति । शिष्टाभिर्नवभिस्त्वक्षाः कितवश्चैव निंद्यंते ॥

३८. [14]मुष्कवानिंद्र ऋषिः । मुष्कवान् सवृषण[15] इत्यर्थः । ऋषेरिंद्रस्य[16] विशेषणं विज्ञेयमित्येवोक्तं । अस्य च[17] गोत्रं नास्त्यनुपदेशात् । न [18]चांगिरसत्वमब्रह्मर्षित्वात्[19] । देवताजातीयोऽसौ देवताकांडे पाठात् । तर्ह्ययं देवता भवतु सौर्योऽभितपा ऋषिस्त्विति चेन् न तद्धितचतुर्थ्यभावादार्षानुक्रमण्यामिंद्रोऽस्मिन्मुष्कवानित्युक्तेर्दैवतानुक्रमणीबृहद्देवतयोरभावाच्च ॥

३९. घोषा नाम कक्षीवतो दुहिता ॥

[1] W 1; आद्यया P 1, I 2; आद्याय I 4. [2] W 1; सर्वास्त्रिष्टुभः the rest. [3] W 1; °द्रस्य the rest. [4] W 1; °देवतां the rest. [5] W 1; प्रीतः added in the rest. [6] Omitted by W 1. [7] संग्रामयुद्धो नाम इति W 1; संग्रामयुद्धमिति the rest. Cp. Schol. on Pâ*n*. III, i, 12, and Dhâtupâ*th*a, § 35, 68. [8] पुरोडाशमः P 1; पुराडाशेमः I 4; पुरोडाशमत I 2. [9] °शेषण W 1. [10] I 4; उपा° P 1, I 2; अपाकरोद् W 1. [11] W 1; मुज° the rest. [12] Âsv. G*ri*hya-sûtra, II, iii, 4. [13] W 1; एष्वेव नात्र I 2; पृष्ठे नात्र P 1; omitted in I 4. [14] P 1 inserts अत्रेतिहास छंदोगे द्रष्टव्यः. [15] इंद्र W 1. [16] इदं W 1. [17] च omitted in W 1. [18] न वा W 1. [19] °ब्रह्मत्वात् W 1. Cp. Introd. § 2, 3.

४५. वत्सप्रीर्नाम[1] भालंदन इत्युक्तं[2] ॥५६॥

४७. सप्तगुर्नामांगिरसो वैकुंठमिंद्रं तुष्टावाभिस्त्रिष्टुब्भिः । विकुंठाया अपत्यमिति शिवादिभ्योऽण्[3] । इंद्रमिति वैकुंठविशेषणत्वाय[4] । अनादेशादैंद्रत्वं सिद्धं । असत्यस्मिन्विकुंठी[5]देवतात्वं स्यात् । ननूत्तरत्र सप्तगुस्तुतिसंहृष्ट इति दर्शनादस्यामैंद्रत्वं[6] नास्तीति चेत् तर्हि वैकुंठमिंद्रं तुष्टावेति पदत्रयमप्यकर्तुं शक्यं । अथेंद्रस्य वैकुंठत्वमुपपिपादयिषुरितिहासयति । असुरीत्यसुरजातिः । ङीष् । तपः कृच्छ्रचांद्रायणादिकं तेपे कृतवती । अस्याश्च मत्समोऽन्यो मा स्म भूदिति स्वयमेव पुत्रो जज्ञे जातवान्[7] । जनी प्रादुर्भावे । इत्येवमिंद्रस्य वैकुंठत्वं सिद्धं । अथास्यैव वैकुंठस्य सप्तगुस्तुतस्येंद्रस्योत्तरसूक्तत्रयदर्शित्वं स्तुत्यत्वं चाह । जगृभ्मादिसूक्तदर्शिनः सप्तगुनाम्न ऋषेः स्तुत्या सुप्रीतः स वैकुंठ इंद्रो विस्मितः स्वमाहात्म्यं बुबुधर्षिमध्य[8] आत्मानमहं भुवमित्यादिसूक्तत्रयेण तुष्टाव[9] । एवमहमित्यादिसूक्तत्रये देवतात्वमृषित्वं चैंद्रस्येति सिद्धं भवति[10] ॥

५०. द्विजगत्याद्यंतं । आदावंते च द्वे जगत्यौ यस्य तत् । कर्मधारयद्वंद्व[11]गर्भो बहुव्रीहिः । अथ महत्तदुल्बमित्यारभ्य[12] सूक्तत्रयस्यर्षिदैवतज्ञानार्थं कथामाह । स्वधातृप्त्यग्निहोत्रिया[13] वषट्कारेण वज्रभूतेन वृक्णेषु छिन्नेषु सत्स्वेषां कनिष्ठः सौचीक[14]नामाग्निर्वषट्कार[15]हविर्वहनाभ्यां भीतोऽपः प्रविश्य नष्टः । तत्र वाचा प्रदर्शितः सन्नन्वेष्टुमागतैर्देवैः सह समवदत् संवादमुत्तरसूक्तत्रयेण । वषट्कारहविर्[16]वहनभीतिः कनिष्ठत्वं[17] च श्रुत्यंतरात् । अग्नेस्त्रयो ज्यायांसो भ्रातर आसंस्ते देवेभ्यो हव्यं वहंतः प्रामीयंतेत्या[18]दिभिः समामनंति ॥

५१–५३. अत्र नवर्चे द्वितीयादि[19]युजश्चतस्र ऋचो विश्वे देवाः शान्तनेत्युत्तरसूक्तं च यदृचमित्यृचो दशाग्निवाक्यं । तत्रैवायुजः प्रथमाद्याः पंचर्चो यमैच्छाम मनसा सोऽयमित्युत्तरसूक्तं चैकादशकमिति षोडश देवानां[20] वाक्यं । तत्र षोडशसु तदस्य वाचः प्रथमं मसीयेत्याद्या ऋचोऽग्नेर्वाक्यं । अत्र च महत्तदुल्बमित्यादिसूक्तत्रयवर्तिन्यस्त्रिष्टुभः । तत्र तृतीयसूक्त एकादशर्चे तंतुं तन्वन्नित्याद्या जगत्यः । अत्रापि सूक्तस्याष्टमी त्रिष्टुप् । अग्न्युक्तिर्देवदेवत्या । देवोक्तिस्त्वग्निदेवत्या । नात्र गुरुलाघवं चोदनीयं ब्राह्मणानुकरणत्वात् । इत्युत्तरमित्यादि व्यतिरिक्तमस्ति ॥

५४. बृहदुक्थो नाम वामदेव्यः । गर्गादिभ्यो यञ् ॥

[1] P 1 in both text and comm.; the rest वात्सप्रिः; but I 4 reads वात्सप्रीः in the comm. on the next sûtra. [2] Sûtra on IX, 68. [3] Pân. IV, i, 112. [4] W 1; °विशेषितत्वाय the rest. [5] वैकुंठ° W 1. [6] °स्यां नैंद्रत्वं W 1, C. [7] W 1; सूतवान् P 1. [8] ऋषिमध्य omitted in W 1. [9] P 1 here adds a quotation of 9 ślokas from the Brihaddevatâ (see note). [10] P 1 omits this sentence. [11] °द्वंद्व° omitted in W 1. [12] W 1; °त्यादि the rest. [13] W 1; °त्रिवाहु the rest. [14] Cp. M. M., vol. vi, p. 3. [15] W 1; °ग्निवष° P 2, I 2; °ग्निर्नै वषट्कारः P 1, I 4. [16] P 1, P 2, I 2; °रः हवि° I 4; °काराद्व° W 1. [17] W 1; महत्त्वं च the rest. [18] Taitt. Samh. II, vi, 6, 1. [19] °दिषु W 1. [20] देवतानां W 1. [21] शति° W 1.

५७–६०. अत्रिदृष्टे पंचमे मंडलेऽबोध्यग्निः समिधेत्यादौ द्वैपदे द्विपदासूक्तेऽग्ने त्वं नो अंतम इत्यत्रर्चयोऽग्ने त्वं गौपायना लौपायना वा बंधुः सुबंधुः श्रुतबंधुर्विप्रबंधुश्चेत्येवमस्माभिरुक्तास्ते[2] पराणि चत्वारि सूक्तान्यपश्यन्निति शेषः। अथ कथां कथयन्नेव सूक्तचतुष्टयस्य ज्ञातव्यं सर्वमाह। अथ ह खलु पुरैक्ष्वाक इक्ष्वाकुपुत्रः[3]। इक्ष्वाकोरण्यंत्यलोपो दांडिनादौ[4] निपात्यते। राजाभिषिक्तोऽसमातिनामा। अत्रैषां[5] लौपायनत्वं न कर्तव्यं[6]। अपि तु गौपायनत्वमेवेति वक्तुमुक्तं[7]। गौपायनानिति पूर्वमात्मनैव[8] वृतान् बंध्वादीन् बंधुसुबंधुश्रुतबंधुविप्रबंधूंस्त्यक्त्वान्यौ मायाविनौ[9] किरातौ कुली[10] इति बृहद्देवतोक्तनामानौ मायाविनौ श्रेष्ठतमौ मत्वा[11] पुरोदधे पुरोहितत्वेनावृणीत[12]। तमसमातिमितरे बंध्वादयोऽभिचेरुरभिचरितवंतः। अथ मायावहितपुरोहितौ[13] कपोतौ[14] भूत्वेति बृहद्देवताविदः[15]। सुबंधोः प्राणाञ्जीवितं। पुंसि भूम्न्यसवः प्राणा इति नैघंटुकाः। आचिक्षिपतुः। सौच्यावयतां[16]। अथानंतरं। हेति खेदे। अस्य मृतस्य सुबंधोर्भ्रातरस्त्रयो बंधुश्रुतबंधुविप्रबंधवो मा प्र गाम पथो वयमिति षड्टचं गायत्रं स्वस्त्ययनं नष्टप्राणानां पुनःप्राप्तिहेतुं[17] वैश्वदेवं जप्त्वा जपित्वा छांदसत्वादनित्त्वं[18]। ततो यत्ते यममिति द्वादशर्चमानुष्टुभं मनआवर्तनं मनसो जीवितस्य[19] देहान्निर्गतस्य पुनर्देह[20]प्रवेशहेतुं मनोदेवत्यं जेपुः। किंच प्रतारीति दशर्चस्यादितश्चतस्र ऋचो निर्ऋत्यपनोदनार्थं। देहात्प्राणानामाच्यावयित्री[21] देवता निर्ऋतिः। तन्निवृत्त्यर्थं[22] जेपुः। तत्र चतुर्थ्यां निर्ऋतिनिवृत्त्यर्थं[23] जपंत एव सोममप्यस्तुवन्। मृत्योरपगमाय निवृत्तये। उत्तराभ्यां पंचमीषष्ठीभ्यामसुनीतिनाम्नीं[24] देवताम[25]स्तुवन्। सप्तम्यां लिंगोक्तदेवताः पृथिवीद्युरंतरिक्षसोमपूषपथ्यास्वस्त्याख्या अस्तुवन्। इति गताः सप्त त्रिष्टुभः। अथाष्टम्यादिभिः शिष्टाभिस्तिसृभिः पंक्तिमहापंक्तिपंक्त्युत्तराभिर्द्यावापृथिव्यावस्तुवन्। समिंद्रेरय गामित्यनेनार्धर्चेनेंद्रं वा द्यावापृथिव्यौ

[1] *Rigv.* V, 1.

[2] Sûtra on V, 24.

[3] अथ खलु पुरा ऐक्ष्वाकुपुत्रः W 1.

[4] Cp. Pâ*n*. VI, iv, 174.

[5] W 1; नात्रैकापां P 1; नात्रैकार्चा P 2, I 2; नात्रैकाष् I 4.

[6] W 1; लोपायति कर्तव्यः I 4; लौपायनिक सर्त्तव्यः P 1, P 2, I 2.

[7] उक्तं in W 1 only.

[8] I. e. in sûtra on V, 24.

[9] W 1, I 4; मायाद्विजौ P 1; द्विजौ P 2, I 2.

[10] कुलि इति W 1; द्वौ किरातौ कुली नाम ततो मायाविनौ द्विजौ। असमातिः पुरोधत्त BD. VII, 858.

[11] W 1; श्रुत्वा the rest.

[12] °तेति W 1.

[13] W 1; तामपि नवपुरोहितौ P 1; तावपि नवपुरोहितौ P 2, I 2; तानपि नवपुरोहिते I 4.

[14] काश्यपौ तौ W 1; omitted in the rest.

[15] तौ कपोतौ द्विजौ भूत्वा गत्वा गौपायनानभि BD. VI, 859.

[16] अ° W 1 corr. for आ°.

[17] W 1; अविनाशप्राप्तिहेतुं the rest.

[18] °त्वादनि इत्वं W 1; छंदसादित्वादिह P 1; छंदसादित्वाह P 2, I 2; omitted in I 4.

[19] Omitted in W 1.

[20] देह° omitted in W 1.

[21] W 1; प्राणानच्यावयतीति P 1, P 2; प्राणाव्यावर्तयतीति I 4.

[22] P 1; तं नि° W 1, P 2, I 2; स्वं नि° I 4.

[23] W 1; तत्र मो पुषः सोमेत्यस्मान्निर्ऋतिनिवृत्त्यर्थं the rest.

[24] °सुनीतीतिनाम्नीं W 1.

[25] W 1; देवीम् the rest.

षोऽस्तुवन् । समिंद्रेरयेति दशमी पंक्त्युत्तरा । एकाधिका भुरिग्विशेषणेयं वेदितव्या । आ जनं त्वेष संदृशमिति द्वादशर्च आनुष्टुभ आदितश्चतसृभिरसमातिं राजानमस्तुवन् यदभिचारात्सुबंधोर्मृतिः[3] । सर्वमूलभूते राज्ञि प्रसन्ने सर्वं प्रसन्नं भवेदिति । अथेंद्रक्षत्रेति पंचम्येंद्रमस्तुवन् । अगस्त्यस्य नप्त्र इति षष्ठ्यागस्त्यस्य स्वसैषां बंध्वादीनां माता राजानमसमातिं स्वपुत्रानुग्रहार्थमस्तौत् । पराभिरयं मातायं पितेत्यादिभिः पंचभिः सुबंधोर्मृतस्य शयानस्य जीवं जीवितं[4] दूरस्थमाह्वयन्[5] आह्वयंत । अथांत्यायां मे हस्त इत्येतया हस्तस्तुतिरूपया लब्धसंज्ञं लब्धप्राणं सुबंधुमस्पृशन् स्पृष्टवंतः । अत्र गौरवं न चोदनीयं । ब्राह्मणवाक्याभिप्रायेणात्र पठ्यत इति ॥

६८. आद्याः षडंगिरसां स्तुतिर्वा विश्वे देवा एव वा । श्रूयते हि । इदमित्था रौद्रं गूर्तवचा ये यज्ञेन दक्षिणया समक्ता इति वैश्वदेवं नाभानेदिष्ठं शंसतीति[6] ॥

६९. गयो नाम प्लतेः पुत्रो न तु प्लतस्य । एवा प्लतेः सूनुरवीवृधदिति[7] लिंगात् । प्लातवचनं त्वामग्ने गय[8] इतिवदस्यात्रेयत्वं[9] मा भूत् । स्वस्ति नस्त्रिष्टुब्वा त्रिष्टुबंतन्यायेन जगती वा । स्वस्ति नः पथ्यास्विनीयं पंचदशी सहोत्तरया स्वस्तिरिद्धीत्यनया सह पथ्यास्वस्तिदेवत्या । उभे अपि पथ्यास्वस्तिदेवत्ये इत्यर्थः । श्रूयते हि । स्वस्ति नः पथ्यासु स्वस्तिरिद्धि प्रपथे श्रेष्ठेति पथ्यास्वस्तेस्त्रिष्टुभाविति[10] ॥

७०. आप्रमित्युक्तेराप्रीदेवताः । द्वितीयस्तनूनपाद्वर्ज्यते[11] तत्स्थाने नराशंसः ॥

७१. बृहस्पतिर्नामांगिरसः । ज्ञानं स्तूयते । तुष्टावेत्यनुक्रमण्यनुकरणं । उक्तं हि बृहद्देवतायां ।

यज्ज्योतिरमृतं[12] ब्रह्म यद्योगात्समुपाश्नुते ।
तज्ज्ञानमभि[13]तुष्टाव सूक्तेनाथ बृहस्पतिः[14] ॥ इति ॥५८॥

७२. लौक्यः । लोकनाम्नोऽपत्यमिति गर्गादियञ् । दाक्षायणी । दक्षाद् अत इञ्[15] ततः फक् स्वार्थे । जातौ ङीष् । गोत्रं च चरणैः सहेति जातित्वं[16] ॥

७३. गौरिवीतिर्नाम शाक्त्यः । व्ययैमा पंचोना गौरिवीतिः शाक्त्य[17] इति ह्युक्तं[18] । श्रूयते हि । गौरिवीतिर्हि वै शाक्त्यो नेदिष्ठमिति[19] ॥

[1] W 1; वा ह्रे the rest. Cp. M. M., vol. vi, p. xxiv. [2] Omitted in W 1. [3] सुबंधुर्मृतः I 4. [4] जीवातवे W 1. [5] W 1; यममुष- स्वाह्वयं P 1; यममुपाह्वयन् P 2, I 2; यमपुरत्येक्तं स्वाह्वयन् I 4. [6] Ait. Br. V, xiii, 12–xiv, 1. [7] Ver. 17. [8] Sûtra on V, 9. [9] W 1; इति गयस्य प्लातत्वं the rest. [10] Ait. Br. I, ix, 7 (where the reading is पथ्यायाः स्वस्तेः). [11] W 1; वर्जे the rest. [12] W 1, M 1-3; परमं the rest. [13] अपि तु° W 1. [14] BD. VII, 877. [15] Pân. IV, i, 95. [16] See kârikâ quoted by Böht., Pân., vol. ii, p. 462, s. v. जाति. [17] Sûtra on V, 29. [18] P 1; इत्युक्तं P 2, I 2, I 4; इति सूक्तं W 1. [19] Ait. Br. III, xix, 4.

७६. सर्पो जातितः। जरत्कर्णो नामैरावतपुत्रः। ग्राव्णः प्रस्तरान्[1] अस्तौत्[2] स्तुतवानित्यर्थः। तद्देवत्यमिदं सूक्तं ॥

८१. वैश्वकर्मणं। विश्वकर्मदेवत्यं। अग्यन्निति[3] प्रकृतिभावः ॥

८५. सूर्या नामर्षिका सवितृसुता। आत्मदैवतं स्वदेवत्यं सोमाद्यपवादाभावे। आनुष्टुभं सूक्तमपश्यदिति शेषः[4]। षष्ठ्यादिभिरेकादशभिः स्वविवाहमस्तौत्[5]। विंश्याद्या नव नृणां मनुष्याणां प्रायेण विवाहमंत्रा विवाहविषया मंत्रा आशिषश्च भवंति। ततः परा देहि शामुल्यम् अश्रीरा तनूर्भवतीति द्वे वध्वा विवाहकालपरिहितवाससो यः स्पर्शस्तस्य[6] मोचिन्यौ[7]। विवाहकालपरिहितं वासो न स्प्रष्टव्यमि[8]त्याहुरित्यर्थः। अथ ये वध्वश्चंद्रं वहतुमित्यादि दंपत्योर्यक्ष्मणः क्षयरोगस्य नाशिनी ॥५९॥

८६. वृषाकपिर्नामेंद्रस्य पुत्रः शचीसपत्न्यां जातः। इंद्राणींद्रपत्नींद्रश्च स्वयमिति त्रयः समूदिरे संहत्योदिरे[9] विवादं कृतवंतः। पांक्तं पंचपदया पंक्त्या व्याप्तं।

उपदेशेष्वनुक्तेष्व वक्तृभेदो न दर्शितः।
अथाप्यृष्यादिज्ञानार्थमर्थतस्त्वत्र[10] वर्ण्यते ॥

वि हि सोतोरित्याद्येंद्रस्य वाक्यं। परा हींद्र किमयं त्वां यमिमं त्वं प्रिया तष्टानि न मत्स्त्रीति पंचें[11]द्राण्याः। उवे अंबेति[12] वृषाकपेः। किं सुबाहो[13] इतींद्रस्य। अवीरामिव संहोत्रमिति[14] द्वे इंद्राण्याः। इंद्राणीमासु नाहमिंद्राणीति[15] द्वे इंद्रस्य। वृषाकपायीति[16] वृषाकपेः। उक्ष्णो[17] हीतींद्रस्य। वृषभो न न सेशे यस्य रंबते न सेशे यस्य रोमशम् अयमिंद्रेति[18] चतस्र इंद्राण्याः। अयमेमि धन्व च यत् पुनरेहि यदुदंच[19] इति चतस्र इंद्रस्य। अर्शुंहं नामेत्यंत्या त्रयोविंशी वृषाकपेरिति। सर्वं सूक्तमैंद्रं। श्रुतौ तु वार्षाकपे हि वृषाकपिं शंसतीत्यादिरेकदेश[20] ऋषिणास्य सूक्तस्य व्यवहारः ॥

८८. मूर्धन्वान्नाम। अस्य गोत्रं विकल्पयति। आंगिरसो वामदेव्यो वेति। आंगिरसत्वेऽनुक्रसिद्धेऽपि वचनं पायुनाम्नोऽनुवृक्षिर्मा भूदिति। असत्यस्मिन् मूर्धन्वान् वामदेव्यो वेत्युक्तेः पायुर्भारद्वाजो वेति प्रसज्येत। सौर्यवैश्वानरीयं। सूर्यदेवत्यं वैश्वानरगुणाग्निदेवत्यं चेति वक्तुं[21] समासनिर्देशः ॥

[1] W 1; पाषाण the rest. [2] स्तु° to end omitted in W 1. [3] अग्नि सन्विति W 1; सन्निति I 4, P 2, I 2; सनन्विति P 1. [4] W 1; सूक्तशेषः the rest. [5] W 1 has two marginal notes: मंत्रप्रतिपाद्योऽर्थो देवता and तत्र प्रतिपाद्योऽर्थो देवता. [6] च added in W 1. [7] मोचन्यौ P 1. [8] W 1; पुनर्न स्प्रष्टव्यम् I 4; न पुनर्द्रष्टव्यं P 1, P 2. [9] संहत्य ऊदिरे MSS. [10] W 1; त्वथ the rest. [11] Verses 2-6. [12] Ver. 7. [13] Ver. 8. [14] Verses 9-10. [15] Verses 11-12. [16] Ver. 13. [17] Ver. 14. [18] Verses 15-18. [19] Verses 19-22. [20] Cp. Ait. Br. V, xv, and VI, xxii. [21] Omitted in W 1.

९०. नारायणो नाम। नास्य गोत्रमुपदेशेष्वनुक्तेः। यथोपदेशमिति सूक्तं। पौरुषं पुरुषदेवत्यं। इतिहासादिसिद्धोऽयं पुरुषः पंचविंशकः। उक्तं हि।

इतिहासादिसिद्धो यः[2] पंचविंशः पुमान् स तु।
इह योग्यतया स्तुत्यो न जातिपुरुषोऽभ्यवत्॥ इति॥

९२. शार्यातो नाम मनुपुत्रः। वैश्वदेवमिदमुत्तरं च। जगतीछंदस्कं। श्रूयते हि। यज्ञस्य वो रथ्यं विश्पतिमित्यारभ्य तदु शार्यातमित्यंतं[3][4]॥

९३. तान्वो नाम पार्थ्यः पृथुपुत्रः। पृथोरुत्तापत्यार्थे। प्रस्तारपांक्तं। उत्तरपदवृद्धिश्छांदसी॥

९४. सर्पो जातितोऽर्बुदो नामतः काद्रवेयः। कद्र्वाः स्त्रीभ्यो ढकि ढे लोपोऽकद्र्वा[5] इति निषेधः। ग्राव्णः शस्यल्लोपोऽनः। पंचमी सप्तमी चतुर्दशी चेति तिस्रस्त्रिष्टुभः। संत्यापंचमी-सप्तम्यस्त्रिष्टुभ इति नोक्तं विशेषाभावात्। तथानुक्त्वैवं[6] किमिति चेच्छिशुभावोऽयं[7] ॥६०॥

९५. उर्वशीं नामाप्सरसं। ऐलः। मनोः पुत्रस्येलस्य[8] वरुण[9]शापात्प्रतिवर्षं प्राप्त[10]षण्मासि-कस्त्रीत्वकाले[11] बुधेन जनितः पुत्रः पुरूरवा नाम महाराजः। पूर्वोर्मितां स्वनगरे प्रतिष्ठानाख्ये चत्वारि वर्षाणि कृतवासां[12] स्वसमयभंगा[13]दात्मानं त्यक्त्वा गतामितश्चेतश्च। कामादत्यंताभिलाषादन्वेषणं कुर्वन्कदाचिन्मानससरस्तीरे दृष्ट्वा। तामासाद्य पुनरपि स्वप्रासादेऽवरोद्धुं वासयितुमिच्छन्दुराशां कृतवान्। सा चोर्वशी तेन प्रार्थ्यमानानिच्छंती निःस्पृहा प्रत्याचष्टे प्रत्याख्यानं[14] कृतवती। न त्वयोक्तं मया करिष्यत इति। हये जाये[15]। इषुर्न श्रिय इषुधेः[16]। या सुजूर्णिः[17]। कदा सूनुः[18]। सुदेवो अद्य[19]। अंतरिक्षप्रां रजसः[20]। सचा यदासु[21] इत्याद्यास्तिस्रश्चेति नवैलस्य पुरूरवसो वाक्यं। शिष्टा नवोर्वश्या वाक्यं। ऐलवाक्यमित्युपसमस्तमर्थ्य[22]पेक्षया संबध्यते। यस्य वाक्यं स ऋषिः। या तेनोच्यते सा देवता।

ऐलोर्वशीतिहासोऽत्र वैस्पष्ट्याय प्रवर्ण्यते[23]।
मित्रश्च वरुणश्चोभौ दीक्षितौ प्रेक्ष्य चोर्वशीं ॥१॥
चलच्चित्तौ ततश्चैतौ[24] कुंभे निहितशुक्रकौ[25]।

[1] Introd. § 1. [2] W 1; यं the rest. [3] Ait. Br. IV, xxii, 6-7. [4] °त्यादि W 1.
[5] Pân. IV, i, 120, and VI, iv, 147. [6] तथा मुक्त्वैवं W 1; तथा मुक्त्वैवं I 4; तथा उक्त्वैवं P 2, I 2; तथा सुक्त्वैवं P 1. [7] W 1; शिशुपाचोद्ययसि P 1; शिशुपाचोद्ययं P 2, I 2; शिशुमाचोद्ययसि I 4.
[8] पुत्रस्यैलस्य MSS. [9] W 1; रुद्राणी° the rest. [10] W 1; प्राप्तप – ते। प्राप्तवते I 4; प्राप्तयेपते P 2, I 2. [11] W 1; उमासस्त्रीत्वस्य स्त्रीत्वकाले तु P 1, P 2, I 2, I 4.
[12] W 1; °वासीं P 1; °वासं P 2, I 2; वासी I 4. [13] W 1; °गर्भाद् the rest. [14] W 1, I 4; प्रत्या – – षा – P 1; प्रत्याभाषणं P 2, I 2. [15] Ver. 1. [16] Ver. 3. [17] Ver. 6.
[18] Ver. 12. [19] Ver. 14. [20] Ver. 17. [21] Verses 8–10. [22] W 1; इति the rest. [23] प्रदर्श्यते W 1. [24] W 1; चलितौ तदुक्तेश्च P 1, P 2, I 2; रेतः सिषिचतुः सद्यस् I 4. [25] W 1; निहित – – कौ P 1; निहितरेतसौ P 2, I 2; तत्कुंभे न्यदधुस्तदा I 4.

तां शमवंतौ मनुष्य[1]भोग्या[2] भूम्यां वसेति ह ॥२॥
अत्रांतर इलो राजा मनुपुत्रैश्च[3] संयुतः ।
मृगयां संचरन्साश्वो[4] देव्याः[5] क्रीडं विवेश ह ॥३॥
यत्र[6] देवं गिरिसुता[7] सर्वैर्भावैरतोषयत् ।
तत्राविशन्[8]पुमान् स्त्री स्यादित्युक्त्वा तत्र चाविशत् ॥४॥
स्त्रीभूत्वा[9] क्रीडितः सोऽगाच्छरणं शिवमंजसा ।
इयं प्रसाद्यतां राजन्नित्युक्तः[10] शंभुना नृपः ॥५॥
जगाम शरणं देवीमात्मनः पुंस्त्वसिद्धये ।
अकरोत्सा नृपं देवी षण्मासात्प्राप्त[11]पुंस्त्वकं ॥६॥
ततः कदाचित्स्त्रीकाले बुधः सौंदर्यमोहितः ।
अप्सरोभ्यो विशिष्टां तां चकमे नृपयोषितं[12] ॥७॥
तत्रैळायां[13] सोमपुत्राज्जातो राजा पुरूरवाः ।
तमूर्वशी तु चकमे प्रतिष्ठानपुरे[14] स्थितं ॥८॥
तल्पादन्यत्र[15] नग्नं त्वां दृष्ट्वा यामि यथागतं ।
सुतावुरणकौ[16] तत्र[17] समीपे[18] कुरु मे दृढं[19] ॥९॥
इति सा समयं कृत्वा रमयामास तं नृपं ।
चतुरब्दे गते रात्रौ देवैर्हरणकद्वयं ॥१०॥
हृतं[20] तस्य ध्वनिं श्रुत्वा नग्न एव स भूपतिः ।
उत्थाय जित्वागच्छेयमित्येवं तल्पतोऽन्यतः[21] ॥११॥
विद्युता दर्शितोऽप्यास्मै नग्न एव पुरूरवाः ।

[1] P 1; मनुज I 4; मानुष्य° W 1, P 2, I 2. [2] I 4, P 1; भोग्य° W 1, P 2, I 2. [3] °पुत्रौश्च P 1, I 4; °पुत्रश्च P 2, I 2; पुत्रेश्च W 1. [4] P 1, I 4; स्वश्च P 2, I 2; सार्श्वे W 1. [5] W 1; देर्वीं I 4; देवी° P 1, P 2, I 2. [6] तत्र W 1. [7] देवीं गिरिसुतां P 2, I 2. [8] °शत् W 1. [9] °भूतो W 1. [10] W 1, I 4; नेत्युक्तः P 1, P 2, I 2. [11] W 1, I 4; °स्त्रीत्व° P 1, P 2, I 2. [12] W 1; तां – – – म नृपयापियां तं P 1; तामिलां तां नृपयोषितां P 2, I 2; तामिलां संगतवान्मुदा I 4, marg. corr. in W 1. [13] तदे° I 4. [14] W 1, I 4; प्रतिष्ठानगरी° P 1; प्रतिष्ठाननगरी° P 2; प्रतिष्ठानपुरी° I 2. [15] W 1; तदन्यत्र P 1; तदन्यां च तथा P 2, I 2; तदान्यत्र च I 4. [16] W 1, P 1; सुता उरणको I 4; सुतावरूणकौ P 2, I 2; उरण ऊर्णावान् भवति marg. note in W 1. [17] W 1; तस्य P 1, P 2, I 2; त्वं च I 4. [18] W 1; समीपे the rest. [19] W 1; दृशं P 1; द्रुतं P 2, I 2, I 4. [20] हतं W 1. [21] W 1; जित्वा भावागच्छ – – – ल्पतो न्य – तः P 1; जित्वा वा गच्छेत्येवं जल्पति क्वो न्यतः P 2, I 2; जित्वा भगवन् गच्छेत्येवं जयन्यतः I 4.

अथ सा नष्ट[1]समया ह्यु[2]र्वशी तु दिवं ययौ ॥१२॥
तत उन्मत्तवद्राजा दिदृक्षुस्तामितस्ततः ।
कुर्वन्नन्वेषणं तीरे सरसो मानसस्य तां ॥१३॥
विचरंतीम्[3]प्सरोभिः सहापश्यत्पुरूरवाः ।
पुनः स चकमे भोक्तुमुर्वशीं पूर्ववन्नृपः[4] ॥१४॥
सा स्वशापस्य मुक्तत्वा[5]त्प्रत्याचष्टे व्रजेति तं[6] ।
इत्युर्वश्यै[7]ल[8]संवादमिममेषोऽप्यसूचयत्[9] ॥१५॥

९६. वरुर्नामांगिरसः । अथवा सर्वहरिर्नाम स चैंद्रः । इंद्रस्य पुत्रः । हरिस्तुतिः । हरिरि-
तींद्राह्वनाम[10] । द्वे त्रिष्टुभावंते यस्य तत्[11] । शिष्टा[12] जगत्यः । वरौ रोहेत्सन्महासूक्तं जागतं
चेति[13] तु प्राधान्यं जगतीनां भूयस्त्वात् ॥

९७. भिषङ्नामाथर्वणः पुत्रः । अन्नणीति प्रकृतिभावः । ओषधयोऽत्र स्तूयंते ॥

९८. देवापिर्नाम ऋष्टिषेणपुत्रः । देवान् बृहस्पतिमित्रादीन् वृष्टिकामः सन् सस्यवृद्धये स्तुत-
वान्[14] ॥

१०१. बुधो नाम सोमपुत्रः । पितरि देवतावदुपचारात् सोमाद्यृण् । ऋत्विकस्तुतिर्वा वैश्वदेवं
वा[15] । ऋत्विक्स्तुतिरिति[16] बृहद्देवतायामुक्तेर्दैवतानुक्रमण्यां वैश्वदेवत्वोक्तेश्च विकल्पः[17] ॥

१०२. मुद्गलो नाम भार्म्यश्वः । भृम्यश्वनाम्नः पुत्रः[18] । द्रुघणेन मुद्गरेण[19] । वृषभेण बलीवर्देन
च । आजिं युद्धं । जिगाय जितवान् । इति हेतौ । अतो हेतोर्द्रुघणदेवत्यं । चेत्युक्तेरैंद्रं वा ।
मुद्गलस्य हृता गावश्चोरैस्त्यक्ता जरद्गवं ।
स शिष्टं शकटे कृत्वा युक्त्वैकत्र जरद्गवं[20] ॥१॥

[1] W 1; दृष्ट° the rest. [2] P 1, I 4; no particle W 1, P 2, I 2. [3] W 1; विहरंतीम् the rest. [4] W 1; च पुरूरवाः the rest. [5] W 1; साश्वः सापश्यदुक्ता च I 4; साश्वः सापश्यदुक्ता च P 2, I 2; साश्वः सापश्यमुक्ता च P 1. [6] तां P 2, I 2. [7] °श्यैव W 1. [8] संवादं मन्यते यास्क इतिहासं तु शौनकः BD. VIII, 916. [9] This story is quoted by Sâyana. See also M. M., vol. vi, p. 18. [10] P 1 adds: आयुधं वाहनं वापि स्तुतौ यस्येह दृश्यते । तमेव च स्तुतं विद्यात्तस्या बहुधा हि सः । [11] I 4; आरोद-सीति तिस्रस्त्रिष्टुभोऽंते तेनेदं त्रित्रिष्टुबंतं P 1; एकादशी द्वादशी त्रयोदशी त्रिष्टुभः अंते यस्य तत् P 2, I 2. [12] I 4; आदौ दश P 1; आद्या दश P 2. P 1, P 2, I 2 read त्रित्रिष्टुबंतं in the text. [13] Ait. Br. VI, xxv, 5. [14] An itihâsa (12 slokas) is here quoted in P 1 from BD. VII, 916-920, VIII, 921-927. [15] तुशब्दाद्वैश्वदेवं ऋत्विक्स्तुतिर्वा P 1. [16] BD. VII, 828. [17] उक्तः added in P 2, I 2, I 4. This comm. omitted in P 1. [18] भृम्यश्वपुत्रः W 1. Cp. Nirukta, IX, 24. [19] W 1; मुद्गलेन the rest. [20] W 1; युक्त्वैक अभ्युराहव the rest.

दुघणं युयुजेऽन्यत्र चोरमार्गानुसारतः[1] ।
दुघणं चाग्रतः कृत्वा[2] चोरेभ्यो जगृहे स्वगाः[3] ॥२॥

इति कथात्र सूचिता ॥

१०३. अप्रतिरथो नामेंद्रपुत्रः । उपांत्या द्वादश्यप्यादेवी । अप्याख्या देव्यत्र स्तूयते । नञृतश्चेति[4] कब्भावश्छांदसः ॥

१०४. अष्टको नाम विश्वामित्रपुत्रः । श्रूयते हि । विश्वामित्रः पुत्रानामंत्रयामास ।

मधुच्छंदाः शृणोतन ऋषभो रेणुरष्टकः । इति[5] ॥

१०५. कौत्सः कुत्सपुत्रो नाम्ना दुर्मित्रः । दुर्मित्र इत्यस्य नामेत्यर्थः । गुणतः सुमित्रः । एष्वयमेव सुमित्र इत्युच्यते शुभमित्रयोगात्[6] । एतद्वा विपरीतं । नाम्ना सुमित्रो गुणतो दुर्मित्र इति दुर्ज्ञान-गुणानि यस्य[7] बहुगुणत्वादिति । विकल्पितस्य च लिंगं[8] । शतं वा यदसुर्य प्रति त्वा सुमित्र इत्यास्तौद्दुर्मित्र इत्यास्तौदित्यर्थानवधारणं[9] । आर्षानुक्रमण्यां चात एष नामविकल्पः ।

दुर्मित्रो वा सुमित्रो वा कौत्सः[10] सूक्तं कदा पसो । इति ।

तस्यैवात्रापि सुमित्रो दुर्मित्रो वेत्येषोऽर्थोऽस्त्विति चेद्दुर्मित्रनाम्नः[11] स्तोतृत्वे सुमित्रनाम्नः स्तोतृत्वायोगात्[12] । ऋगर्थस्यासंबंधता मा प्रसांक्षीदि[13]त्यन्यतरस्यां गुणतयैव योगो वाच्य एवेति हि मन्यते ॥ इदं चौष्णिहं । तत्र हरी यस्य सुयुजा[14] वज्रं यश्चक्र[15] इति पिपीलिकमध्ये । उष्णिगधिकारे[16] न त्वनुष्टुब्बृहत्यधिकारे[16] । कुत एतत् । औष्णिहमिति बुद्ध्यनुसंधानात्सा[17]हचर्याच्च । साहचर्यादपि ह्यर्थनियम इति[18] । रामशब्दो हि कृष्णलक्ष्मणकृतवीर्यसा[19]हचर्याद्रेवतीरमणं जानकीकांतं जामदग्न्यं च बोधयति ॥६१॥

१०७. दिव्यो नामांगिरस ऋषिः । दक्षिणा नाम प्रजापतेः सुता चर्षिका । दक्षिणां यजमानैर्ऋत्विग्भ्यो दीयमानां तद्दातॄन् दक्षिणाया दातॄन् यजमानान् वास्तौद्याजकादित्वात् । तृजकाभ्यां कर्तरीति[20] न षष्ठीसमासप्रतिषेधः ॥

[1] W1, I4; °कः P1, P2, I2. [2] W1; क्षिप्त्वा the rest. [3] Quoted by Sâyana; cp. Nir. IX, 23. [4] Pân. V, iv, 153. [5] Ait. Br. VII, xvii, 7. [6] W1; सुमित्रगुणयोगो त्र the rest. [7] W1; °गणान्यस्य मित्राणि च° the rest. [8] W1; विकल्पस्य च लिंगं P1, I4; विकल्पश्च लिंगात् P2, I2. [9] W1; °त्यस्यानवधारणं P1, P2, I2; °त्यस्यमेवधारणं I4. [10] कौत्सः comes before सुमित्रः in W1. [11] W1; एषो पि स्थिति चेन्ना P1; एषोपस्थिते चेन्नाम्ना P2, I2; एषो पि स्थितित्वा I4. [12] W1; °त्वयोगात् P1, P2, I2; °त्वगात् I4. [13] W1; प्रजीहृ P1, I4; प्रजाहृ P2, I2. [14] Ver. 2. [15] Ver. 7. [16] W1; °कारजे the rest. [17] W1, P1; बुध्यनुबंधनात् I4; इत्यबुध्यनुसंधामाच्च P2, I2. [18] W1; साहचर्यमप्यर्थे नियमय वि P1; साहचर्यमप्यर्थं नियमाय वि P2, I2; साहचर्य्यमध्याय्यर्थो नियमय वि I4. [19] W1; कृतभ्रात° P1; कृतव्रण P2, I2; कृत° I4. [20] Pân. II, ii, 15.

१०८. अथर्षिदेवताज्ञानाय कथां कथयति । कथा चैवं । पुरा खलु बृहस्पतेरिंद्रपुरोहितस्य गावो बलासुरभृ[1]कुटीतटैः पणिनामकासुरैर्हृता बलपुरं प्राप्य सुगुप्त[2]स्थाने स्थापिता आसन् । अथ बृहस्पतिप्रेरितेनेंद्रेण नष्टान्वेषणं कृत्वा[3] सरमा नाम देवशुनी प्रहिता[4] बभूव । सा च[5] बलपुरंस[6]मीपे[7] रसाख्यां महानदीमुत्तीर्य बलपुरं प्राप्य सर्वं विचिंत्य[8] गुप्ते स्थाने ता[9] गा ददर्शेति । तत्र पणिनामभिरसुरैर्बृहस्पतिगृहादाहृत्य[10] निरूळ्हा[11] बलपुरे गुप्ताः स्थापिता गा अन्वेष्टुम् अन्वेषितुम् (तीषुसहेति[12] विकल्पितः) इंद्रेण प्रहितां सरमां देवशुनीं स्वजातीयां[13] देवतां[14] मृगयादिष्विंद्र[15]स्य साधनभूतामस्य सूक्तस्यायुग्भिरृग्भिः[16] पंचभिराद्यातृतीयादिभिः[17] पणयो मित्रीयंतो देवशुन्या सह मित्रत्वमात्मन इच्छंतः (मित्रात् क्यचि ईत्वं[18] शतरि जसि च रूपं) प्रणयपूर्वकमूचुरुक्तवंतः । सा च देवशुनी तान् युग्मांत्याभि[19]र्युग्माभिर्द्वितीयाचतुर्थ्यादिभिरेकादशभिरेकादश्या चेति षड्भिः प्रत्याचष्टे ।

पण्युक्तौ सरमा देवी[20] तदुक्तौ पणयस्तथा ॥

१०९. ब्रह्मणो जाया जुहूर्नामर्षिका । अथवा ब्रह्मपुत्र ऊर्ध्वनाभा नामर्षिः ॥

११०. जमदग्निर्नाम भार्गवः । अथवा तत्सुतस्तस्य जमदग्नेः पुत्रो रामो नाम परशुराम इत्याख्यातः । आप्रीसूक्तमिदं । आप्रीत्यु[21]क्तेस्तनूनपाद्द्वितीयं । अथोत्तरसूक्तदर्शिनामृषीणां चतुर्णां गोत्रमाह । परे चत्वारो वैरूपाः । अत ऋषेः परे चत्वार ऋषयो गोत्रतो वैरूपा वेदितव्याः । लाघवार्थमिदं । प्रत्यृषिवैरूपोक्तेरिदं हि लघु । तर्हि प्राग्घर्माद्वैरूपा इत्येवास्तु प्राङ् मत्स्यात्काण्व[22] इतिवत् किं परे चत्वार इति । तत्रानुक्रमण्यंतरानुकरणं ॥

१११. सप्रिर्नाम वैरूपः । अथवा घर्मो नाम तपसः पुत्रः ॥

११५. उपस्तुतो नाम वृष्टिहव्यपुत्रः । इति त्वाग्ने वृष्टिहव्यस्य पुत्रा उपस्तुतास ऋषयोऽवोचन्[23]निति किं बहुवचनं । पूजार्थमित्यनुमन्यते[24] । उपपन्नं चेदमार्षा[25]नुक्रमण्यामपि तथैव दर्शनात् ।

[1] W 1; भु° P 2, I 2; भृ° P 1, I 4. [2] °गुप्ते W 1. [3] W 1 (corr. for दत्वा), I 4; दत्वा P 1; ज्ञात्वा P 2, I 2. [4] प्रेरिता P 2, I 2. [5] W 1, I 4; – – त्या P 1; आगत्य P 2, I 2. [6] W 1; पुर° the rest. [7] गत्वा added on the marg. in W 1. [8] W 1; सर्वत्र विदित्य P 1, P 2, I 2; सर्वत्र विहित्य I 4. [9] गता W 1. [10] W 1; आगत्य the rest. [11] P 1; निगूळ्हा P 2, I 2, W 1; गूळ्हा I 4. [12] Cp. Pâ*n*. VII, ii, 48. [13] W 1; अजातीयां P 1; जातीयावह P 2, I 2; अजातीया I 4. [14] W 1; °ता the rest. [15] मृगयादींद्र° W 1; मृगादिष्विं° P 1; मृगादिविं° I 4; मृगादेवतादिष्विं° P 2, I 2. [16] ऋग्भिः omitted in W 1. [17] आद्यातृतीयादिभिः in W 1 only. [18] Cp. Pâ*n*. VII, iv, 33. [19] I 4; युग्मांताभिः P 1, W 1; omitted in P 2, I 2. [20] W 1; देवतं P 1, P 2, I 2; देवता I 4. [21] आप्री इत्यु° W 1; आप्रमित्यु° the rest. [22] Introd. paribhâshâ to Ma*n*d. VIII. [23] Verse 9. [24] W 1; इति तमनाते P 1, P 2, I 2; तमनोते I 4. [25] W 1; उपपंनं चैतत् P 1; उपयमनं चैतत् P 2; नुपयं चैतत् I 4.

उपस्तुतो वार्ष्टिहव्यो नवकं[1] चित्र इच्छिशोः। इति ॥

११६. स्यौरः स्यूर[2]नाम्नः पुत्रः। अग्नियुतो[3] नाम। अथवा स्यौर एवाग्नियूपो नाम ॥

११७. भिक्षुर्नामांगिरसो धनस्यान्नस्य च दानं[4] प्रकर्षेणादातृनिंदापूर्वकं[5] प्रशशंस स्तुतवान् ॥

११८. उरुक्षयो नामामहीयवः[6]। आमहीयुंगोत्रजः। रक्षोहेत्यग्नेर्गुणः। गायत्रमिदमुत्तरं च। श्रूयते हि। स यदि न जायेत यदि चिरं जायेत राक्षोघ्नी गायत्र्यो ऽनूच्या[7] अग्ने हंसि न्यत्रिण-मित्येता[8] इति[9] ॥

११९. [10]इंद्रस्यायमित्यैंद्रः। तत्स्वीकृतत्वात्। लबो लबरूपमात्मानं स्वयमेव स्तुतवान्। इंद्रो हि लबरूपमास्थाय सोमऋजीषं पिबनृषिभिर्दृष्टः[11] सोमस्यातिप्रियत्वं स्ववैभवं च वै [12]वर्णयन्नात्मान-मनेन सूक्तेन स्तुतवानितीतिहासविदः प्राहुः[13]। एवं च[14] लाबमैंद्रं ततः[15] कायमिति देवतानुक्र-मणीयं[16] संगच्छते। इति वै लाबमैंद्रमिति[17] बृहद्देवता[18] च।

तथा। उरुक्षयो[19] लबस्त्वैंद्र इति वा इति मे मनः।

इत्यार्षानुक्रमणी[20] ॥६२॥

१२१. हिरण्यगर्भो नाम प्रजापतिपुत्रः। कायं। कदेवत्यं। हिरण्यगर्भः समवर्तताग्र इति षट् प्राजापत्या इति[21] सूत्रं प्राजापत्य इडादधः प्रजापते न त्वदेतान्यन्य[22] इतिवत् कायत्वापवादः। अत एव कया नश्चित्र आ भुव[23]द्धिरण्यगर्भः समवर्तताग्र इति[24] कदेवत्ये विनियुंक्ते। प्राजापत्यया चर्चेति ब्राह्मणं तु सुकीर्तिवृषाकपिवरुनाभानेदिष्ठवदृषिणा निर्देशः ॥

१२४. उत्तमैंद्रदेवत्या। अंत्येत्यनुक्तिश्चित्रार्षी। अग्निवरुणसोमानां निहवस्तुत्युक्तिः। कर्तरि षष्ठी। ह्वेञ् स्पर्धायां शब्दे च। ह्वः संप्रसारणं च न्यभ्युपविष्विं[25]त्यप्। तत्राद्याग्निदेवत्या। अथ

[1] W 1; नवकः P 1, P 2, I 2. The quotation is omitted in I 4. [2] स्युर° P 1. [3] P 1, P 2, I 4, both text and comm.; °यूतो W 1. Cp. Aufrecht's noto in his Index. Gagannâtha: अग्नियुतो वाग्नियूपो वा स्यौरः. [4] दातृप्रशंसा W 1. [5] प्रकर्षेणादातृनि-दानपूर्वकः P 1; प्रकर्षेण दातृनिदानपूर्वकः P 2, I 2; प्रकर्षेणादातृनिंदां दानपूर्वकं I 4. [6] W 1, I 4; °हीय° P 1; °हीयुव° P 2; °हियव° I 2. [7] P 1, I 4; अनूच्याग्ने W 1, P 2, I 2. [8] Ait. Br. I, xvi, 9–10. [9] एता इति in W 1 only. [10] लबो पश्यदिंद्रपुत्रः here inserted in P 1. [11] W 1; °जीपतृसं पिबनदृष्टः ऋषिभिर्दृष्ट सन् P 1; °जिषहृसं पिबनदृष्टः। ऋषि-भिर्दृष्ट सन् P 2, I 2; °जीषीप नृसं पिबनदृष्टः। ऋषिभिर्दृष्टः सन् I 4. [12] चावर्णयन् W 1. [13] W 1; आहुः the rest. [14] W 1; इति च the rest. [15] P 1, P 2, I 2; लाबमैंद्रतः W 1; लाबमैंद्र ततः I 4. [16] W 1; °णी the rest. [17] W 1; लाबमैंद्रं तदिति P 1; लाबमैंद्रं सदिति I 4; लबमैंद्रं। तदिति P 2, I 2. [18] BD. VIII, 956. [19] W 1; तयोरुयोर् P 1; तयोरुभयोर् P 2, I 2, I 4. [20] °णीति W 1. [21] Âsv. Sr. III, viii, 1. [22] Ibid. II, xiv, 11–12. [23] *Rigv.* IV, 31. [24] Âsv. Sr. II, xvii, 15. [25] Pân. III, iii, 72.

तिस्रोऽग्नेरात्मस्तवः । आसामग्निर्ऋषिर्देवता चेत्यर्थः । शिष्टा ऋचो यथानिपातं । यो यत्र स्तुतत्वे[1] निपतति स तत्र स्तुत इत्यर्थः । आद्यां पंचम्यादिपंचेति षट् संभूया[2]पश्यन्नग्निवरुणसोमाः ॥

१२५. वाङ्नामांभृणी । अंभृणस्य महर्षेः पुत्री[3] । आत्मानं तुष्टाव । स्वयमेव[4]र्षिका देवता चेत्यर्थः ॥

१२६. कुल्मुल[5]र्बर्हिषो नाम शिलूषपुत्रः । बाह्वादित्वादिञ् । उपरिष्टाद्बार्हतं । उत्तरपदवृद्धिश्छांदसी ॥

१२७. कुशिको नाम सोभरिपुत्रः । अथवा रात्रिर्नाम भरद्वाजस्य पुत्र्यृषिका । रात्रिस्तवं । रात्रिदेवतायाः स्तवं स्तुतिर्यत्र सूक्ते तत् ॥

१२९. प्रजापतिर्नाम परमेष्ठी गुण[6]विशिष्टः । विशेषणं च[7] वाच्यत्वं वैश्वामित्रत्वं चास्य प्रजापतेर्माभूदिति । अन्यथा क्वचित्कथंचिन्न्यायेन प्रसज्येत[8] । प्रजापतिरगोत्रोऽयमुपदेशेष्वनुक्तः । भाववृत्तं । भावानां पदार्थानां[9] वृत्तिः सृष्ट्यादिप्रवृत्ति[10]र्यस्य देवता तद्भाववृत्तीयमिति प्राप्ते छार्थेऽण् ॥

१३१. सुकीर्तिर्नाम कक्षीवतः पुत्रः । सूक्तस्य मध्ये या चतुर्थी सानुष्टुप् । उत्तरा पंचमीति द्वे अश्विदेवत्ये ॥

१३५. कुमारो नाम यमगोत्रः[11] । नडादित्वात्फक् ॥

१३९. विश्वावसुर्नाम । एष च देवानां गंधर्वो गायकत्वेन देवानां संबंधी जातितश्च गंधर्व इत्यर्थः । पूर्वार्धं तृतीयार्धे । अस्य सूक्तस्य पूर्वार्धेन । आद्यतृचेनेति यावत् स्तुतवान् सवितारं । उत्तरेण तृचेनात्मानमस्तौत् ॥

१४०. सूक्तस्यादौ द्वे विष्टारपंक्ती[12] । अथ तिस्रः सतोबृहत्यः[13] । षष्ठ्युपरिष्टाज्ज्योतिः[14] ॥

[1] W 1; स्तुत्यत्वेन P 1, P 2, I 2; स्तुतित्वेन I 4. [2] W 1; संख्याया° the rest. [3] W 1, P 2, I 2; पुत्रा P 1; दुहिता I 4. [4] स्वयमस्य W 1. [5] कुल्मुल° P 1; कुल्मल° P 2, I 2, I 4, both text and comm., W 1 in comm. only. Gagannâtha reads कुल्मुल°. [6] Sic MSS. [7] च omitted in W 1. [8] W 1, I 4; °ज्येत् P 1, P 2, I 2. [9] W 1, P 2, I 2; पदानां P 1, I 4; वियदादि marg. note in W 1. [10] W 1; °वृत्तिर् the rest. W 1 adds on the margin: वियदादीनां सृष्टिस्थितिप्रलयादीनामत्र प्रतिपाद्यत्वादत्र परमात्मा देवतेत्यर्थः, apparently taken from Sâyana. P 1 here adds: महाप्रलयाद्युपपर्यायमेव भाववृत्तं वदंति तत्. Cp. Aufrecht, note. [11] °पुत्रः P 1. [12] P 1; आद्ये विष्टारपंक्ती I 4; आद्ये द्वे विष्टारपंक्ती Gagannâtha; आद्या विष्टारपंक्तिः W 1, P 2, I 2. W 1 has a marg. note: मूलभाष्ययोर्भ्रमः । आद्ये विष्टारपंक्ती इति युक्ततरः पाठः । अत्र संहिताभाष्येऽपि भ्रमः । [13] W 1, I 4, P 2, I 2; ऊर्जो नपादिति तिस्रः सतोबृहत्यः P 1; तृतीयाद्यास्तिस्रः सतोबृहत्यः I 3; P 2, I 2 add तृतीया चतुर्थी पंचमी सतोबृहत्यः. [14] P 2, I 2, I 4; ऋतावानामित्युपरिष्टाज्ज्योतिस्त्रिष्टुप् P 1; अंत्या उपरिष्टाज्ज्योतिषंस्त्रिष्टुप् I 3; पंचम्युपरिष्टाज्ज्योतिः । अंत्यानुक्ते त्रिष्टुप् W 1.

१४२. शार्ङ्गा जातितः। शार्ङ्गा इति पक्षिविशेषस्याख्या। ते चत्वारो दृषाश्च प्रत्येकं क्रमेण दृषद्दर्शिनः। तेषामाद्यो जरिता नाम। द्वितीयो द्रोणः। तृतीयः सारिसृक्वः[1]। चतुर्थः स्तंबमित्रः ॥६३॥

१४३. अग्निर्नाम संस्थस्यापत्यं भौमत्वापवादः। अग्निरन्यो ह्ययं भौमादुपदेशेषु[2] दर्शनात् ॥

१४४. सुपर्णो नाम तार्क्ष्यपुत्रः। अथवोर्ध्वकृशनो[3] नाम यामायनः ॥

१४५. इंद्राण्यृषिका। उपनिषत्संज्ञं सत्[4] सपत्नीबाधनं च। सपत्नी बाध्यतेऽनेन सूक्तेनेह जपादिना। तेनास्य तदेव देवता ॥

१४६. देवमुनिर्नाम। इरंमदपुत्रः। अरण्यानीं महारण्या[5]भिमानिनीं देवतां तुष्टाव। हिमारण्ययोर्महत्व[6] इति ङीष् आनुक् च ॥

१४७. सुवेदा नाम शिरीषपुत्रः। बाह्वादित्वादिञ् ॥

१४८. पृथुर्नाम वेनपुत्रः। अणो यञ् ॥

१५१. श्रद्धा नामर्षिका। सा च कामायनी[7]। कामान्नडादिभ्यः[8] फकि जातिङीष्। गोत्रं च चरणैः सहेति जातित्वं[9] ॥

१५३. देवजामयः। देवानां स्वसृभूता इंद्रमातरो नामर्षिकाः ॥

१५५. अलक्ष्मीघ्नं।

> अलक्ष्मीनाशकं[10] सूक्तं जपहोमादिभिस्त्विदं।
> तत्राद्योपांत्ययोरश्रीनाश एव प्रकीर्तितः ॥१॥
> द्वितीया च तृतीया च ब्रह्मणस्पतिदेवते।
> उपाद्ये इति किं नोक्तमिति चेत्पृच्छ तं मुनिं ॥२॥

१५७. भुवननामाप्त्यपुत्रः। अथवा भुवनस्य पुत्रः साधनसंज्ञः। द्विपदया व्याप्तं द्वैपदं। विंशत्यक्षरा विराजो मा भूवन्निति त्रैष्टुभमित्युक्तं। श्रूयते हि। इमा नु कं भुवना सीषधामेति द्विपदाः शंसतीति[11] ॥

१५८. चक्षुर्नाम सूर्यपुत्रः। सौर्य इति मानवनिवृत्त्यर्थं। चक्षुर्मानव[12] इति ह्युक्तं ॥

१५९. पुलोमतनया शची नामेंद्रस्य महि[13]ष्यृषिका भूत्वा स्वयमात्मानमेव तुष्टाव स्तुतवती ॥

१६१. यक्ष्मनाशनो नाम प्रजापतिपुत्रः। राजयक्ष्मघ्नमिदं। राजयक्ष्मा क्षयव्याधिः। राजय-

[1] I 4 °क्वः in text, °क्कः in comm. [2] °ब्वद° I 4. Cp. comm. to V, 76. [3] °कृशानो P 2, I 2. [4] W 1; उपनिषत्संज्ञमिदं I 4; उपनिषत्संज्ञकमिदं P 2; उपनिषत् रहस्यविद्यासंज्ञमिदं P 1. [5] W 1, I 4; महारण्यामति° P 1, P 2, I 2. [6] Cp. Pân. IV, i, 49. [7] कामायिनी I 4, text and comm.; P 1 comm. [8] काम does not occur in the Gana नडादि (B.'s Pânini). [9] See kârikâ quoted in B.'s Pân., vol. ii, p. 462. [10] W 1; अश्रीघ्नं नाशकरं the rest. [11] Ait. Br. V, xix, 12. [12] In sûtra on IX, 106. [13] पत्नी W 1.

ष्णेति च सर्वव्याधिप्रशमनं । गृह्ये हि सूच्यते[1] । अथ व्याधितस्यातुरस्य यक्ष्मगृहीतस्य वा पंचा[2]-हुतिश्चरुर्मुंचामि त्वा हविषा जीवनाय कमित्येतेनेति[3] । अनादेशादिंद्रो देवता । अत्र बृहद्देवतायां विकल्प उक्तः ।

ऐंद्राग्नं मन्यते यास्क एके लिंगोक्तदैवतं । इति[4] ।

नैतदस्ति । यत्रान्येषां मतमुक्तं । स्वयं शौनकस्त्वैंद्रः । एक इत्यादेशादैंद्रत्वमेवानेनांगीकृतं[5] ॥

१६२. रक्षोहा नाम ब्रह्मपुत्रः । गर्भसंस्रावे गर्भस्य निहितस्य स्रावे पातविषयभूते तस्य प्रायश्चित्तं समाधायकं । गर्भसमाधानमत्र[6] देवता ॥

१६३. विवृहा नाम काश्यपगोत्रः[7] । यक्ष्मघ्नं । यक्ष्मा क्षयरोगः[8] । तस्य नाशनमस्य वाच्यं ॥

१६४. प्रचेता नामांगिरसः । आदितो द्वे चतुर्थी चानुष्टुभः । त्रितीया त्रिष्टुप् । पंचमी पंक्तिः । दुःस्वप्नघ्नमिति तत्फलमुपचारेणोक्तं । दुःस्वप्ननाशनं ॥

१६५. कपोतो नाम निर्ऋतिपुत्रः । कपोतेन गृहादेरुपहता[9]वभिभवे सति जपहोमाभ्यां प्रायश्चित्तमिदं[10] । गृह्येऽपि[11] सूच्यते । कपोतश्चेदगारमुपहन्यादनुपतेद्वा देवाः कपोत इति प्रत्यृचं जुहुयाज्जपेद्वेति[12] ॥

१६६. ऋषभो नाम । वैराजोऽयं शाक्वरो वा । अत्र चाद्या प्रकृतिस्तु विराट् । वैराजो शाक्वरो वा । नात्र कैश्चिन्निरणायि । सपत्नघ्नं । शत्रुनाशनमनेनोच्यते[13] ॥

१६७. तृतीया सोमस्य राज्ञ इत्येषा वरुणधातृ[14]विधातृसोमबृहस्पति[15]लिंगोक्तदेवता[16] ॥

१६८. अनिलो नाम वातगोत्रः[17] । वातात्तडादिफक्[18] ॥

१६९. शबरो नाम कक्षीवद्गोत्रः[19] । गोदेवत्यमिदं ॥

[1] गृहे हि सूच्यते P 1; गृह्य हि सूच्यते I 4; गृह्ये सूच्यते P 2, I 2; गृह्यादौ सूच्यते W 1. [2] पंच W 1. [3] Âsv. Grihya-sûtra, III, vi, 3-4. [4] BD. VIII, 979. [5] W 1; एक इत्ययमादेशादैंद्रत्वमेवानेन स्वीकृतं I 4; एतेष्ट इत्ययमादेशादैंद्रत्वमेवानेनाशीहृतं (°तः P 2, I 2), P 1, P 2, I 2. [6] °मंत्र P 1, I 4. [7] W 1; कश्यपपुत्रः the rest. [8] यक्ष्म राजयक्ष्म-रोगः W 1. [9] W 1; °हते P 1, P 2, I 2. [10] P 1, P 2, I 2 here add: तादर्थ्यात्ताच्छ-ब्द्यमायुर्घृतमिति शेषः P 1; तादर्थ्या ता – छब्द्य आयुर्घृतमितिवत् P 2, I 2. [11] W 1; यथा गृह्ये हि P 1, P 2, I 2. [12] Âsv. Grihya-sûtra, III, vii, 7. Instead of this comm., I 4 has कपोतौपहतौ यदि गृहं प्रविशेत् । अनेन सूक्तेनाज्यं होतव्यं. [13] शत्रुक्षयकरदेवत्यं I 4, which adds हंतारं शत्रूणामिति लिंगात्. [14] °धातृ° in W 1 only. [15] P 1; °तिलिं° W 1; °बृहस्पत्यनुमति° P 2, I 2; इत्येषा लिंगोक्तदेवता I 4. [16] P 1, P 2, I 4 add वा in the text, with the comm. ऐंद्री वा P 1, P 2, I 2; पक्षे इंद्र एव देवता I 4. Cp. M. M., vol. vi, p. 24. [17] वातायनः W 1. [18] This comm. omitted in W 1. वात does not occur in this Gana. [19] काक्षीवतगोत्रजः W 1.

१७२. संवर्तो नामांगिरसोऽनादेशात् । श्रूयते हि । ऐंद्रेण महाभिषेकेण संवर्त आंगिरसो मरुत्तमाविक्षितमभिषिषेचेति[1] ॥

१७३. ध्रुवो नामांगिरसः । राजस्तुतिरिदमुत्तरं च । उक्तं हि बृहद्देवतायां ।

आ त्वा[2] राज्ञेऽभिषिक्ताय द्वे सूक्ते अभिमंत्रणे[3] । इति[4] ॥

१७५. ऊर्ध्वग्रावा नामार्बुदसर्पपुत्र ऋषिः[5] । अत इञोऽपवाद ऋष्यणोऽपवादो बाह्वादित्वादिञ्[6] । ग्राव्णोऽस्तौत् स्तुतवान्[7] ॥

१७६. सूनुर्नाम । ऋभुपुत्रः । तत्राद्यर्भुदेवत्या ॥

१७७. पतंगो नाम प्रजापतिपुत्रः ॥

१७८. अरिष्टनेमिर्नाम तार्क्ष्यपुत्रः । तार्क्ष्याद्वृष्यण् । तार्क्ष्यदेवत्यं । तार्क्ष्याद्देवताण्[8] । श्रूयते हि । त्यमूषु वाजिनं देवजूतमिति तार्क्ष्योऽच्युत[9] इति ॥

१७९. उशीनरपुत्रः शिबिर्नाम । काशिराजः काशीनां राजा प्रतर्दनो नाम । दैवोदासिः प्रतर्दनः । रुशदश्वपुत्रो[10] वसुमनाः । इतीमे त्रयो राजानः । एकर्चाः । एकैकस्या ऋचः क्रमेण द्रष्टारः ॥

१८०. जयो नामेंद्रपुत्रः[11] । अत इञ्[12] न ह्यैंद्र ऋषिः । ननु संवाद इंद्रादितिवामदेवानामिंद्रागस्त्ययोः[13] संवाद[14] इंद्राणींद्रश्च समूदिर[15] इति दर्शनादृषिरेवेंद्र इति चेत्तर्हि[16] बाह्वादित्वादिञ् ॥

१८१. लस्याप्पृथयश्चैकर्चाः प्रथसप्रथधर्माः । एते च वसिष्ठभरद्वाजसूर्यपुत्राः ॥

१८३. प्रजावान्नाम प्रजापतिपुत्रः । अन्वृचं । ऋचमृचमनु क्रमेण प्रत्यृचमित्यर्थः । ऋक्पूरित्यकारः[17] । यजमानस्य पत्न्या होतुश्चाशिषः[18] । तथा च सूत्रं । अपश्यं त्वेत्येतस्याद्यया यजमानमीक्षते द्वितीयया पत्नीं तृतीययात्मानमिति[19] । होतुरिदं विधानं ॥

१८४. गर्भाणां कर्तृभूतस्त्वष्टा नामर्षिः । नास्य गोत्रमनुपदेशात् । अथवा प्रजापतिपुत्रो विष्णुर्नामर्षिः । गर्भार्थाशीरत्र प्रार्थ्यते । विष्णुस्त्वष्टा प्रजापतिः सिनीवाली सरस्वत्यश्विनाविति लिंगोक्तदैवतमिदं ॥

[1] Ait. Br. VIII, xxi, 12. The quotation is omitted in I 4. [2] उक्तं to त्वा (incl.) in W 1 only. [3] चानुमंत्रणे M 1-3. [4] BD. VIII, 987. [5] अर्बुदसर्पऋषिपुत्रः W 1. [6] अत इञपवादे ऋष्यण् ॥ बाह्वादीञ् W 1. [7] W 1; ग्राव्णां प्रशंसा स्तुतवान् I 4; राज्ञशास स्तुतवान् P 1; राज्ञा शासः ग्रावाणं स्तुतवान् P 2, I 2. सोमाभिषवार्थात् marg. note in W 1. [8] तार्क्ष्य आदित्यः marg. note in W 1. [9] Ait. Br. IV, xxxi, 14. [10] रुशदश्व° W 1, P 1, P 2, I 2; रुशिदश्व° I 4. रौशदश्व° is the reading of P 2, I 2, रोशिदश्व° of I 4, रौशाश्व° of P 1, in the text. W 1 रौशि° corr. to रौश°; °श° corr. to हि in the margin. The copyist of C, misunderstanding the correction, has रौहिषदश्व°. [11] °द्रः corr. to °द्रिः in W 1 (marg.). The rest °द्रः in the text. [12] Pâ*n*. IV, i, 95. [13] See sûtra on IV, 18. [14] See sûtra on I, 170. [15] X, 86. [16] तर्हि in W 1 only. [17] Cp. Pâ*n*. V, iv, 74. [18] यजमानादयो देवता! marg. note in W 1. [19] Âsv. Sr.-sûtra, IV, vi, 3.

१८७. सत्यधृतिर्नाम वरुणपुत्रः । वरुणाद्ब्राह्मणादित्वादिञ् । न त्वृषित्वादत इञ्[1] । निह्नवो ऽग्निवरुणसोमानामिति वरुणस्यर्षित्वस्य दृष्टत्वात्[2] । आदित्यं । अदितिदेवत्यं । यस्मै पुत्रासो अदितेरिति लिंगात् । स्वस्त्ययनं । अविनाशगमनसाधनं । सूच्यते गृह्ये । महि त्रीणामित्यनुमंत्र्यैवमतिसृष्टस्य न कुतश्चिद्भयं भवतीति विज्ञायत[3] इति ॥

१८८. श्येनो नामाग्निपुत्रः । जातवेदा इत्यग्नेरधिकृतस्य गुणः ॥

१८९. सार्पराज्ञी नामर्षिका[4] । आत्मदेवत्यं । स्वदेवत्यं[5] यथा तथापश्यत्[6] । सूर्यदेवत्यं वा यथा तथापश्यत्[6] ॥

१९०. भाववृत्तदेवत्यं । भाववृत्तार्थ उक्तः[7] ॥

१९१. संवननो नामांगिरसः । संज्ञानं सम्यग्ज्ञानं[8] । ततोऽण् । तृतीया त्रिष्टुप् तृतीया त्रिष्टुबिति शास्त्रांते[9] द्विरुक्तिः[10] समाप्तिसूचनार्था[11] । यथा पाणिनीयांते अ अ[12] इति । परे पूर्वं परे पूर्वमिति[13] छंदोविचित्यंते । तत्र च सूत्रांते प्रकृतिभावे प्रकृतिभावे । नमो ब्रह्मणे नमो ब्रह्मणे । नम आचार्येभ्यो नम आचार्येभ्य[14] इति । तथा च गृह्यांते । मध्यमियान्मध्यमियात् । नमः शौनकाय नमः शौनकायेति[15] । तथा चतुर्थ्यारण्यकांते । ब्रह्म भवति ब्रह्म भवतीति[16] । एते च ब्राह्मणाभि-[17]दृष्टमेवानुकुर्वंतीति[18] । तथा हि । क्षिप्रं हैवैनं स्तृणुते स्तृणुत[19] इति दृश्यते[20] । ब्राह्मणारण्यकसूत्रगृह्यचतुर्थारण्यकेषु तु प्रत्यध्यायसमाप्तावपि द्विर्वचनं दृष्टं । वागुदिता भवति भवतीत्यादि[21] ॥

अथ ऋग्वेद इत्यादि तृतीयात्रिष्टुबंतकं ।
इदं शास्त्रमधीयानः प्रणवाद्यर्थतामियात् ॥१॥
ऋषिच्छंदोदैवतादि[22] विज्ञानं फलमुच्यते ।
ऋषिर्ना[23]मार्षगोत्रश्च ऋषेः संस्थानता[24]मियात् ॥२॥
एकैकस्य ऋषेर्ज्ञाना[25]त्सहस्राब्दा स्थिति[26]र्भवेत् ।

[1] W 1 and I 4 omit this remark.
[2] See sûtra on X, 124.
[3] Âsv. Grihya-sûtra, III, x, 7-8.
[4] ब्रह्मवादिनी added in P 1.
[5] W 1; omitted in P 2, I 2; आत्मस्तवमित्यर्थः P 1. सार्पराज्ञीदेवत्यमित्यर्थः marg. note in W 1.
[6] यथा तथापश्यत् in W 1 only.
[7] See comm. on X, 129. P 1 here repeats the former comm.
[8] W 1.
[9] W 1 only.
[10] शास्त्रसमा° P 1, P 2, I 2; शास्त्रपरिसमा° I 4.
[11] °र्थे P 1, P 2, I 2.
[12] Pân. VIII, iv, 68.
[13] Piṅgala *Kh*anda*h*-sûtra, VIII, 33.
[14] Âsv. Sr.-sûtra, XII, xv, 12-13.
[15] Âsv. Grihya-sûtra, IV, viii, 43-44.
[16] Ait. Âr. V, iii, 3, 19.
[17] ब्राह्मणमुखएवा° P 1, P 2, I 2, I 4.
[18] This remark omitted in W 1.
[19] Ait. Br. VIII, 28, 20.
[20] This quotation omitted in W 1.
[21] Ait. Br. I, vi, 12. This quotation in P 1 and I 4 only.
[22] °तानि W 1.
[23] ऋषेर्ना° W 1.
[24] W 1; संस्थानं P 1; ऋषिसंस्थितिमित्ययात् P 2, I 2; omitted in I 4.
[25] P 1, I 4; नाम्ना P 2, I 2; दिव्य° W 1.
[26] W 1; सहस्राब्दातिथिर्भवेत् P 1, P 2, I 2, I 4.

छंदसां चैव[1] सालोक्यं छंदोज्ञानादवाप्नुयात् ॥३॥
तस्यास्तस्या देवतायास्तद्भावं प्रतिपद्यते[2]।
यां यां विजानाति नरो देवतामिति[3] निर्णयः ॥४॥

किं च। ऋष्यादिविज्ञानफलमनुभूय सुपूजितः।
स्वाध्यायस्य फलं पश्चाच्छ्रुत्यादृष्टं प्रपद्यते[4] ॥५॥
ज्ञानेस्मरणसंयुक्तो[5] जायते यदि जायते।
नन्वेतज्ज्ञानसूत्रेण[6] चादावेव[7] महात्मना ॥६॥
उक्तमन्यस्य[8] नैष्फल्यं सर्वकर्मसु सर्वदा।
किंच[9] स्वयं शौनकोऽपि ब्रवीत्यत्र फलं महत्[10] ॥७॥
ऋषिनामार्षगोत्रज्ञऋषिभ्योऽस्तु सदा नमः।
ऋषीणां विषयज्ञस्तु यः शरीरात्प्रमुच्यते ॥८॥
सोऽतीत्य तमसः पारं स्वर्गलोके महीयते।
सहस्रयुगपर्यंतमहर्यद्ब्राह्मणमुच्यते[11] ॥९॥
नाकस्य पृष्ठे तं[12] कालं दिवि सूर्येव[13] रोचते।
स्वाध्यायं मुनियोऽधीते[14] मंत्रदैवतविच्छ्रुतेः[15] ॥१०॥
सह[16] सद्भिर्वसे[17]त्स्वर्गे तत्र[18] सद्भिरपी[19]ज्यते।
सर्वानुक्रमणी सैषा कात्यायनमुनेः कृतिः[20] ॥११॥
तस्या वृत्तिरियं चापि समाप्ता षड्गुरोः कृतिः।
वेदार्थदीपिका नाम[21] षड्गुरूणां प्रसादतः ॥१२॥

[1] P 2, I 2; नु च I 4; तु P 1; छंदसामृत° W 1. [2] W 1; तावद्भाव्यं प्रपद्यते I 4; स्वाभाव्यत्वं प्रपद्यते P 1; ताद्भाव्यत्वं प्रतीयते P 2, I 2. [3] W 1; श्रियं वांछति I 4; देवमिच्छथि P 2, I 2; देवाच्छिति P 1. [4] W 1 omits this line and the following. [5] P 2, I 2; ज्ञाति P 1, I 4. [6] W 1, P 2, I 2; नन्वेतदनुज्ञानसूत्रेण P 1, I 4. See Introd. § 1. [7] W 1; –रेवं P 1, I 4; समवैव P 2, I 2. [8] W 1; महास्य P 1, P 2; – – स्याज्ञाने I 4. [9] W 1 alone. [10] W 1; भवतीत्यत्र फलमाह the rest. [11] W 1; ब्राह्मं यदु° P 1, I 4; ब्राह्मणं P 2, I 2. [12] नाकपृष्ठे वसेत् P 2, I 2. [13] सूर्य इव P 1, W 1, I 4; सूर्यैर्विराजते P 2, I 2. [14] मुनयो धीते P 2, I 2; मनुयो धीते P 1; मुनयो धीय I 4; मुनयो पीते W 1. [15] °वच्छ्रुतिः P 1; निच्छ्रुतिः P 2; °विच्छ्रुतिः I 2; °वच्छ्रुतिः I 4; °विच्छ्रिषी W 1. [16] स तत्र W 1; स तस – I 4; सतस्य – P 1; स तं सति P 2, I 2. [17] दिवस W 1; सदिग्व P 1, I 4; दिग्वसेत् P 2, I 2. [18] सत्र W 1; सत P 1, I 4; स तं P 2, I 2. [19] W 1; अभिर् the rest. [20] W 1 here adds षड्विंश्येकाध्ययवती; P 1, P 2, I 4 समानैकाध्यायवती (°न्यैकाध्ययनवैः P 2, I 2)। षट् सर्मत्रिकब्राह्मिका (°व्यया I 4). [21] नाम्ना W 1.

खगोत्याम्नेषुमायेति[1] कल्यहर्गणने[2] सति ।
सर्वानुक्रमणीवृत्तिर्जाता वेदार्थदीपिका ॥१३॥
लक्षाणि पंचदश वै[3] पंचषष्टिसहस्रकं ।
सप्तत्रिंशच्छतं चेति दिनवाक्यार्थ ईरितः[4] ॥१४॥
विनायकः शूलपाणिर्मुकुंदः[5] सूर्यो व्यासः शिवयोगीति षड्वै[6] ।
नमामि तान् सर्वदा पांतु मां ते यैर्वै षड्भिः सप्त विद्यास्तु दत्ताः[7] ॥१५॥
आद्या सर्वानुक्रमणी[8] द्वितीया महाव्रतं चोपनिषद्द्वयं च ।
महाव्रतं सूत्रमासां तृतीया चत्वारिंशद्ब्राह्मणं[9] वै चतुर्थी ॥१६॥
सूत्रं पंचम्यत्र[10] षष्ठी तु गृह्यं शाकल्यस्य संहिता सप्तमीति ।
इमा दत्ता[11] विद्यास्तु सद्भिर्यैर्वै षड्भ्यो गुरुभ्यो हि नमोऽस्तु तेभ्यः ॥१७॥
इति षड्गुरुशिष्येण कृता वेदार्थदीपिका ।
सर्वानुक्रमणीवृत्तिः समाप्तेष्टार्थपुष्टये[12] ॥१८॥

॥ इति षड्गुरुशिष्यविरचितायां सर्वानुक्रमणीवृत्तौ वेदार्थदीपिकायां प्रथमोऽध्यायः समाप्तः[13] ॥

[1] W 1; गांत्यांमेषमासेति P 1; गणांत्यामेषमासेति P 2, I 2 (I 4 omits verses 12–18). [2] कल्यंहोगणने W 1; कलिशुद्धदिनहोगणने P 1; किलशुद्धदिनहोगणने P 2, I 2. [3] W 1; ल-पंचदश वै P 1; लक्षपंचदशपदैः P 2, I 2. [4] W 1; °र्थं हीरितः P 1, P 2, I 2. These two *s*lokas (13 and 14), which give the date of the Vedârthadîpika, are fully explained by Weber, Ind. Stud. vol. viii, p. 160, note. [5] P 1, P 2, I 2; मुकुंदात्मयो W 1. In the Introd. to Sha*dg*.'s comm. (Weber's Catal., p. 14) *S*ûlapâ*n*i is called *S*ûlâṅka, and Mukunda is called Govinda. [6] षड्भ्यो P 1, P 2, I 2; पड्भ्यो W 1. [7] P 1, W 1; प्रदत्ताः P 2, I 2. [8] P 1, P 2, I 2; आद्यानुक्रमणी W 1. [9] °र्शं P 1. [10] W 1; सूत्रं पंचम्यु- P 1; तद्वत्सुत्रं पंचमी वै निरुक्तं P 2, I 2. [11] P 1, P 2, I 2 add सप्त. [12] W 1; चार्थपुष्टये P 1; आत्मतुष्टये P 2, I 2. [13] P 1, I 4 add समाप्तमिदं शास्त्रं समाप्ता चेयं वृत्तिः सर्वानुक्रमणीवृत्तिः ।

॥ अथ षड्गुरुशिष्यविरचितानुवाकानुक्रमणीवृत्तिः ॥

३. तादर्थ्ये प्रणम्य । प्रयतः । जितेंद्रियः । द्विविधं शौचं । मृज्जलाभ्यां बाह्यं । आंतरमर्थशुद्धिः । प्रणम्य । ततः किं ॥

४. ऋजु । वर्तमानानां च ऋजु[2] । अतंद्रितः । तारकादिभ्य इतच्[3] ॥

५. आदि[4] सूक्तपरिमाणं । परी[5]दीर्घश्छांदसः[6] । संख्यां[7] सर्वविषयक्रममेव च । इदमस्यां[8]परमिति । यावंतः । अनुवाकाः ॥

६. तत्सर्वं वक्ष्यामीत्यन्वयः । अनुवाकस्य नित्याध्ययने प्रयोजनमित्याह ॥

७. ब्रह्म कृण्वंतः परिवत्सरीणमिति श्रुतेः[9] । अस्य तु नित्याध्ययनस्य[10] ॥

८. देवान् प्रजापत्यादीन्[11] मंत्रस्य । ऋषीन् । शतर्च्यादिमहासूक्तांतान् । पितॄन् सुमंत्वादि प्रतिपुरुषं पितॄन्[12]नित्यंतान् । तदर्थं[10] ॥

९. शैशिरीयायां । शिशिरनाममहर्षिप्रोक्तायां । शिशिरर्तुसमाप्यायां[13]मित्यन्ये । शाकलस्य[14] संहितायामित्यर्थः । प्रमाणं निबोधनं[15] प्रतिपादनमित्यर्थः । शास्त्र[16] उक्तं हि ।

प्रमाणं बोधनेयत्ता[17]मर्यादाशास्त्रहेतुषु ।
सम्यगुक्तावेव[18] च ॥

इति । अनुवाकानां सूक्तैः । सहेति शेषः । शृणुत हे शाकलाः । के ते । सर्वेषां शाकलत्वमाप्रीद्वारेण वक्तुमाप्रीद्रष्टॄ[19]नाह ॥

१०. आप्रीद्रष्टार एते । इदं शास्त्रं शाकलानामेव[20] संबंधन[21]मित्यन्ये । जमदग्निरयोक्षरं । दशममाप्रीसूक्तं जमदग्निर्ददर्श । प्राजापत्ये पशौ सर्वेषामाप्रियो जामदग्न्य[22] इति सर्वे शाकलाः ॥

११. सुसमिद्धो न आ वह[23] । समिद्धो अग्न आ वह[24] । समिद्धो अद्य राजसि[25] । समिद्धो

[1] ऋजुर्व° W 1, C. [2] W 1, C; ऋजुः C 1. [3] See Kâsikâ Vritti on Pân. V, ii, 36. [4] W 1, C, C 1. [5] W 1, C; परि C 1. [6] °स W 1, C, C 1. [7] ता added in W 1, C, C 1. [8] हृदमस्या W 1, C; हृदयमस्या C 1. [9] *Rigv.* VII, 103, 8. [10] Introducing the next verse. [11] C 1; प्राजापत्यादेव W 1, C. [12] Âsv. Grihya-sûtra, III, iv, 4–5. [13] °समाप्यम् W 1, C; समाप्याम् C 1. [14] शाक्षरस्य W 1, C, C 1. [15] बोधनं W 1, C. [16] C 1; शास्त्रे मुक्तं W 1, C. [17] बोधनेयता C 1. [18] सम्यगुक्तैरिवे च MSS. [19] °द्रष्टुम् W 1, C; द्रष्टृम् C 1. [20] शाकलाय नामेव C 1. [21] संबद्धम् C 1. [22] Cp. Âsv. Sr.-sûtra, III, ii, 8. [23] (12) *Rigv.* I, 13. [24] (13) I, 142. [25] (11) I, 188.

अग्निर्निहितः[1] । समित्समित्सुमनाः[2] । सुसमिद्धाय शोचिषे[3] । जुषस्व नः समिधमग्ने अद्य[4] । समिद्धो विश्वतस्पतिः[5] । इमां मे अग्ने समिधं जुषस्व[6] । समिद्धो अद्य मनुषो दुरोणे[7] । अथारभते[8] ॥

१५. अग्निमीळे त्रिसूक्तस्तु । अनुवाकविशेषः । सुरूपेंद्र चतुःसूक्तो । अनुवाकविशेष इत्यादि यथायोगमुत्तरत्रापि वेदितव्यं । सुरूपकृत्नुमूतये[9] । एंद्र सानसिं रयिं[10] । अग्निं दूतं[11] । सोमानं स्वरणं[12] । कस्य नूनं[13] ॥

१६. पंचकं । अनुवाकं पंचसूक्तं । त्वमग्ने प्रथमो अंगिराः[14] । प्र वो यह्वं[15] । अग्ने विवस्वद् अभि त्यं नूचिदिति ये त्रयोऽनुवाकाः सप्तसूक्तकाः । अग्ने विवस्वदुषसः[16] । अभि त्यं मेषं[17] । नूचित्सहोजाः[18] ॥

१७. पश्वा न तायुं[19] । उप प्रयंतो अध्वरं[20] । एकादशसूक्तं विद्यादित्येव । नन्वत्र[21] मध्ये खिलमार्षानुक्रमण्यादिवत्[22] किं[23] नोच्यत इत्याह । अस्मिन्ननुवाकानां ग्रंथे खैलिकानामनुवाकानामनादेशः । अनुक्ता हि ॥

१८. योऽनुवाकश्चर्चायते सम्यगभ्यस्यते । चर्चैवास्त्रतीति क्वङ् । यद्वा चर्चयाभ्यसनेनायते । आभिमुख्येन बद्धः । यमु बंधने क्तः । वेदे । वेदपारायणाध्ययने[24] तस्य संख्या विज्ञेयेति । नः । अस्माकं । श्रुतिः । उपदेशः । अतोऽत्रोत्तरत्रापि खिलवर्जमृगुच्यत इति भावः ॥ प्र ये शुंभंते जनयः[25] । इमं स्तोमं[26] ॥

१९. इंद्रं मित्रं वरुणं[27] । अत्र दश सूक्तानि । नासत्याभ्यां बर्हिरिव[28] । कदित्था नॄन्[29] । अग्निमित्यपरोऽनुवाकः सप्तसूक्तकः । अग्निं होतारं मन्ये[30] । आ त्वा जुवो रारहाणाः[31] ॥

२०. वेदिषदे प्रियधामाय[32] । अबोध्यग्निर्ज्मः[33] । कया शुभा[34] । त्रिपंचसूक्तः । पंचदशसूक्त इति यावत् । युवो रजांसि[35] ॥

२१. चत्वारो विंशतिश्चैव । अनुवाकाः । अथ बाष्कलकेऽस्य[36] विशेषमाद्यमंडल आह । उपप्रयंतो नासत्याभ्याम् अग्निं होतारं इमं स्तोमं वेदिषद इति बाष्कलकः क्रम इत्यर्थः । उपप्रयंत इमं स्तोमं नासत्याभ्याम् अग्निं होतारं वेदिषद इति शाकलकः क्रमः[37] । अत्रैवमुक्तेरुत्तरमंडलनवकेऽनुक्रमविपर्यासः[38] ॥

॥ इति प्रथमं मंडलं समाप्तं ॥

[1] (11) *Rigv.* II, 3. [2] (11) III, 4. [3] (11) V, 5. [4] (11) VII, 2. [5] (11) IX, 5. [6] (11) X, 70. [7] (11) X, 110. [8] There is no commentary on the last five lines of the Introd. [9] *Rigv.* I, 4. [10] I, 8. [11] I, 12. [12] I, 18. [13] I, 24. [14] I, 31. [15] I, 36. [16] I, 44. [17] I, 51. [18] I, 58. [19] I, 65. [20] I, 74. [21] C 1; यत्र W 1, C. [22] Cp. Meyer, *Rigv.*, p. xx, note. [23] MSS. add किमिति. [24] Cp. Ind. Stud. III, 251. [25] *Rigv.* I, 85. [26] I, 94. [27] I, 106. [28] I, 116. [29] I, 121. [30] I, 127. [31] I, 134. [32] I, 140. [33] I, 157. [34] I, 165. [35] I, 180. [36] °क अस्या W 1, C, C 1. [37] This comm. omitted in C 1. [38] See M. M., A. S. L., p. 229, note.

२२. त्वमग्ने द्युभिः[1] । यो जात एव[2] । गणानां त्वा[3] । आ ते पितः[4] । गणानां तृतीये सूक्तानि दश । त्वं यो आ त इत्यन्ये त्रयोऽनुवाका एकादशसूक्तकाः ॥

॥ इति द्वितीयं मंडलं ॥

सोमस्य मा तवसं[5] । प्र वो देवाय[6] ॥

२३. इच्छंति त्वा[7] । इंद्रं मतिर्हृद आ वच्यमाना[8] । पंचदशक इत्यर्थः । इमं महे विदथ्याय[9] ॥

॥ इति तृतीयं मंडलं ॥

त्वां ह्यग्ने सदमित्[10] । भद्रं ते अग्ने[11] । यन्न इंद्रः[12] ॥

२४. प्र ऋभुभ्यो दूतमिव[13] । अग्रं पिबेत्येष चापि त्रयोदश । अग्रं पिब मधूनां[14] ॥

॥ इति चतुर्थं मंडलं ॥

अबोध्यग्निः समिधा[15] । प्र वेधसे कवये[16] ॥

२५. महि महे[17] । बिदा दिवो विष्यन्[18] । तथा द्वादशक इति यावत् । आ रुद्रास इंद्रवंतः[19] । यदद्य स्यः[20] पंचदश ॥

॥ इति पंचमं मंडलं ॥

त्वं ह्यग्ने प्रथमो मनोता[21] । त्वमग्ने यज्ञानां[22] । वृषा मद इंद्रे[23] । यो रयिवो रयिंतमः[24] ॥

२६. हुवे वो देवीं[25] द्वादश । स्तुषे नरा[26] षष्ठे मंडले यः षष्ठोऽनुवाकश्चतुर्दशसूक्तः ॥

॥ इति षष्ठं मंडलं ॥

अग्निं नरो दीधितिभिः[27] । त्वे ह यत्पितरः[28] । प्र शुक्रा[29] ॥

२७. क ईं व्यक्ता नरः[30] । अप स्वसुरुषस[31] एकोनविंशतिः । प्र वीरया शुचयः[32] ॥

॥ इति सप्तमं मंडलं ॥

मा चिदन्यद्वि शंसत[33] । अथ सप्त । महाँ इंद्रो य ओजसा[34] । अष्ट । इंद्र सुतेषु[35] । वयमु त्वामपूर्व्य[36] ॥

२८. यो यजाति[37] । इमे विप्रस्य[38] । हकारः पूरणः । अग्न आ याह्यग्निभिः[39] । यो राजा चर्षणीनां[40] । उतेति पूरणः । आ तू न इंद्र क्षुमंतं[41] । गौर्धयति मरुतां[42] । विद्यादिति शेषः ।

[1] Rigv. II, 1. [2] II, 12. [3] II, 23. [4] II, 33. [5] III, 1. [6] III, 13. [7] III, 30. [8] III, 39. [9] III, 54. [10] IV, 1. [11] IV, 11. [12] IV, 22. [13] IV, 33. [14] IV, 46. [15] V, 1. [16] V, 15. [17] V, 33. [18] V, 45. [19] V, 57. [20] V, 73. [21] VI, 1. [22] VI, 16. [23] VI, 24. [24] VI, 44. [25] VI, 50. [26] VI, 62. [27] VII, 1. [28] VII, 18. [29] VII, 34. [30] VII, 56. [31] VII, 71. [32] VII, 90. [33] VIII, 1. [34] VIII, 6. [35] VIII, 13. [36] VIII, 21. [37] VIII, 31. [38] VIII, 43. [39] VIII, 60. [40] VIII, 70. [41] VIII, 81. [42] VIII, 94.

यस्तमिति च । अष्टममिति च । अतः परो दशको गोर्धयतीत्यर्थः । तमष्टममंडलस्यांतं विद्यात् । अतः पंचाशको गोर्धयत्ययमित्यन्ये पठंति ॥

॥ इत्यष्टमं मंडलं ॥

२९. स्वादिष्ठया मदिष्ठया[2] चतुर्विंशति[3]सूक्तः । पवस्व दक्षसाधनः[4] । त्रिंशत् सप्तद्वः । स्त्रीत्वा-भाव[5]श्छांदसः । षट्त्रिंशत्सूक्तकः । अया वीती परि स्रव[6] । प्र देवमच्छा[7] । प्र त आशवः[8] । अस्य प्रेषा हेमना[9] । सखाय आ नि षीदत[10] ॥

॥ इति नवमं मंडलं ॥

३०. अग्ने बृहन्नुषसां[11] । त्वष्टा दुहित्रे[12] । प्र देवत्रा ब्रह्मणे[13] । अच्छा म इंद्रं[14] । इदमित्था रौद्रं[15] । भद्रा अग्नेः[16] । सत्येनोत्तभिता[17] । सं जागृवद्भिः[18] । इंद्र दृह्य[19] ॥

३१. तमस्य द्यावापृथिवी सचेतसा[20] । नासदासीदि[21]त्येष परोऽनुवाकस्त्रयोविंशतिसूक्तकः । अस्मिन्मंडले द्वादशक ऋग्वेदांत्यो योऽनुवाकः शास इत्येत्यादि तत्रानुवाके सूक्तानि चत्वारिंशत् । शास इत्था महाँ असि[22] ॥

॥ इति दशमं मंडलं ॥

३२. अथ मंडलेष्वनुवाकसंख्यामाह । यत् । तत्रेति शेषः । द्वितीयं मंडलं यच्चतुरनुवाकं । द्वे पंचके । अतः परमित्येव । अतः परे द्वे तृतीयचतुर्थमंडले पंचानुवाके भवतः । पराणि त्रीणि मंडलानि पंचमषष्ठसप्तमानि षडनुवाकानि । अष्टमं । तत्र दशानुवाकाः संति । नवमं यत्तत्र सप्तानुवाकाः । दशममंत्यं मंडलं यत्तत्र द्वादशानुवाकाः ॥

३३. अथ मंडलेषु सूक्तसंख्यामाह । एकनवत्यधिकशतं सूक्तानि भवंतीत्यर्थः । द्वितीयं त्रिच-त्वारिंशत्सूक्तं । द्वे सूक्ते । द्व्यधिकषष्टिरिति यावत् ॥

३४. अपि तु यच्चतुर्थं तत्राष्टा[23]धिकपंचाशत्सूक्तानीत्याहुः । अतः परं स्यात् । अतः पंचमं मंडलं । पंचाधिका सप्ततिरुत्तरं तु । उत्तरं षष्ठं । वासिष्ठं सप्तमं मंडलं चतुरधिकं शतं सूक्तं ॥

३५. अष्टमं । द्विनवतिः[24] सूक्तानि यानि । नवमं मंडलं शतं भवेद्ध अथ[25] यानि चतुर्दश सूक्तानि[26] चाचाहुश्चतुर्दशाधिकशतं भवेदित्याहुरित्यर्थः । अथाधिकानीति[27] ।

वष्टि भागुरिरल्लोपमवाप्यो[28]रुपसर्गयोः[29] ।

चतुर्दश त्वाहुरथाधिकानीत्यन्ये पठंति । एकनवत्यधिकशतं सूक्तानि वदंति दशमे मंडल इत्यर्थः ॥

[1] गोर्धयदित्यर्थः W 1. [2] *Rigv.* IX, 1. [3] C 1; °ति: W 1, C. [4] *Rigv.* IX, 25. [5] स्त्रीत्वादाव W 1, C. [6] *Rigv.* IX, 61. [7] IX, 68. [8] IX, 86. [9] IX, 97. [10] IX, 104. [11] X, 1. [12] X, 17. [13] X, 30. [14] X, 43. [15] X, 61. [16] X, 69. [17] X, 85. [18] X, 91. [19] X, 100. [20] X, 113. [21] X, 129. [22] X, 152. [23] °र्थात् । अष्ट° W 1; °र्थं तत् अष्ट° C 1. [24] °ति MSS. [25] अथो W 1; omitted in C 1. [26] C 1; शतानि W 1. [27] अथो यानीति MSS. [28] C 1; °ल्लोपयमवास्योरु° W 1. [29] See kârikâ, giving a rule of Bhâguri, quoted by Sâyana, *Rigv.* II, 4, 5, and III, 26, 1.

३६. अथ सर्वमंडलसूक्तसंख्यामाह । एतासूक्तजालं सप्तदशाधिकं सहस्रं सूक्तानि । बाष्कलके[1] संहितापाठे[2]ऽतः शाकलादधिकान्यष्टौ सूक्तानि पंचविंशत्यधिकसहस्रमित्यर्थः[3] । खिलेष्वनुवाका[4] नेत्युक्तं[5] । तन्नैस्पष्टयाय[6] पुनराह । तानुक्तानुवाकान्[7] शाकले शैशिरीये पारायणे वेदपारतीरकर्मसमाप्तौ । करणे ल्युट् । अन्नादिमोक्षांतफलपारप्राप्तिहेतौ । शिशिरशब्दाद् गहादिछात्[8] प्रोक्ताद्यण्[9] स्वार्थे[10] । शिष्टाः परमहर्षयो[11] विप्रा मेधाविनः । शिष्टा अनुवाकान्[12] खिलम्शाकल एव वदंति न खिलेष्वित्यर्थः । अतः खिलानामनुवाको नोक्त इति भावः । तान्पारणे शाकले शैशिरीया वदंति शिष्टा न खिलेषु विप्रा इति पठंत्यन्ये[13] ॥

३७. सर्वमंडलमिलितानुवाकसंख्यामाह । दाशतये[14] । दशमंडलयोगिनि[15] वेदे । संख्याया अवयवे तयप्[16] । ततः स्वार्थेऽण् । ऋग्वित् । ऋगर्थवित् । वेदतोऽधीते सः । वेदिताध्येता च । नाकपृष्ठं स्वर्गं । शश्वत् सदा । भजते भजेत । लिङर्थे लट् । ह प्रसिद्धौ । इतोऽमुं लोकमेत्य तस्माच्च च्यवते[17] हीत्यर्थः ॥

३८. वर्गाः षडधिकद्विसहस्रमित्यर्थः ॥

३९. खिलरहितसूक्तानि सप्तदशाधिकसहस्रं । संख्यातं । पुरा महर्षिभिरिति शेषः । वयमपि तच्छाकल्यदृष्ट इत्यादिना[18] वक्ष्यामः ॥

४०. एकर्चः । जातवेदसे[19] । नवर्च एको वर्गः । आपो हि ष्ठा मयोभुवः[20] । तृचौ । अग्ने त्वं नो अंतमः[21] । आ याहि वनसा सह[22] । तृचवर्गाः सप्तनवतिः । उत त्यं चमसं नवमित्यादि[23] ॥

४१. चतुर्थ्यैव[24]वर्गजातं चतुःसप्तत्यधिकशतं । यदंग दाशुषे त्वमित्यादि[25] । सप्ताधिकशतत्रयसहस्रं पंचका वर्गाः । अग्निमीळ इत्यादि[26] ॥

४२. अश्विना यज्वरीरिष[27] इत्यादि । सप्तकानां । एकोनविंशत्यधिकशतं सप्तर्चाः । यच्चिद्धि सत्य सोमपा[28] इत्यादि । एकोनषष्टिरष्टकवर्गाः[29] । ऊना षष्टिरष्टकानामित्यन्ये पठंति । इंद्रं विश्वा अवीवृधन्नित्यादि[30] ॥

४३. सहस्राण्यृचामिति संबंधानुकरणं छंदोऽनुवाकानुकरणं पारणं वेदसमापनकर्मर्षिभिः संप्रकीर्तितं । पादश्च भद्रं न[31] इति ॥

[1] C I; बाष्कले W I. [2] C I; °पाठके W I. [3] See A. S. L., p. 229. [4] W I; °के C I. [5] Ver. 17. [6] W I; °ष्टाय C I. [7] तानुवाकान् C I; तानुक्तानुवाकानां W I, C. [8] °शब्दानुग्रहादिछान् MSS. [9] W I; प्रोक्ता यण् C I. [10] स्वार्थो MSS. [11] C I; शिष्टा महर्षयः W I, C. [12] शिष्टाः अनुवाकाः C I; शिष्टानुवाका W I. [13] W I, C; °न्ये पठंति C I. [14] °तय्ये MSS. [15] W I; °गीन C I. [16] Pâṇ. V, ii, 42. [17] W I; प्रच्यवते C I. [18] दृष्टेत्या° MSS. See verse 45. [19] *Rigv.* I, 99. [20] X, 9. [21] V, 24. [22] X, 172. [23] I, 20, 6. [24] C I; चतुर्था च W I, C. [25] *Rigv.* I, 1, 6. [26] I, 1. [27] I, 3. [28] I, 29. [29] C I; अष्टवर्गाः W I, C. [30] *Rigv.* I, 11. [31] X, 20. Cp. A. S. L., pp. 220–221.

४४. मुनिभिः पुरा। दृष्टमिति शेषः। द्वात्रिंशदधिकशतद्वयाधिकमेकविंशतिसहस्रमर्धर्चाः पादश्चैक इत्यर्थः ॥

४५. शाकल्यदृष्टे वेदे चर्चितान्यभ्यस्तान्यधीतानि पदानि षड्विंशत्यधिकाष्टशतयुक्तत्रिसहस्राधिकपंचाशत्सहस्राधिकशतसहस्रमित्यर्थः ॥

४६. अथ क्रमसंख्यामाह। चर्चापदानि क्रमरूपेणाभ्यस्तानि पदानीत्यर्थः। चतुरधिकसप्तशतदशसहस्राधिकलक्षं क्रमसंख्येत्यर्थः ॥ वावेति खल्वित्यर्थः। द्वात्रिंशत्सहस्राधिकचतुर्लक्षमक्षराणीत्यर्थः। द्विरुक्तिः समाप्तिज्ञापनार्था। एष वा ऋग् एष वा अर्धर्च एष वै पदम्[2] एष वा अक्षरमित्यादि सर्वेषां ब्रह्म[3]रूपत्वोक्तेरारण्यके[4]। अत्रापि सर्वं संयक् संख्यातं भगवता शौनकेन वक्तृषसिंहेन वेदितव्यं ॥

॥ षड्गुरुशिष्यविरचितानुवाकानुक्रमणीविवृत्तिः समाप्ता ॥

[1] वसि खल्वित्यर्थः W 1, C; सि खल्वित्यर्थः C 1; all three adding वावेति पाठेऽपि स एवार्थः। [2] C 1; पाद W 1. [3] ब्रह्म° C 1. [4] Ait. Âr. II, ii, 2, 7–10.

APPENDICES.

I. EXPLANATORY NOTES.

II. INDEX OF PRATÎKAS AS GIVEN IN THE SARVÂNUKRAMA*N*Î.

III. INDEX OF METRES.

IV. LIST OF VERSES FROM THE *RI*GVEDA, QUOTED BY SHA*D*-GURU*S*ISHYA AS EXAMPLES OF METRES.

V. LIST OF AUTHORS AND WORKS QUOTED BY SHA*D*GURU-*S*ISHYA.

VI. LIST OF ITIHÂSAS RELATED BY SHA*D*GURU*S*ISHYA.

VII. INDEX OF WORDS OCCURRING IN THE SARVÂNUKRAMA*N*Î, THE ANUVÂKÂNUKRAMA*N*Î, AND IN SHA*D*GURU*S*ISHYA.

I.

EXPLANATORY NOTES.

§ 1, 1. The quotation छादयंति ह वा एनं छंदांसि पापात्कर्मणः is from the Ait. Âr. II, i, 6, 4. (W 1 alone reads छादयंतीह.)

शौनकोपदेशानुक्रमणीदशक°: as to the thirteen books on which the Sarvânukrama*n*î is based, see A. S. L., p. 234. Note that the ten works of *S*aunaka are here mentioned under the generic term 'Anukrama*n*î.'

§ 1, 3. महाबलिम्: Bali the son of Prahlâda. अपत्यप्रत्ययः: with reference to the importance here attributed to patronymic suffixes in connexion with the names of seers, a line is curiously enough introduced from the story of Syâvâ*s*va in the B*r*ihaddevatâ, containing the fanciful statement that 'a seer considers the composer of hymns a father of the Veda.' This is supported by a forced interpretation of *R*igv. X, 66, 14, which is understood to mean 'the Vasish*th*as composed this as fathers' instead of 'as their fathers did before them.' The reading ऋषिः, which I have chosen because a subject is necessary both here and in the BD., is also supported by the corruption तमुकर्णो (P 2, I 2); this no doubt stands for वसुकर्णो, the author of the verse quoted. Probably the same name has been shortened to कएव in P 1 to force it into the metre. W 1 has किंच.

§ 2, 3. कौशिकत्वं कथादिना: the reference is to the introductory sûtra to ma*nd*. III.

नारायणस्य गोत्रं: cp. comm. to X, 90.

§ 2, 6. यदक्षरपरिमाणं तच्छंद: none of the MSS. containing the commentary have this sûtra (except W 1, where it is written on the margin), nor is there any comment. It is, therefore, perhaps, a later addition, it being necessary for the sake of completeness, with reference to the three words *r*ishi, daivata, *kh*anda*h*, mentioned in the first sûtra of § 1.

§ 2, 16. नैय्यायकाः seems to have no point, and is probably a corruption for ऐतरेयकाः, P 1 being an incorrect MS. I cannot make any sense out of the reading of W 1, I 4.

§ 2, 20. The conjectural reading क्षार, 'acid,' is preferable to a vague word like रस (W 1, I 4), 'liquid.' All the MSS. have a long vowel in सूत्रायंते: 'the sûtras, like the Brâhma*n*as, explain the connexion of the Veda.'

§ 2, 22. अभ्यागतपूजनं (P 2, I 2) is, perhaps, a preferable reading to that of the other MSS., आगत° : besides this curious explanation of Nipâta, Shadg. gives another elsewhere (see comm. to III, 6). What follows I explain thus: 'moreover, if after this (scil. this introduction, i.e. in the main part of the Sarvânukramanî which refers to the mantras) an Indra metre is to be recited, it is always connected with the Maruts, as the verse itself shows. Hence though *Ri*gv. I, 6 contains six verses to the Maruts, the employment of it as an Indra hymn by the Brâhma*n*â*kh*amsi priest is undoubted.' This passage shows, I think, pretty clearly the connexion between MSS. P 2 and P 1. मारुतषड्वान्वये पि must be the correct reading. P 1 (1392 A.D.) reads मारुतः कान्वये पि (षड् having dropped out). The writer of P 2, who no doubt knew the pratîkas of the *Ri*gveda by heart, being unable to make sense of the words as they stand, turned them into नेयासु ये पि रोदसी (adding the last word), which is a Marut verse (VIII, 94, 11), but has no connexion whatever with the hymn here under discussion.

§ 3, 10. The quotation न ह्येकस्मादक्षराद्वाधयंति is from the Pa*ñk*avi*m*sa Br. XV, xii, 5, where the reading is विराधयंति.

§ 11, 4. माहावृहत: the MSS. are all corrupt; this must, however, be what Sha*dg*. considered the correct grammatical formation: v*ri*ddhi of the first syllable of the first word, and no v*ri*ddhi in the second.

§ 11, 6. मा विज्ञायि: a rare use of the aorist passive as an imperative. अनुष्टुम्मुखास्तृचाः: the Sarvânukrama*n*î (VIII, 68 and 74) agrees with the *Kh*ando*nukrama*n*î in stating that there are eight of these pragâthas in the *Ri*gveda. These are not given in the table of metres in the preface (p. xviii); if they had been there mentioned, 8 would have to be subtracted from the total of the anush*t*ubh, and 16 from that of the gâyatrî verses in ma*nd*ala VIII.

Page 76, line 4. The MSS. are here corrupt, doubtless owing partly to the similarity of य and थ when indistinctly written, and partly to the ambiguity of उक्तं. The passage as emended gives a perfectly clear and satisfactory meaning: 'It is to be understood that, because 14 is considered to be the number of metres in this *S*âkalya Sa*m*hitâ, there is no mention, either at the beginning, of the five metres ukta, etc., nor at the end, of the seven metres beginning with k*ri*ti and ending with utk*ri*ti.'

P. 76, l. 8. उक्तं साति मध्यं प्रतिष्ठा सु च। This sûtra does not occur in the extant text of Piṅgala. Prof. Weber (Ind. Stud. VIII, p. 283) thinks it is impossible to reconcile two of these words with the names of the five metres just mentioned by Sha*d*g., viz. उक्तं अत्युक्तं मध्यं प्रतिष्ठा सुप्रतिष्ठा. Their identity seems to me to be perfectly clear. उक्तं certainly does not occur in any of the MSS., but it may easily be restored without any violence; for that an ambiguous word like this, which might mean 'it has been said,' should easily have dropped out after सूच्यते, especially when not अत्युक्तं

follows, but सातिं, is obvious; then सातिं would be = स + अति [उक्तं], a form quite in keeping with Pingala's style; मध्यं and प्रतिष्ठा show no variation, while the last words सु च are clearly = सु[प्रतिष्ठा] च.

P. 77. प्रकृतिः। I have been unable to trace the verse quoted as an example of this metre: it is probably from the Taittirîya Brâhma*n*a. (Cp. M. M., *R*igv. Prâtis., p. cccxxvii.)

I, 23, l. 6. The words मरुद्भिरस्त्वान् occur in Nir. IV, 25.

P. 85, verse 9. शुनःशेपपशुं must be the correct reading: 'a râ*g*asûya sacrifice in which *S*una*h*sepa played the part of the sacrificial animal.' Ver. 12. The reading अन्याः (देवताः) is more natural than that of W 1: the meaning being, 'I will address myself to the other gods,' not to Varu*n*a, to whom he does not pray till afterwards (ver. 13).

I, 28. The MSS. are very corrupt in the three metrical lines, but the sense requires the emendations I have made.

I, 50. सूत्रवृत्तौ: this is the only reference to another comm. (Ait. Âr.) in Sha*d*g. उपनिषत्: the fanciful etymology of this word here given upa[itya] ni[yuktâya] sad[yate] reminds one of the jocular derivation of 'cadaver' from ca[ro] da[ta] ver[minibus].

I, 51. अभ्यध्यायत्: the MSS. are so corrupt here that it is almost impossible to make out what the commentator meant. According to my emendation the meaning would be: 'instead of the impf. अभ्यध्यायत् the aor. अभ्यध्यात् should have been used, the employment of the present base being Vedic:' none of the MSS., however, read लुङि, all pointing to लङि. The point appears to lie in the use of the present stem, not in the difference of meaning in the tenses. Sha*d*g. does here and there speak of one tense being wrongly used for another in the case of तुष्टाव (see Index), which, he says, is owing to the influence of another anukrama*n*î, and should have been अस्तौत्. This may, however, only be due to the fact that there is one *mora* less in this word. It is not clear to me whether Sha*d*g. made a distinction in the *meaning* of the tenses.

I, 99. Sha*d*g. comments at some length on the curious statement in the text that this hymn, consisting of one verse, is the first of a thousand hymns composed by Kasyapa. He quotes the Ârshânukrama*n*î as the authority for Kâtyâyana's statement. He says: 'These are Khila hymns: we read (in the *R*igveda) the first of them which consists of one verse; this is stated by *S*aunaka himself in the *R*ishi Anukrama*n*î, where he says, "*g*âtavedase" is the first of the hymns composed by Kasyapa, which increase (in the number of their verses) by one up to one thousand.' The verses, however, ending with the hymn "sa yo v*r*ishâ" [*R*igv. I, 100, the following hymn. Sha*d*g. uses anta with an excluding sense in the introd. to ma*nd*. VIII also, this ma*nd*ala being said to end with svâdish*th*ayâ, which is the first hymn of ma*nd*. IX] are in the midst of the Veda, appertaining to the Akhila sûktas.' [The MSS. are very corrupt in this line.] 'But the number of verses [contained in these 1000 hymns] will amount to 500,500 diminished by one (a half verse being subtracted at the beginning and the end), according to the calculation of Âryabha*tt*a, just as the sum of (the arithmetical progression) 1 to 10 is stated to be 55.' The sum of the progression 1 to 1000 *is* 500,500. Meyer, *Ri*gvidh., p. xx, note, is therefore not right in saying that there is nothing to support the statement of Max Müller (*Ri*gv., vol. ii) that the Khilas seem to have been mentioned in Saunaka's Ârshânukrama*n*î. In fact this very point is distinctly stated in the comm. on the Anuvâkânukrama*n*î (verse 17). Other references to the Khilas will be found in the Anuvâkânukrama*n*î (see Index) and Meyer, *Ri*gvidh., pp. xxi, note 2, and xxvii.

I, 111. Perhaps it would have been better to retain the reading of the MSS., उपनिषदित्युक्तार्थे, supplying पदं to account for the neuter.

I, 120. The only practical difference in the reading which I have adopted (this being supported by all the MSS. except W 1) is that W 1 states verse 2 to be ush*n*ih *or* gâyatrî, while the rest state it to be ush*n*ih (kakubh) only.

I, 132. It is clear from the comm. that Sha*d*g. read ऐंद्रापर्वत (without v*ri*ddhi of the second word), which should therefore be restored. The MSS. have followed Pâ*n*ini.

I, 164, p. 97, l. 4. सूच्यते refers to the sûtra portion of the Âra*n*yaka, this quotation being explained by the following quotation from the Brâhma*n*a portion (cp. comm. on I, 50, l. 3, and X, 28, l. 2). Line 11. संज्ञा चैकर्षाः केशिनः, the reading of the remaining MSS., केशिनः, should be corrected to कैशिनं (W 1), this word being quoted from the sûtra on X, 136. The meaning is that the name Kesina*h* has the same signification as it has in that sûtra, where Agni, Sûrya, and Vâyu are the deities, and the hymn is stated to be कैशिनं.

I, 165. The structure of the three lines quoted from the Devatânukrama*n*î is irregular, and similar to that in the Anuvâkânukrama*n*î.

II, 33, verse 5. हित्वा जहुः 'fled and forsook him' (the one verb being intransitive, the other transitive,) 'while the Maruts assisted him.'

II, 41. The last three lines of the comm. are difficult, as the last part is in W 1 only, and besides being very corrupt, is written on the margin. In accordance with my emendations I explain the passage इत्येष हि. etc. as follows: Sha*d*g. says that the Sûtrakâra by the sûtra VII, vi, 2–3 means 'in assigning a triplet to each of the praüga deities, each of whom claims a triplet, he gives five triplets or 15 verses (4–18) to the gods beginning with Mitrâvaru*n*a and ending with Sarasvatî; while as regards the first triplet, he assigns to Vâyu (who in *R*igv. II, 41, 1–2 obtains two verses), as obtaining only one verse in I, 23, 1, and to Indra-Vâyu (who in *R*igv. II, 41, 3 obtains one verse), as obtaining two verses in I, 23, 2–3, the verse तीव्राः (for Vâyu) and the two verses उभा (for Indra-Vâyu) respectively.' The sense seems to require लब्धद्वयाभ्यां. I do not know what to make of the corrupt word वार्येम्. द्वाभ्यां would be superfluous.

IV, 3. The quotation given in the foot-note from MS. I 2 is written on the margin in another hand. As it is not to be found in P 2, the passage must have been copied from some other source. Its presence in this form does not invalidate the evidence that this MS. is a copy of P 2.

IV, 18, ver. 9. विवेकत्वे etc.: 'the meaning is explained because it is necessary to distinguish in order to ascertain who are the *R*ishis and who the deities.'

IV, 23. The comm. is corrupt. साधनाः, if correct, is used like प्रतिपादकाः, 'these verses are addressed to *R*ita because they mention him in the sense of a deity; or they are addressed to Indra.' It is perhaps better to omit देवे.

IV, 33. It is necessary to read प्र ऋभुभ्यः owing to the grammatical remark which follows (this could not refer to the Sandhi of वा ऋभुः); but Sha*dg*. does not otherwise comment on the Sandhi of the pratîkas of the hymns.

IV, 57. The comm. distinctly shows that Sha*dg*. read क्षैत्रपत्यः (not क्षैत्रपत्याः), the fem. of क्षैत्रपत।

V, 61, ver. 9. The last four words are corrupt, but make good sense as emended: 'A man who is not a *R*ishi cannot be our son-in-law; this man (is not one) for he has not seen mantras; let our daughter be given to a *R*ishi, *in order that she may become a mother* (अंबा) *of the Veda;* for a seer (Vasukar*n*a) considers that one who has seen mantras to be a father of the Veda.' This is of course very fanciful, but at the same time very Indian. (Cp. comm. on § 1, 3, p. 58.)

Ver. 30. प्रत्याचक्षि must be the correct reading though none of the MSS. have it: 'because I refused you before.'

Ver. 35. वाच्यत्वे: 'then, because it was necessary to praise the Maruts in the form of a question, those deities are praised in the four verses ke sh*th*â (V, 61, 1–4) and the six verses ya îm' (verses 11–16).

V, 73. 'This seer is a citizen, from a city. He is not Paura by name as Bahuvr*i*kta, for instance, is called Bâhuvr*i*kta. There are no two *R*ishis having the name of Pura (i. e. I suppose there is no *R*ishi named Pura, nor one with the patronymic Paura). The name of the *R*ishi is not even mentioned.' The MSS. have न स्तो षिनामापि नोच्यते. The corruption must have arisen from the ऋ being mistaken for an अ, which would then drop out after अः.

V, 78. The words सर्वोऽस्त्वार्षं केचित् are a quotation from the sûtra on V, 27. समुदायोपदेशत्वात्: 'the singular (upanishad) is used, as in the expression, "the Vedas are the authority," because he wishes to give (upadâ) the aggregate of five verses.'

P. 123, l. 2. The emendation प्रसववेदनानां I take as a bahuvrîhi: 'of women in the travail of childbirth.' Verse 2. The conjecture निष्पेक्ष्यन् I derive from निष्पिष् in the sense of 'wishing to stamp out, annihilate.'

VI, 27. अभ्यावर्तिनः: 'of king *K*âyamâ*n*a, who has obtained the epithet of the "returning" hero, after having gone to meet his foes in battle.'

VI, 52. द्वैमातुरः; this, he means, is not an uncommon thing, for a man may have a step-mother; but how is द्विपितृकाः to be explained? For according to the well-known Indian custom a widow might not marry again. Verse 4. If मत is the correct reading, the meaning would be: 'the one called Sa*m*varta was widely renowned in India as one of good repute.'

P. 127, ver. 5. अवोचदुत्तरं: without being addressed. Cp. the biblical expression, 'answered and said.'

VII, 32. एकपुरोडाश°: I do not understand the reference. It is meant as an illustration from some sacrificial usage, to show that if two verses, a b*r*ihatî and a satob*r*ihatî, were left over, neither should be taken as the metre of a single verse at the end, but trish*t*ubh, the regular metre when no other is specified, would take their place; while by applying another method of reasoning, that of taking the first of two and leaving the last, verse 27 would be b*r*ihatî. This difficulty is, however, hypothetical only, for verse 3 being a virâ*t*, no single verse is left over to be accounted for at the end.

P. 131, last line. शाख्यात् seems a necessary correction as the reading of the MS. does not construe.

VII, 55. उपनिषच्च भवति: Sha*d*g. regularly puts the verb in the sing. after plural subjects, when it is immediately preceded by a noun in the singular. Cp. § 3, 6: द्वे अक्षरे एकमक्षरं क्रियते; I, 65: द्वे द्विपदे एकर्ग् भवति.

VII, 90. According to this comm. the first verse should also have Indra and Vâyu for their deities; this is not mentioned in the Indices of Aufrecht or Max Müller.

VIII, 1. Cp. with this discussion, showing that ma*nd*ala VIII begins here, though it is not expressly stated in the Sarvânukrama*n*î, the introd. to ma*nd*ala X, where the Anuvâkânukrama*n*î is also referred to, as here.

VIII, 4. अदर्शनात् is a necessary correction because of the meaning. 'Kâtyâyana must not be supposed to be infringing the rule "yathopadesam" owing to nothing being said about this in the Devatânukrama*n*î; for it is expressly stated in another authority, the B*r*ihaddevatâ.'

VIII, 11. त्रिष्टाजगतीत्व: a curious compound frequently employed by Sha*d*g.

VIII, 14. Shad*g*. expressly states here that the names are properly Goshûkti and A*s*vasûkti (not ending in न्), because that is the form they have in the Sâmans. The names are quoted without न् in Ind. Stud. I, p. 293, but with न् in III, p. 215.

VIII, 15. I do not see the relevancy of the quotation.

VIII, 91. The readings are so corrupt in the first line that it is impossible to emend them satisfactorily. In the first place the sense requires इंद्रं instead of यां. सामगाः may be right: it might easily have become corrupted owing to the similarity of the following word. Cp. the passage in Max Müller's *R*igv. quoted in foot-note 10.

P. 146, l. 1. सोमदेवता. The verses which have Soma for their deity have the quality of 'pavamâna.' All the MSS. but W 1 read सर्वदेवत्याः; this would refer to what is said in the introd. to this ma*nd*ala, that any other deity occurring in this ma*nd*ala has this quality also. This reading is, therefore, after all, perhaps preferable to the other; it being less obvious, for Soma himself in the introductory paribhâshâ is expressly stated to be pavamâna. It is only an inference with regard to the other gods.

P. 146, ll. 4-6. Now follows a discussion as to the propriety of placing the paribhâshâ जागतमूर्ध्वं प्रागशनसः before 68 instead of before 72. It may be objected, says Sha*dg*., that by placing it where it is, it states over again for these four hymns (68-71) what already follows from the paribhâshâ about hymns ending in a trish*t*ubh. But, he answers, nothing is really gained by placing it either in one place or the other. However, he adds, even if you lay stress on the argument as to sûktas ending in trish*t*ubhs, it really implies a praise (scil. of Kâtyâyana in placing the sûtra here, because, I suppose, it confirms the paribhâshâ, while nothing at all would be gained by placing it after the four hymns).

IX, 86. The mysterious word निवावरी must be a nom. plur. agreeing with सिकताः, and should, I suppose, be written with a visarga (i.e. निवावरीरिति) as a Vedic plur., though the MSS. without exception read निवावरी इति.

X, 17. सारण्यौ must be the correct dual fem. of the masc. सारण्य (not सारण्य), an adj. formed from सरण्यू according to the analogy of सरयू in Pâ*n*. VI, iv, 174.

X, 18. The reasoning appears to be this: 'If this verse is called aniruktâ because the name of a god does not appear in it, then the same would apply to *R*igv. VII, 59, 12, and to *R*igv. IV, 40, 5. But this is not so, because Kâtyâyana considers this to be anirukta as being enjoined as such in the Veda. Well then, he continues, *R*igv. I, 43, 6 is in the Ait. Br. specially stated to be aniruktâ, and yet it is not mentioned by Kâtyâyana. The answer is, that the verse under discussion must not be taken to be aniruktâ, because cited as such in a Brâhma*n*a, but it (tad scil. aniruktatvam) is pointed out by the verse (tayâ) itself.' This verse has no meaning, being quite disconnected. (See Grassmann, *R*igv., p. 468, note.)

P. 157, ver. 9. See on this Max Müller, *R*igv., vol. vi, p. 18.

X, 50. The quotation from the BD. is at the end of the comm. on this hymn (not 149), and is introduced with the words भाष्यांतरे पि वृद्धाचार्यो प्याह । वैश्वानरे गृहपतौ यविष्ठे ग्नौ च पावके etc. BD. VII, 839–855 (17 slokas, not 9).

X, 98. The quotation from the BD. in P 1 is simply introduced with अत्रेतिहासः । and begins with the words आर्ष्टिषेणो देवापि शंतनुश्चापि कारवौ (sic).

X, 105. दुर्ज्ञानगुणानि etc.: 'called Durmitra as an epithet because his virtues are difficult to know owing to their great number.'

ऋग्गर्थस्य etc.: 'Kâtyâyana thinks the optional connexion of either name with the other epithet should be mentioned without urging the want of connexion in the sense of the verse.'

बलासुरभ्रूकुटीतटैः etc.: 'by Asuras named Pani, protected by the frown of the Asura Bala;' Bala being their protector. All the MSS. read °तटैः. It may possibly be a corruption for कटैः (= करैः), in which case the compound would mean 'performing the (frowns =) commands of Bala,' i. e. the servants of Bala.

X, 106. P 1 alone at the end of the comm. introduces a short story of three lines with the words अत्रेतिहासः । भूतांशः किल प्रजाकामः कर्माणि चकारः । What follows is corrupt.

X, 121. The meaning seems to be: 'The hymn is sacred to Ka. A sûtra, it is true, mentions this verse as prâ*g*âpatyâ, which would be an exception to Ka. Hence this hymn, as well as *Ri*gv. IV, 31, is employed as a Ka hymn, and when in a Brâhma*n*a it is spoken of in connexion with a prâ*g*âpatyâ verse it is merely alluded to by the name of the *Ri*shi, like Sukîrti and the rest.'

X, 140. The evidence of the MSS., both in the text and the comm., is altogether in favour of the two first verses being vish*t*ârapaṅkti, and the last therefore uparish*t*â*gg*yoti*h*.

X, 161. Shad*g*. thinks that Saunaka also, in the B*ri*haddevatâ, considering Indra to be the deity, quotes the opinion of Yâska and of certain persons (eke) merely to show that he differs from them.

X, 166. The MSS. are very corrupt in the comm. W 1 reads अत्र चान् प्रकृतिस्तु विराड्वैराजं शाक्वरी वा शाक्वरं वा; P 1, अत्र चाण् प्रकृतिस्तु विराट् । वैराजं वा शाक्वरं वा । न कैश्चिदपि किरणायि; P 2, अत्र चाण् । प्रकृतिस्तु विराट् । वैराजं वा शाक्वरं वा नात्र कैश्चदण्यापि किरणापि; all the comm. in I 4 is ऋषभो नाम विराजपुत्रः । अथ शाक्वरा वा ऋषभः । The passage as emended means: 'here we have the suffix अण्, while the base is विराट्; but the meaning of "Vairâ*g*a or Sâkvara" has been made out by no one.'

X, 179. There can be no doubt from the evidence of the MSS. in both text and comm. that the patronymic is Rausadasva.

X, 180. The ĭ of Aindri*h* has dropped out of the text in all the MSS. Aindra*h*, however, would not be incorrect if Indra be considered a *R*ishi, which, as is here pointed out, he may be.

X, 185. P 1 reads नानृषित्वादत इम् (= न त्वृषित्वादत इम्); P 2, न तु ऋषित्वादत इम्. This remark is omitted in W 1 and I 4, but corresponds to what is said in the comm. to X, 180.

X, 191. संज्ञानं । ततोऽण् W 1, P 2 (संज्ञानं - - - P 1; संज्ञानं ततो I 4); according to this the text should have सांज्ञानं.

P. 167, ver. 11. सह सद्भिर् etc.: the readings of the MSS. in this line are very corrupt; the conjecture is not violent, and gives a good sense: 'he will dwell in heaven with the good, and even be worshipped there by them.'

P. 168, ver. 16. महाव्रतं सूत्रं must refer to the sûtra portion of the Aitareya Âra*n*yaka, the *S*rauta and the G*ri*hya Sûtra being afterwards mentioned as the fifth and the sixth branch of knowledge taught to Sha*d*gurusishya by his six teachers.

ANUVÂKÂNUKRAMA*N*Î.

Verse 5. परीदीर्घश्छांदसः, 'the length of pari is Vedic,' shows that the text must have read परीमाणम् originally.

Verse 9. प्रमाणं etc.; this is apparently a quotation from one of the Kosas. For the meanings of प्रमाण here given, cp. A. Boroooah's Grammar of the Sanskrit Language, vol. iii, part i, p. 287; also the *S*âsvata Ko*s*a.

Verse 17. This reference to the mention of the Khilas in the Ârshânukrama*n*î confirms what Sha*d*g. says in his comm. to Sarv. I, 99.

Verse 18. चर्षेवाचरतीति क्यङ्: cp. Schol. to Pâ*n*. III, i, 10. The alternative explanation is that *k*ar*k*âyate is a compound of *k*ar*k*â + âyate, loc. sing. of the past participle of â-yam.

Verse 21. The only difference in the order of the Bâshkalas is that the hymns of Kutsa (beginning with इमं स्तोमं) come last but one instead of second.

Verse 35. If the अ of अपि is dropped according to the rule of Bhâguri, the reading would of course be °धिकानि प्याह्वे. अथो यानीति, the reading of the MSS., makes no sense, and must be a corruption for अथाधिकानीति, under the influence, perhaps, of the words अथो यानि in the previous line. The only point in which the reading of 'others' differs from that given in the text, is apparently the dropping of अपि altogether.

Verse 36. Why Meyer, *Ri*gvidhâna, p. xxvii, wishes to read शिशान् अखिलेषु, I cannot understand, for no sense can be made out of the words if so divided.

शिशिरशब्दाद् etc.: the corruption of the MSS. is easily explained from शिशिरशब्दात् गहादिछात्. The meaning is clearly this: 'after the suffix छ of the ga*n*a gahâdi (Pâ*n*. IV, ii, 136) following the word शिशिर, is added the suffix अण् coming under the sûtra तेन प्रोक्तं (Pâ*n*. IV, iii, 101), without any change of meaning.' छ would give शिशिरीय, which अण् changes to शैशिरीय. The form शैशिरि, occurring in the ga*n*a gahâdi, must be wrong for शिशिर.

II.

INDEX OF PRATÎKAS

AS GIVEN IN THE SARVÂNUKRAMA*N*Î.

III.

INDEX OF METRES.

Gâyatrî (24).

Ma*nd*ala I, 1, 1–9; 2, 1–9; 3, 1–12; 4, 1–10; 5, 1–10; 6, 1–10; 7, 1–10; 8, 1–10, 9, 1–10; 12, 1–12; 13, 1–12; 14, 1–12; 15, 1–12; 16, 1–9; 17, 1–9[1]; 18, 1–9; 19, 1–9; 20, 1–8; 21, 1–6; 22, 1–21; 23, 1–18, 21[2]; 24, 3–5; 25, 1–21; 26, 1–10; 27, 1–12; 28, 7–9; 30, 1–15[3], 17–22; 37, 1–15; 38, 1–15; 41, 1–9; 42, 1–10; 43, 1–8; 46, 1–15; 50, 1–9; 74, 1–9; 75, 1–5; 78, 1–5; 79, 7–12; 84, 13–15; 86, 1–10; 90, 1–8; 91, 5–16; 93, 9–11; 97, 1–8; 120, 1, 10–12; 133, 5; 172, 1–3; 187, 2, 4, 8–10; 188, 1–11. [472]

II, 6, 1–8; 7, 1–6; 8, 1–5; 41, 1–15, 19–21. [37]

III, 11, 1–9; 12, 1–9; 24, 2–5; 27, 1–15; 28, 1, 2, 6; 37, 1–10; 40, 1–9; 41, 1–9; 42, 1–9; 51, 10–12; 52, 1–4; 53, 13; 59, 6–9; 62, 4–18. [104]

IV, 8, 1–8; 9, 1–8; 10, 1–3[4], 4, 6, 7[5]; 15, 1–10; 30, 1–7, 9–23; 31, 1[6]–15; 32, 1–24; 46, 1–7; 49, 1–6; 52, 1–7; 55, 8–10; 56, 5–7. [119]

V, 5, 1–11; 13, 1–6; 14, 1–6; 19, 1–2; 26, 1–9; 28, 5–6; 51, 1–4; 53, 8, 12; 61, 1–4, 6–8, 10–19; 68, 1–5; 70, 1–4; 71, 1–3; 82, 2–9. [79]

VI, 16, 1[7]–26, 28–45; 45, 1–32[8]; 47, 24; 52, 7–12; 53, 1–7, 9–10; 54, 1–10; 55, 1–6; 56, 1–5; 57, 1–6; 60, 4–12; 61, 4–12. [137]

VII, 15, 1–15; 31, 1–9; 55, 1; 59, 9–11; 66, 1–9, 17–19; 89, 1–4; 94, 1–11; 96, 4–6; 102, 1–3. [61]

VIII, 2, 1–27, 29–42; 3, 22–23; 5, 1–36; 6, 1–48; 7, 1–36; 9, 2, 3, 20–21; 11, 1[9]–9; 14, 1–15; 16, 1–12; 17, 1–13; 25, 23[10]; 26, 16–19, 21, 25; 28, 1–3, 5; 30, 1; 31, 1–8, 10[11]–13; 32, 1–30; 33, 16–18; 34, 16–18; 38, 1–10; 43, 1–33; 44, 1–30; 45, 1–42; 46, 1[11], 2–4, 6, 10, 23, 29, 33; [55, 1, 2, 4; 56, 1–4]; 63, 2, 3, 6, 8–11; 64, 1–12; 65, 1–12; 67, 1–21; 68, 2–3, 5–6, 8–9, 11–19; 69, 4–6; 71, 1–9; 72, 1–18; 73, 1–18; 74, 2–3, 5–6, 8–9, 11–12; 75, 1–16; 76, 1–12; 77, 1–9; 78, 1–9; 79, 1–8; 80, 1–9; 81, 1–9; 82, 1–9; 83, 1–9; 84, 1–9; 85, 1–9; 92, 2–33; 93, 1–34; 94, 1–12; 101, 3; 102, 1–22; 103, 10[12]. [733]

IX, 1, 1–10; 2, 1–10; 3, 1–10; 4, 1–10; 5, 1–7; 6, 1–9; 7, 1–9; 8, 1–9;

[1] 4 and 5 pâdani*kri*t. [2] Pratish*th*â. [3] 11 pâdani*kri*t. [4] Padapaṅkti. [5] (3) padapaṅkti or ush*n*ih. [6] 3 pâdani*kri*t. [7] 1 and 6 vardhamânâ. [8] 29 atini*kri*t, 31 pâdani*kri*t. [9] 1 pratish*th*â, 2 vardhamânâ. [10] Ush*n*iggarbhâ. [11] Pâdani*kri*t. [12] Hrasîyasî.

9, 1-9; 10, 1-9; 11, 1-9; 12, 1-9; 13, 1-9; 14, 1-8; 15, 1-8; 16, 1-8; 17, 1-8; 18, 1-7; 19, 1-7; 20, 1-7; 21, 1-7; 22, 1-7; 23, 1-7; 24, 1-7; 25, 1-6; 26, 1-6; 27, 1-6; 28, 1-6; 29, 1-6; 30, 1-6; 31, 1-6; 32, 1-6; 33, 1-6; 34, 1-6; 35, 1-6; 36, 1-6; 37, 1-6; 38, 1-6; 39, 1-6; 40, 1-6; 41, 1-6; 42, 1-6; 43, 1-6; 44, 1-6; 45, 1-6; 46, 1-6; 47, 1-5; 48, 1-5; 49, 1-5; 50, 1-5; 51, 1-5; 52, 1-5; 53, 1-4; 54, 1-4; 55, 1-4; 56, 1-4; 57, 1-4; 58, 1-4; 59, 1-4; 60, 1, 2, 4; 61, 1-30; 62, 1-30; 63, 1-30; 64, 1-30; 65, 1-30; 66, 1-17, 19-30; 67, 1-15, 19-26, 28-29; 101, 2-3; 108, 13[1]. [600]

X, 9, 1-7[2]; 19, 6; 20, 3-8; 33, 4-9; 57, 1-6; 60, 1-5; 62, 10; 101, 4, 6; 105, 1[3]; 118, 1-9; 119, 1-13; 127, 1-8; 144, 1, 3-4; 153, 1-5; 156, 1-5; 158, 1-5; 171, 1-4; 175, 1-4; 176, 2; 185, 1-3; 186, 1-3; 187, 1-5; 188, 1-3; 189, 1-3. [108]

Ush*n*ih (28).

I, 23, 19[4]; 79, 4-6; 84, 7-9; 91, 17; 92, 13-18; 120, 2[5], 5[6], 6[7]; 150, 1-3; 187, 1[8]. [21]

III, 10, 1-9; 28, 1. [10]

IV, 10, 8; 57, 5[9]. [2]

V, 40, 1-3; 51, 5-10; 53, 1, 10, 11[10], 4[11]; 72, 1-3; 78, 1-3. [19]

VI, 43, 1-4; 48, 13, 18[12]; 51, 13-15. [9]

VII, 66, 16[13]. [1]

VIII, 4, 21; 9, 5[14]; 12, 1-33; 13, 1-33; 15, 1-13; 18, 1-22; 19, 34, 36[14]; 22, 11[14]; 23, 1-30; 24, 1-29; 25, 1-22, 24; 26, 1-15, 22-24; 28, 4[15]; 30, 2; 46, 5[16], 15[17]; 31, 1-3; 69, 2; 70, 13, 15[15]; 98, 1-12[18]; 103, 8, 12[16]. [228]

IX, 60, 3[15]; 67, 30[15]; 102, 1-8; 103, 1-6; 104, 1-6; 105, 1-6; 106, 1-14. [42]

X, 26, 1, 4; 105, 2-10[19]; 132, 1. [12]

Anush*t*ubh (32).

I, 10, 1-12; 11, 1-8; 23, 20, 22-24; 28, 1-6; 43, 9; 45, 1-10; 49, 1-4; 50, 10-13; 84, 1-6; 90, 9; 93, 1-3; 120, 3[20], 4[21], 8[22], 9[23]; 126, 6-7; 133, 2-4; 142, 1-13; 149, 1-5[24]; 158, 6; 164, 51; 170, 2-4; 175, 2-5; 176, 1-5; 187, 3, 5-7, 11[25]; 191, 1-9, 14-16. [117]

II, 5, 1-8; 8, 6; 32, 6-8; 41, 16-17. [14]

III, 8, 3, 7; 13, 1-7; 21, 2-3; 22, 4; 24, 1; 25, 1-5[26]; 29, 1, 4, 10, 12; 33, 13; 37, 11; 53, 12, 20, 22. [27]

IV, 7, 2-6; 10, 5[27]; 24, 10; 30, 8, 24; 37, 5-8; 39, 6; 47, 1-4; 48, 1-5; 57, 1, 4, 6, 7. [27]

V, 7, 1-9; 9, 1-4, 6; 10, 1-3, 5-6; 16, 1-4; 17, 1-4, 18, 1-4; 19, 3-4; 20, 1-3; 21, 1-3; 22, 1-3; 23, 1-3; 25, 1-9; 27, 4-6; 28, 4; 35, 1-7; 38, 1-5; 39, 1-4; 40, 5, 9; 50, 1-4; 51, 14-15; 52, 1-5, 7-15; 53, 3; 61, 5; 64, 1-6; 65, 1-5; 66, 1-6; 67, 1-5; 73, 1-10; 74, 1-10;

[1] Yavamadhyâ. [2] Vardhamânâ, 7 pratish*th*â. [3] Or ush*n*ih. [4] Puraüsh*n*ih. [5] Kakubh. [6] Tanu*s*irâ. [7] Aksharai*h*. [8] Anush*t*ubgarbhâ. [9] Puraüsh*n*ih. [10] (3) kakubh. [11] Puraüsh*n*ih. [12] Puraüsh*n*ih (2). [13] Puraüsh*n*ih. [14] Kakubh. [15] Puraush*n*ih. [16] Kakubh. [17] Nyaṅku*s*irâ. [18] 7, 10, 11 kakubh; 9, 12 puraush*n*ih. [19] 2 and 7 pipîlikamadhyâ. [20] Kâvirâ*t*. [21] Nash*t*arûpî. [22] K*ri*ti. [23] Virâ*t*. [24] Virâ*t*. [25] Or b*ri*hatî. [26] Virâ*t*. [27] Mahâpadapaṅkti.

B*ri*hatî (36).

Paṅkti (40).

[1] Virâ*t*. [2] Pipîlikamadhyâ. [3] Virâ*t*. [4] Vish*t*ârab*ri*hatî. [5] Skandhogrîvî. [6] Uparish*t*âdb*ri*hatî. [7] Vishamapadâ. [8] Or anush*t*ubh. [9] (11) purastâdb*ri*hatî. [10] Urob*ri*hatî. [11] Nyaṅkusârinî. [12] Purastâdb*ri*hatî. [13] Uparish*t*âdb*ri*hatî. [14] (2) prastârapaṅkti. [15] Prastârapaṅkti. [16] *K*atushpadâ virâ*t*. [17] Satob*ri*hatî and virâ*d*rûpâ, v. comm. [18] Satob*ri*hatî. [19] (4) satob*ri*hatî.

VI, 20, 7[1]; 44, 7–9[1]; 75, 17. [5]
VII, 96, 3[2]. [1]
VIII, 10, 4[3]; 19, 35[4], 37; 31, 15–18; 35, 22, 24; 46, 9[4], 12[5], 21, 22, 24, 32; [56, 5]; 62, 1–6, 10–12; 69, 11, 16; 91, 1–2; 96, 4[1]; 101, 4[4]; 103, 7, 9, 11, 13[6]. [33]
IX, 108, 14[4]; 112, 1–4; 113, 1–11; 114, 1–4. [20]
X, 18, 11[2]; 21, 1–8[3]; 24, 1–3[3]; 25, 1–11[3]; 59, 8; 60, 8–9; 86, 1–23; 93, 1, 4–8, 10, 12, 14[7], 9[8]; 132, 2, 6[2]; 134, 7; 140, 1–2[9], 3–5[4]; 144, 5[4], 6[9]; 145, 6; 164, 5; 170, 4[3]. [72]

Trish*t*ubh (44).

I, 24, 1–2, 6–15; 27, 13; 30, 16; 31, 8, 16, 18; 32, 1–15; 33, 1–15; 34, 9, 12; 35, 2–8, 10–11; 51, 14–15; 52, 13, 15; 53, 10–11; 54, 6, 8–9, 11; 58, 6–9; 59, 1–7; 60, 1–5; 61, 1–16; 62, 1–13; 63, 1–9; 64, 15; 71, 1–10; 72, 1–10; 73, 1–10; 76, 1–5; 77, 1–5; 79, 1–3; 84, 16–18; 85, 5, 12; 88, 2–5[10]; 89, 6[11], 8–10; 91, 1–4, 18–23; 92, 5–12; 93, 4–7, 8[12], 12; 94, 15–16; 95, 1–11; 96, 1–9; 98, 1–3; 99, 1; 100, 1–19; 101, 8–11; 102, 11; 103, 1–8; 104, 1–9; 105, 8[13], 19; 106, 7; 107, 1–3; 108, 1–13; 109, 1–8; 110, 5, 9; 111, 5; 112, 24–25; 113, 1–20; 114, 10–11; 115, 1–6; 116, 1–25; 117, 1–25; 118, 1–11; 121, 1–15; 122, 1–15[14]; 123, 1–13; 124, 1–13; 125, 1–3, 6–7; 126, 1–5; 130, 10; 133, 1; 136, 7; 139, 11; 140, 10[12], 12–13; 141, 12–13; 143, 8; 145, 5; 146, 1–5; 147, 1–5; 148, 1–5; 152, 1–7; 153, 1–4; 154, 1–6; 157, 5–6; 158, 1–5; 161, 14; 162, 1–2, 4–5, 7–22; 163, 1–13; 164, 1–11, 13–14, 16–22, 24–28, 30–35, 37–40, 43–50, 52; 165, 1–15; 166, 14–15; 167, 1–11; 168, 8–10; 169, 1, 3–8; 170, 5; 171, 1–6; 173, 1–13; 174, 1–10; 175, 6; 176, 6; 177, 1–5; 178, 1–5; 179, 1–4, 6; 180, 1–10; 181, 1–9; 182, 6, 8; 183, 1–6; 184, 1–6; 185, 1–11; 186, 1–11; 189, 1–8; 190, 1–8; 191, 13[15]. [742]
II, 3, 1–6, 8–11; 4, 1–9; 9, 1–6; 10, 1–6; 11, 1–21[16]; 12, 1–15; 13, 13; 14, 1–12; 15, 1–10; 16, 9; 17, 8–9; 18, 1–9; 19, 1–9; 20, 1–9[17]; 21, 6; 23, 15, 19; 24, 12, 16; 27, 1–17; 28, 1–11; 29, 1–7; 30, 1–10; 31, 7; 33, 1–15; 34, 15; 35, 1–15; 38, 1–11; 39, 1–8; 40, 1–6; 42, 1–3. [230]
III, 1, 1–23; 4, 1–11; 5, 1–11; 6, 1–11; 7, 1–11; 8, 1–2, 4–6, 8–11; 9, 9; 14, 1–7; 15, 1–7; 17, 1–5; 18, 1–5; 19, 1–5; 20, 1–5; 21, 1, 4; 22, 1–3, 5; 23, 1–2, 4–5; 26, 7–9; 28, 4; 29, 2–3, 5, 7–9, 13, 16; 30, 1–22; 31, 1–22; 32, 1–17; 33, 1–12; 34, 1–11; 35, 1–11; 36, 1–11; 38, 1–10; 39, 1–9; 43, 1–8; 46, 1–5; 47, 1–5; 48, 1–5; 49, 1–5; 50, 1–5; 51, 4–9; 52, 5, 7–8; 53, 1–9, 11, 14–15, 17, 19, 21, 23, 24; 54, 1–22; 55, 1–

[1] Virâ*t*. [2] Prastârapaṅkti. [3] Âstârapaṅkti. [4] Satobr*i*hatî. [5] Viparîtâ. [6] (4) satobr*i*hatî. [7] (9) prastârapaṅkti. [8] Aksharai*h*. [9] Vish*t*â*r*apaṅkti. [10] Ver. 5 virâ*d*rûpâ. [11] Virâ*t*sthânâ. [12] Or *g*agatî. [13] Mahâbr*i*hatî yavamadhyâ. [14] 5 and 6 virâ*d*rûpâ. [15] Mahâbr*i*hatî. [16] 1–20 virâ*t*sthânâ. [17] 3 virâ*d*rûpâ.

[1] Virâ*d*rûpâ. [2] Virâ*t*pûrvâ. [3] Yavamadhyâ mahâb*ri*hatî. [4] Madhye*g*yoti*h*. [5] Uparish*t*â*g*gyoti*h*. [6] Mahâb*ri*hatî. [7] Virâ*d*rûpâ.

IX, 68, 10; 69, 9–10; 70, 10; 71, 9; 74, 8; 81, 5; 82, 5; 85, 11–12; 87, 1–9; 88, 1–8; 89, 1–7; 90, 1–6; 91, 1–6; 92, 1–6; 93, 1–5; 94, 1–5; 95, 1–5; 96, 1–24; 97, 1–58. [149]

X, 1, 1–7; 2, 1–7; 3, 1–7; 4, 1–7; 5, 1–7; 6, 1–7; 7, 1–7; 8, 1–9; 10, 1–14; 11, 7–9; 12, 1–9; 13, 1–4; 14, 1–12; 15, 1–10, 14–16; 16, 1–10; 17, 1–12; 18, 1–10, 12; 20, 10; 22, 15; 23, 1, 5[1], 7; 27, 1–24; 28, 1–12; 29, 1–8; 30, 1–15; 31, 1–11; 32, 6–9; 33, 1; 34, 1–6, 8–14; 35, 13–14; 36, 13–14; 37, 10; 39, 14; 42, 1–11; 43, 10–11; 44, 1–3, 10–11; 45, 1–12; 46, 1–10, 47, 1–8; 48, 7, 10–11; 49, 2, 11; 50, 3–5[2]; 51, 1–9; 52, 1–6; 53, 1–5, 8; 54, 1–6; 55, 1–8; 56, 1–3, 7; 59, 1–7, 10[3]; 61, 1–27; 62, 11; 63, 15[4]–17; 64, 12, 16–17; 65, 15; 66, 15; 67, 1–12; 68, 1–12; 69, 3–12; 70, 1–11; 71, 1–8, 10–11; 73, 1–11; 74, 1–6; 77, 1–4, 6–8; 78, 1, 3–4, 8; 79, 1–7; 80, 1–7; 81, 1–7; 82, 1–7; 83, 2–3; 84, 1–3; 85, 14, 19–21, 23–24, 26, 36–37, 44; 87, 1–21; 88, 1–19; 89, 1–18; 90, 16; 91, 15; 94, 5, 7, 14; 95, 1–18; 96, 12–13; 98, 1–12; 99, 1–12; 100, 12; 101, 1–3, 7–8, 10–11; 102, 2, 4–11; 103, 1–12; 104, 1–11; 105, 11; 106, 1–11; 107, 1–3, 5–11; 108, 1–11; 109, 1–5; 110, 1–11; 111, 1–10; 112, 1–10; 113, 10; 114, 1–3, 5–10; 115, 8; 116, 1–9; 117, 3–9; 120, 1–9; 121, 1–10; 122, 1, 5; 123, 1–8; 124, 1–6, 8–9; 125, 1, 3–8; 126, 8; 128, 1–8; 129, 1–7; 130, 2–7; 131, 1–3, 5–7; 132, 3[5]–5; 133, 7; 139, 1–6; 140, 6[6]; 142, 3–6; 147, 5; 148, 1–5; 149, 1–5; 150, 4–5[7]; 160, 1–5; 161, 1–4; 164, 3; 165, 1–5; 168, 1–4; 169, 1–4; 177, 2–3; 178, 1–3; 179, 2–3; 180, 1–3; 181, 1–3; 182, 1–3; 183, 1–3; 191, 3. [901]

Gagatî (48).

I, 31, 1–7, 9–15, 17; 34, 1–8, 10–11; 35, 1, 9; 51, 1–13; 52, 1–12, 14; 53, 1–9; 54, 1–5, 7, 10; 55, 1–8; 56, 1–6; 57, 1–6; 58, 1–5; 61, 1–14; 82, 6; 83, 1–6; 85, 1–4, 6–11; 87, 1–6; 89, 1–5, 7; 92, 1–4; 94, 1–14; 101, 1–7; 102, 1–10; 106, 1–6; 110, 1–4, 6–8; 111, 1–4; 112, 1–23; 114, 1–9; 119, 1–10; 125, 4–5; 140, 1–9, 11; 141, 1–11; 143, 1–7; 144, 1–7; 145, 1–4; 151, 1–9; 155, 1–6; 156, 1–5; 157, 1–4; 159, 1–5; 160, 1–5; 161, 1–13; 162, 3, 6[8]; 164, 12, 15, 23, 29, 36, 41; 166, 1–13; 168, 1–7; 182, 1–5, 7; 191, 10–12[9]. [356]

II, 1, 1–16; 2, 1–13; 3, 7; 13, 1–12; 16, 1–8; 17, 1–7; 21, 1–5; 23, 1–14, 16–18; 24, 1–11, 13–15; 25, 1–5; 26, 1–4; 30, 11; 31, 1–6; 32, 1–5; 34, 1–4; 36, 1–6; 37, 1–6; 43, 1, 3. [142]

III, 2, 1–15; 3, 1–11; 26, 1–6; 28, 5; 29, 6, 11, 14–15; 51, 1–3; 52, 6; 53, 10, 16; 60, 1–7. [50]

IV, 7, 1; 36, 1–8; 40, 2–5; 45, 1–6; 50, 10; 53, 1–7; 54, 1–5; 58, 11. [33]

[1] Abhisârinî. [2] 3 and 4 abhisârinî. [3] Panktyuttarâ. [4] 15 or gagatî. [5] 3 virâdrûpâ. [6] Uparishtâggyotih. [7] Uparishtâggyotih, 4 or gagatî. [8] Quoted as trishtubh by Shadg. [9] Mahâpankti.

V, 8, 1–7; 11, 1–6; 28, 2; 34, 1–8; 36, 3; 44, 1–13; 46, 1, 3–7; 48, 1–5; 51, 11–13[1]; 54, 1–13, 15; 55, 1–9; 57, 1–6; 59, 1–7; 60, 7–8; 63, 1–7; 81, 1–5; 83, 2–4. [103]

VI, 7, 6–7; 8, 1–6; 15, 1–2, 4–5, 7–9; 28, 2–4; 47, 27; 48, 6; 52, 14; 58, 2; 61, 1–3, 13; 68, 9–10; 70, 1–6; 71, 1–3; 75, 6, 10. [39]

VII, 41, 1; 44, 1; 46, 1–3; 50, 1–3; 82, 1–10; 83, 1–10; 89, 5; 104, 1–6, 7, 18, 21, 23. [39]

VIII, 9, 12; 36, 7[2]; 37, 2–7[2]; 39, 1–10[2]; 40, 1, 3–11[2]; 41, 1–10[2]; 46, 17; 47, 1–18; 48, 5; [59, 1–7]; 86, 1–5; 97, 15; 100, 6. [65]

IX, 68, 1–9; 69, 1–8; 70, 1–9; 71, 1–8; 72, 1–9; 73, 1–9; 74, 1–7, 9; 75, 1–5; 76, 1–5; 77, 1–5; 78, 1–5; 79, 1–5, 80, 1–5; 81, 1–4; 82, 1–4; 83, 1–5; 84, 1–5; 85, 1–10; 86, 1–48. [166]

X, 11, 1–6; 13, 5; 15, 11; 18, 13; 23, 2–4, 6; 32, 1–5; 34, 7; 35, 1–12; 36, 1–12; 37, 1–9, 11–12; 38, 1–5; 39, 1–13; 40, 1–14; 41, 1–3; 43, 1–9; 44, 4–9; 48, 1–6, 8–9; 49, 1, 3–10; 50, 1–2, 6–7; 53, 6–7, 9–11; 56, 4–6; 59, 9[2]; 62, 1–4; 63, 1–14; 64, 1–11, 13–15; 65, 1–14; 66, 1–14; 69, 1–2; 71, 9; 75, 1–9; 76, 1–8; 77, 5; 78, 2, 5–7; 83, 1, 4–7; 84, 4–7; 85, 18, 27, 43; 91, 1–14; 92, 1–15; 94, 1–4, 6, 8–13; 96, 1–11; 100, 1–11; 101, 9–12; 107, 4; 113, 1–9; 114, 4; 115, 1–7; 117, 1–2; 122, 2–4, 6–8; 124, 7; 125, 2; 128, 9; 130, 1; 132, 7[3]; 133, 4–6[2]; 134, 1–6[2]; 138, 1–6; 142, 1–2; 147, 1–4; 166, 5[2]; 167, 1–4; 170, 1–3; 177, 1. [351]

Ati*g*agatî (52).

IV, 1, 2. [1]

V, 41, 16–17; 87, 1–9. [11]

VI, 48, 15. [1]

VIII, 37, 1; 97, 10, 13. [3]

*S*akvarî (56).

IV, 27, 5. [1]

V, 2, 12. [1]

VI, 2, 11; 14, 6; 15, 3, 15; 31, 4; 49, 15. [6]

VII, 50, 4[4]. [1]

VIII, 36, 1–6; 40, 2. [7]

X, 115, 9; 133, 1–3. [4]

Ati*s*akvarî (60).

I, 129, 8–9; 137, 1–3. [5]

II, 22, 2, 3, 4[5]; 43, 2[5]. [4]

VI, 15, 6. [1]

Ash*t*i (64).

I, 129, 11; 134, 6; 135, 7–8. [4]

II, 22, 1. [1]

IV, 1, 1. [1]

Atyash*t*i (68).

I, 127, 1–5, 7–11; 128, 1–8; 129, 1–7, 10; 130, 1–9; 131, 1–7; 132, 1–6; 133, 7; 134, 1–5; 135, 1–6, 9; 136, 1–6; 138, 1–4; 139, 1–4, 6–10. [80]

IX, 111, 1–3. [3]

Dh*ri*ti (72).

I, 133, 6. [1]

IV, 1, 3. [1]

Atidh*ri*ti (76).

I, 127, 6. [1]

[1] Or trish*t*ubh. [2] Mahâpaṅkti. [3] Mahâsatob*ri*hatî. [4] Or ati*g*agatî. [5] Or ash*t*i.

Dvipadâ (20).

I, 65, 1–5; 66, 1–5; 67, 1–5; 68, 1–5; 69, 1–5; 70, 1–6. [31]
V, 24, 1–4. [4]
VI, 10, 7; 17, 15[1]; 47, 25. [3]
VII, 17, 1–7[2]; 32, 3; 34, 1–21; 56, 1–11. [40]
VIII, 19, 27; 29, 1–10; 46, 13[3], 30. [13]
IX, 67, 16–18[4]; 107, 3, 16; 109, 1–22. [27]
X, 157, 1–5[2]; 172, 1–4. [9]

Ekapadâ (10).

IV, 17, 15. [1]
V, 41, 20; 42, 17; 43, 16. [3]
VI, 63, 11[5]. [1]
X, 20, 1. [1]

Pragâtha.

a. Barhata (36 and 40).

I, 36, 1–20; 39, 1–10; 40, 1–8; 44, 1–14; 47, 1–10; 48, 1–16; 84, 19–20. [80]
III, 16, 1–6. [6]
V, 56, 2–3, 6–7[6]. [4]
VI, 46, 1–14; 48, 1–4, 9–10. [20]
VII, 16, 1–12; 22, 1–2, 4–27; 59, 1–6; 66, 10–15; 74, 1–6; 81, 1–6; 96, 1–2. [64]
VIII, 1, 1–4; 3, 1–20; 4, 1–20; 10, 5–6; 17, 14–15; 22, 1–6; 27, 1–22; 46, 25–28; [49, 1–10; 50, 1–10; 51, 1–10; 52, 1–10; 53, 1–8; 54, 1–8]; 60, 1–20; 61, 1–18; 66, 1–14; 70, 1–6; 71, 10–15; 77, 10–11; 87, 1–6; 88, 1–6; 89, 1–4; 90, 1–6; 99, 1–8; 101, 1–2, 5–12; 103, 6–7. [188]
IX, 107, 1–2, 4–7, 10–15, 17–26. [22]
X, 23, 2–3; 62, 6–7. [4]

b. Kâkubha (28 and 40).

V, 53, 5–6, 15–16[6]. [4]
VI, 48, 11–12, 16–17. [4]
VIII, 19, 1–26, 28–33; 20, 1–26; 21, 1–18; 22, 9–10, 13–18. [84]
IX, 108, 1–12, 15–16. [14]

c. Mahâbârhata (44 and 48).

VI, 48, 7–8. [2]

[1] Trish*t*ubh. [2] Dvaipadam traish*t*ubham. [3] *K*aturvi*ms*ikâ. [4] Dvipadâ gâyatrya*h*.
[5] Ekapadâ trish*t*ubh. [6] Not specially stated to be pragâtha in the text.

IV.

LIST OF VERSES FROM THE *RI*GVEDA,

QUOTED BY SHA*D*GURU*S*ISHYA AS EXAMPLES OF METRES IN HIS COMMENTARY ON THE INTRODUCTION TO THE SARVÂNUKRAMA*N*Î, §§ 3–11.

*Ri*g-veda.

I, 1, 1, gâyatrî, § 4, 1.
1, 2, gâyatrî ni*kri*d, 3, 4.
1, 8, virâ*d* gâyatrî, 3, 5.
7, 4, (vyûha), 3, 6.
10, 1, anush*t*ubh, 6, 1.
11, 1, anush*t*ubh, 6, 1.
17, 4, gâyatrî pâdani*kri*d, 4, 4.
23, 19, puraüsh*n*ih, 5, 2.
35, 9, *g*agatî ni*kri*d, 3, 5.
40, 1, b*ri*hatî, 7, 1.
47, 1, b*ri*hatî, 11, 2.
47, 2, satob*ri*hatî, 11, 2.
57, 4, *g*agatî, 9, 8.
80, 1, paṅkti, 8, 1.
81, 1, paṅkti, 8, 1.
89, 6, virâ*t*sthânâ, 9, 5.
94, 1, *g*agatî, 10, 1.
94, 2, *g*agatî, 9, 2.
105, 8, yâvamadhyâ, 9, 10.
120, 2, bhurig gâyatrî, 3, 4.
120, 3, kâvirâ*d*, 6, 5.
120, 4, nash*t*arûpâ, 6, 6.
120, 5, tanu*s*irâ, 5, 5.

I, 120, 7, vish*t*ârab*ri*hatî, 7, 5.
120, 8, k*ri*ti anush*t*ubh, 6, 3.
120, 9, virâ*d* anush*t*ubh, 6, 8.
122, 5, virâ*d*rûpâ, 9, 6.
122, 6, virâ*d*rûpâ, 9, 6.
127, 1, 'atyash*t*i,' 11, 6.
127, 6, 'atidh*ri*ti,' 11, 6.
133, 6, 'dh*ri*ti,' 11, 6.
162, 6, trish*t*ubh, 9, 3.
162, 12, trish*t*ubh, 9, 2.
175, 1, nyaṅku*s*irâ, or '*sk*andhogrîvî,' or 'urob*ri*hatî,' 7, 3.
187, 1, anush*t*ubgarbhâ, 5, 7.
187, 11, b*ri*hatî, 7, 9.
191, 10, mahâpaṅkti, 10, 3.
191, 13, mahâb*ri*hatî, 9, 9.
II, 7, 6, (vyûha of y), 3, 6.
11, 1, virâ*t*sthânâ, 9, 5.
22, 1, 'ash*t*i,' 11, 6.
22, 3, 'ati*s*akvarî,' 11, 6.

III, 21, 4, virâ*d*rûpâ, 9, 6.
62, 10, (vyûha of y), 3, 6.
62, 10, gâyatrî, 4, 5.
IV, 10, 1, padapaṅkti gâyatrî, 4, 2.
10, 2, padap. gây., 4, 1.
10, 5, mahâpadapaṅkti, 6, 2.
19, 1, (vyûha of r), 3, 6.
31, 3, pâdani*kri*d gâyatrî, 4, 4.
V, 86, 6, paṅktyuttarâ, or virâ*t*pûrvâ, 9, 11.
87, 1, 'ati*g*agatî,' 11, 6.
VI, 16, 1, vardhamânâ gâyatrî, 4, 7.
28, 8, (vyûha), 3, 6.
44, 8, paṅkti virâ*t*, or trish*t*ubh, 8, 3.
45, 29, atini*kri*d gâyatrî, 4, 5.
45, 29, supratish*th*â, 11, 6.
47, 27, (vyûha of y), 3, 6.
48, 6, mahâsatob*ri*hatî, 10, 2.
48, 7–10, bârhata pragâtha, 11, 4.

VII, 22, 1, virâ*d* anush*t*ubh, 6, 7.
32, 22, b*ri*hatî, 7, 1.
32, 23, satob*ri*hatî, 8,
36, 1, (vyûha), 3, 6.
VIII, 10, 2, madhyegyoti*h*, 9, 8.
11, 1, pratish*th*â gâyatrî, 4, 8.
11, 2, vardhamânâ gâyatrî, 4, 7.
12, 1, ush*n*ih, 5, 1.
16, 7, (vyûha), 3, 6.
21, 1, kakubh, 11, 3.
21, 1, ush*n*ih kakubh, 5, 3.
21, 2, satob*ri*hatî, 11, 3.
22, 12, madhyegyoti*h*, 9, 8.
25, 23, ush*n*iggarbhâ gâyatrî, 4, 3.
29, 1, 'dvipadâ', 8, 8.
35, 1, uparish*t*âggyoti*h*, 9, 8.
35, 23, mahâb*ri*hatî, 9, 9.
46, 11, uktam, 11, 6.
46, 11–12, viparîtottara pragâtha, 11, 5.
VIII, 46, 12, viparîtâ, 8, 5.
46, 14, pipîlikamadhyâ b*ri*hatî, 7, 7.
46, 15, kakum nyańku*s*irâ, 5, 4.
46, 20, vishamapadâ b*ri*hatî, 7, 8.
61, 17, (vyûha), 3, 6.
68, 1–3, anush*t*ummukha, 11, 6.
69, 1, 'anush*t*ubh,' 5, 8.
69, 2, ush*n*ih, 5, 8.
69, 8, 'anush*t*ubh,' 5, 8.
69, 13, ush*n*ih, 5, 8.
84, 1, atini*kri*d gâyatrî, 4, 5.
84, 7, trish*t*ubh, 9, 1.
103, 10, atini*kri*d gâyatrî 4, 5.
103, 10, hrasîyasî gâyatrî, 4, 9.
IX, 108, 13, yavamadhyâ gâyatrî, 4, 9.
110, 1, pipîlikamadhyâ b*ri*hatî, 6, 4.
110, 4, ûrdhvab*ri*hatî, 7, 6.
IX, 110, 8, ûrdhvab*ri*hatî, 7, 6.
X, 18, 11, prastârapańkti, 8, 6.
21, 1, âstârapańkti, 8, 7.
22, 1, purastâdb*ri*hatî, 7, 2.
22, 3, purastâdb*ri*hatî, 7, 2.
23, 5, abhisâri*n*î trish*t*ubh, 9, 4.
26, 4, ush*n*ih, 5, 8.
59, 9, mahâpańkti, 10, 3.
103, 6, (vyûha), 3, 6.
105, 2, ush*n*ik pipîlikamadhyâ, 5, 6.
117, 7, (vyûha), 3, 6.
126, 1, uparish*t*âdb*ri*hatî, 7, 4.
133, 1, '*s*akvarî,' 11, 6.
134, 1, mahâpańkti, 10, 3.
140, 1, vish*t*ârapankti, 8, 9.
140, 6, uparish*t*âggyoti*h*, 9, 8.
157, 1, 'dvipadâ,' 8, 8.
172, 1, 'dvipadâ,' 8, 8.
172, 3, sa*m*stârapańkti, 8, 8.

THE FOLLOWING VERSES ARE FROM OTHER VEDAS.

Vâ*g*asaneyi Sa*m*hitâ.

III, 9, atyuktam, 11, 6.
VIII, 10, pratish*th*â, 11, 6.
XIX, 82, madhyegyoti*h*, 9, 8.
XXI, 43, utk*ri*ti, 11, 6.
XXXI, 42, vik*ri*ti, 11, 6.
58, abhik*ri*ti, 11, 6.

Taittirîya Brâhma*n*a.

III, v, 9, 1, sańk*ri*ti, 11, 6.

Taittirîya Âra*n*yaka.

IV, xxi, 1, k*ri*ti, 11, 6.
xliv, 32, âk*ri*ti, 11, 6.

V.

LIST OF AUTHORS AND WORKS

QUOTED BY SHAḌGURUŚISHYA.

The figures refer to the numbering of the sûtras and commentary corresponding to the hymns of the *Ri*gveda ; §§ refer to the introduction of the Sarvânukrama*n*î.

Anukrama*n*îs.

1. Anuvâkânukrama*n*î :
   (Verse 32) VIII, 1.
   (Verses 43–44) X, 1 and 20.
2. Ârshânukrama*n*î :
   I, 24 (p. 86, ver. 20), 99, 100, 105 ; II, 1 ; III, 31, 36, 38 ; V, 1, 18 ; IX, 66 ; X, 38, 105, 115, 119.
3. *Kh*ando*nukrama*n*î :
   § 3, 5 ; III, 21.
4. Devatânukrama*n*î :
   I, 22, 28, 112, 165 ; VII, 100 ; VIII, 4, 68 ; X, 38, 101, 119.
5. Pâdânukrama*n*î :
   § 11, 6.

Âra*n*yakas.

1. Aitareya :
   (I, ii, 6, 1) X, 28.
   (I, ii, 6, 6–8) VI, 15.
   (I, v, 1, 10) VIII, 40.
   (I, v, 3, 7–8) I, 164,
   (II, i, 6, 4) § 1, 1 and § 2, 14.
   (II, ii, 2, 2–4) VIII, 1.
   (II, ii, 2, 7–8) A. 46.
   (III, ii, 3, 12) § 2, 15.
   (V, i, 1, 8) X, 28.
   (V, ii, 5) § 5, 4 and § 11, 6 (p. 76).
   (V, iii, 2, 14) I, 164.
   (V, iii, 3, 6) I, 50.
   (V, iii, 3, 19) X, 191.
2. Taittirîya :
   (IV, xxi, 1) § 11, 6.
   (IV, xliv, 32) § 11, 6.

*Ri*gvidhâna.

(II, iv, 2) III, 53.
(II, xvii, 1–4) V, 78.
(II, xxii, 2–4) V, 47.

Nigha*n*tu.

§ 2, 12.

Nirukta.

(I, 5) I, 170.
(II, 10) § 2, 7.
(II, 11) § 2, 4.
Quoted generally : Introd. § 2, 12.

VI.

LIST OF ITIHÂSAS

RELATED BY SHA*D*GURU*S*ISHYA.

Agastya[1], son of Mitra and Varu*n*a, I, 166.

Apâlâ (cured of skin-disease by Indra), VIII, 91.

Âsaṅga and his wife *S*a*s*vatî (their sex changed), introd. to ma*nd*. VIII.

Urva*s*î[1] and Mitrâvaru*n*au, I, 166; and Purûravâ Ai*l*a, X, 95.

Kakshîvân, son of Dîrghatamas and the slave U*s*i*g*, I, 116.

Gâthin[1] (Indra), son of Ku*s*ika Aishîrathi and father of Vi*s*vâmitra, introd. to ma*nd*. III.

Gaupâyanas[1], household priests to king Asamâti, X, 57–60.

Pâyu, son of Bharadvâ*g*a, renders *K*âyamâna and Prastoka victorious over the Pâra*s*ikhas, VI, 75.

Pragâtha[1], son of Ghora, is adopted by his elder brother Ka*n*va, introd. to ma*nd*. VIII.

Maruts, sons of Diti, adopted by Rudra, II, 33.

Vasish*th*a, son of Mitra and Varu*n*a, I, 166.

Vasukra[1], son of Indra, and his wife converse with Indra, X, 28.

Vâk Sasarparî and Vi*s*vâmitra, III, 53.

Vâmadeva, his conversation, before birth, with Indra and Aditi, IV, 18.

Viku*nth*â[1], an Asurî, becomes the mother of Indra, X, 47.

Vi*s*vâmitra and Vâ*k*, III, 53.

*S*akti[1], son of Vasish*th*a, burnt at the instigation of Vi*s*vâmitra, VII, 32.

*S*una*h*sepa, son of A*g*îgarta, saved from the stake by the gods, cures king Hari*s*k*a*ndra, and is adopted by Vi*s*vâmitra, I, 24.

*S*yâvâ*s*va, son of Ar*k*anânas, obtains the daughter of king Rathavîti, V, 61.

Saramâ[1] recovers the cows of B*ri*haspati, X, 108.

Savya[1] (Indra) becomes the son of Aṅgiras, I, 51.

Suhotra[1], *S*unahotra, Nara, Garga, *Ri*gi*s*vâ, the five sons of Bharadvâ*g*a, who, being the son of B*ri*haspati, was adopted by Bharata, VI, 52.

Sau*k*îka Agni[1], X, 50.

[1] Shortly told in the text of the Sarvânukrama*n*î also.

VII.

INDEX OF WORDS

OCCURRING IN THE SARVÂNUKRAMANÎ, THE AṄUVÂKÂNUKRAMANÎ, AND IN SHADGURUSISHYA.

A. refers to the Anuvâkânukramanî. An asterisk indicates that the word occurs in Shadgurusishya only; inverted commas, that it is to be found in a quotation. Nouns are often, verbs always, given as they occur, so that it may be seen at a glance what forms occur. The names of Rishis and Deities are, as a rule, excluded, because these are given in Max Muller's and Aufrecht's Indexes; the principal metres are also excluded, these being given in Appendix III.

CORRIGENDA.

The figures in parentheses refer to the numbers of the sûtras.

Page 1, line 6, for °गच्छतीति read °गच्छति
,, 10, line 1, for ककप् read ककुप्
,, 13, line 10, *dele* the figure [3]
,, 16, third line from the bottom, read °पत्य° for °पत्प°
,, 17, second line from the bottom, read °सोमं for °सौमं
,, 24, line 8 (74), read सोम° for सौम°
,, 27, line 8 (104), read °सोमं for °सौमं
,, 27, third line from the bottom, read दत्त्वा for दत्वा
,, 28, third line from the bottom, read कात्यायनौ for कात्त्यायनौ
,, 31, line 6, insert गायत्रे after चानुष्टुभो
,, 33, line 9 (1), read मधुच्छंदाः for मधुच्छाः
,, 36, line 1 (104), read काश्यप्यौ for काश्यपौ
,, 41, line 1, read गृभ्णामीति for गृभ्नामीति
,, 45, line 9 (165), *dele* इदं after प्रायश्चित्तं
,, 46, line 1, read रौशदश्वो for रौहिदश्वो
,, 46, line 2 (180), read ऐंद्रिः for ऐंद्रः
,, 79, line 3, read गायत्रं for गामत्रं
,, 96, line 5, read नराशंस° for नाराशंस°
,, 97, line 11, read कैशिनं for केशिन
,, 106, line 8, read °वचनीयको for °वचयीयको
,, 111 (46), read चेंद्र° for चंद्र°
,, 112 (50), read बृहस्पति° for वृहस्पति°
,, 155 (86), line 6, read संहोत्रम् for संहीत्रम्
,, 157, verse 8, read तमुर्वशी for तमूर्वशी